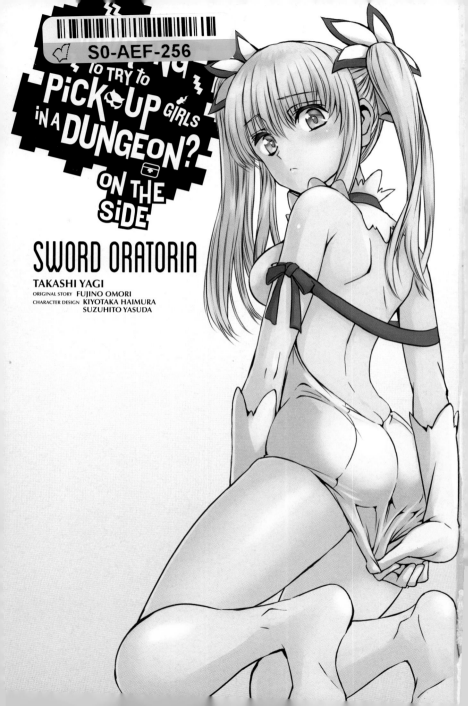

to TRY to PiCK UP GIRLS iN A DUNGEON? ON THE SiDE

SWORD ORATORIA

TAKASHI YAGI
ORIGINAL STORY FUJINO OMORI
CHARACTER DESIGN KIYOTAKA HAIMURA
SUZUHITO YASUDA

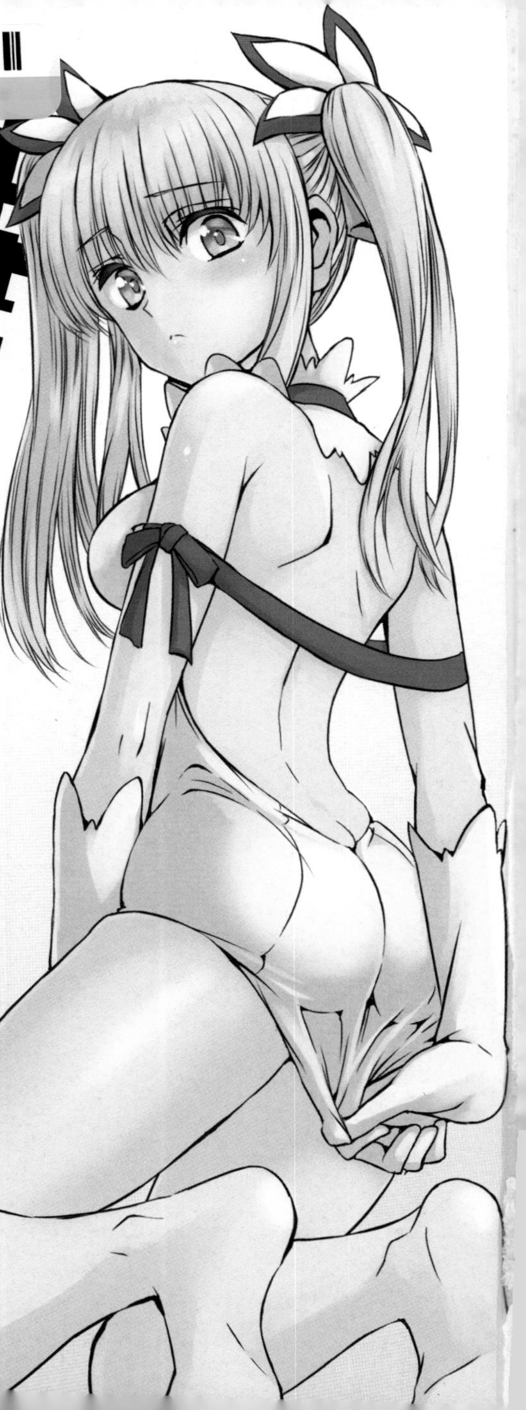

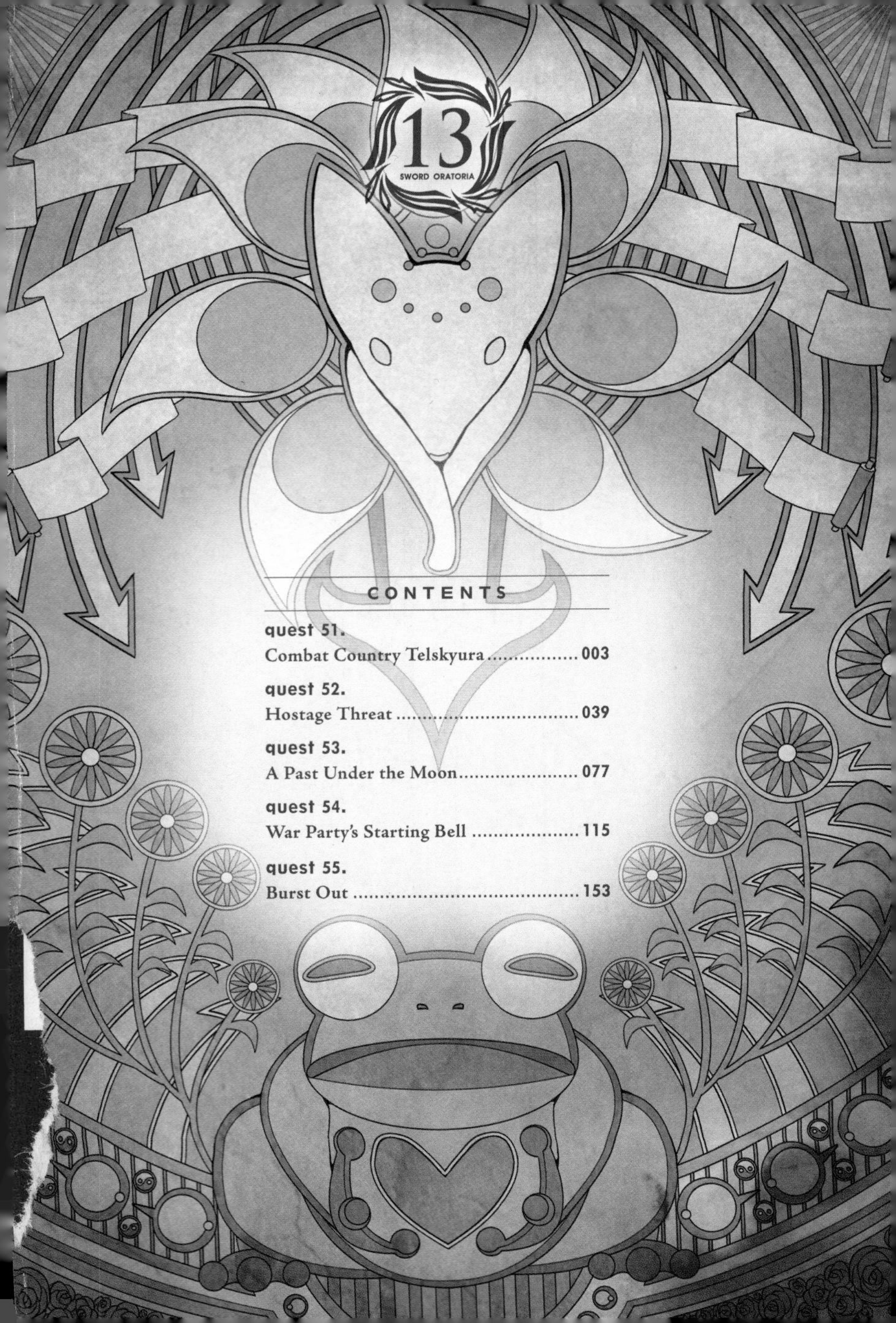
13
SWORD ORATORIA

CONTENTS

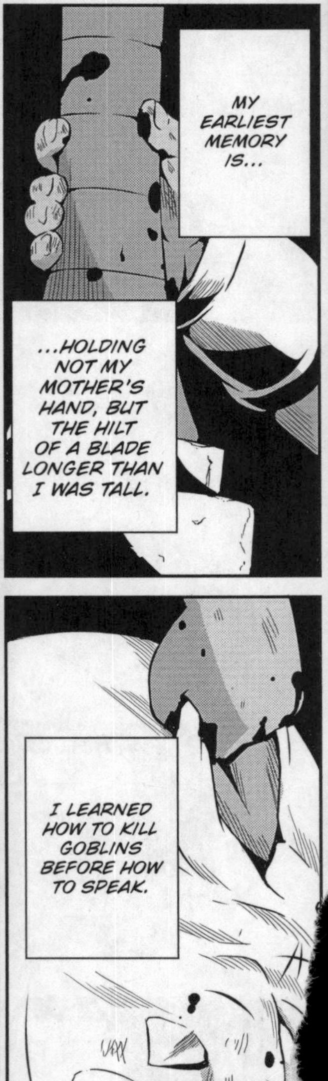
MY EARLIEST MEMORY IS...
...HOLDING NOT MY MOTHER'S HAND, BUT THE HILT OF A BLADE LONGER THAN I WAS TALL.
I LEARNED HOW TO KILL GOBLINS BEFORE HOW TO SPEAK.

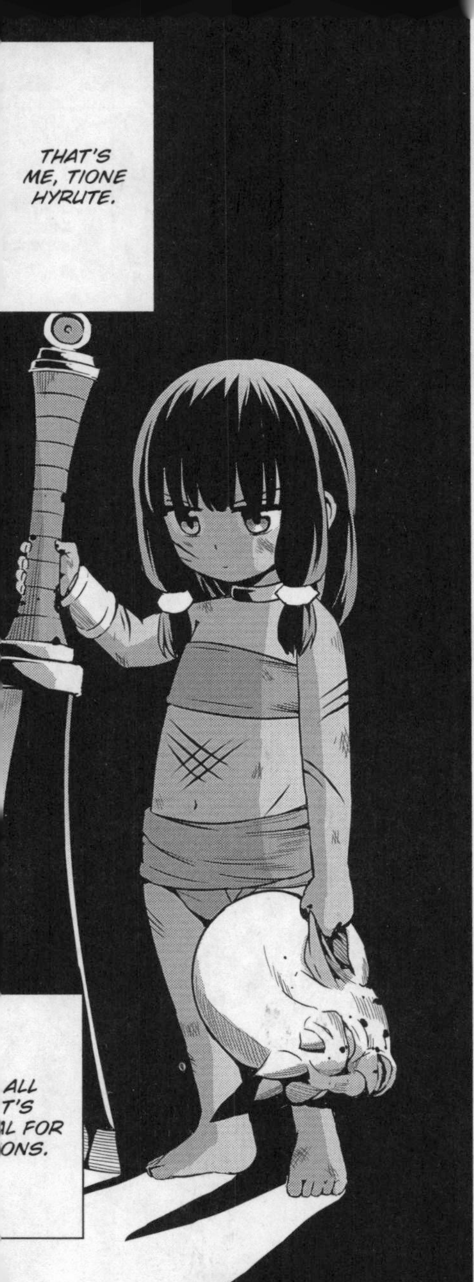
THAT'S ME, TIONE HYRUTE.
ALL T'S AL FOR ONS.

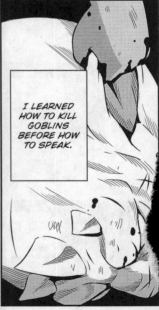

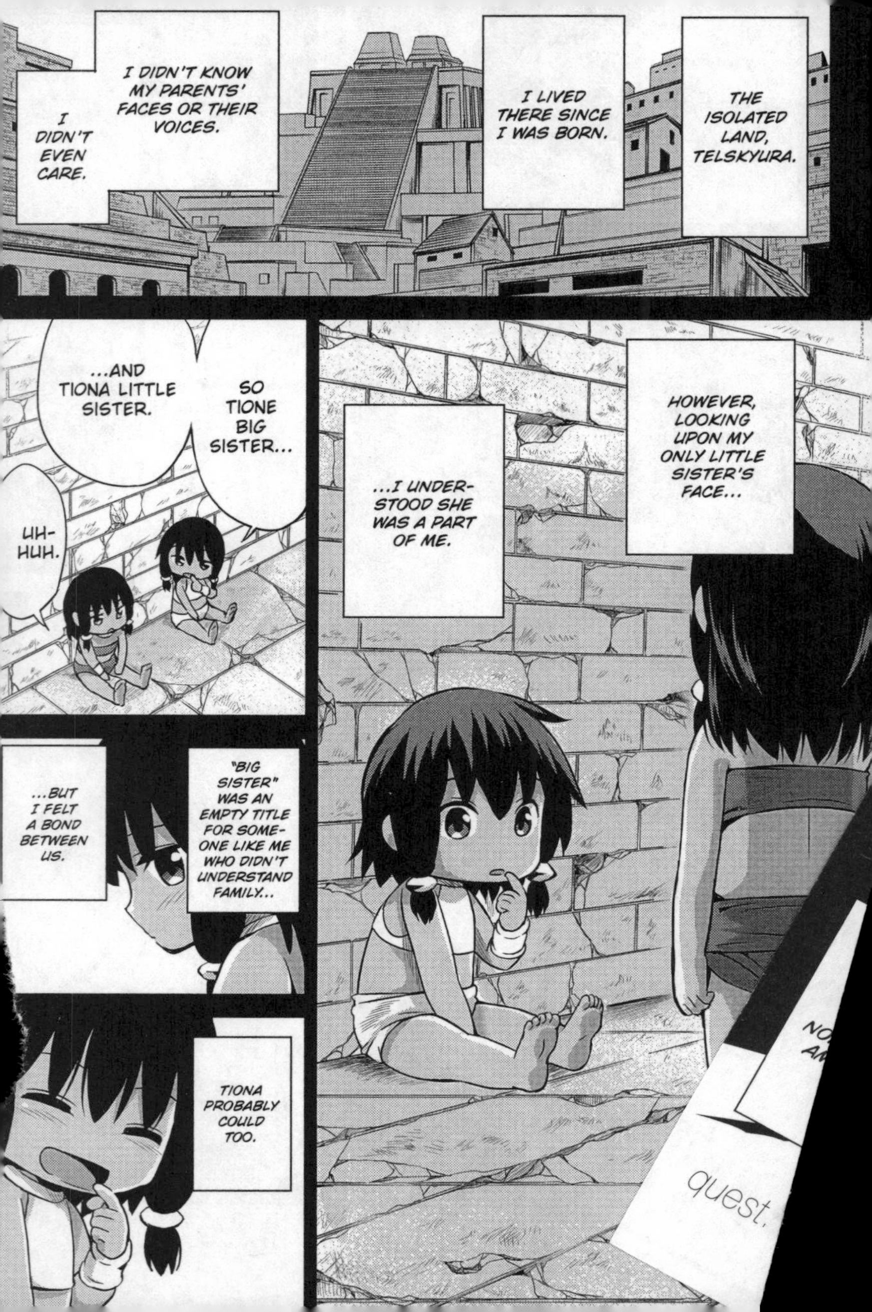
THE ISOLATED LAND, TELSKYURA.
I LIVED THERE SINCE I WAS BORN.
I DIDN'T KNOW MY PARENTS' FACES OR THEIR VOICES.
I DIDN'T EVEN CARE.
HOWEVER, LOOKING UPON MY ONLY LITTLE SISTER'S FACE...
...I UNDERSTOOD SHE WAS A PART OF ME.
SO TIONE BIG SISTER...
...AND TIONA LITTLE SISTER.
UH-HUH.
"BIG SISTER" WAS AN EMPTY TITLE FOR SOMEONE LIKE ME WHO DIDN'T UNDERSTAND FAMILY...
...BUT I FELT A BOND BETWEEN US.
TIONA PROBABLY COULD TOO.

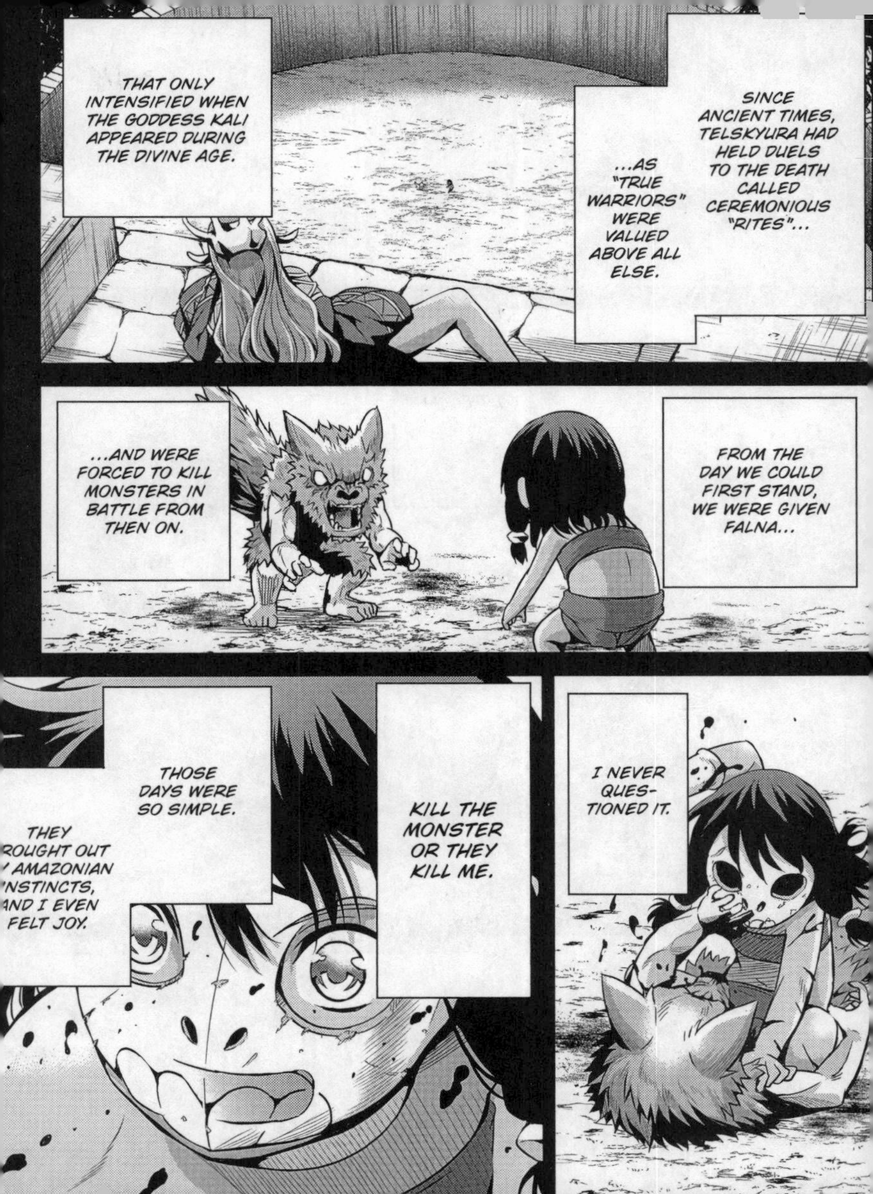
SINCE ANCIENT TIMES, TELSKYURA HAD HELD DUELS TO THE DEATH CALLED CEREMONIOUS "RITES"...
...AS "TRUE WARRIORS" WERE VALUED ABOVE ALL ELSE.
THAT ONLY INTENSIFIED WHEN THE GODDESS KALI APPEARED DURING THE DIVINE AGE.
FROM THE DAY WE COULD FIRST STAND, WE WERE GIVEN FALNA...
...AND WERE FORCED TO KILL MONSTERS IN BATTLE FROM THEN ON.
I NEVER QUES- TIONED IT.
KILL THE MONSTER OR THEY KILL ME.
THOSE DAYS WERE SO SIMPLE.
THEY ROUGHT OUT AMAZONIAN NSTINCTS, AND I EVEN FELT JOY.

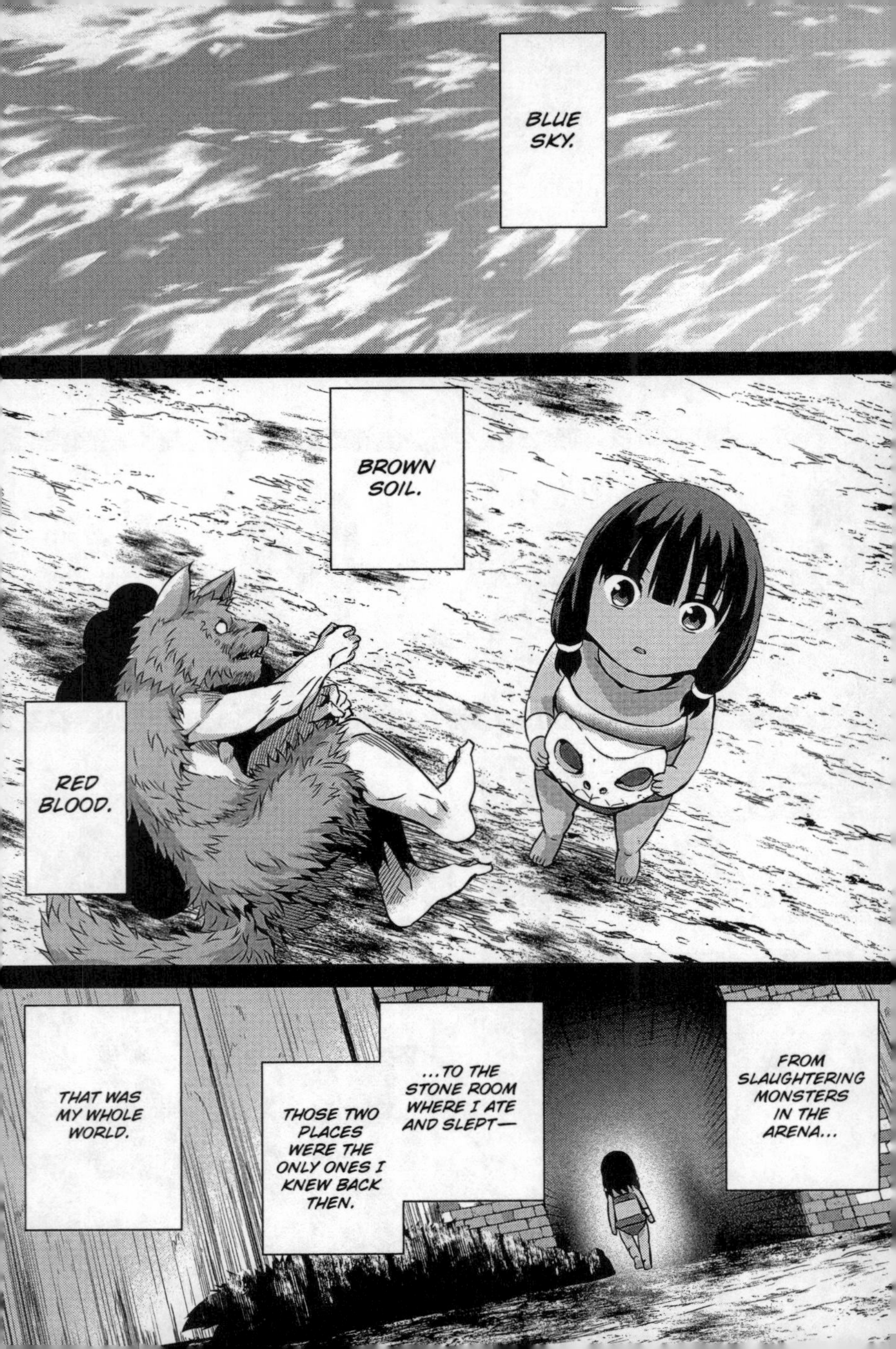
BLUE SKY.
BROWN SOIL.
RED BLOOD.
FROM SLAUGHTERING MONSTERS IN THE ARENA...
...TO THE STONE ROOM WHERE I ATE AND SLEPT—
THOSE TWO PLACES WERE THE ONLY ONES I KNEW BACK THEN.
THAT WAS MY WHOLE WORLD.

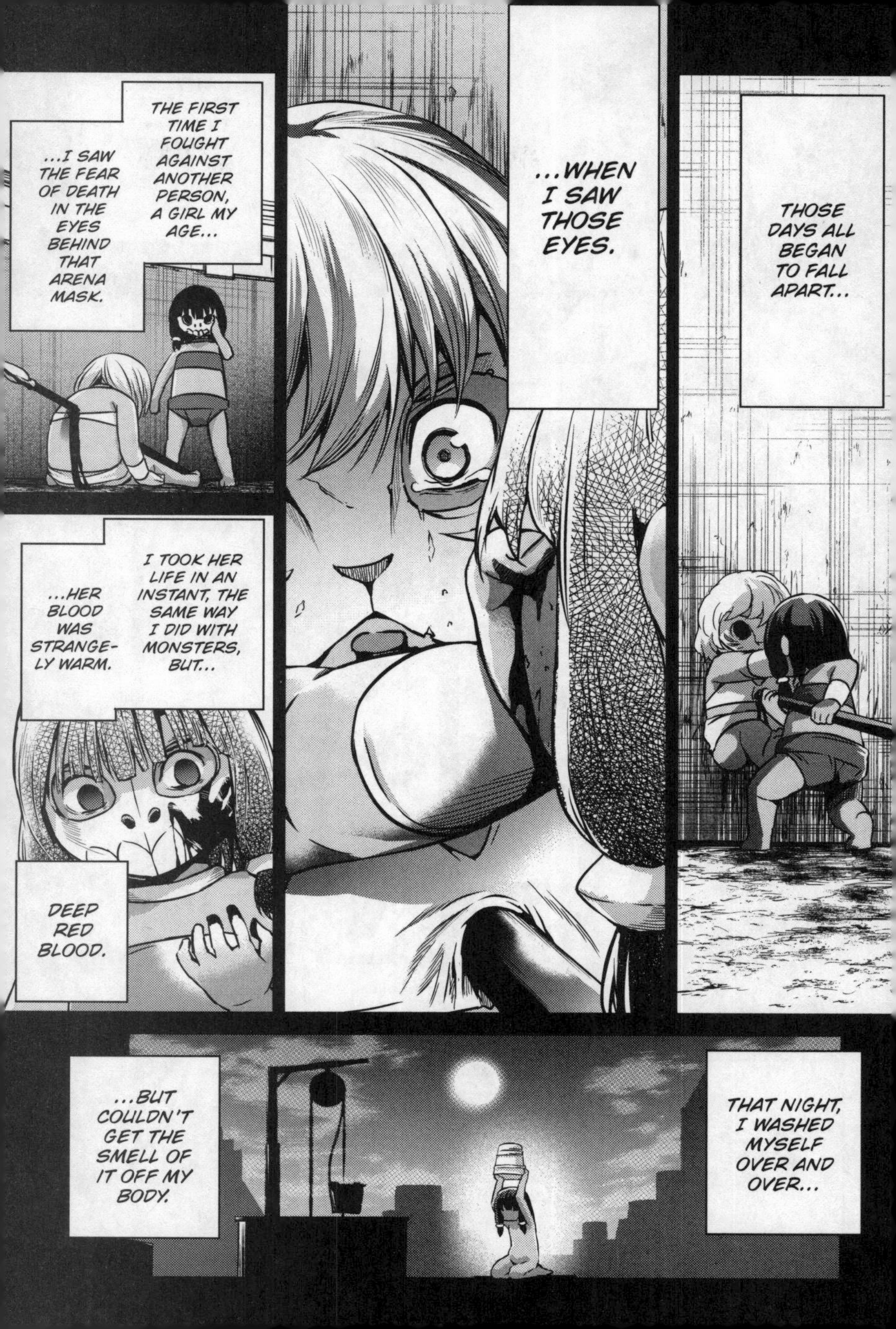
THOSE DAYS ALL BEGAN TO FALL APART...
...WHEN I SAW THOSE EYES.
THE FIRST TIME I FOUGHT AGAINST ANOTHER PERSON, A GIRL MY AGE...
...I SAW THE FEAR OF DEATH IN THE EYES BEHIND THAT ARENA MASK.
I TOOK HER LIFE IN AN INSTANT, THE SAME WAY I DID WITH MONSTERS, BUT...
...HER BLOOD WAS STRANGE-LY WARM.
DEEP RED BLOOD.
THAT NIGHT, I WASHED MYSELF OVER AND OVER...
...BUT COULDN'T GET THE SMELL OF IT OFF MY BODY.

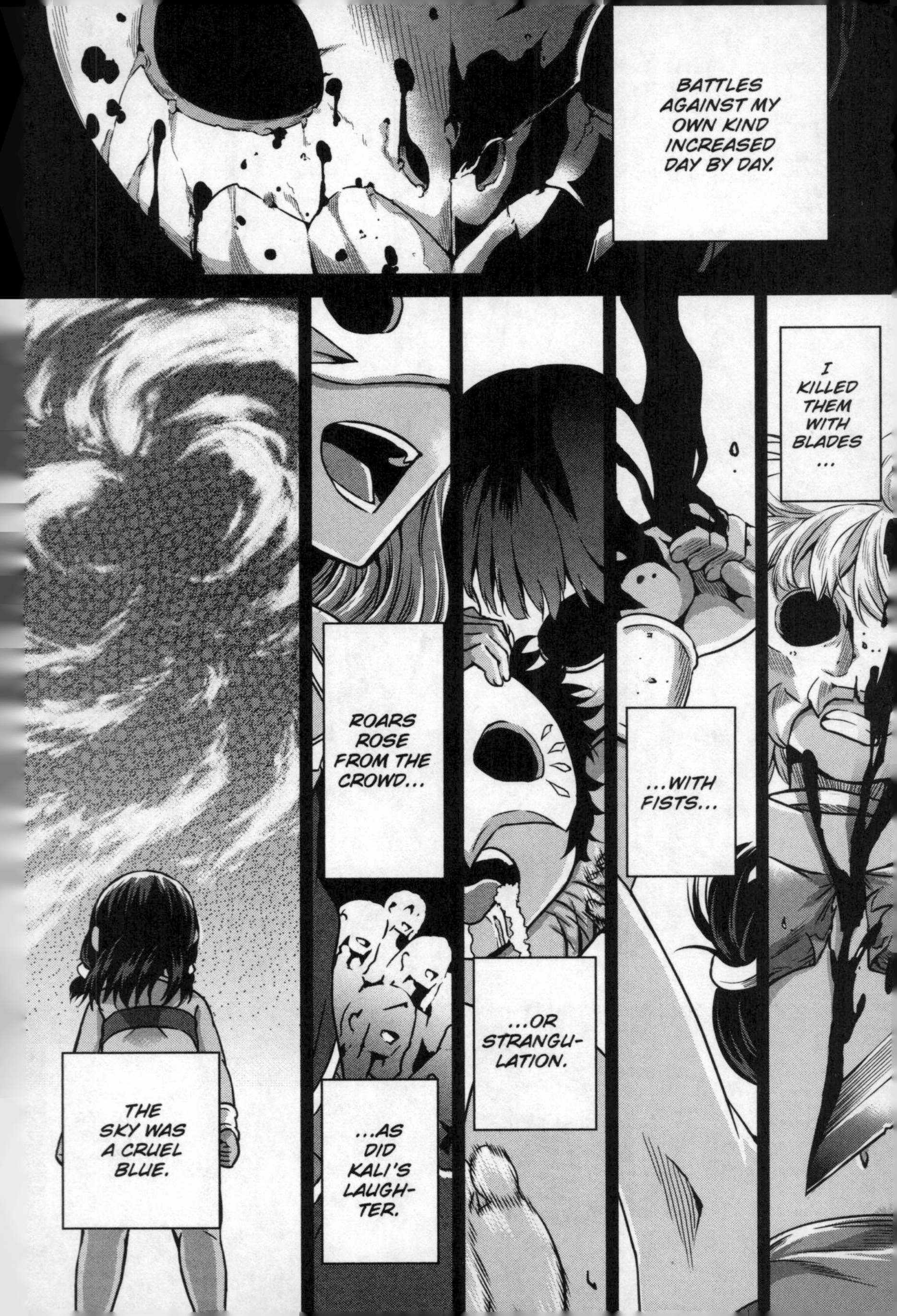
BATTLES AGAINST MY OWN KIND INCREASED DAY BY DAY.
I KILLED THEM WITH BLADES...
...WITH FISTS...
...OR STRANGU-LATION.
ROARS ROSE FROM THE CROWD...
...AS DID KALI'S LAUGH-TER.
THE SKY WAS A CRUEL BLUE.

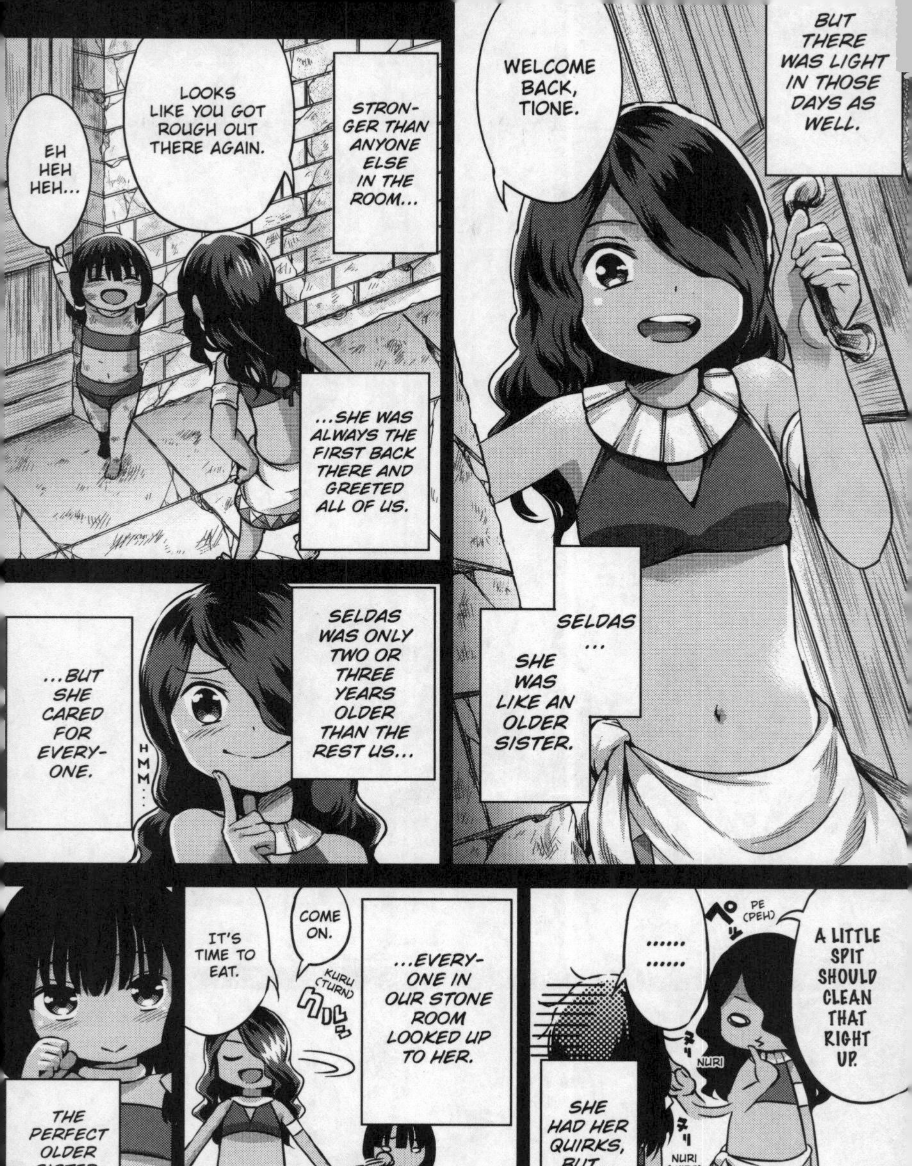
BUT THERE WAS LIGHT IN THOSE DAYS AS WELL.
WELCOME BACK, TIONE.
SELDAS... SHE WAS LIKE AN OLDER SISTER.
STRONGER THAN ANYONE ELSE IN THE ROOM...
LOOKS LIKE YOU GOT ROUGH OUT THERE AGAIN.
EH HEH HEH...
...SHE WAS ALWAYS THE FIRST BACK THERE AND GREETED ALL OF US.
SELDAS WAS ONLY TWO OR THREE YEARS OLDER THAN THE REST US...
HMM...
...BUT SHE CARED FOR EVERYONE.
PE (PEH)
A LITTLE SPIT SHOULD CLEAN THAT RIGHT UP.
......
......
NURI
NURI (WIPE)
SHE HAD HER QUIRKS, BUT...
...EVERYONE IN OUR STONE ROOM LOOKED UP TO HER.
COME ON.
KURU (TURN)
IT'S TIME TO EAT.
THE PERFECT OLDER SISTER.

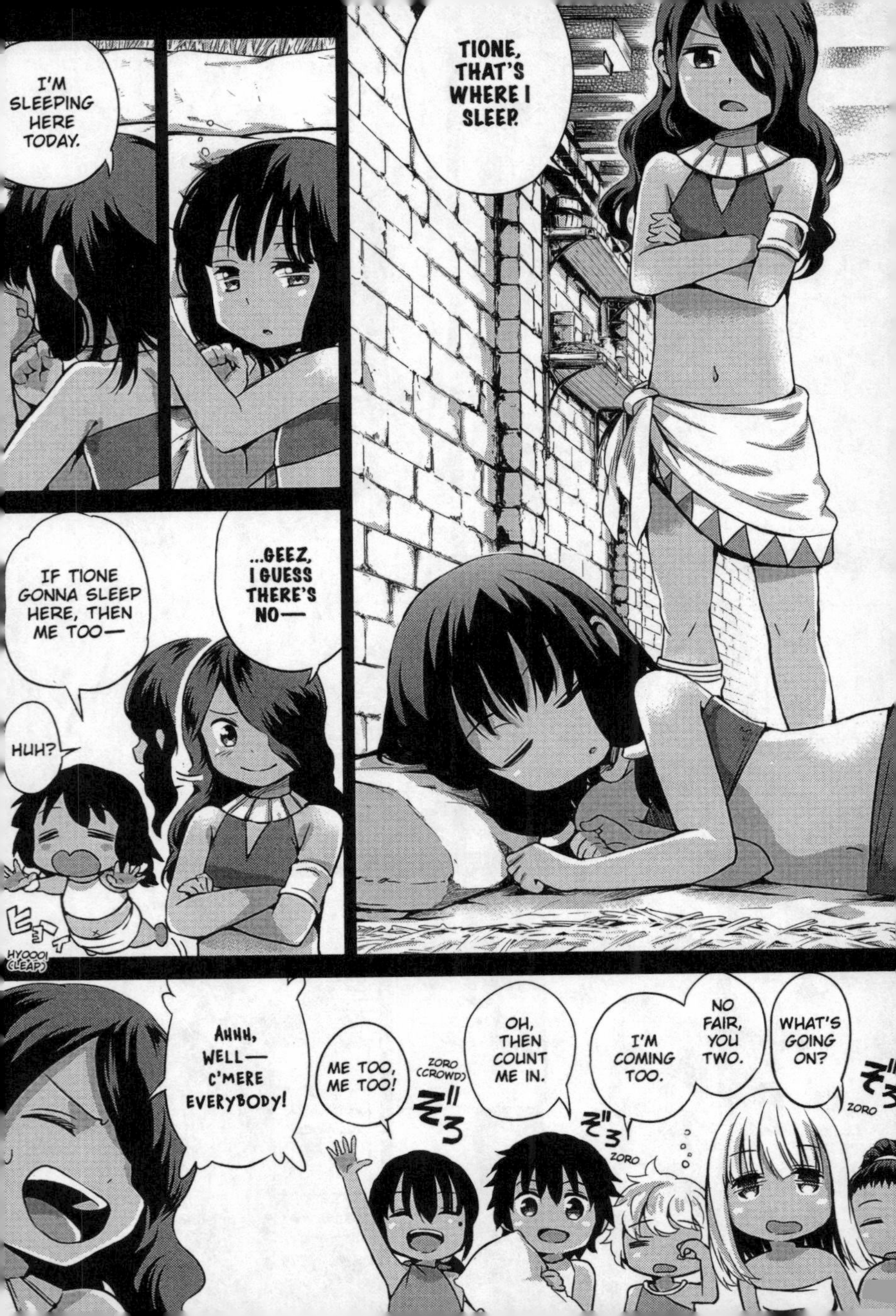
TIONE, THAT'S WHERE I SLEEP.
I'M SLEEPING HERE TODAY.
...GEEZ, I GUESS THERE'S NO—
IF TIONE GONNA SLEEP HERE, THEN ME TOO—
HUH?
HYOOO! (LEAP)
WHAT'S GOING ON?
ZORO
NO FAIR, YOU TWO.
I'M COMING TOO.
ZORO
OH, THEN COUNT ME IN.
ZORO (CROWD)
ME TOO, ME TOO!
AHHH, WELL— C'MERE EVERYBODY!

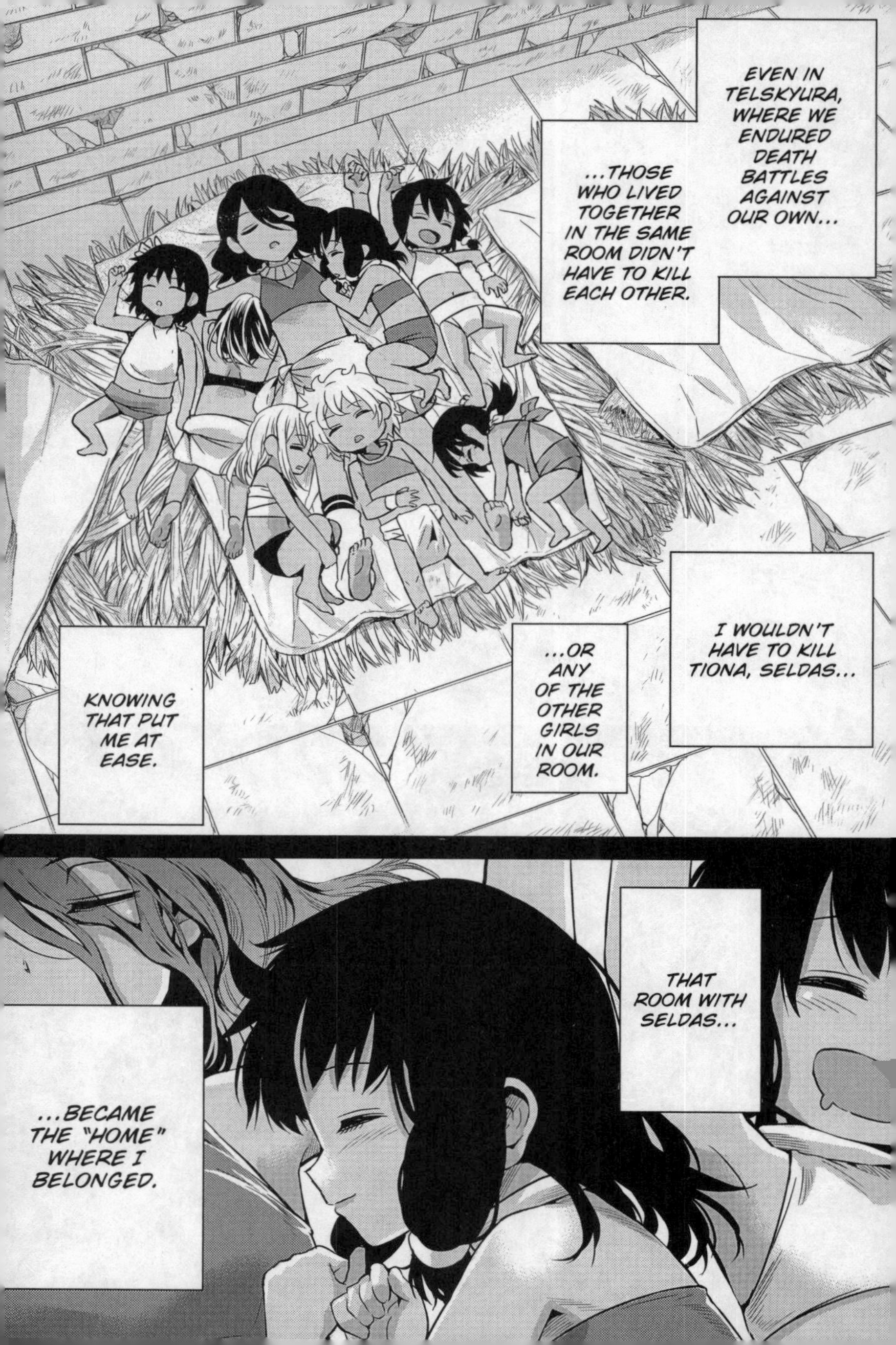
EVEN IN TELSKYURA, WHERE WE ENDURED DEATH BATTLES AGAINST OUR OWN...
...THOSE WHO LIVED TOGETHER IN THE SAME ROOM DIDN'T HAVE TO KILL EACH OTHER.
I WOULDN'T HAVE TO KILL TIONA, SELDAS...
...OR ANY OF THE OTHER GIRLS IN OUR ROOM.
KNOWING THAT PUT ME AT EASE.
THAT ROOM WITH SELDAS...
...BECAME THE "HOME" WHERE I BELONGED.

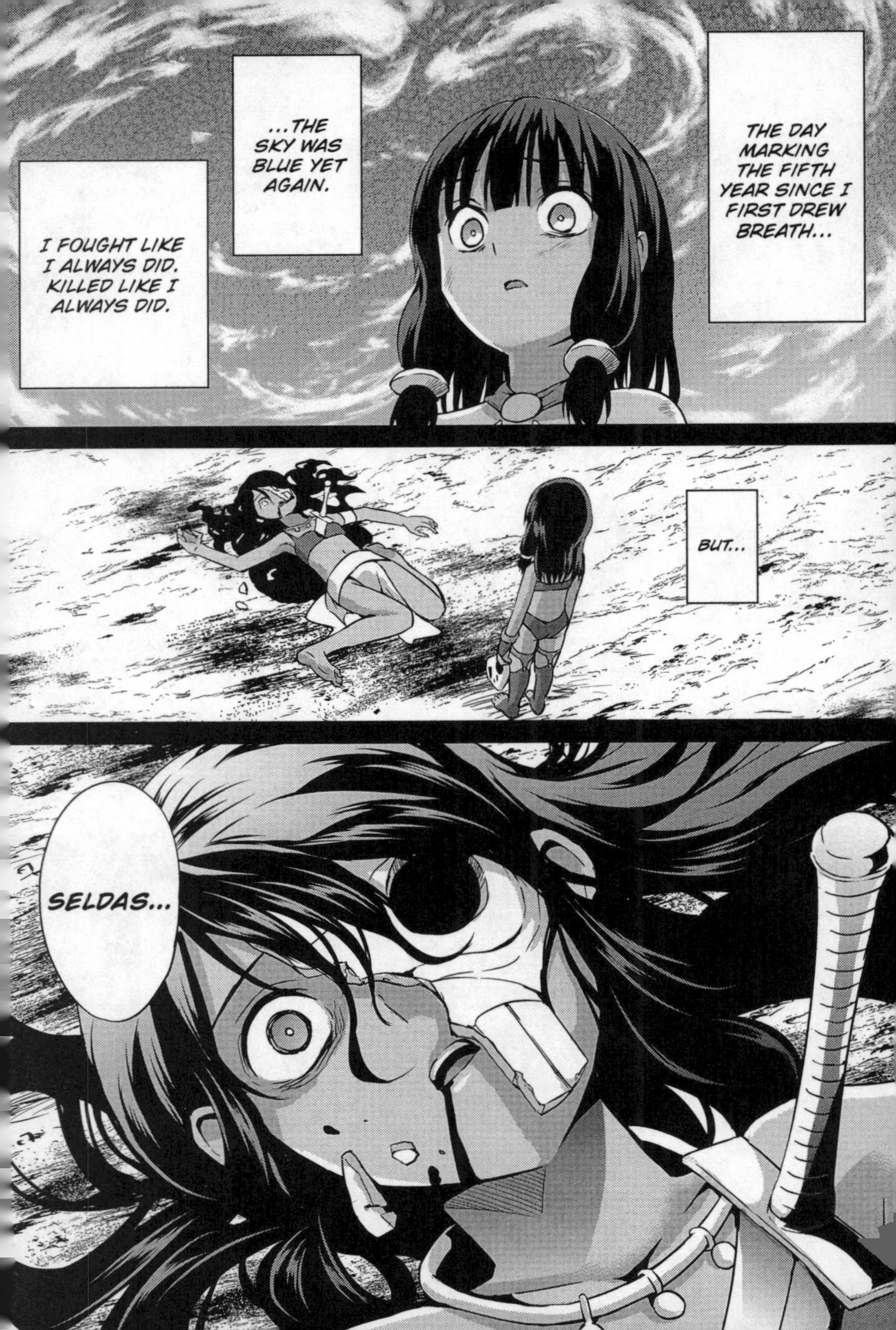
THE DAY MARKING THE FIFTH YEAR SINCE I FIRST DREW BREATH...
...THE SKY WAS BLUE YET AGAIN.
I FOUGHT LIKE I ALWAYS DID. KILLED LIKE I ALWAYS DID.
BUT...
SELDAS...

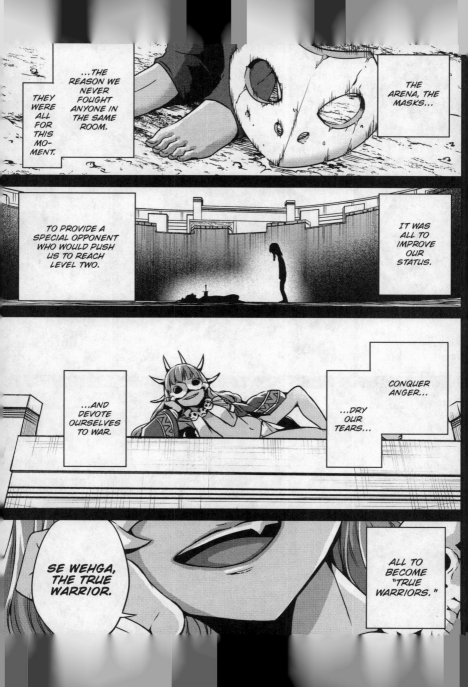

THE ARENA, THE MASKS...
...THE REASON WE NEVER FOUGHT ANYONE IN THE SAME ROOM.
THEY WERE ALL FOR THIS MOMENT.
IT WAS ALL TO IMPROVE OUR STATUS.
TO PROVIDE A SPECIAL OPPONENT WHO WOULD PUSH US TO REACH LEVEL TWO.
CONQUER ANGER...
...DRY OUR TEARS...
...AND DEVOTE OURSELVES TO WAR.
ALL TO BECOME "TRUE WARRIORS."
SE WEHGA, THE TRUE WARRIOR.

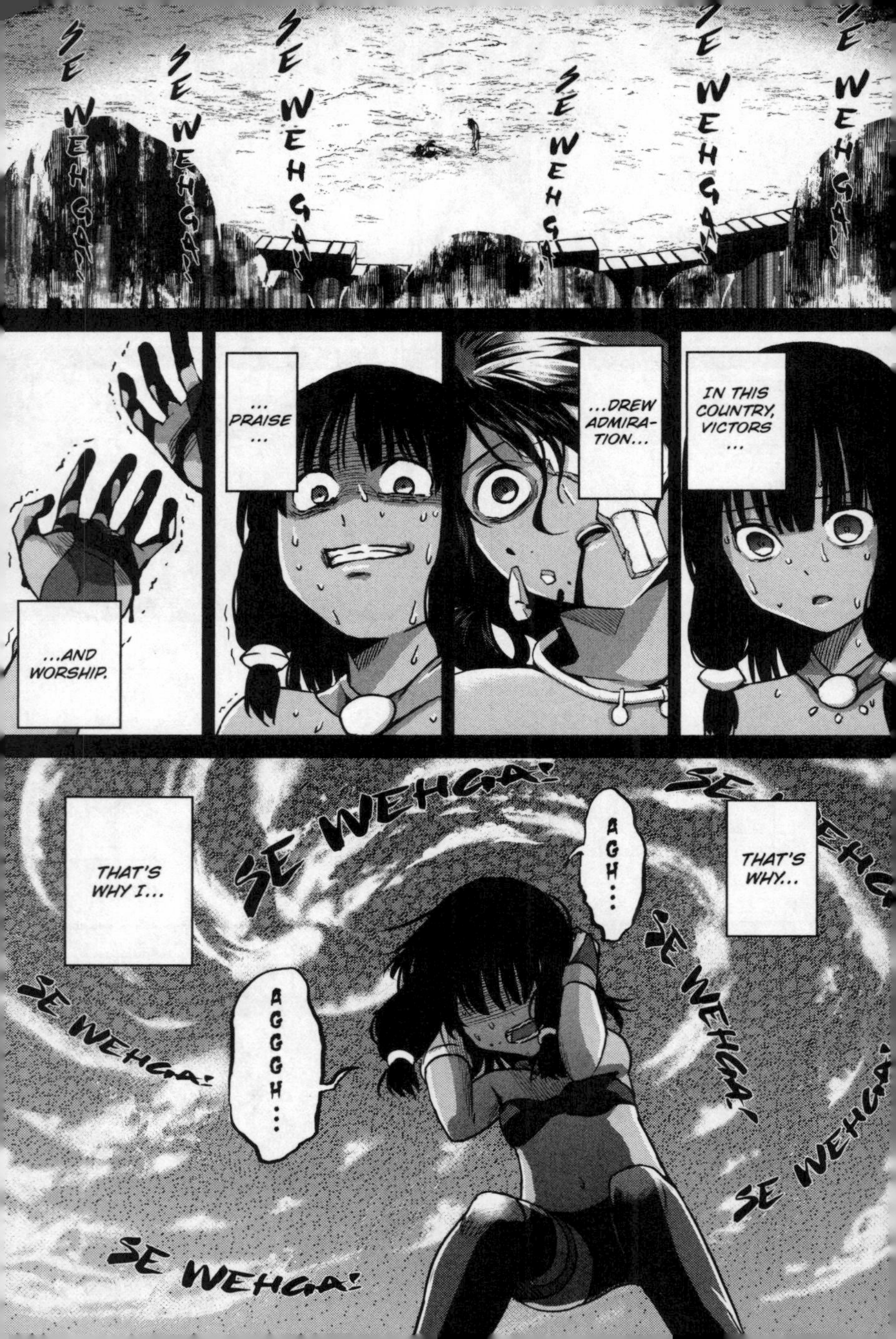
SE WEHGA!
SE WEHGA!
SE WEHGA!
SE WEHGA!
SE WEHGA!
SE WEHGA!
SE WEHGA!
IN THIS COUNTRY, VICTORS...
...DREW ADMIRATION...
...PRAISE...
...AND WORSHIP.
THAT'S WHY...
SE WEHGA!
SE WEHGA!
SE WEHGA!
AGH...
SE WEHGA!
THAT'S WHY I...
AGGGH...
SE WEHGA!
SE WEHGA!

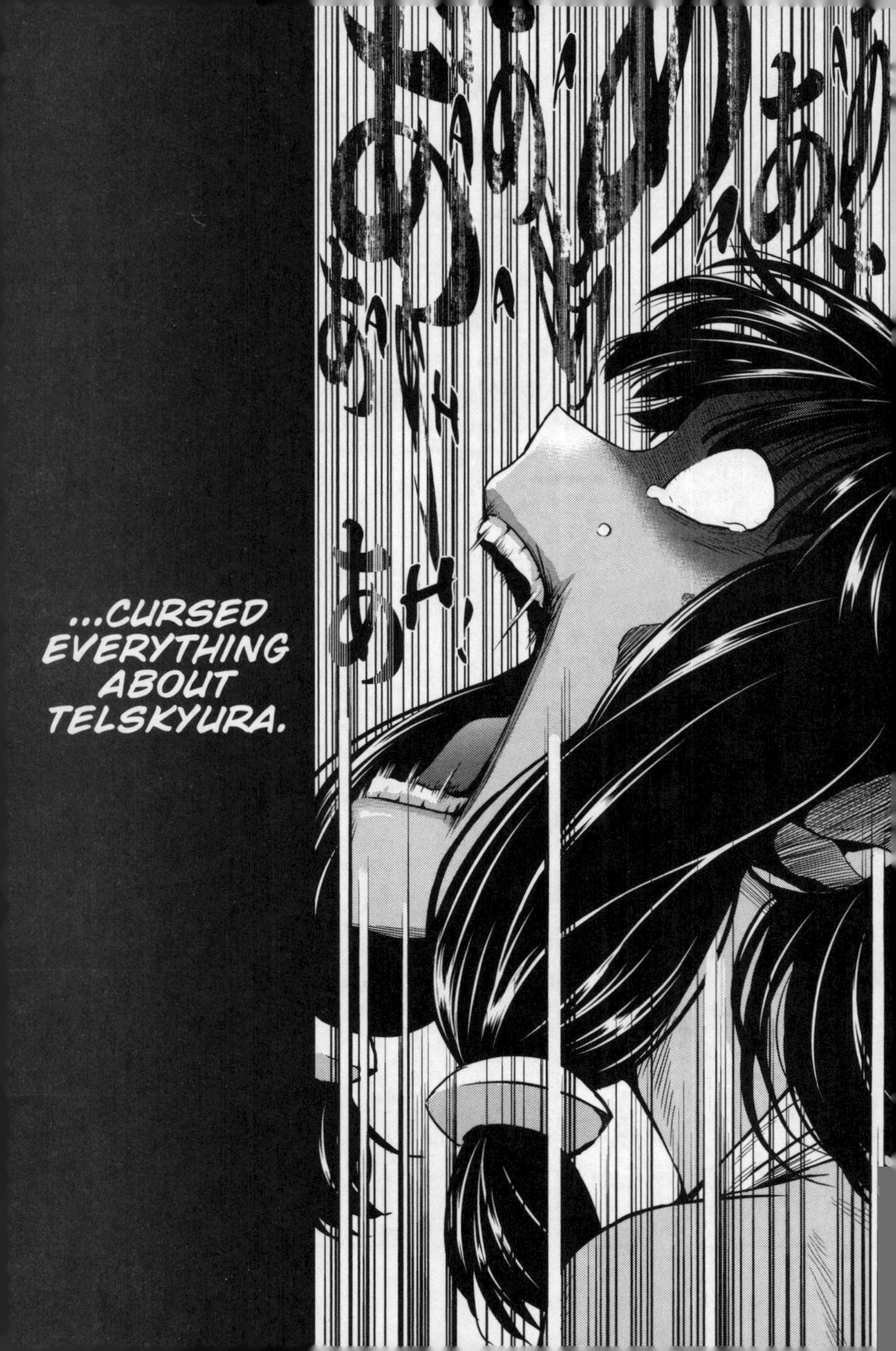
...CURSED EVERYTHING ABOUT TELSKYURA.

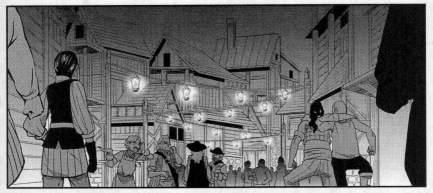

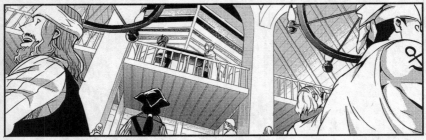

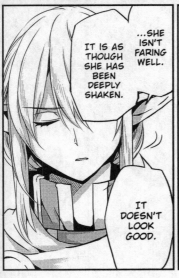

HOW'S TIONE DOIN', RIVERIA?
EVEN WITH TIONA AND AIZ BY HER SIDE...
...SHE ISN'T FARING WELL.
IT IS AS THOUGH SHE HAS BEEN DEEPLY SHAKEN.
IT DOESN'T LOOK GOOD.

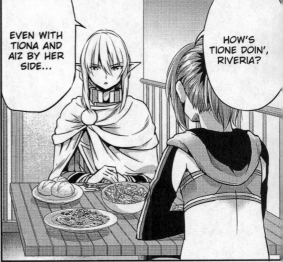

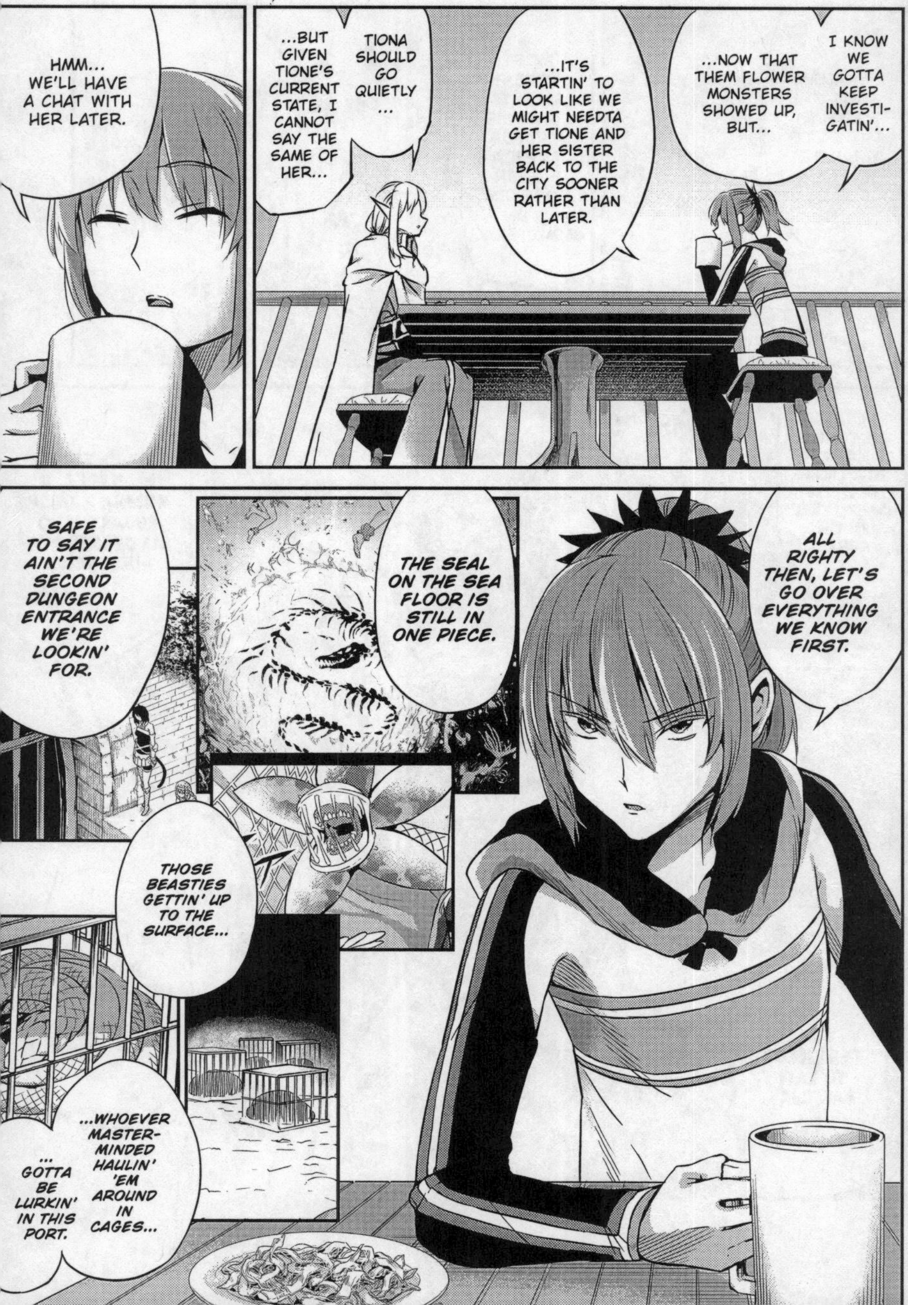
I KNOW WE GOTTA KEEP INVESTI-GATIN'...
...NOW THAT THEM FLOWER MONSTERS SHOWED UP, BUT...
...IT'S STARTIN' TO LOOK LIKE WE MIGHT NEEDTA GET TIONE AND HER SISTER BACK TO THE CITY SOONER RATHER THAN LATER.
TIONA SHOULD GO QUIETLY...
...BUT GIVEN TIONE'S CURRENT STATE, I CANNOT SAY THE SAME OF HER...
HMM... WE'LL HAVE A CHAT WITH HER LATER.
ALL RIGHTY THEN, LET'S GO OVER EVERYTHING WE KNOW FIRST.
THE SEAL ON THE SEA FLOOR IS STILL IN ONE PIECE.
SAFE TO SAY IT AIN'T THE SECOND DUNGEON ENTRANCE WE'RE LOOKIN' FOR.
THOSE BEASTIES GETTIN' UP TO THE SURFACE...
...WHOEVER MASTER-MINDED HAULIN' 'EM AROUND IN CAGES...
...GOTTA BE LURKIN' IN THIS PORT.

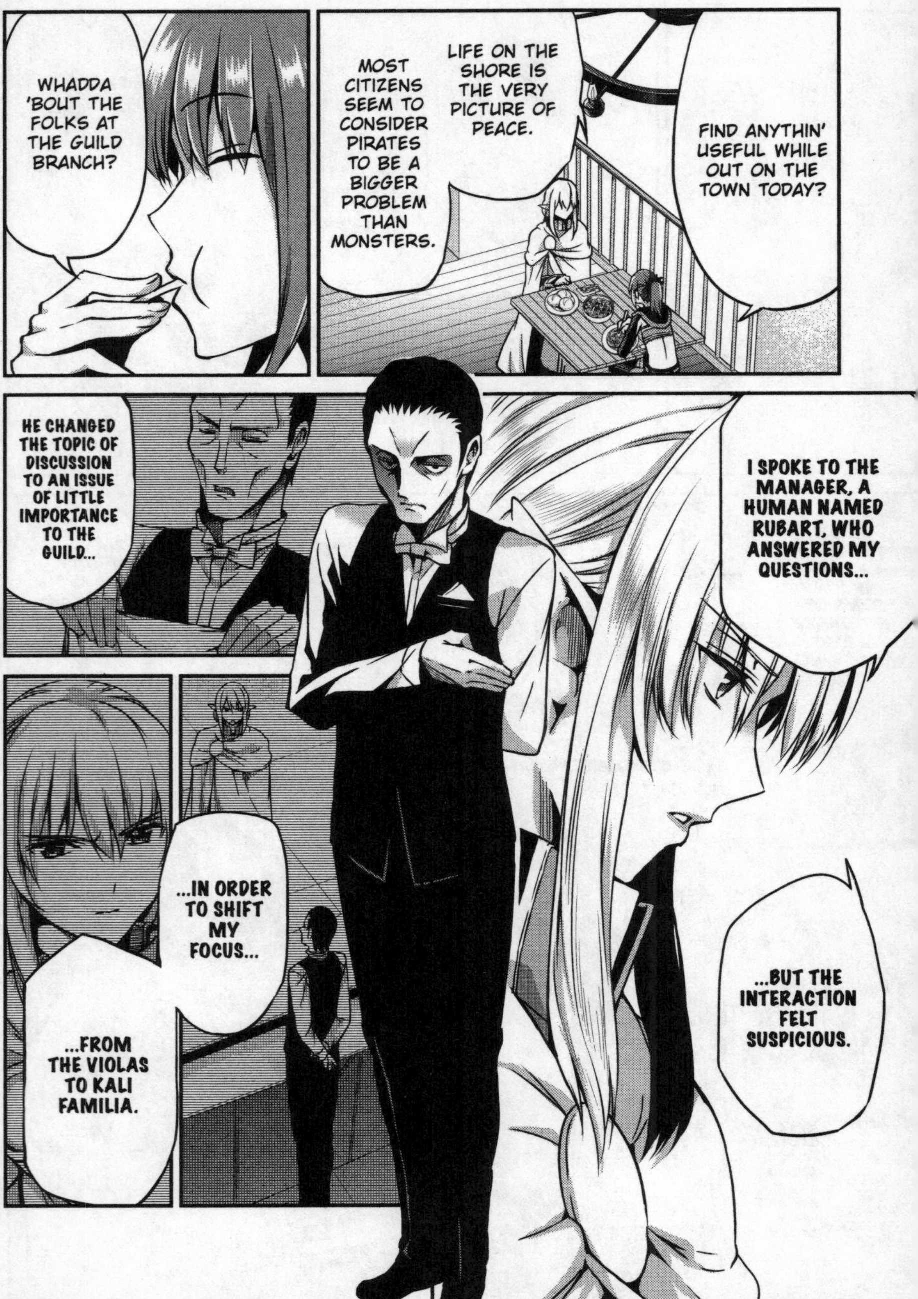
FIND ANYTHIN' USEFUL WHILE OUT ON THE TOWN TODAY?
LIFE ON THE SHORE IS THE VERY PICTURE OF PEACE.
MOST CITIZENS SEEM TO CONSIDER PIRATES TO BE A BIGGER PROBLEM THAN MONSTERS.
WHADDA 'BOUT THE FOLKS AT THE GUILD BRANCH?
I SPOKE TO THE MANAGER, A HUMAN NAMED RUBART, WHO ANSWERED MY QUESTIONS...
...BUT THE INTERACTION FELT SUSPICIOUS.
HE CHANGED THE TOPIC OF DISCUSSION TO AN ISSUE OF LITTLE IMPORTANCE TO THE GUILD...
...IN ORDER TO SHIFT MY FOCUS...
...FROM THE VIOLAS TO KALI FAMILIA.

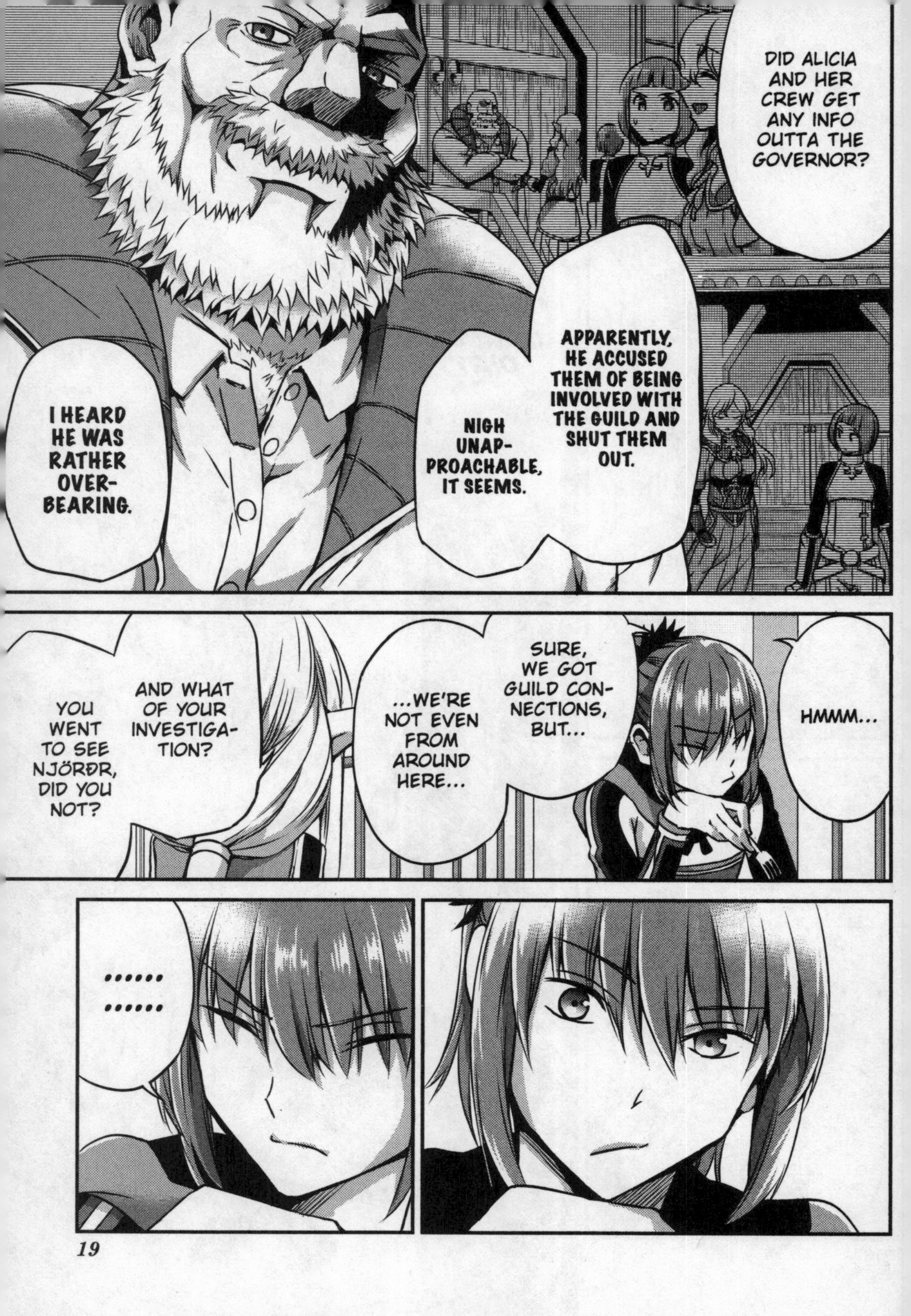
DID ALICIA AND HER CREW GET ANY INFO OUTTA THE GOVERNOR?
APPARENTLY, HE ACCUSED THEM OF BEING INVOLVED WITH THE GUILD AND SHUT THEM OUT.
NIGH UNAP-PROACHABLE, IT SEEMS.
I HEARD HE WAS RATHER OVER-BEARING.
HMMM...
SURE, WE GOT GUILD CON-NECTIONS, BUT...
...WE'RE NOT EVEN FROM AROUND HERE...
AND WHAT OF YOUR INVESTIGA-TION?
YOU WENT TO SEE NJÖRÐR, DID YOU NOT?
......
......

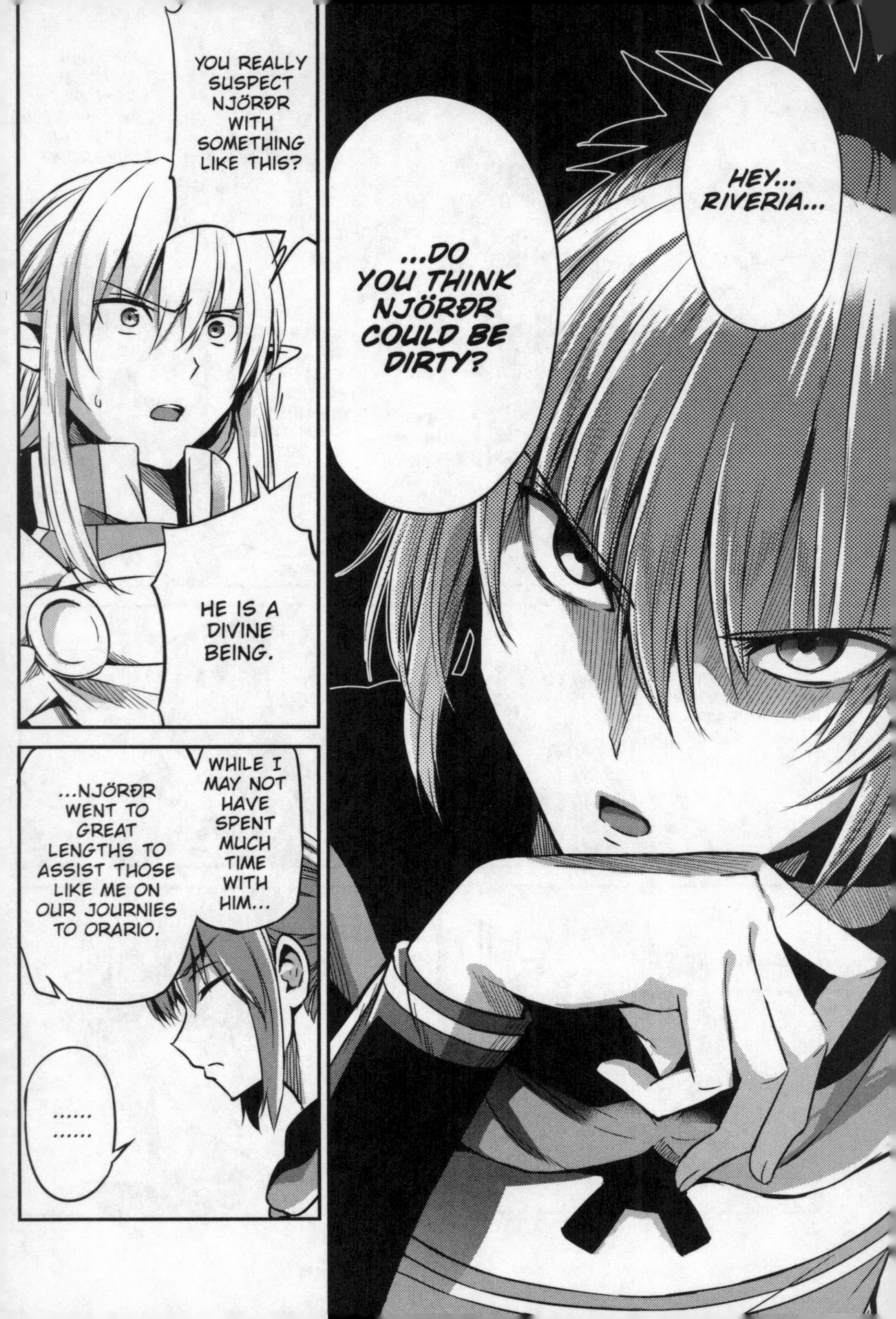
HEY... RIVERIA...
...DO YOU THINK NJÖRÐR COULD BE DIRTY?
YOU REALLY SUSPECT NJÖRÐR WITH SOMETHING LIKE THIS?
HE IS A DIVINE BEING.
WHILE I MAY NOT HAVE SPENT MUCH TIME WITH HIM...
...NJÖRÐR WENT TO GREAT LENGTHS TO ASSIST THOSE LIKE ME ON OUR JOURNIES TO ORARIO.
......
......

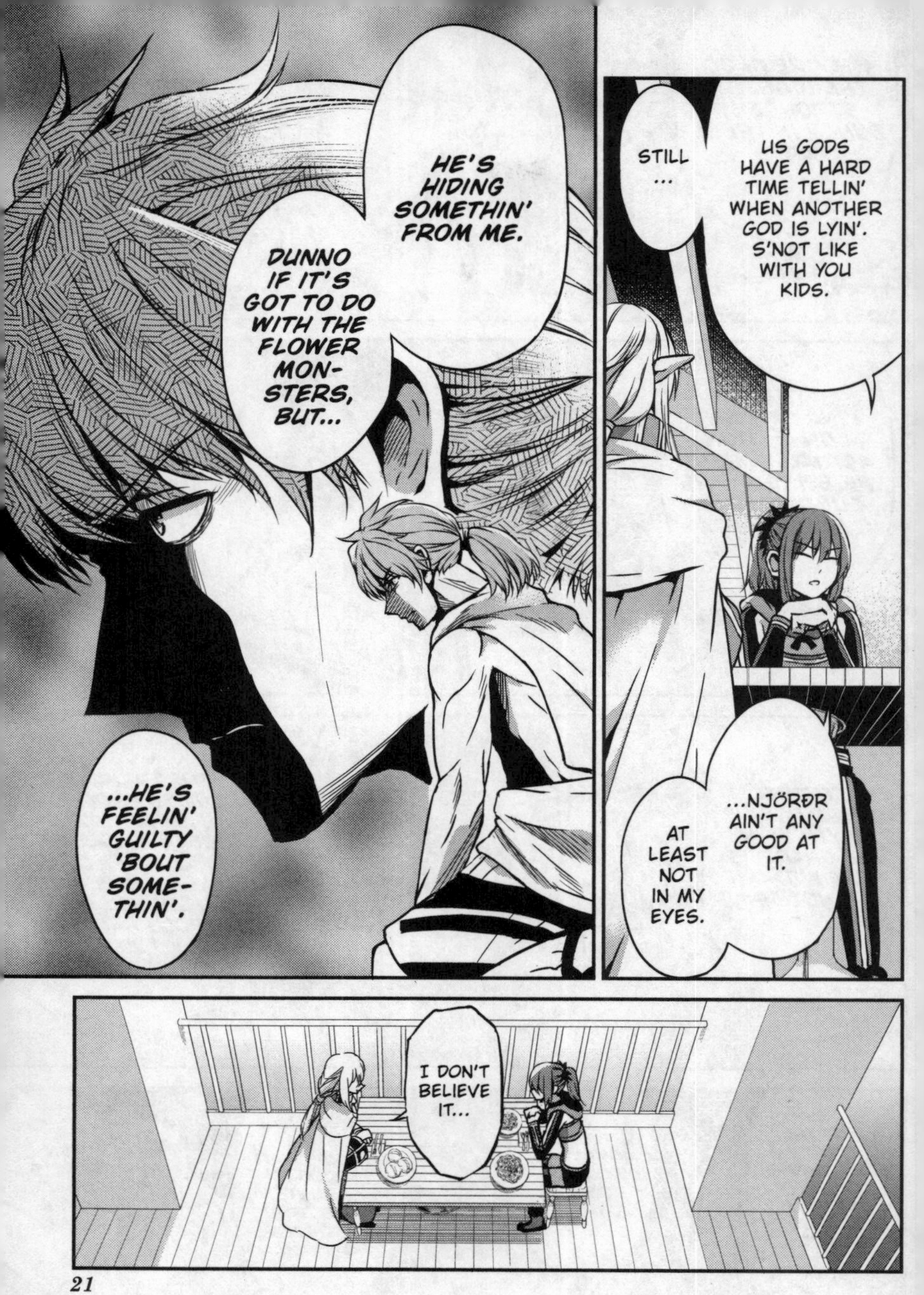
US GODS HAVE A HARD TIME TELLIN' WHEN ANOTHER GOD IS LYIN'. S'NOT LIKE WITH YOU KIDS.
STILL ...
...NJÖRÐR AIN'T ANY GOOD AT IT.
AT LEAST NOT IN MY EYES.
HE'S HIDING SOMETHIN' FROM ME.
DUNNO IF IT'S GOT TO DO WITH THE FLOWER MON-STERS, BUT...
...HE'S FEELIN' GUILTY 'BOUT SOME-THIN'.
I DON'T BELIEVE IT...

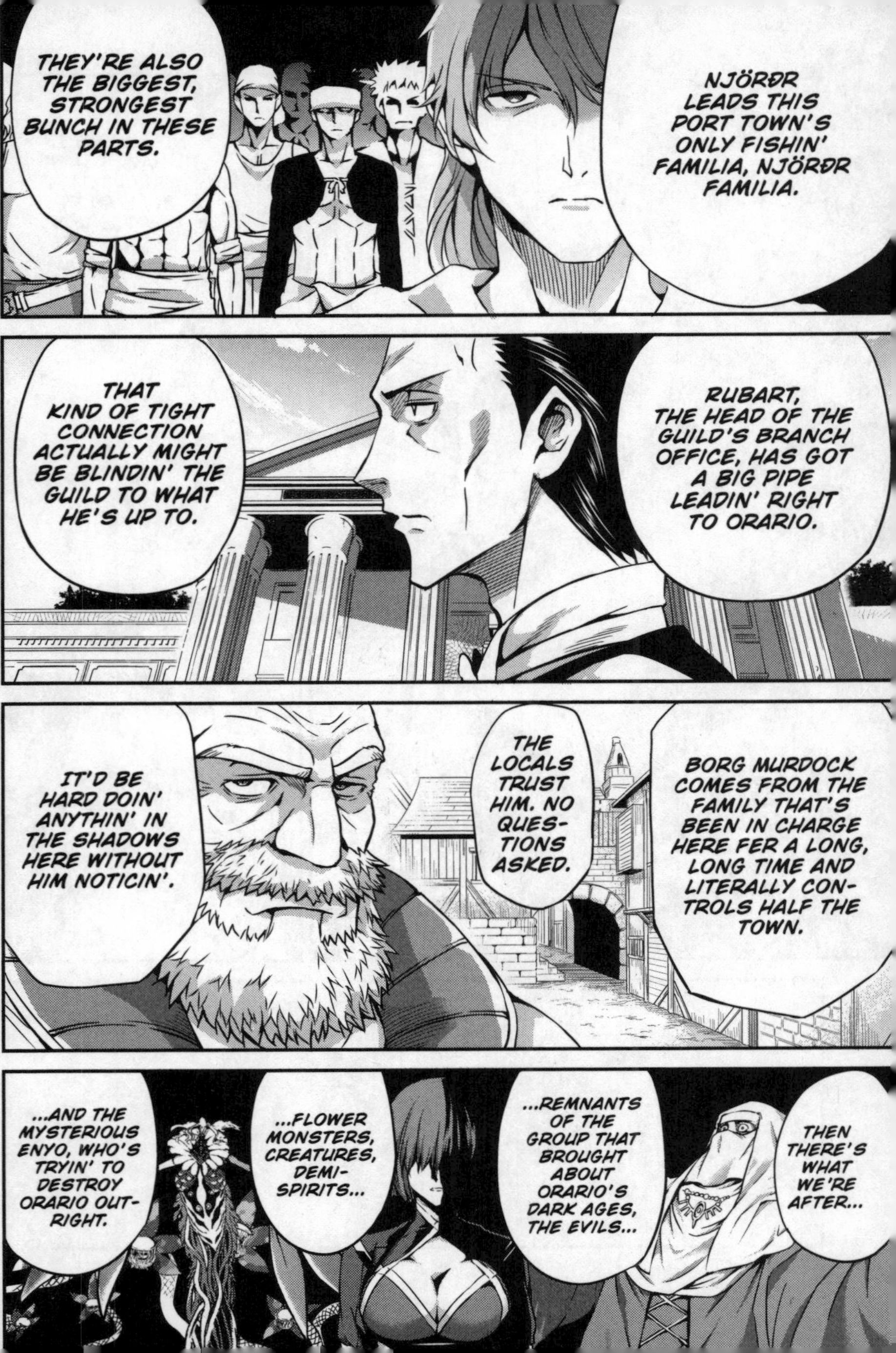
NJÖRÐR LEADS THIS PORT TOWN'S ONLY FISHIN' FAMILIA, NJÖRÐR FAMILIA.
THEY'RE ALSO THE BIGGEST, STRONGEST BUNCH IN THESE PARTS.
RUBART, THE HEAD OF THE GUILD'S BRANCH OFFICE, HAS GOT A BIG PIPE LEADIN' RIGHT TO ORARIO.
THAT KIND OF TIGHT CONNECTION ACTUALLY MIGHT BE BLINDIN' THE GUILD TO WHAT HE'S UP TO.
BORG MURDOCK COMES FROM THE FAMILY THAT'S BEEN IN CHARGE HERE FER A LONG, LONG TIME AND LITERALLY CON-TROLS HALF THE TOWN.
THE LOCALS TRUST HIM. NO QUES-TIONS ASKED.
IT'D BE HARD DOIN' ANYTHIN' IN THE SHADOWS HERE WITHOUT HIM NOTICIN'.
THEN THERE'S WHAT WE'RE AFTER...
...REMNANTS OF THE GROUP THAT BROUGHT ABOUT ORARIO'S DARK AGES, THE EVILS...
...FLOWER MONSTERS, CREATURES, DEMI-SPIRITS...
...AND THE MYSTERIOUS ENYO, WHO'S TRYIN' TO DESTROY ORARIO OUT-RIGHT.

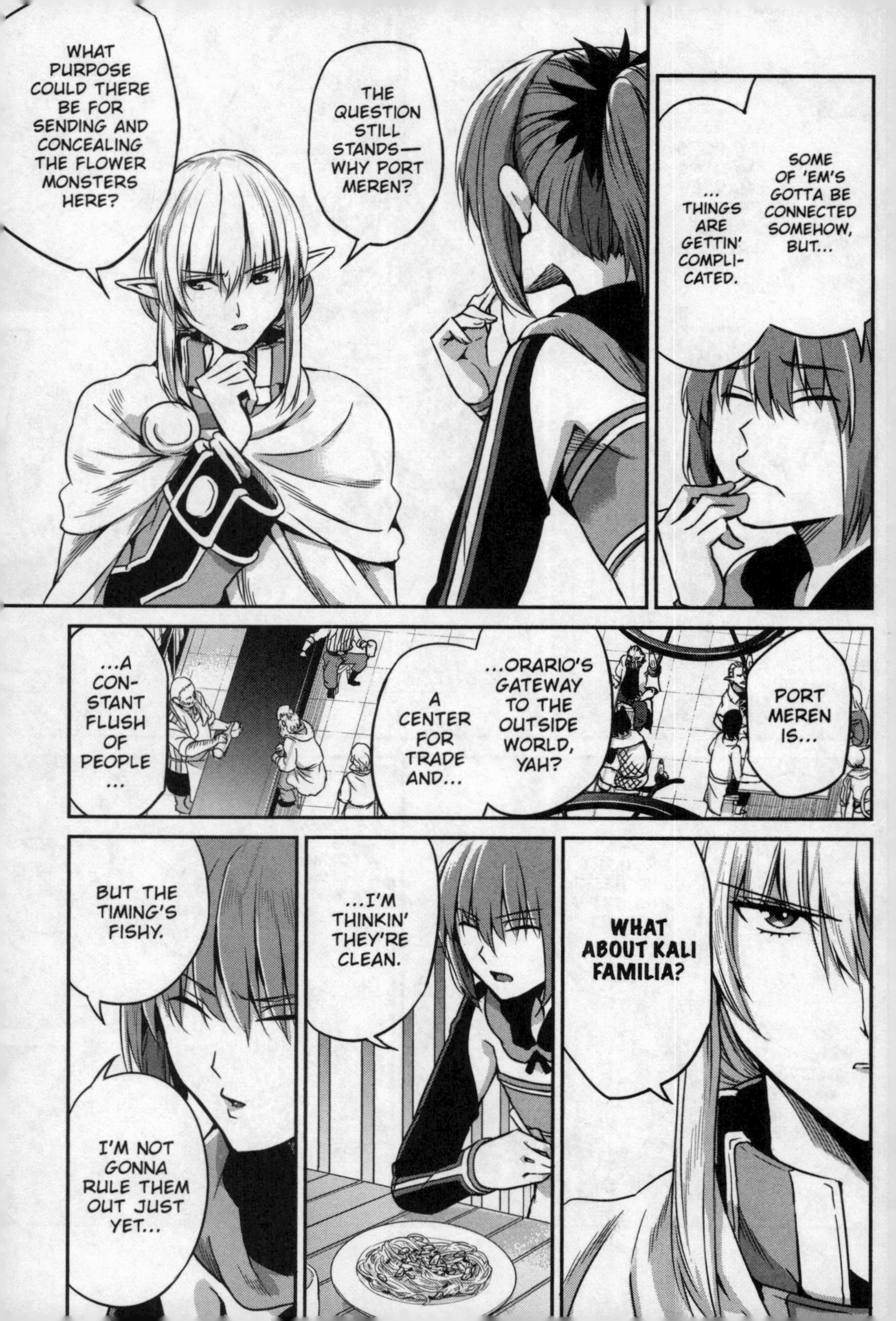
SOME OF 'EM'S GOTTA BE CONNECTED SOMEHOW, BUT...
...THINGS ARE GETTIN' COMPLI-CATED.
THE QUESTION STILL STANDS—WHY PORT MEREN?
WHAT PURPOSE COULD THERE BE FOR SENDING AND CONCEALING THE FLOWER MONSTERS HERE?
PORT MEREN IS...
...ORARIO'S GATEWAY TO THE OUTSIDE WORLD, YAH?
A CENTER FOR TRADE AND...
...A CONSTANT FLUSH OF PEOPLE...
WHAT ABOUT KALI FAMILIA?
...I'M THINKIN' THEY'RE CLEAN.
BUT THE TIMING'S FISHY.
I'M NOT GONNA RULE THEM OUT JUST YET...

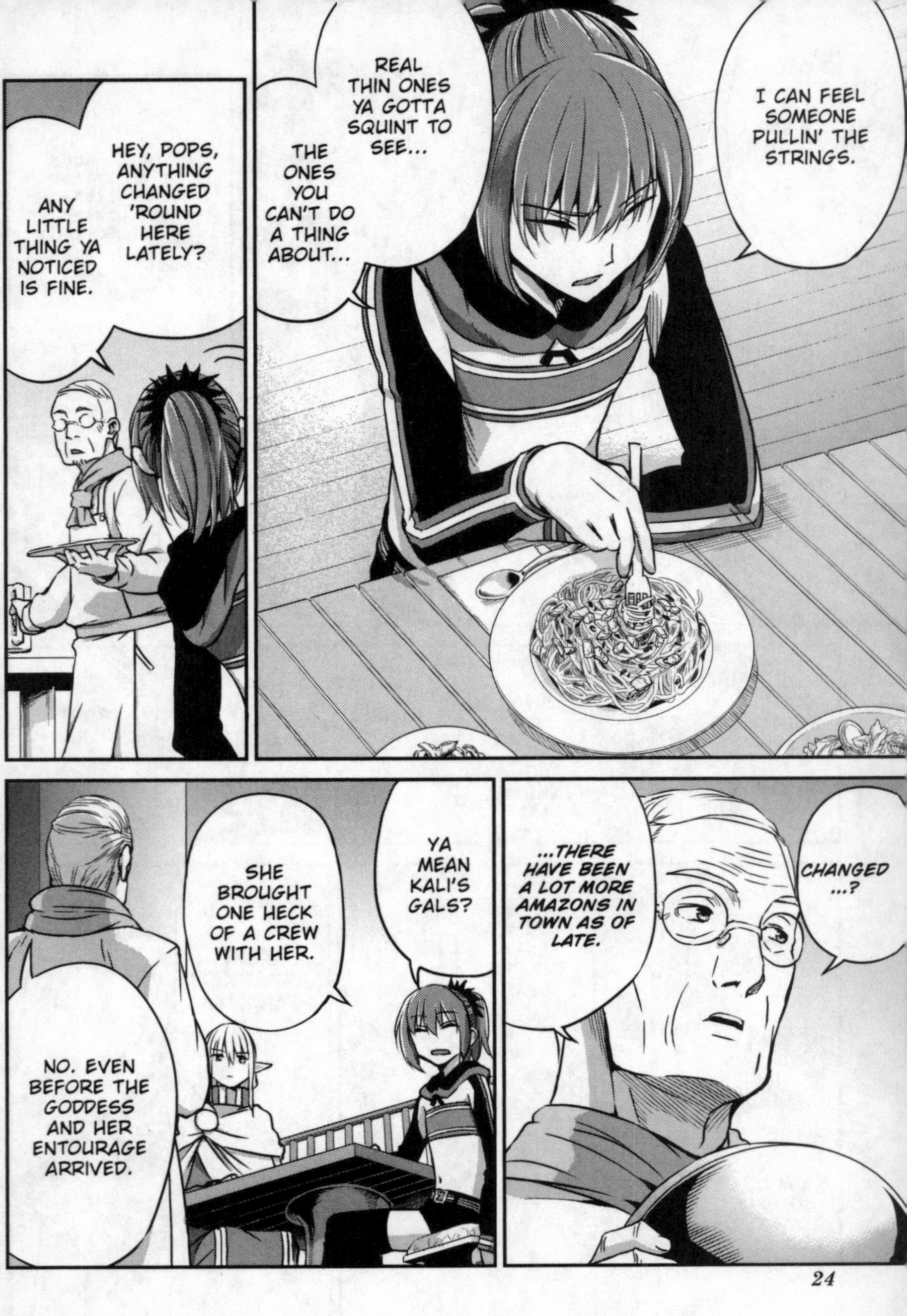
I CAN FEEL SOMEONE PULLIN' THE STRINGS.
REAL THIN ONES YA GOTTA SQUINT TO SEE...
THE ONES YOU CAN'T DO A THING ABOUT...
HEY, POPS, ANYTHING CHANGED 'ROUND HERE LATELY?
ANY LITTLE THING YA NOTICED IS FINE.
CHANGED ...?
...THERE HAVE BEEN A LOT MORE AMAZONS IN TOWN AS OF LATE.
YA MEAN KALI'S GALS?
SHE BROUGHT ONE HECK OF A CREW WITH HER.
NO. EVEN BEFORE THE GODDESS AND HER ENTOURAGE ARRIVED.

IT WAS JUST SURPRISING TO SEE SO MANY NEW FACES ALL THE TIME.

...AMAZONS?

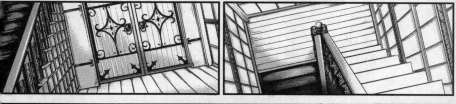

ABOUT TIME YOU GOT HERE...

CREEEAK

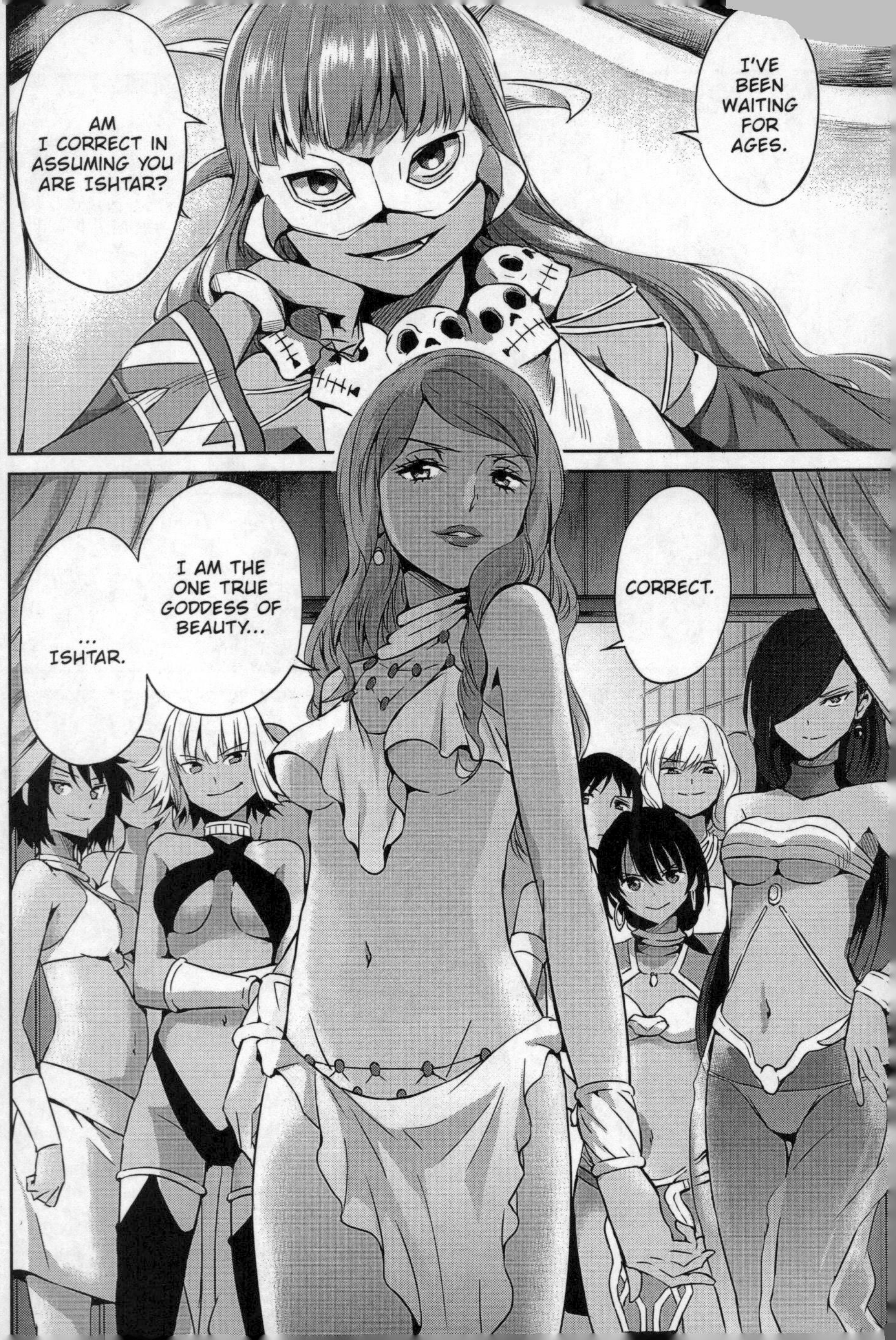
I'VE BEEN WAITING FOR AGES.
AM I CORRECT IN ASSUMING YOU ARE ISHTAR?
CORRECT.
I AM THE ONE TRUE GODDESS OF BEAUTY...
... ISHTAR.

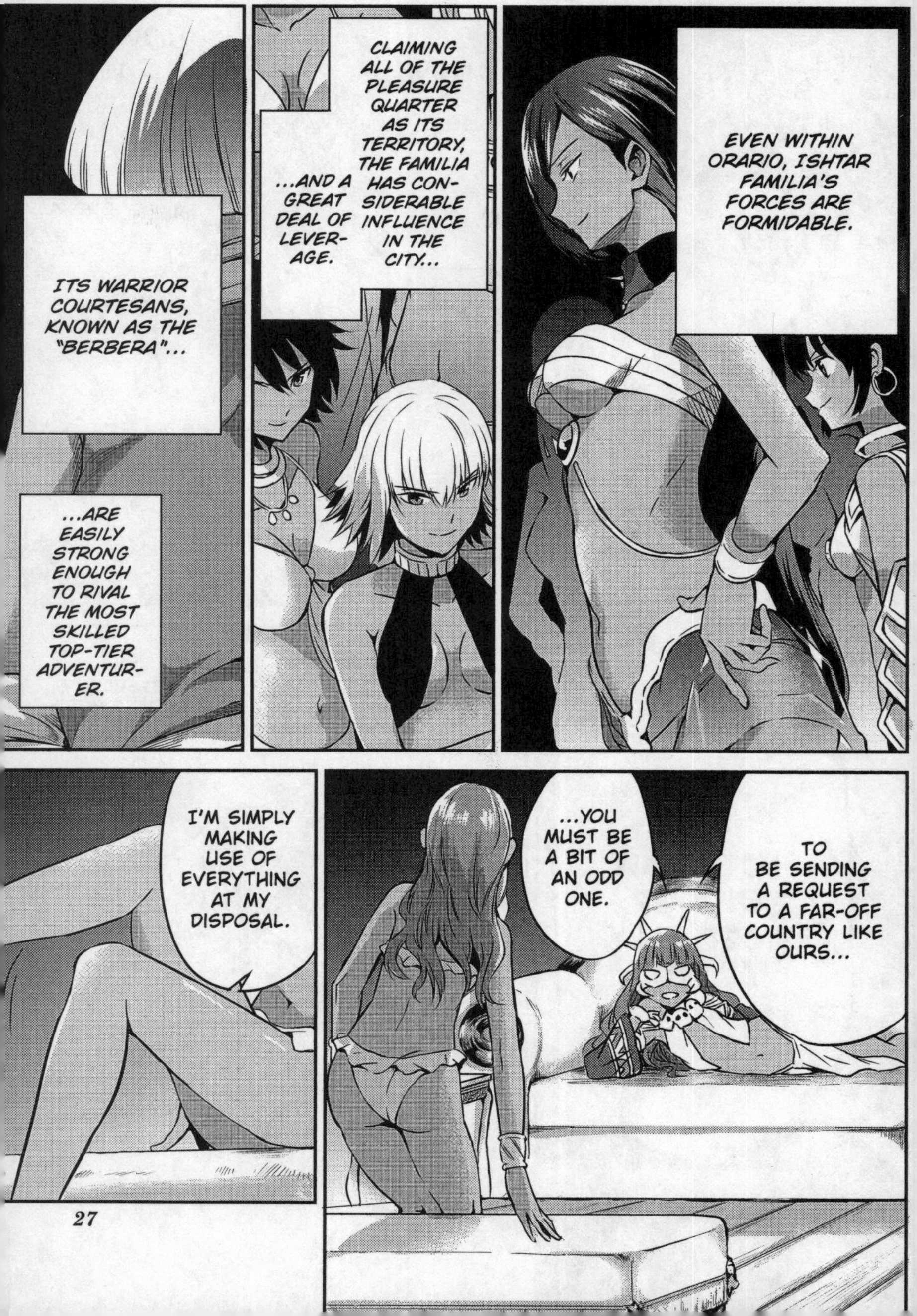
EVEN WITHIN ORARIO, ISHTAR FAMILIA'S FORCES ARE FORMIDABLE.
CLAIMING ALL OF THE PLEASURE QUARTER AS ITS TERRITORY, THE FAMILIA HAS CONSIDERABLE INFLUENCE IN THE CITY...
...AND A GREAT DEAL OF LEVERAGE.
ITS WARRIOR COURTESANS, KNOWN AS THE "BERBERA"...
...ARE EASILY STRONG ENOUGH TO RIVAL THE MOST SKILLED TOP-TIER ADVENTURER.
TO BE SENDING A REQUEST TO A FAR-OFF COUNTRY LIKE OURS...
...YOU MUST BE A BIT OF AN ODD ONE.
I'M SIMPLY MAKING USE OF EVERYTHING AT MY DISPOSAL.

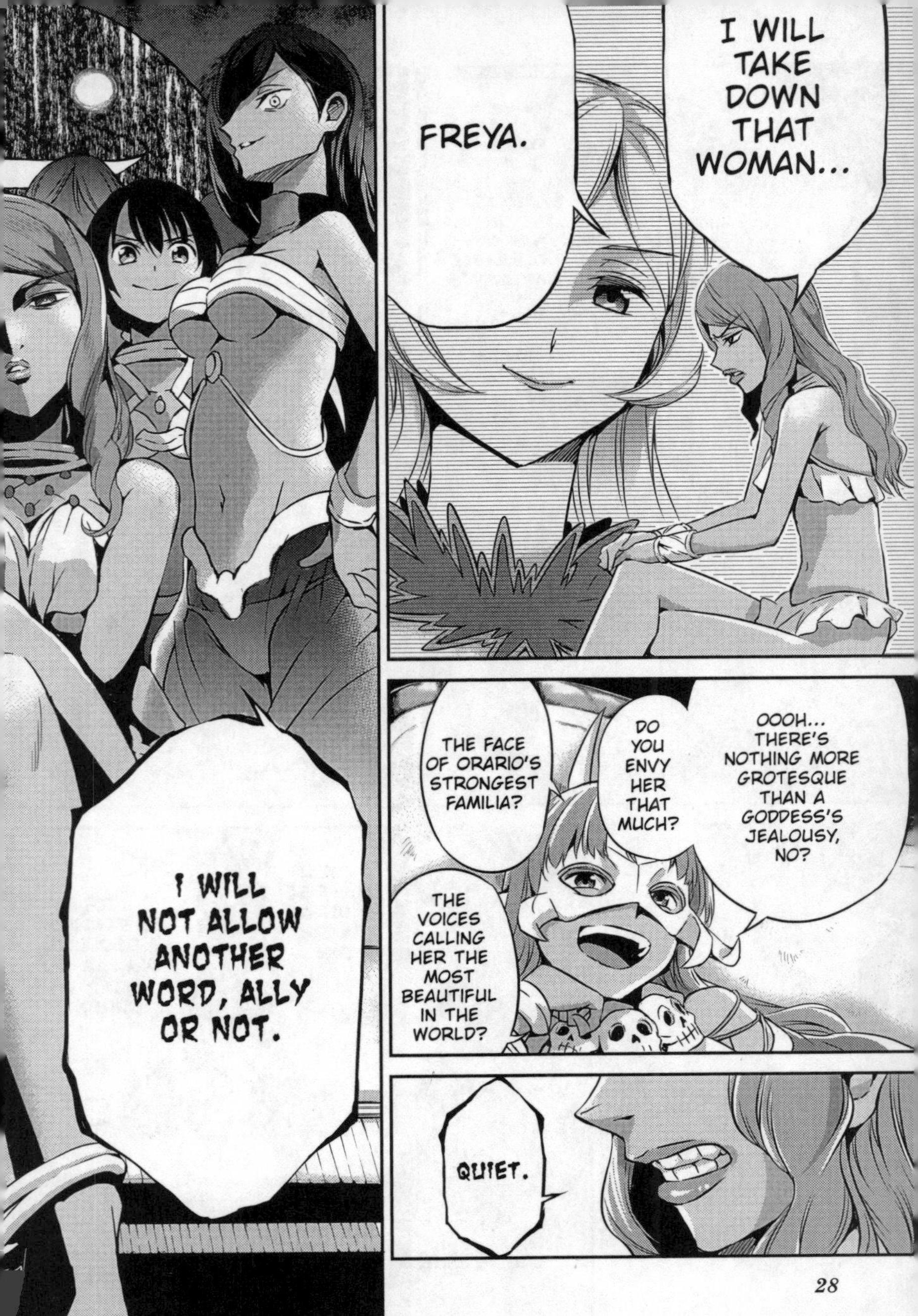
I WILL TAKE DOWN THAT WOMAN...
FREYA.
OOOH... THERE'S NOTHING MORE GROTESQUE THAN A GODDESS'S JEALOUSY, NO?
DO YOU ENVY HER THAT MUCH?
THE FACE OF ORARIO'S STRONGEST FAMILIA?
THE VOICES CALLING HER THE MOST BEAUTIFUL IN THE WORLD?
QUIET.
I WILL NOT ALLOW ANOTHER WORD, ALLY OR NOT.

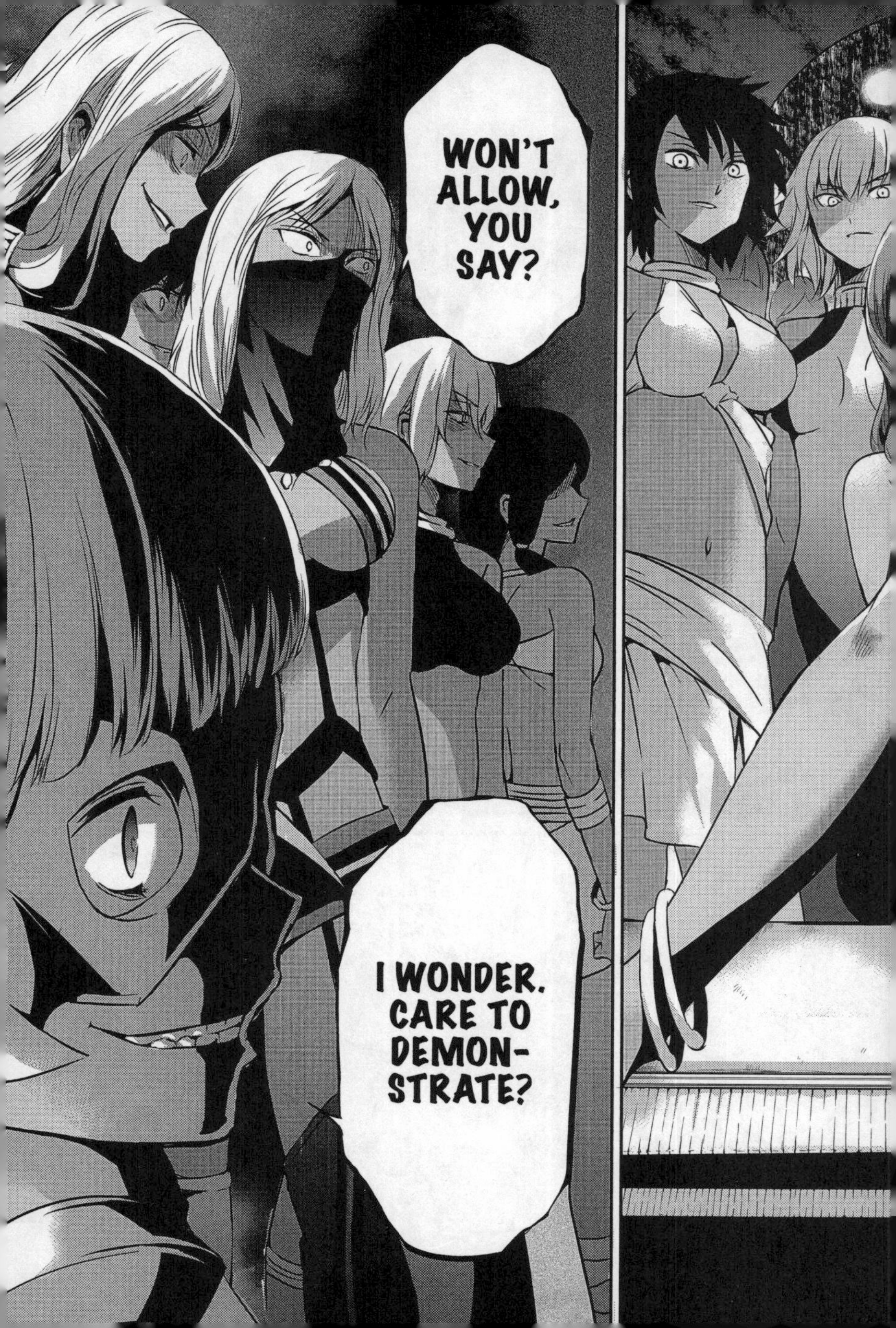
WON'T ALLOW, YOU SAY?
I WONDER. CARE TO DEMON-STRATE?

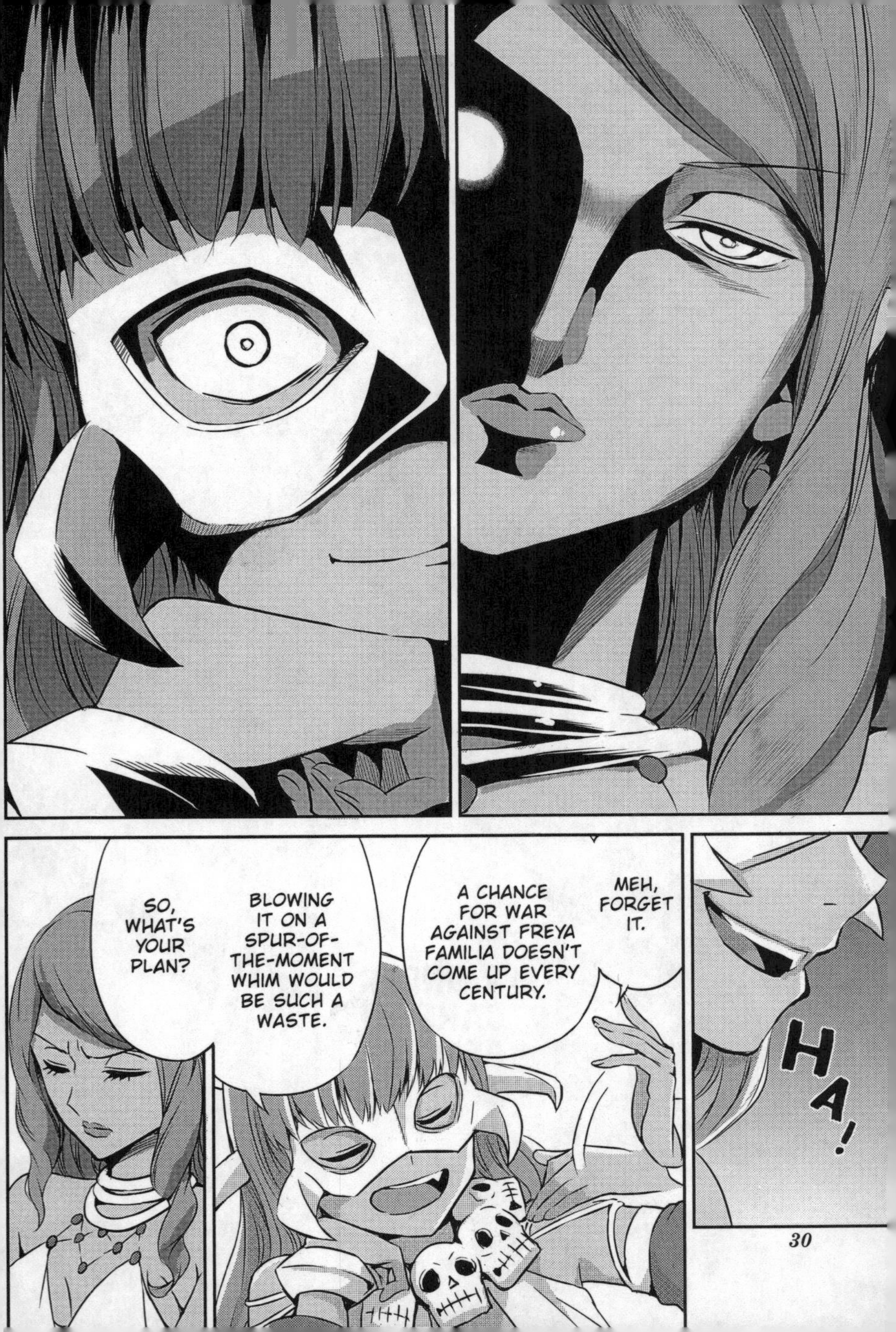
HA!
MEH, FORGET IT.
A CHANCE FOR WAR AGAINST FREYA FAMILIA DOESN'T COME UP EVERY CENTURY.
BLOWING IT ON A SPUR-OF-THE-MOMENT WHIM WOULD BE SUCH A WASTE.
SO, WHAT'S YOUR PLAN?

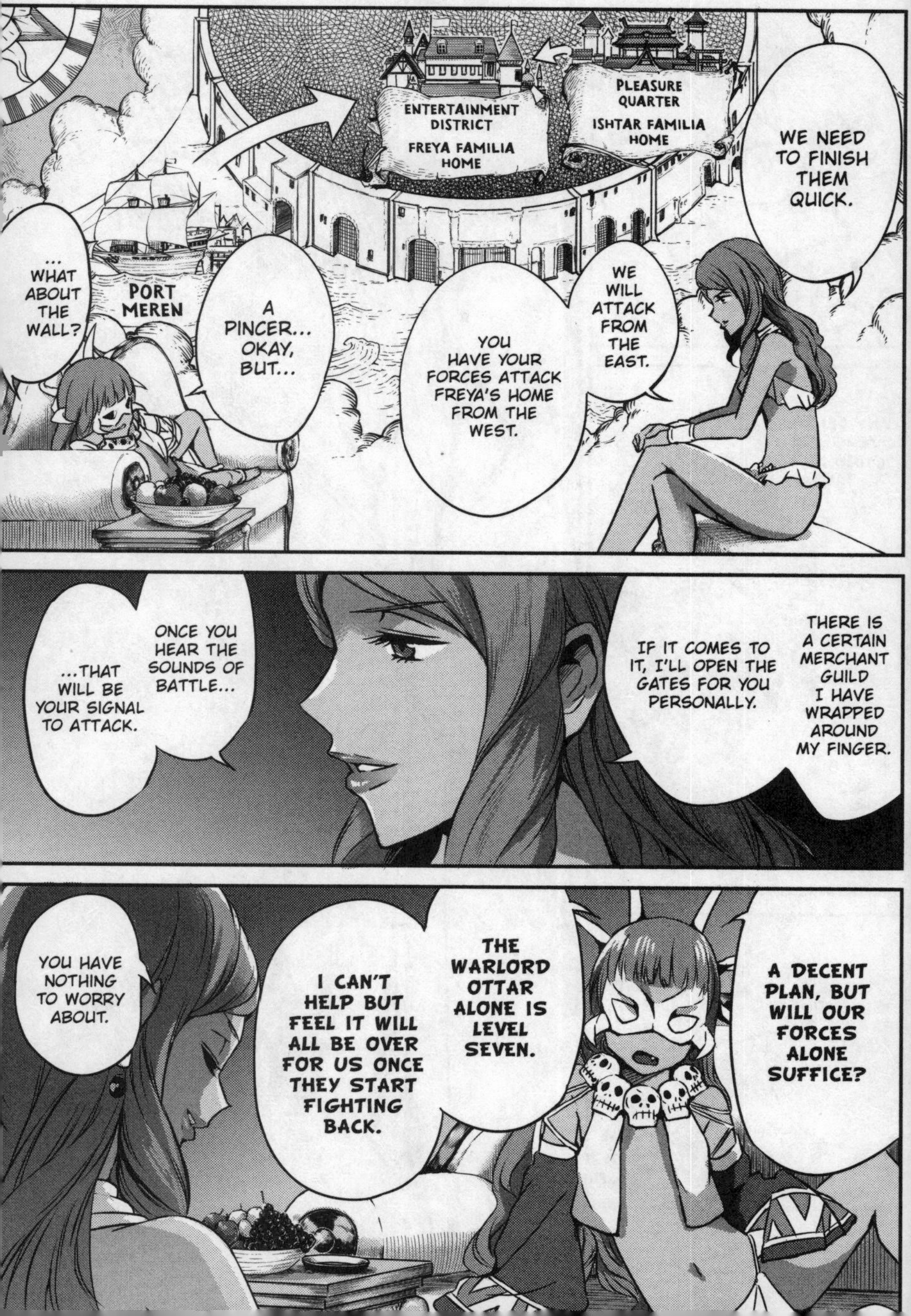
WE NEED TO FINISH THEM QUICK.
PLEASURE QUARTER
ISHTAR FAMILIA HOME
ENTERTAINMENT DISTRICT
FREYA FAMILIA HOME
WE WILL ATTACK FROM THE EAST.
YOU HAVE YOUR FORCES ATTACK FREYA'S HOME FROM THE WEST.
A PINCER... OKAY, BUT...
PORT MEREN
... WHAT ABOUT THE WALL?
THERE IS A CERTAIN MERCHANT GUILD I HAVE WRAPPED AROUND MY FINGER.
IF IT COMES TO IT, I'LL OPEN THE GATES FOR YOU PERSONALLY.
ONCE YOU HEAR THE SOUNDS OF BATTLE...
...THAT WILL BE YOUR SIGNAL TO ATTACK.
A DECENT PLAN, BUT WILL OUR FORCES ALONE SUFFICE?
THE WARLORD OTTAR ALONE IS LEVEL SEVEN.
I CAN'T HELP BUT FEEL IT WILL ALL BE OVER FOR US ONCE THEY START FIGHTING BACK.
YOU HAVE NOTHING TO WORRY ABOUT.

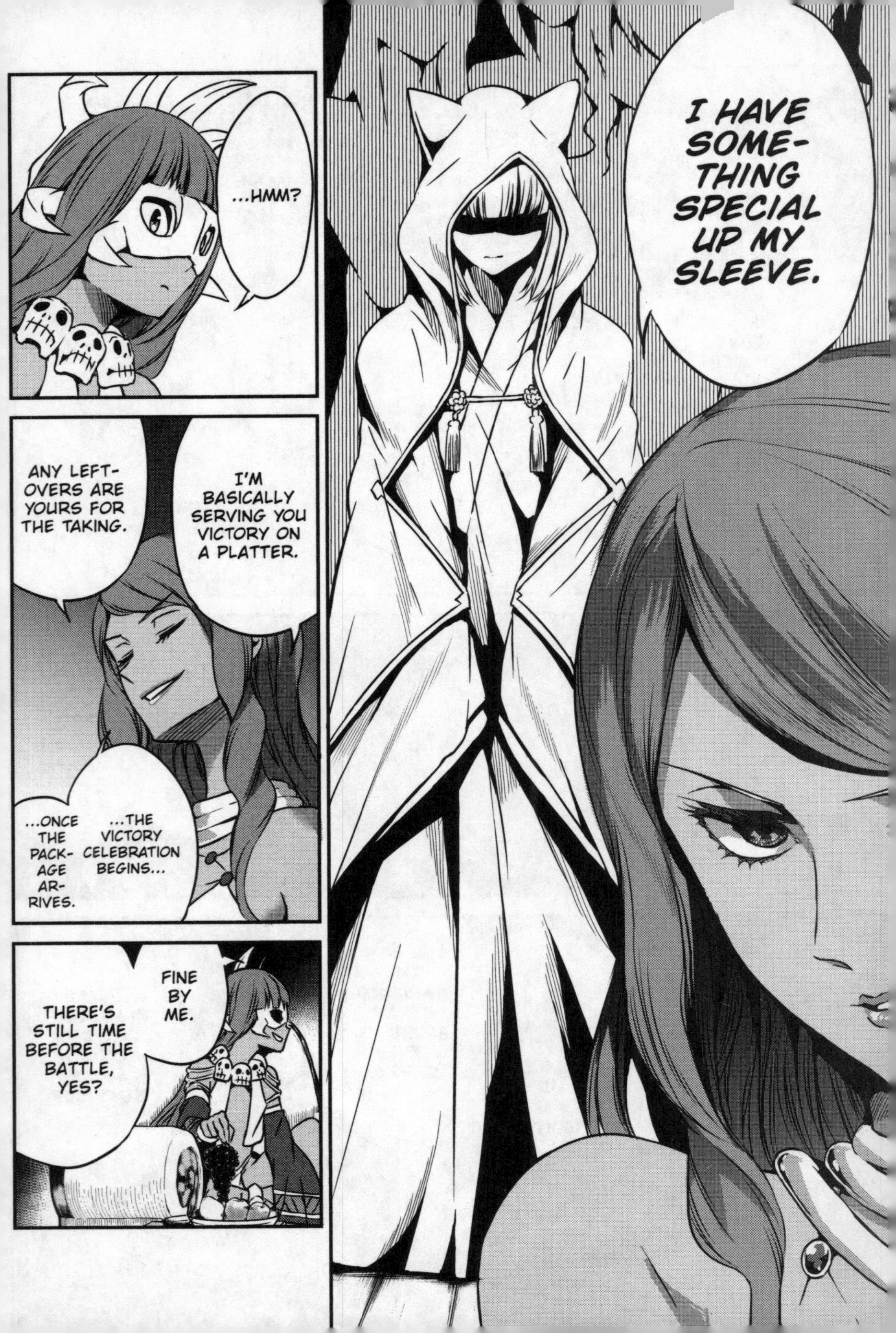
I HAVE SOME-THING SPECIAL UP MY SLEEVE.
...HMM?
I'M BASICALLY SERVING YOU VICTORY ON A PLATTER.
ANY LEFT-OVERS ARE YOURS FOR THE TAKING.
...THE VICTORY CELEBRATION BEGINS...
...ONCE THE PACK-AGE AR-RIVES.
FINE BY ME.
THERE'S STILL TIME BEFORE THE BATTLE, YES?

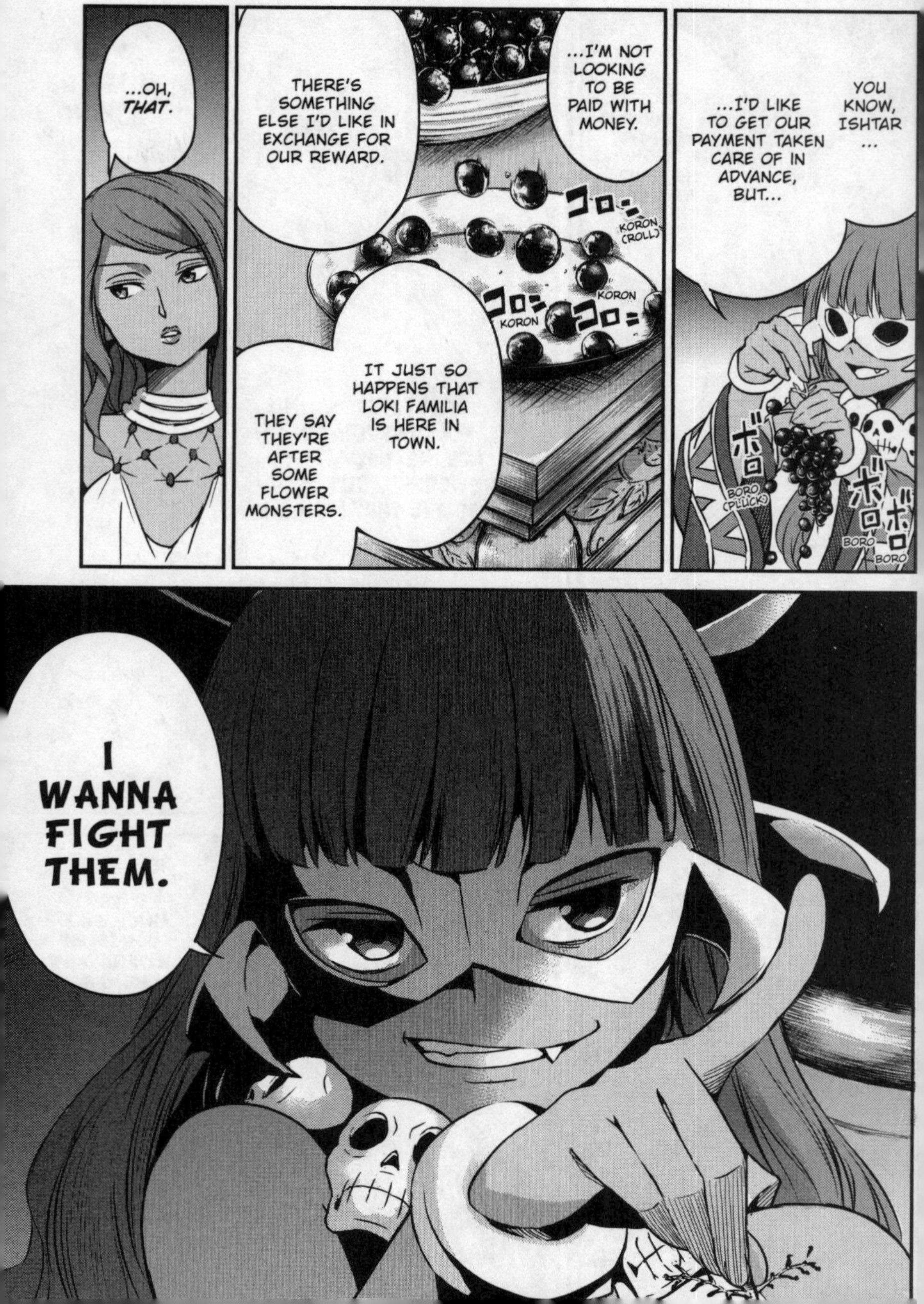
YOU KNOW, ISHTAR...
...I'D LIKE TO GET OUR PAYMENT TAKEN CARE OF IN ADVANCE, BUT...
BORO (PLUCK)
BORO
BORO
...I'M NOT LOOKING TO BE PAID WITH MONEY.
THERE'S SOMETHING ELSE I'D LIKE IN EXCHANGE FOR OUR REWARD.
KORON (ROLL)
KORON
KORON
IT JUST SO HAPPENS THAT LOKI FAMILIA IS HERE IN TOWN.
THEY SAY THEY'RE AFTER SOME FLOWER MONSTERS.
...OH, *THAT*.
I WANNA FIGHT THEM.

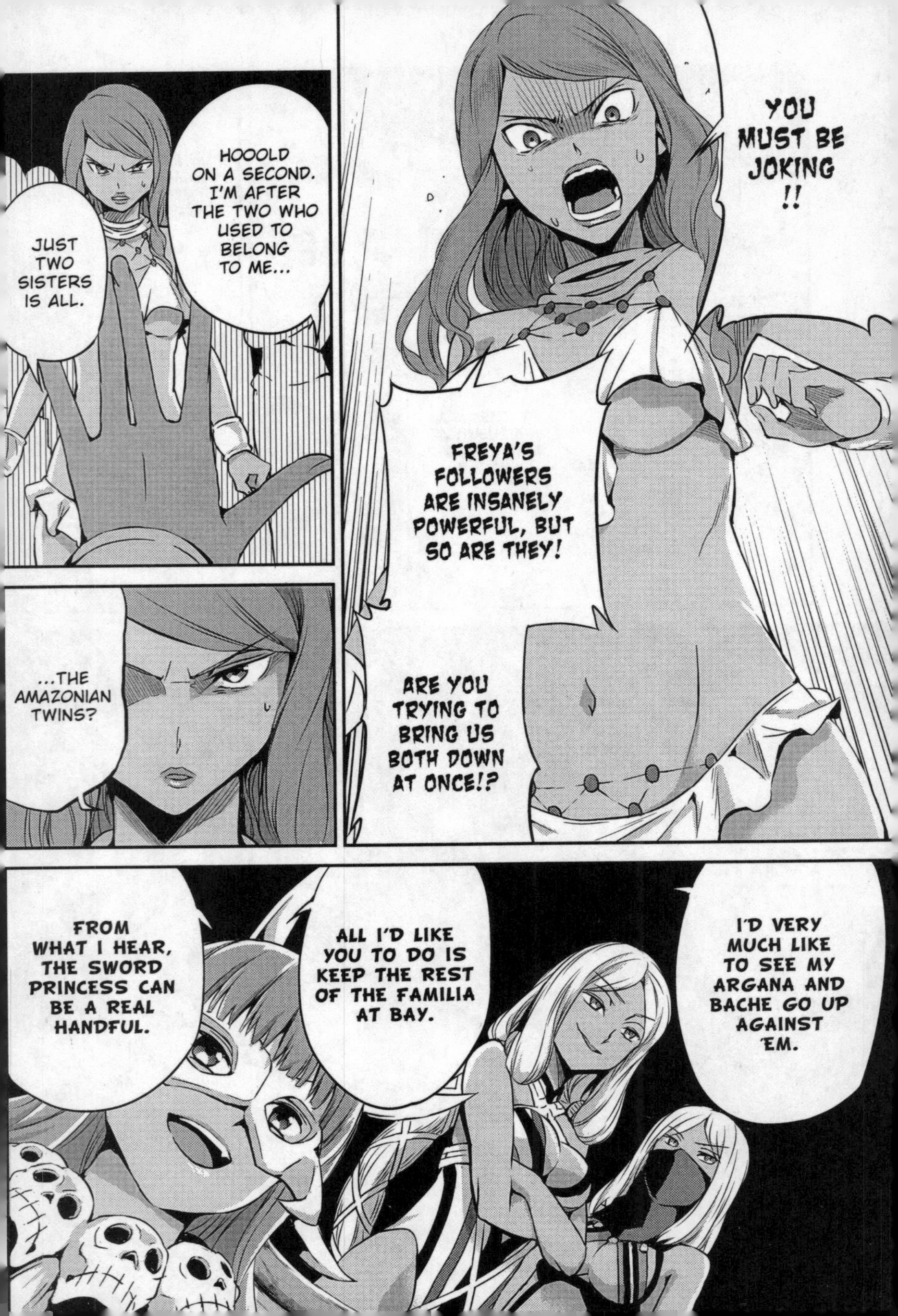
YOU MUST BE JOKING !!
FREYA'S FOLLOWERS ARE INSANELY POWERFUL, BUT SO ARE THEY!
ARE YOU TRYING TO BRING US BOTH DOWN AT ONCE!?
HOOOLD ON A SECOND. I'M AFTER THE TWO WHO USED TO BELONG TO ME...
JUST TWO SISTERS IS ALL.
...THE AMAZONIAN TWINS?
I'D VERY MUCH LIKE TO SEE MY ARGANA AND BACHE GO UP AGAINST 'EM.
ALL I'D LIKE YOU TO DO IS KEEP THE REST OF THE FAMILIA AT BAY.
FROM WHAT I HEAR, THE SWORD PRINCESS CAN BE A REAL HANDFUL.

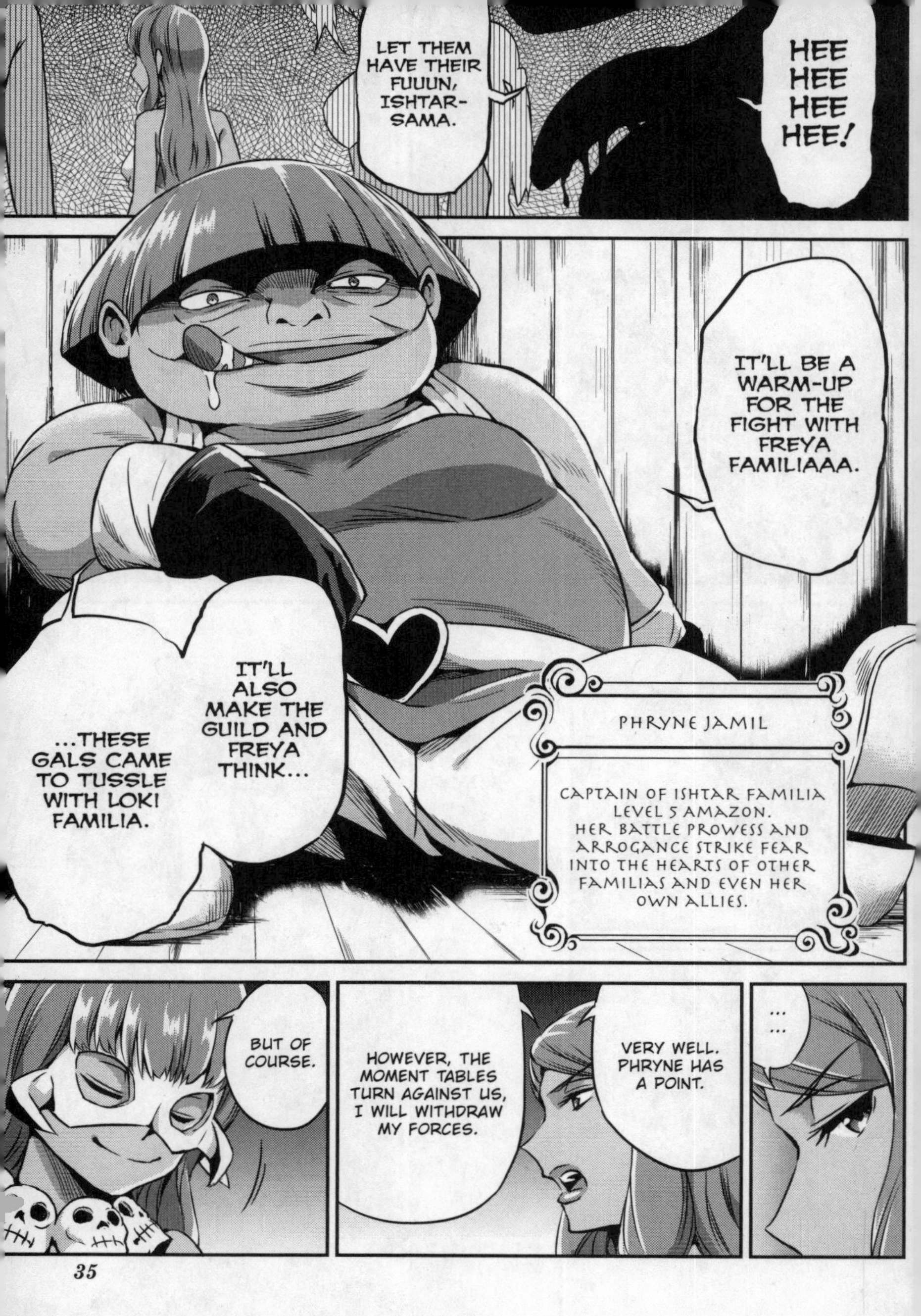
HEE HEE HEE HEE!
LET THEM HAVE THEIR FUUUN, ISHTAR-SAMA.
IT'LL BE A WARM-UP FOR THE FIGHT WITH FREYA FAMILIAAA.
PHRYNE JAMIL
CAPTAIN OF ISHTAR FAMILIA LEVEL 5 AMAZON. HER BATTLE PROWESS AND ARROGANCE STRIKE FEAR INTO THE HEARTS OF OTHER FAMILIAS AND EVEN HER OWN ALLIES.
IT'LL ALSO MAKE THE GUILD AND FREYA THINK...
...THESE GALS CAME TO TUSSLE WITH LOKI FAMILIA.
......
VERY WELL. PHRYNE HAS A POINT.
HOWEVER, THE MOMENT TABLES TURN AGAINST US, I WILL WITHDRAW MY FORCES.
BUT OF COURSE.

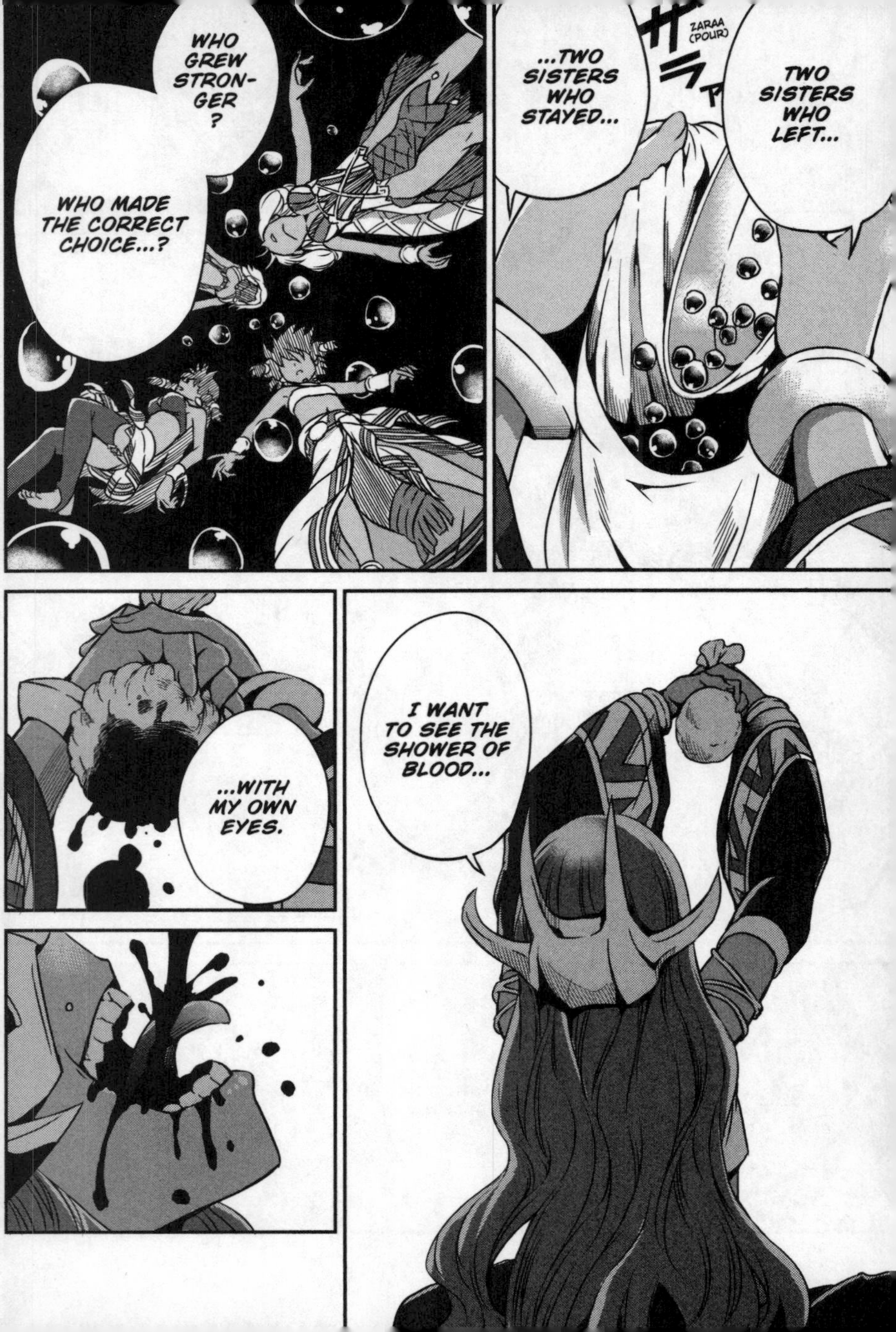
TWO SISTERS WHO LEFT...
ZARAA (POUR)
...TWO SISTERS WHO STAYED...
WHO GREW STRONGER-GER?
WHO MADE THE CORRECT CHOICE...?
I WANT TO SEE THE SHOWER OF BLOOD...
...WITH MY OWN EYES.

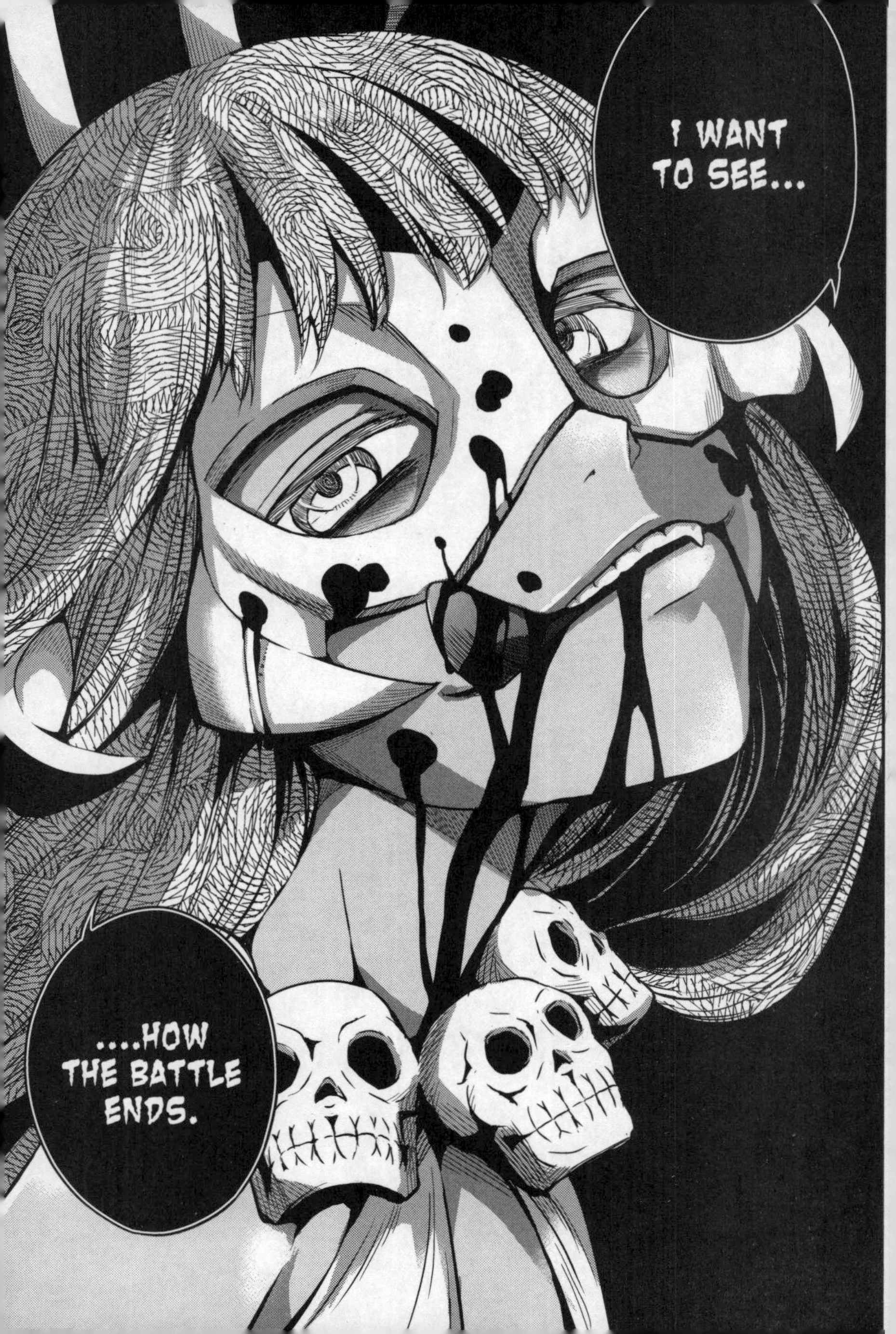
I WANT TO SEE...
....HOW THE BATTLE ENDS.

Is it Wrong to Try to Pick Up Girls in a Dungeon? On the Side

Sword Oratoria

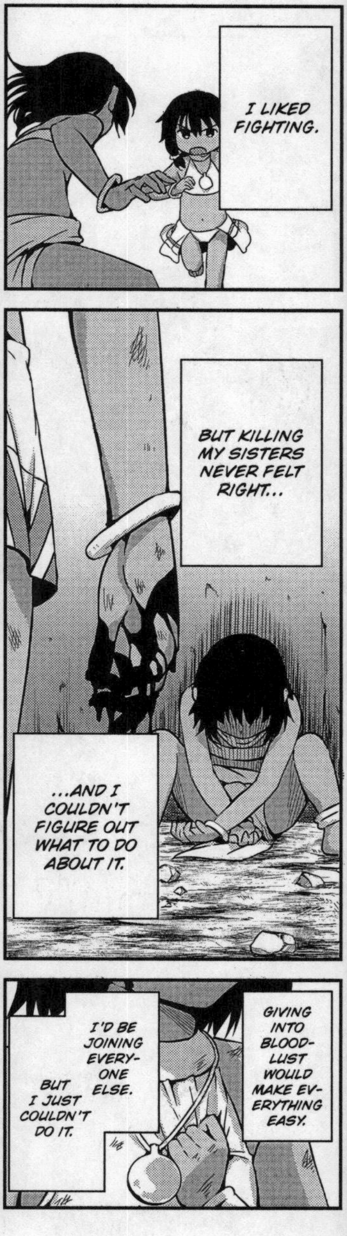
I LIKED FIGHTING.
BUT KILLING MY SISTERS NEVER FELT RIGHT...
...AND I COULDN'T FIGURE OUT WHAT TO DO ABOUT IT.
GIVING INTO BLOOD-LUST WOULD MAKE EV-ERYTHING EASY.
I'D BE JOINING EVERY-ONE ELSE.
BUT I JUST COULDN'T DO IT.

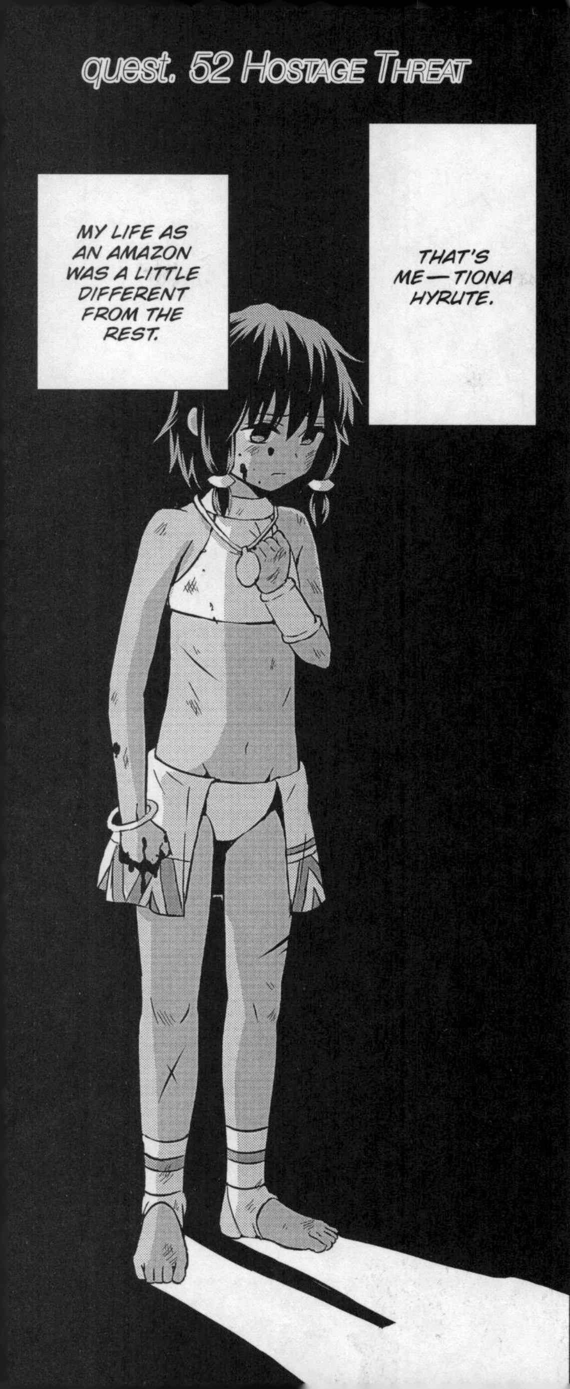
quest. 52 Hostage Threat
THAT'S ME—TIONA HYRUTE.
MY LIFE AS AN AMAZON WAS A LITTLE DIFFERENT FROM THE REST.

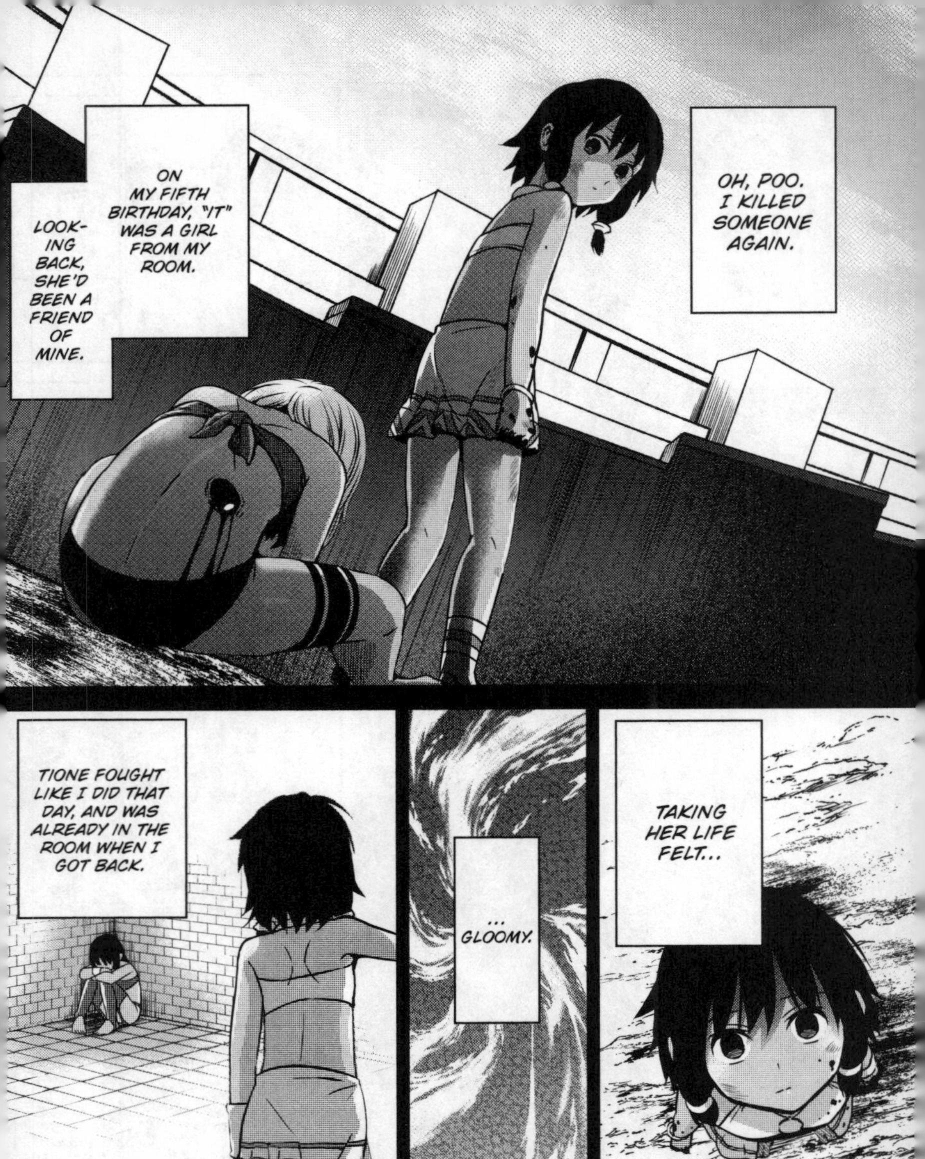
OH, POO. I KILLED SOMEONE AGAIN.
ON MY FIFTH BIRTHDAY, "IT" WAS A GIRL FROM MY ROOM.
LOOKING BACK, SHE'D BEEN A FRIEND OF MINE.
TAKING HER LIFE FELT...
...GLOOMY.
TIONE FOUGHT LIKE I DID THAT DAY, AND WAS ALREADY IN THE ROOM WHEN I GOT BACK.

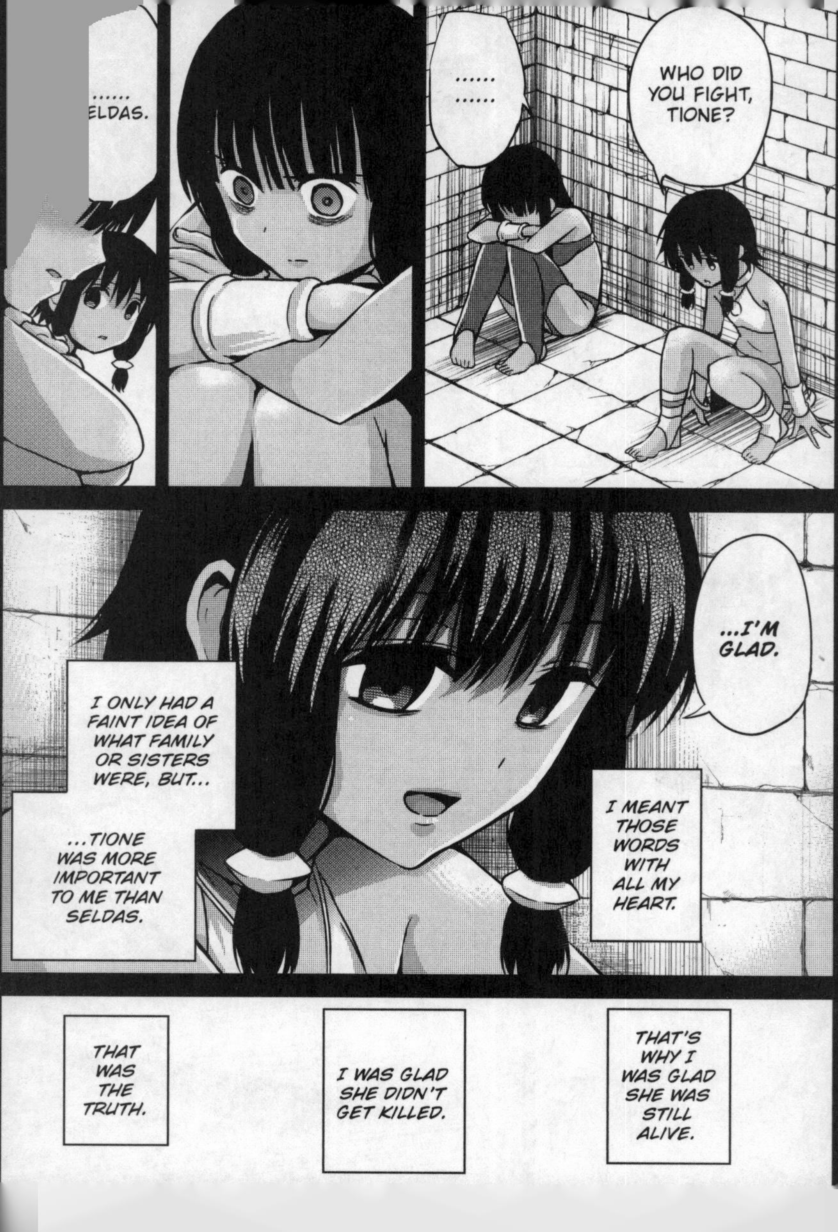
WHO DID YOU FIGHT, TIONE?
......
......
......
ELDAS.
...I'M GLAD.
I MEANT THOSE WORDS WITH ALL MY HEART.
I ONLY HAD A FAINT IDEA OF WHAT FAMILY OR SISTERS WERE, BUT...
...TIONE WAS MORE IMPORTANT TO ME THAN SELDAS.
THAT'S WHY I WAS GLAD SHE WAS STILL ALIVE.
I WAS GLAD SHE DIDN'T GET KILLED.
THAT WAS THE TRUTH.

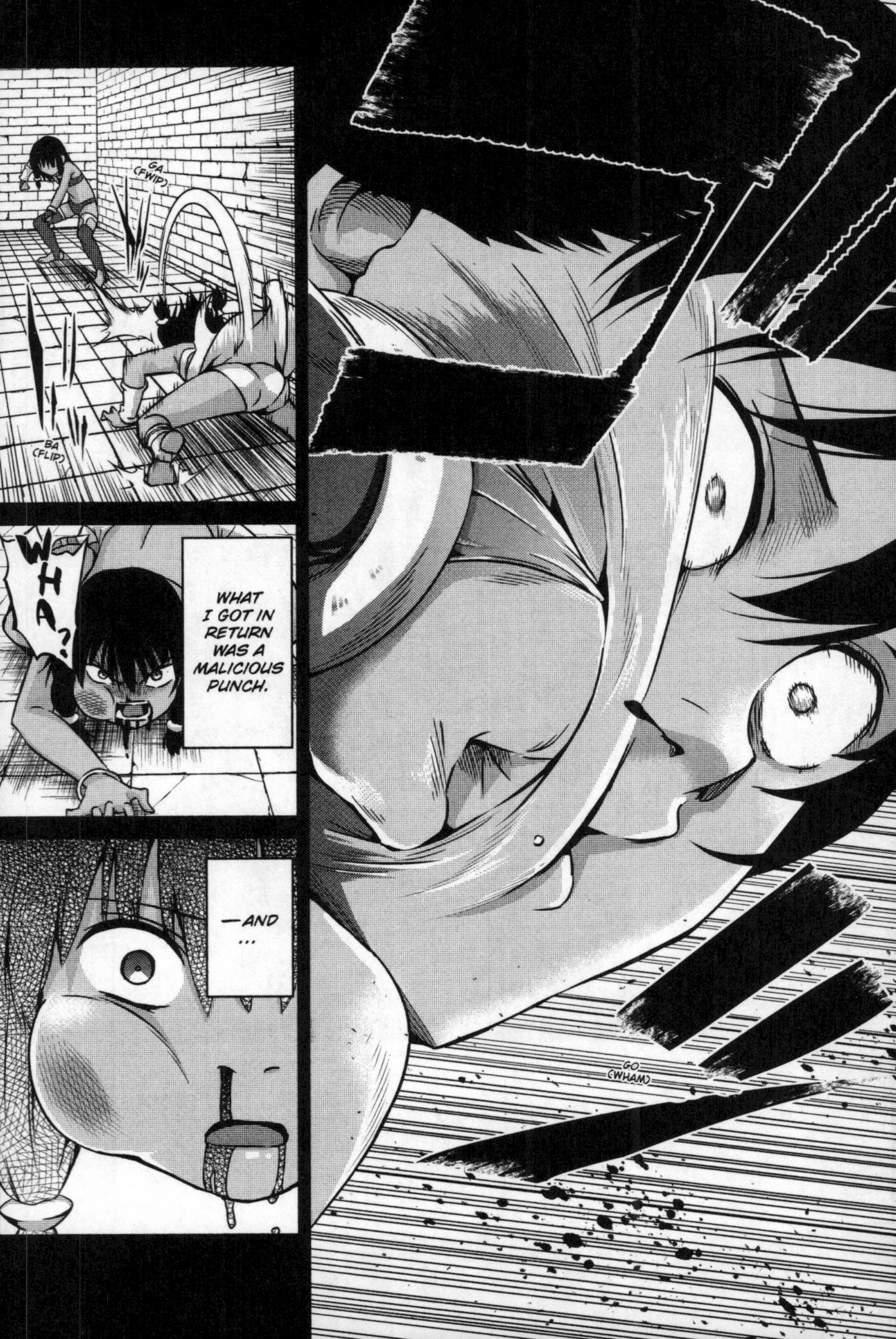
GO (WHAM)
GA (FWIP)
BA (FLIP)
WHA?
WHAT I GOT IN RETURN WAS A MALICIOUS PUNCH.
—AND ...

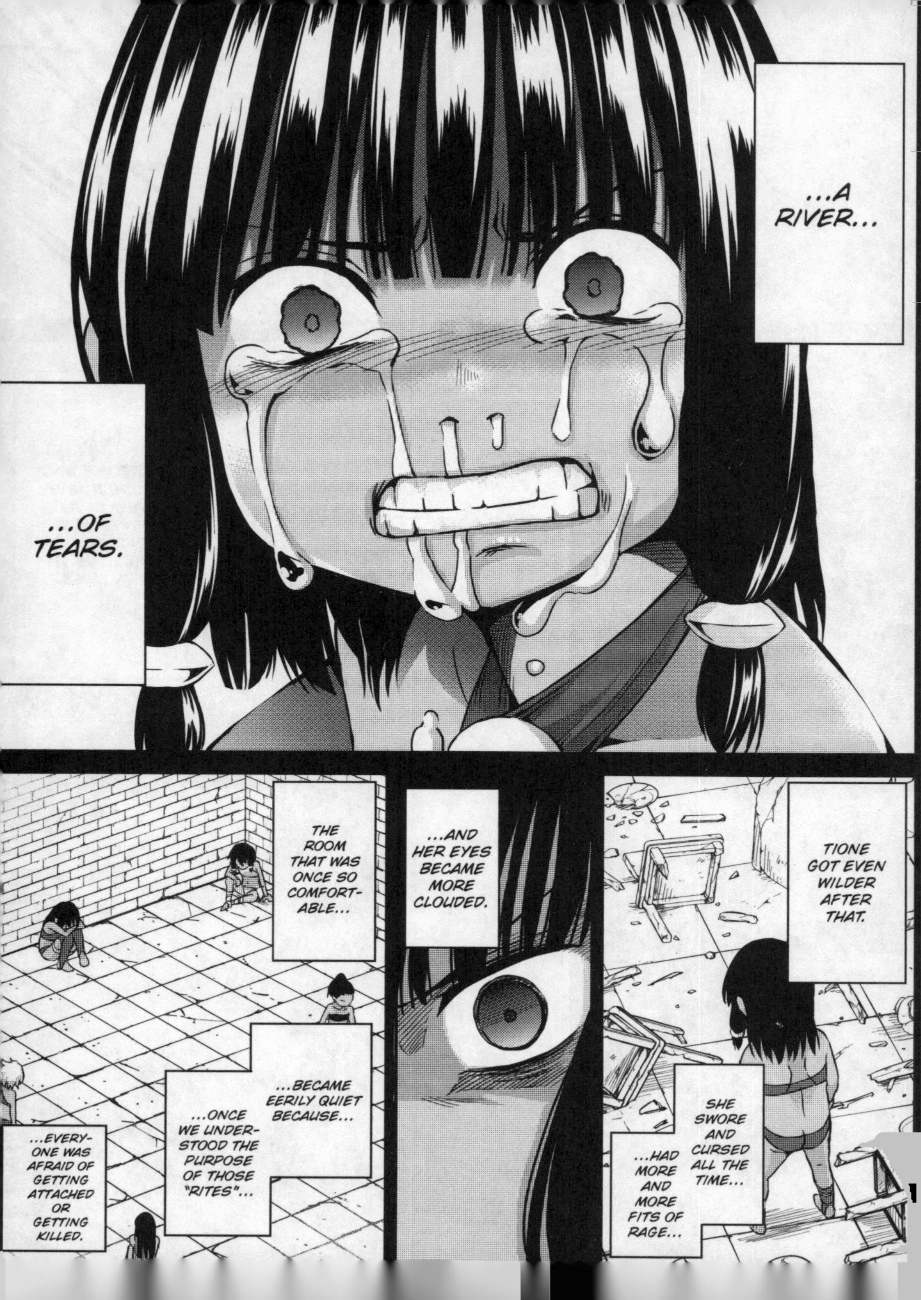
...A RIVER...
...OF TEARS.
TIONE GOT EVEN WILDER AFTER THAT.
SHE SWORE AND CURSED ALL THE TIME...
...HAD MORE AND MORE FITS OF RAGE...
...AND HER EYES BECAME MORE CLOUDED.
THE ROOM THAT WAS ONCE SO COMFORT-ABLE...
...BECAME EERILY QUIET BECAUSE...
...ONCE WE UNDER-STOOD THE PURPOSE OF THOSE "RITES"...
...EVERY-ONE WAS AFRAID OF GETTING ATTACHED OR GETTING KILLED.

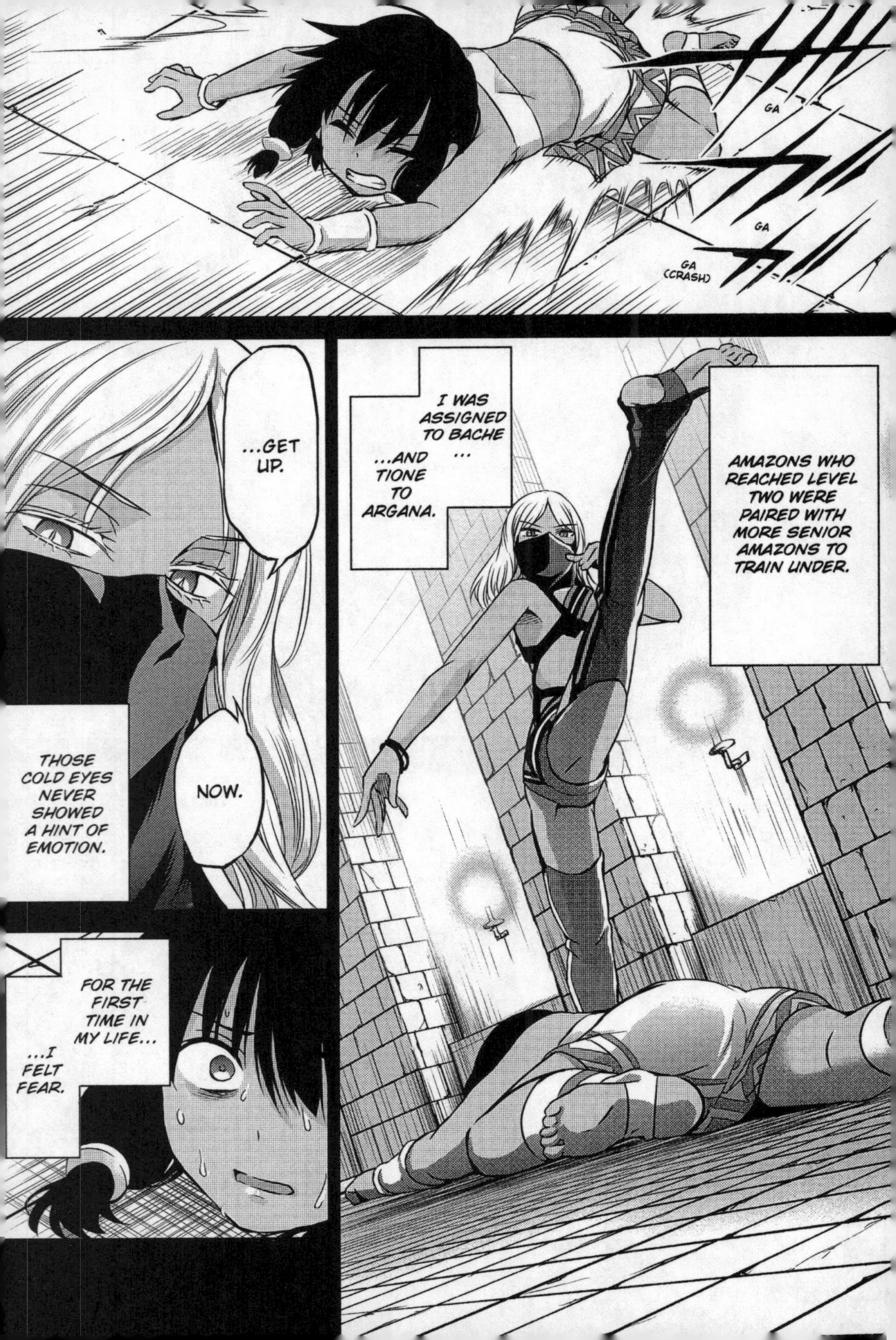
GA
GA
GA (CRASH)
AMAZONS WHO REACHED LEVEL TWO WERE PAIRED WITH MORE SENIOR AMAZONS TO TRAIN UNDER.
I WAS ASSIGNED TO BACHE ...
...AND TIONE TO ARGANA.
...GET UP.
NOW.
THOSE COLD EYES NEVER SHOWED A HINT OF EMOTION.
FOR THE FIRST TIME IN MY LIFE...
...I FELT FEAR.

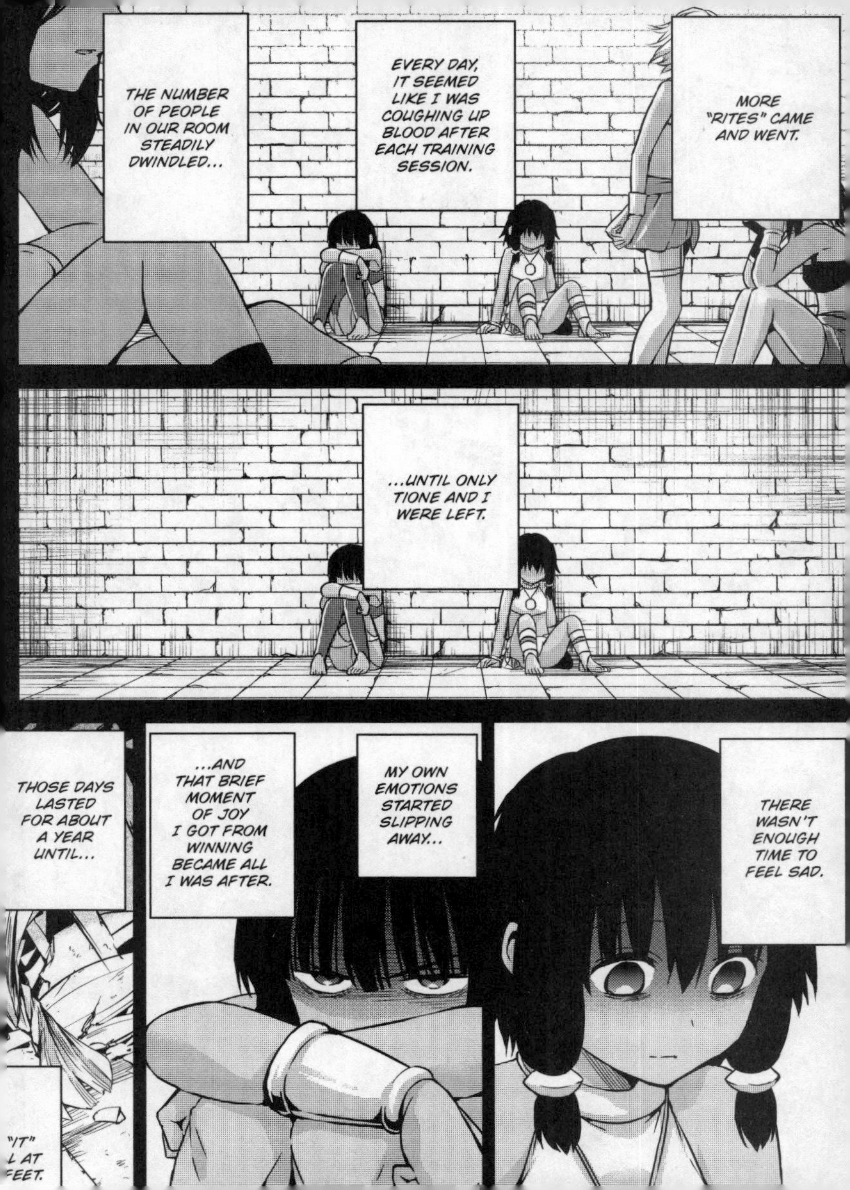
MORE "RITES" CAME AND WENT.
EVERY DAY, IT SEEMED LIKE I WAS COUGHING UP BLOOD AFTER EACH TRAINING SESSION.
THE NUMBER OF PEOPLE IN OUR ROOM STEADILY DWINDLED...
...UNTIL ONLY TIONE AND I WERE LEFT.
THERE WASN'T ENOUGH TIME TO FEEL SAD.
MY OWN EMOTIONS STARTED SLIPPING AWAY...
...AND THAT BRIEF MOMENT OF JOY I GOT FROM WINNING BECAME ALL I WAS AFTER.
THOSE DAYS LASTED FOR ABOUT A YEAR UNTIL...
"IT" L AT FEET.

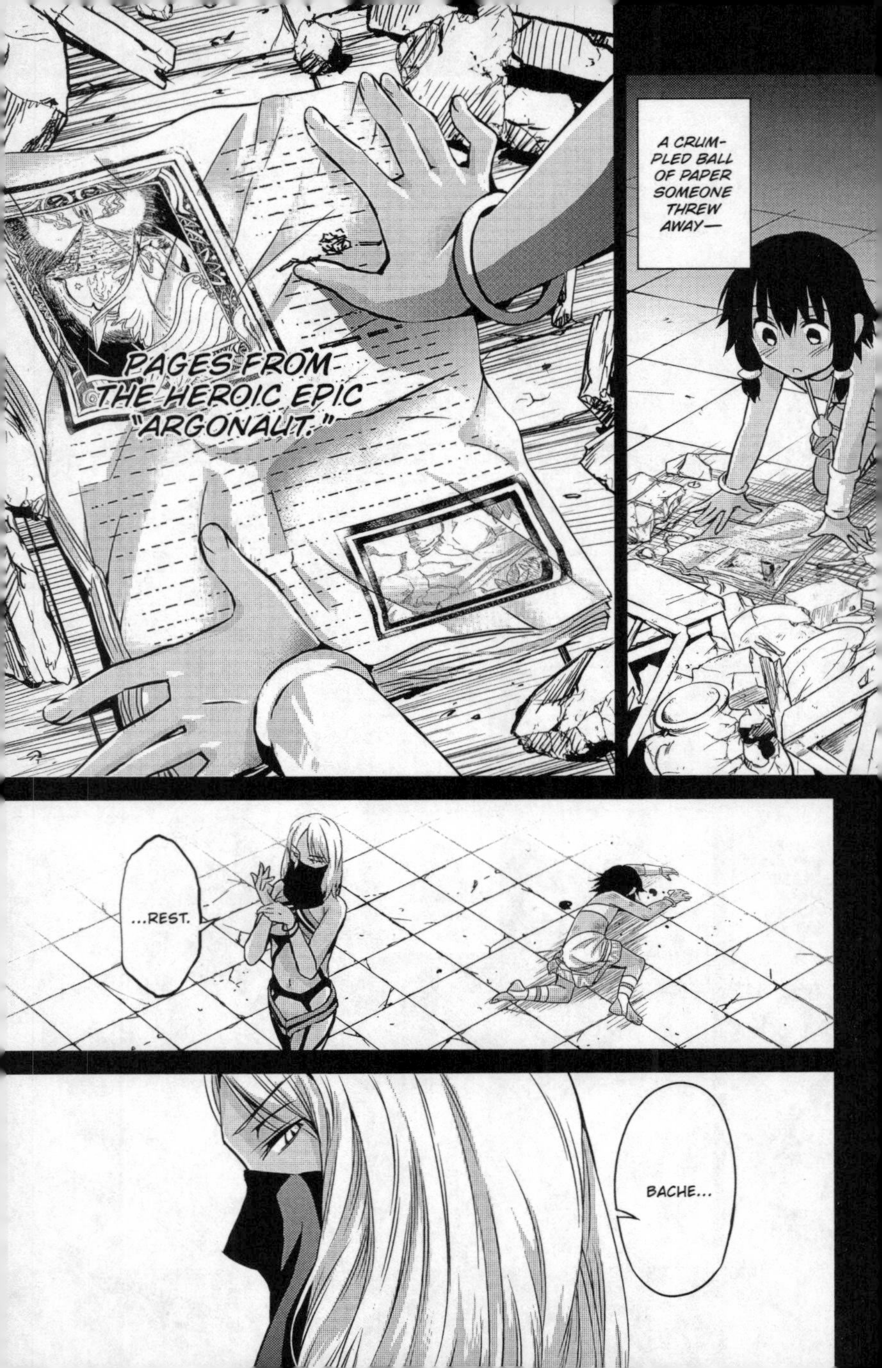
A CRUMPLED BALL OF PAPER SOMEONE THREW AWAY—
PAGES FROM THE HEROIC EPIC "ARGONAUT."
...REST.
BACHE...

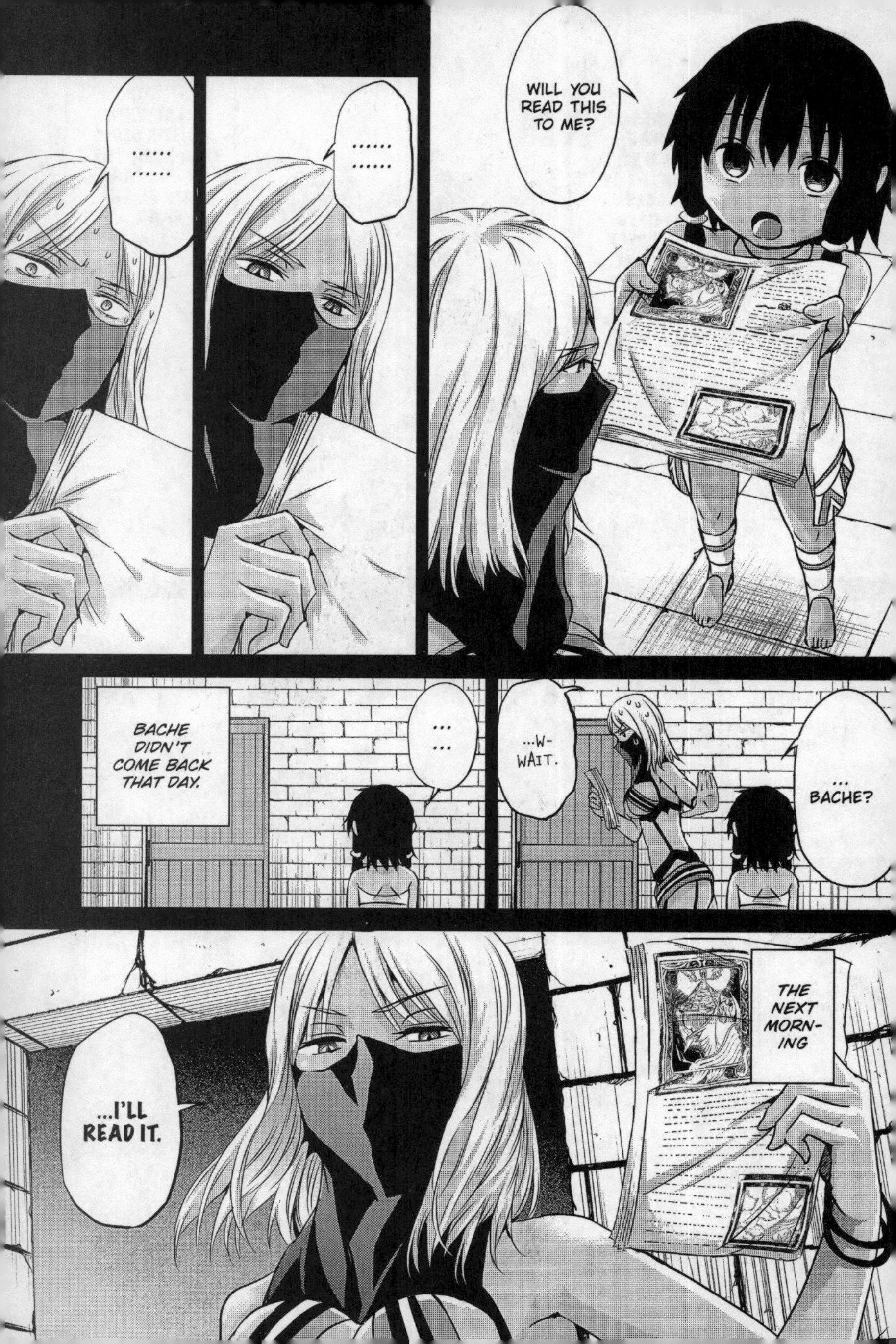
WILL YOU READ THIS TO ME?
....
....
... BACHE?
...W- WAIT.
... ...
BACHE DIDN'T COME BACK THAT DAY.
THE NEXT MORNING
...I'LL READ IT.

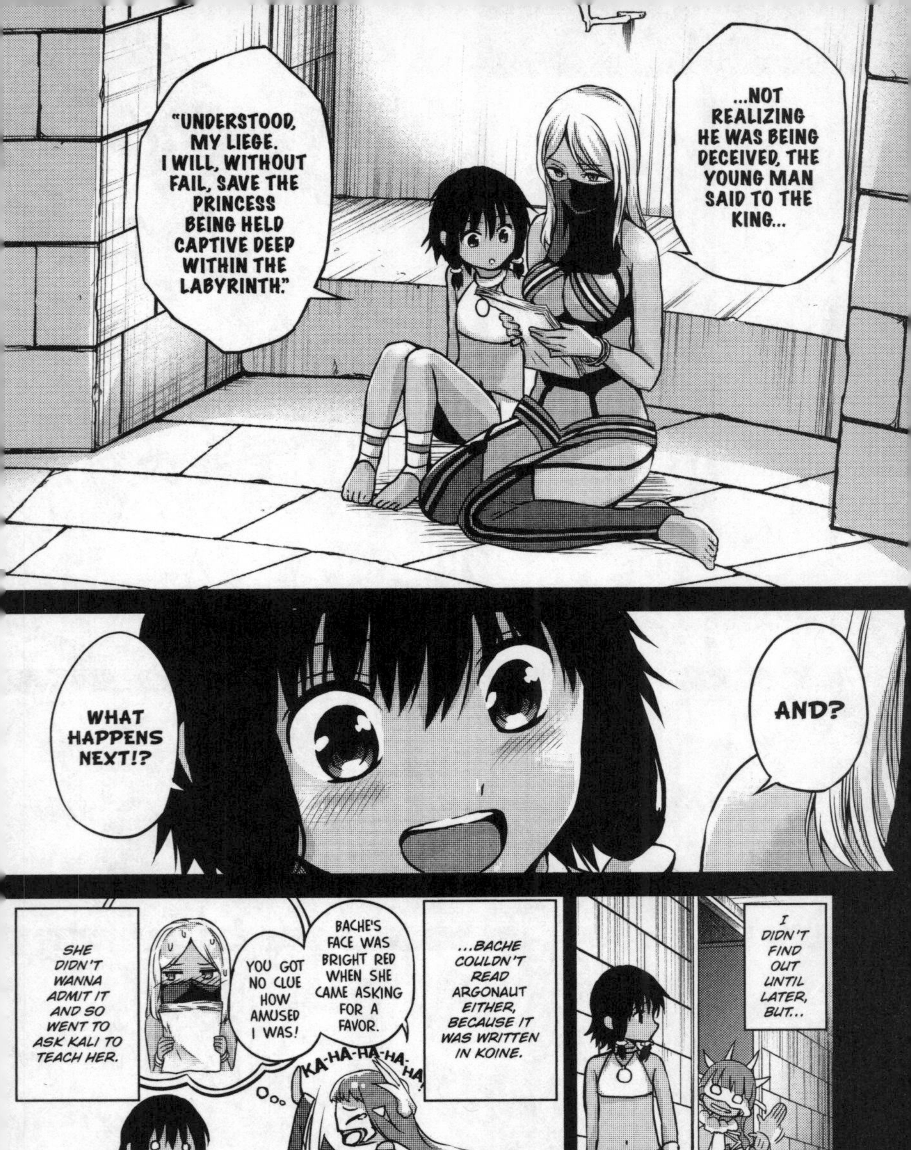
...NOT REALIZING HE WAS BEING DECEIVED, THE YOUNG MAN SAID TO THE KING...
"UNDERSTOOD, MY LIEGE. I WILL, WITHOUT FAIL, SAVE THE PRINCESS BEING HELD CAPTIVE DEEP WITHIN THE LABYRINTH."
AND?
WHAT HAPPENS NEXT!?
I DIDN'T FIND OUT UNTIL LATER, BUT...
...BACHE COULDN'T READ ARGONAUT EITHER, BECAUSE IT WAS WRITTEN IN KOINE.
BACHE'S FACE WAS BRIGHT RED WHEN SHE CAME ASKING FOR A FAVOR.
YOU GOT NO CLUE HOW AMUSED I WAS!
SHE DIDN'T WANNA ADMIT IT AND SO WENT TO ASK KALI TO TEACH HER.
KA-HA-HA-HA-HA!

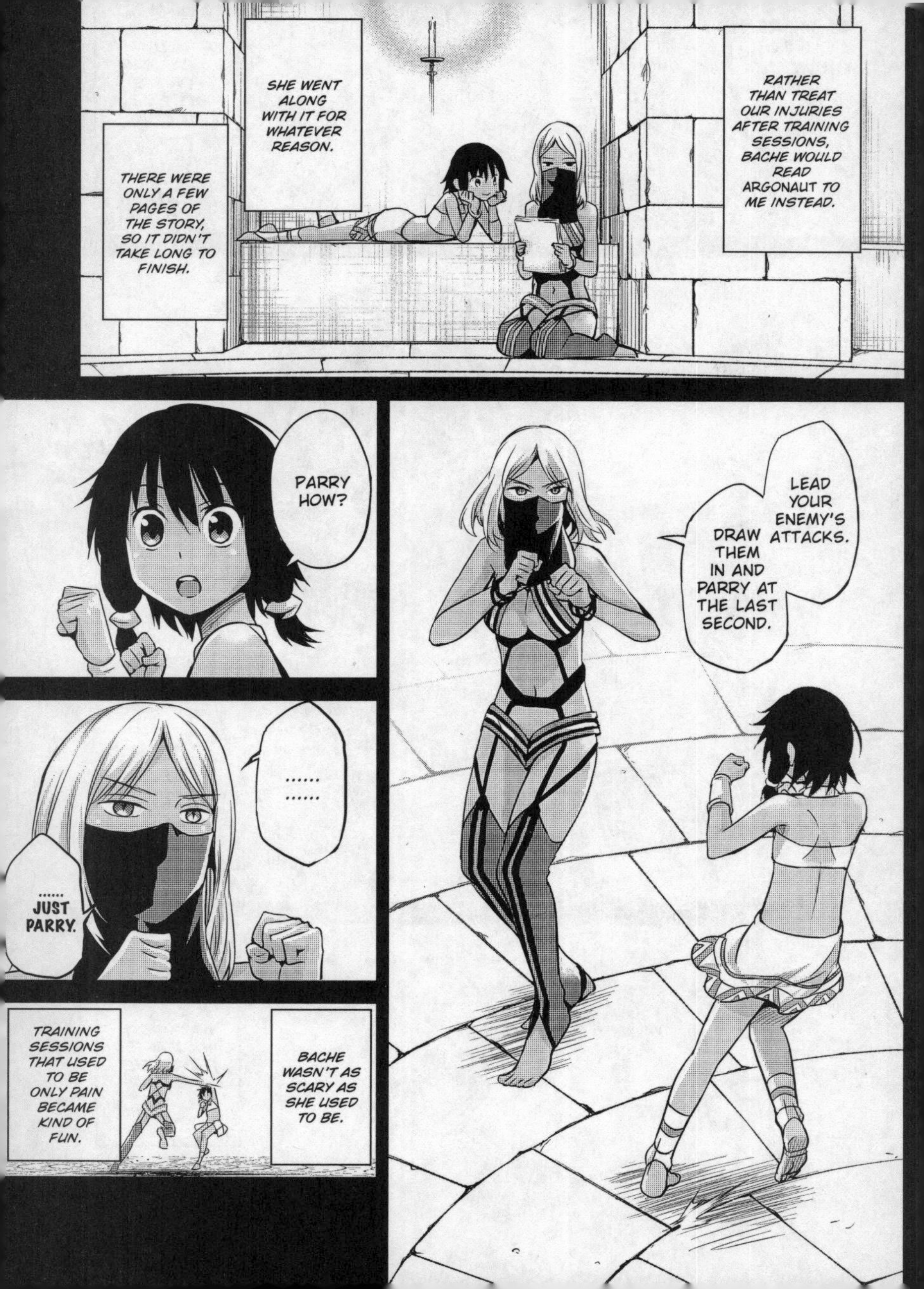
RATHER THAN TREAT OUR INJURIES AFTER TRAINING SESSIONS, BACHE WOULD READ ARGONAUT TO ME INSTEAD.
SHE WENT ALONG WITH IT FOR WHATEVER REASON.
THERE WERE ONLY A FEW PAGES OF THE STORY, SO IT DIDN'T TAKE LONG TO FINISH.
LEAD YOUR ENEMY'S ATTACKS.
DRAW THEM IN AND PARRY AT THE LAST SECOND.
PARRY HOW?
....
...... JUST PARRY.
BACHE WASN'T AS SCARY AS SHE USED TO BE.
TRAINING SESSIONS THAT USED TO BE ONLY PAIN BECAME KIND OF FUN.

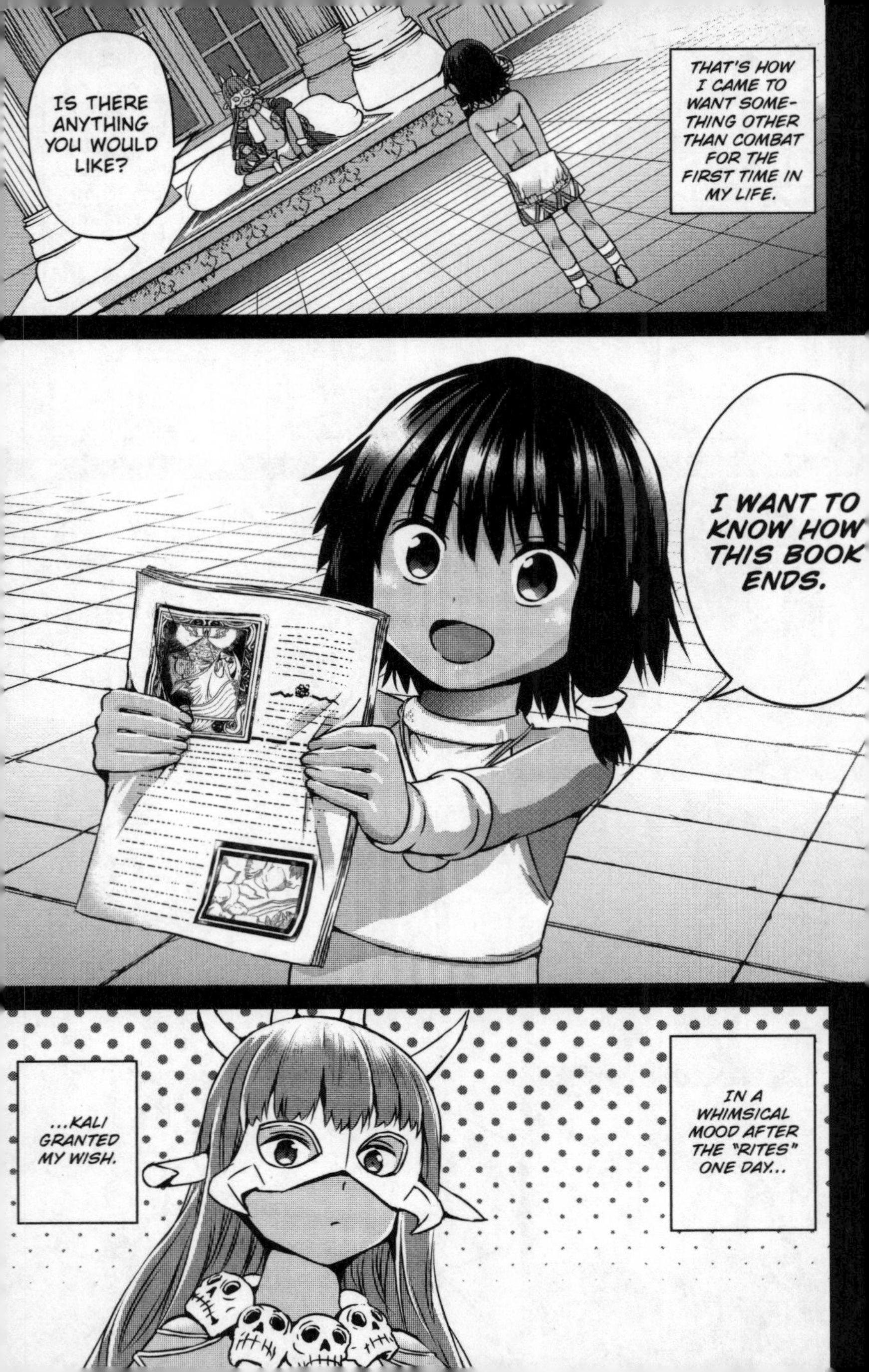
THAT'S HOW I CAME TO WANT SOME-THING OTHER THAN COMBAT FOR THE FIRST TIME IN MY LIFE.
IS THERE ANYTHING YOU WOULD LIKE?
I WANT TO KNOW HOW THIS BOOK ENDS.
IN A WHIMSICAL MOOD AFTER THE "RITES" ONE DAY...
...KALI GRANTED MY WISH.

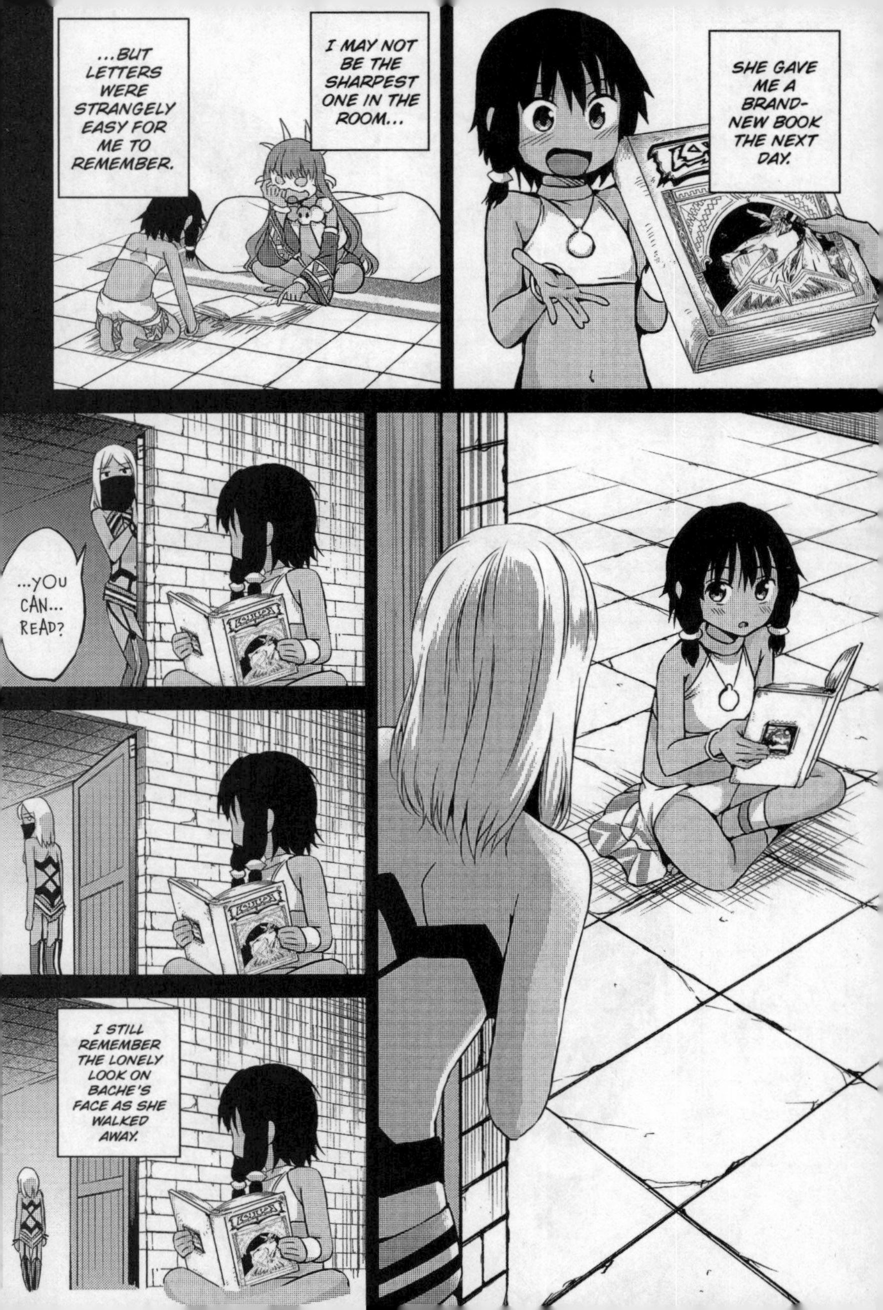
SHE GAVE ME A BRAND-NEW BOOK THE NEXT DAY.
I MAY NOT BE THE SHARPEST ONE IN THE ROOM...
...BUT LETTERS WERE STRANGELY EASY FOR ME TO REMEMBER.
...YOU CAN... READ?
I STILL REMEMBER THE LONELY LOOK ON BACHE'S FACE AS SHE WALKED AWAY.

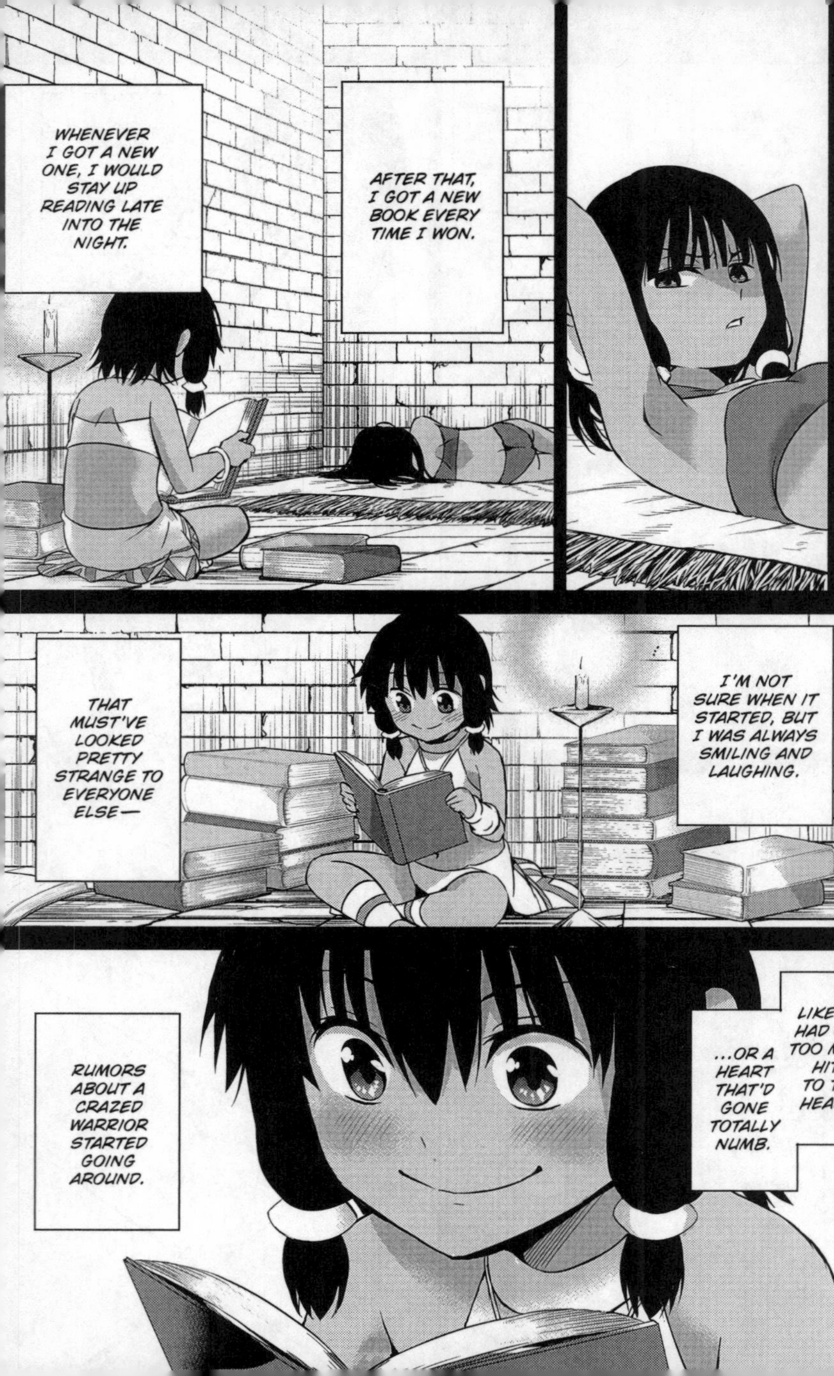

AFTER THAT, I GOT A NEW BOOK EVERY TIME I WON.
WHENEVER I GOT A NEW ONE, I WOULD STAY UP READING LATE INTO THE NIGHT.
I'M NOT SURE WHEN IT STARTED, BUT I WAS ALWAYS SMILING AND LAUGHING.
THAT MUST'VE LOOKED PRETTY STRANGE TO EVERYONE ELSE—
LIKE I'D HAD ONE TOO MANY HITS TO THE HEAD...
...OR A HEART THAT'D GONE TOTALLY NUMB.
RUMORS ABOUT A CRAZED WARRIOR STARTED GOING AROUND.

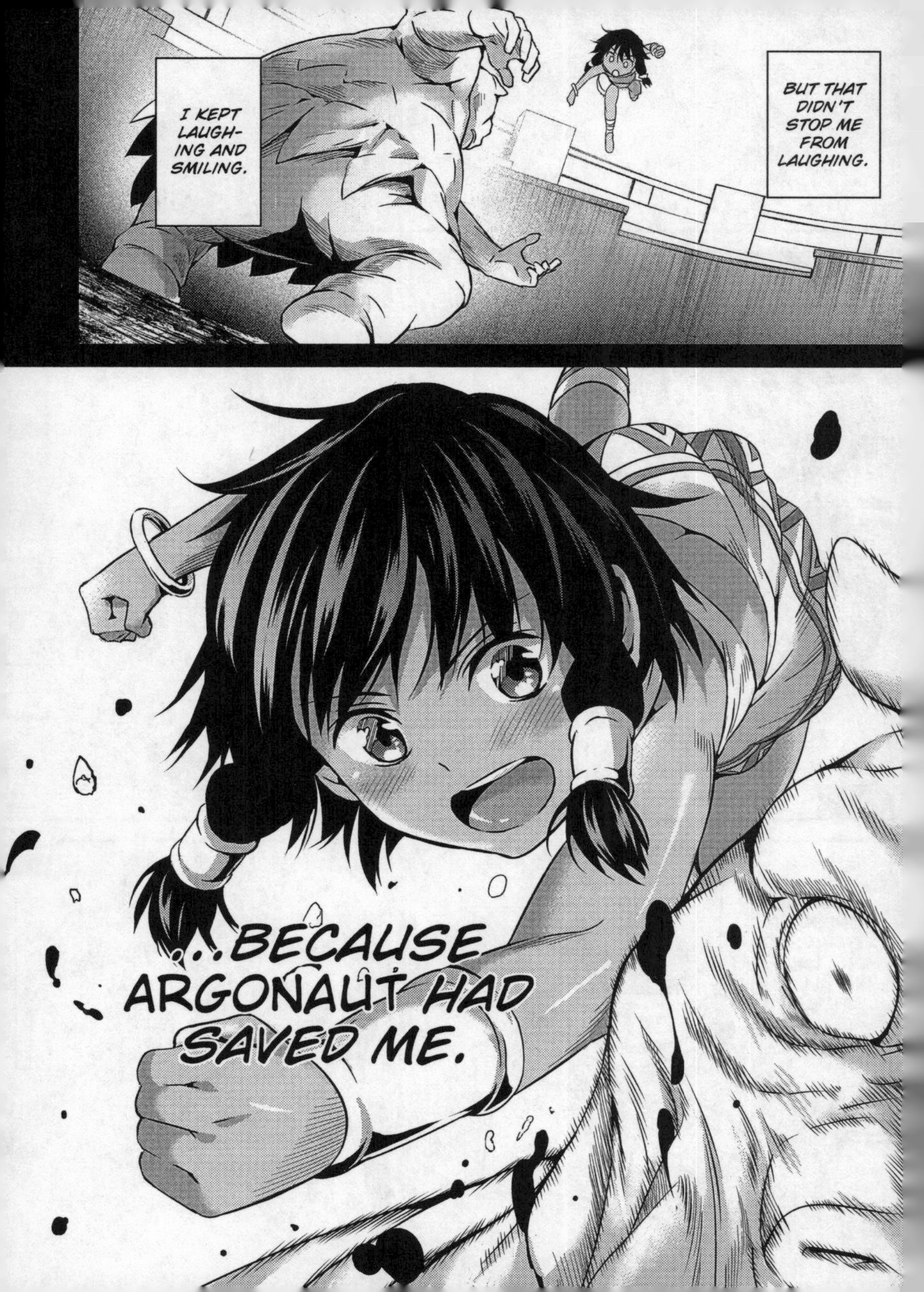
BUT THAT DIDN'T STOP ME FROM LAUGHING.
I KEPT LAUGH-ING AND SMILING.
...BECAUSE ARGONAUT HAD SAVED ME.

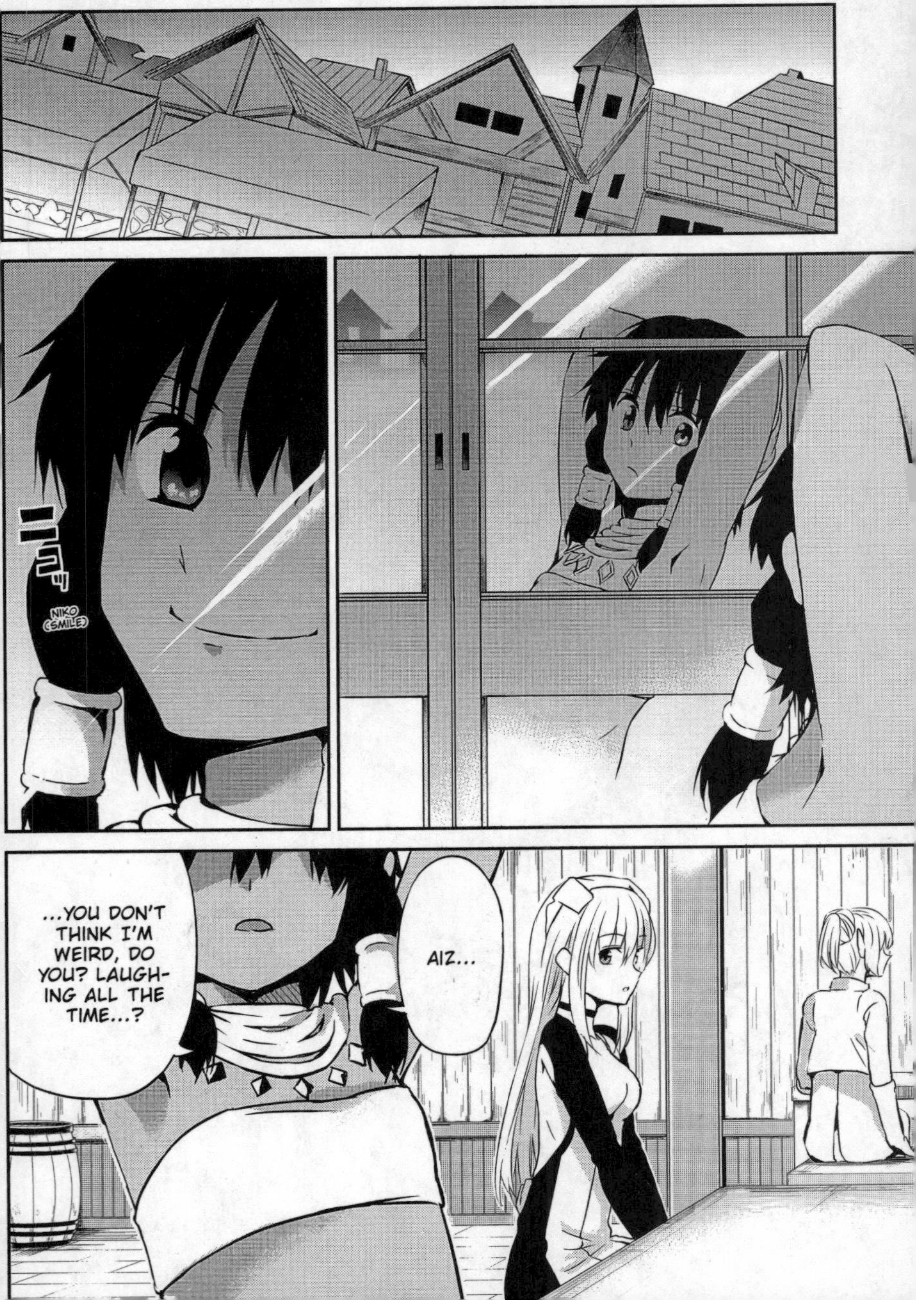
NIKO (SMILE)
AIZ...
...YOU DON'T THINK I'M WEIRD, DO YOU? LAUGHING ALL THE TIME...?

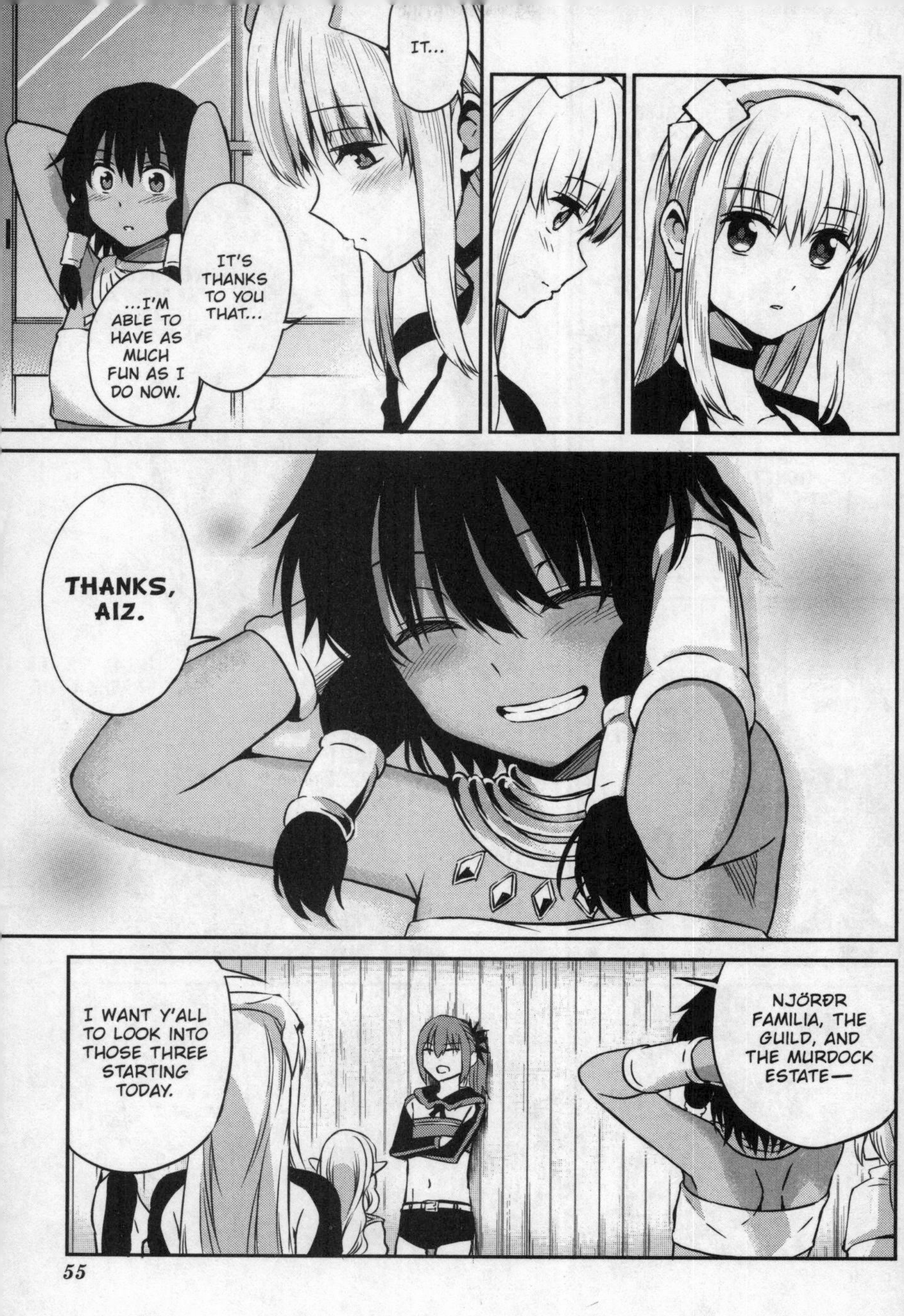
IT...
IT'S THANKS TO YOU THAT...
...I'M ABLE TO HAVE AS MUCH FUN AS I DO NOW.
THANKS, AIZ.
NJÖRÐR FAMILIA, THE GUILD, AND THE MURDOCK ESTATE—
I WANT Y'ALL TO LOOK INTO THOSE THREE STARTING TODAY.

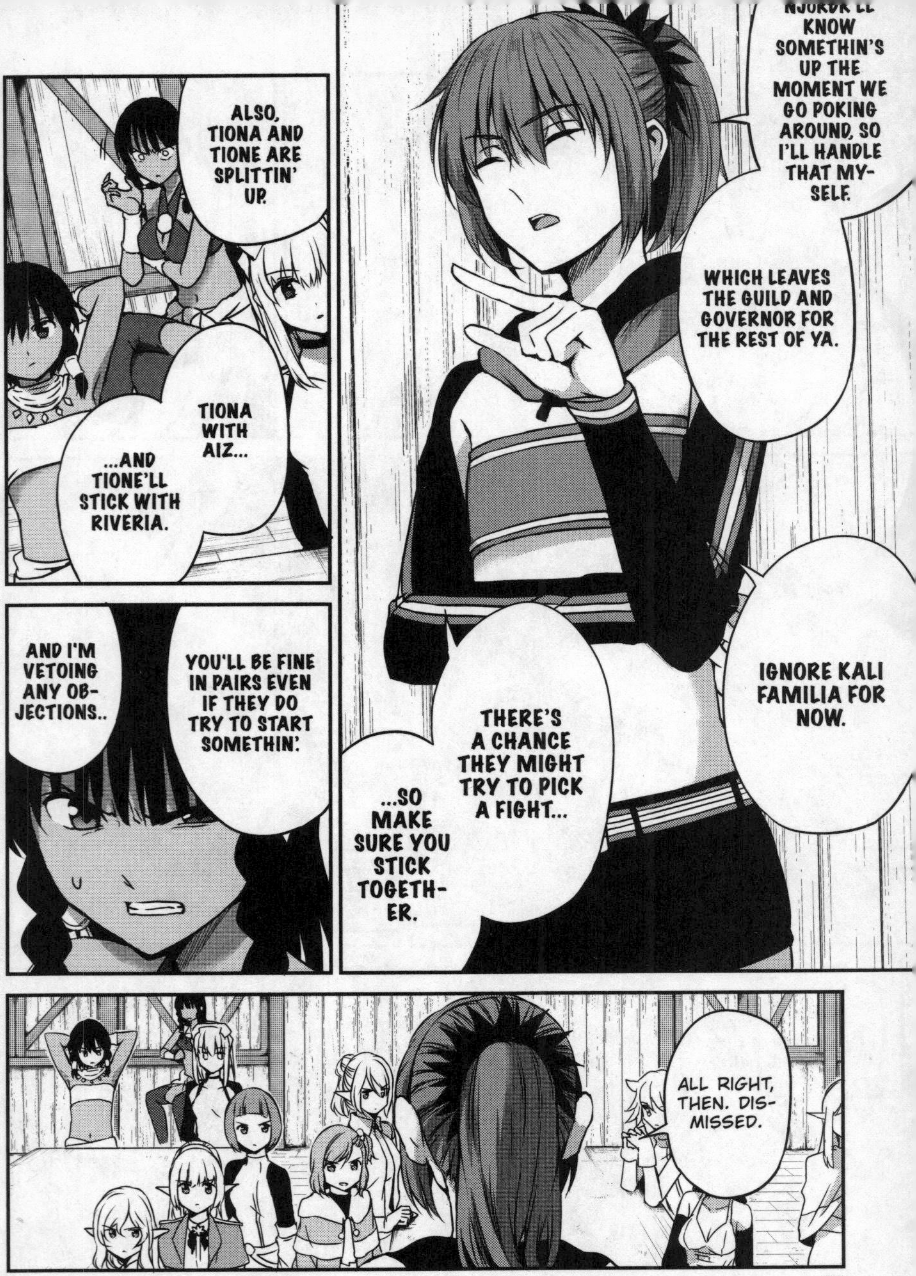
KNOW SOMETHIN'S UP THE MOMENT WE GO POKING AROUND, SO I'LL HANDLE THAT MY-SELF.
WHICH LEAVES THE GUILD AND GOVERNOR FOR THE REST OF YA.
IGNORE KALI FAMILIA FOR NOW.
THERE'S A CHANCE THEY MIGHT TRY TO PICK A FIGHT...
...SO MAKE SURE YOU STICK TOGETH-ER.
ALSO, TIONA AND TIONE ARE SPLITTIN' UP.
TIONA WITH AIZ...
...AND TIONE'LL STICK WITH RIVERIA.
YOU'LL BE FINE IN PAIRS EVEN IF THEY DO TRY TO START SOMETHIN'.
AND I'M VETOING ANY OB-JECTIONS..
ALL RIGHT, THEN. DIS-MISSED.

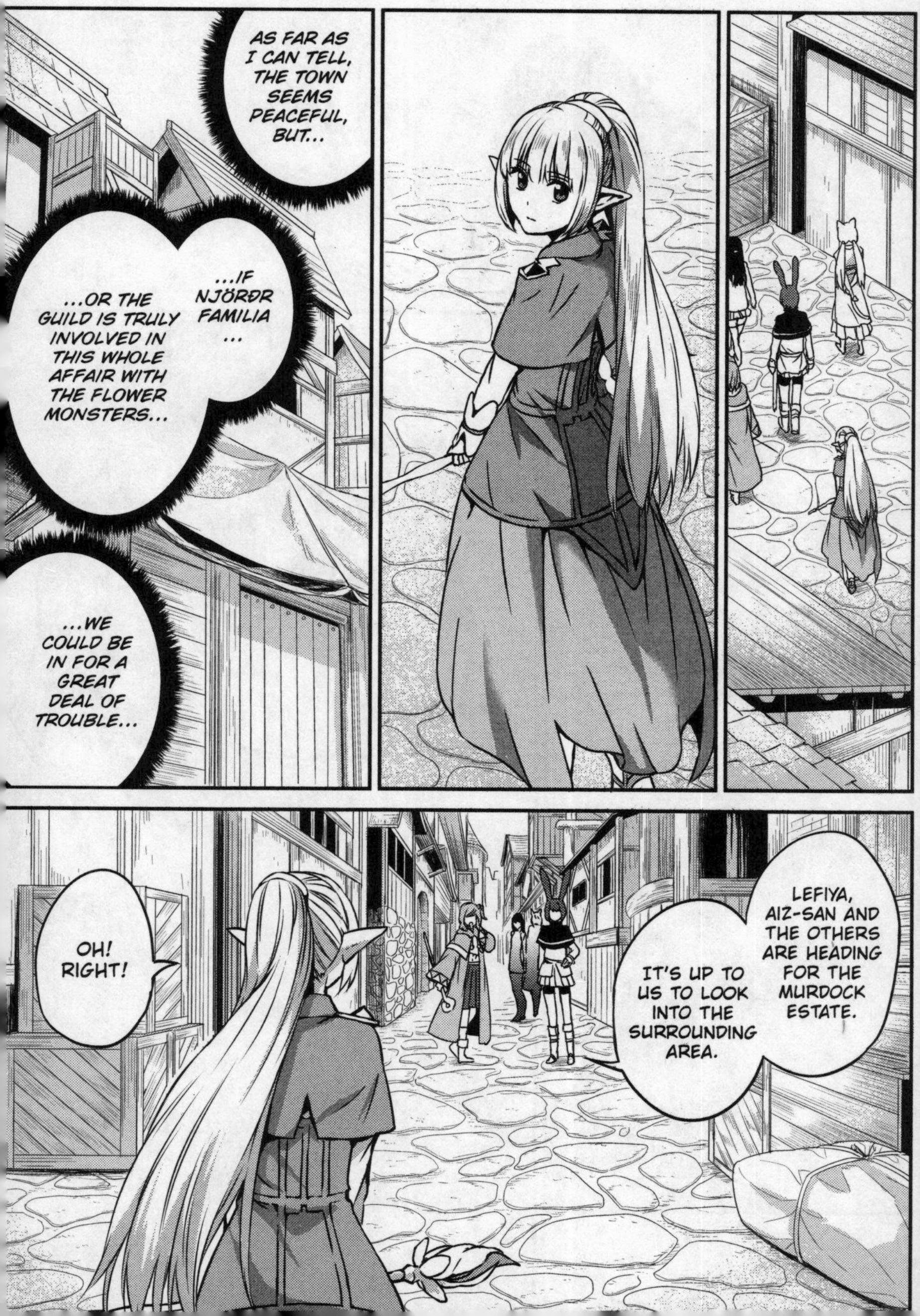
AS FAR AS I CAN TELL, THE TOWN SEEMS PEACEFUL, BUT...
...IF NJÖRÐR FAMILIA ...
...OR THE GUILD IS TRULY INVOLVED IN THIS WHOLE AFFAIR WITH THE FLOWER MONSTERS...
...WE COULD BE IN FOR A GREAT DEAL OF TROUBLE...
LEFIYA, AIZ-SAN AND THE OTHERS ARE HEADING FOR THE MURDOCK ESTATE.
IT'S UP TO US TO LOOK INTO THE SURROUNDING AREA.
OH! RIGHT!

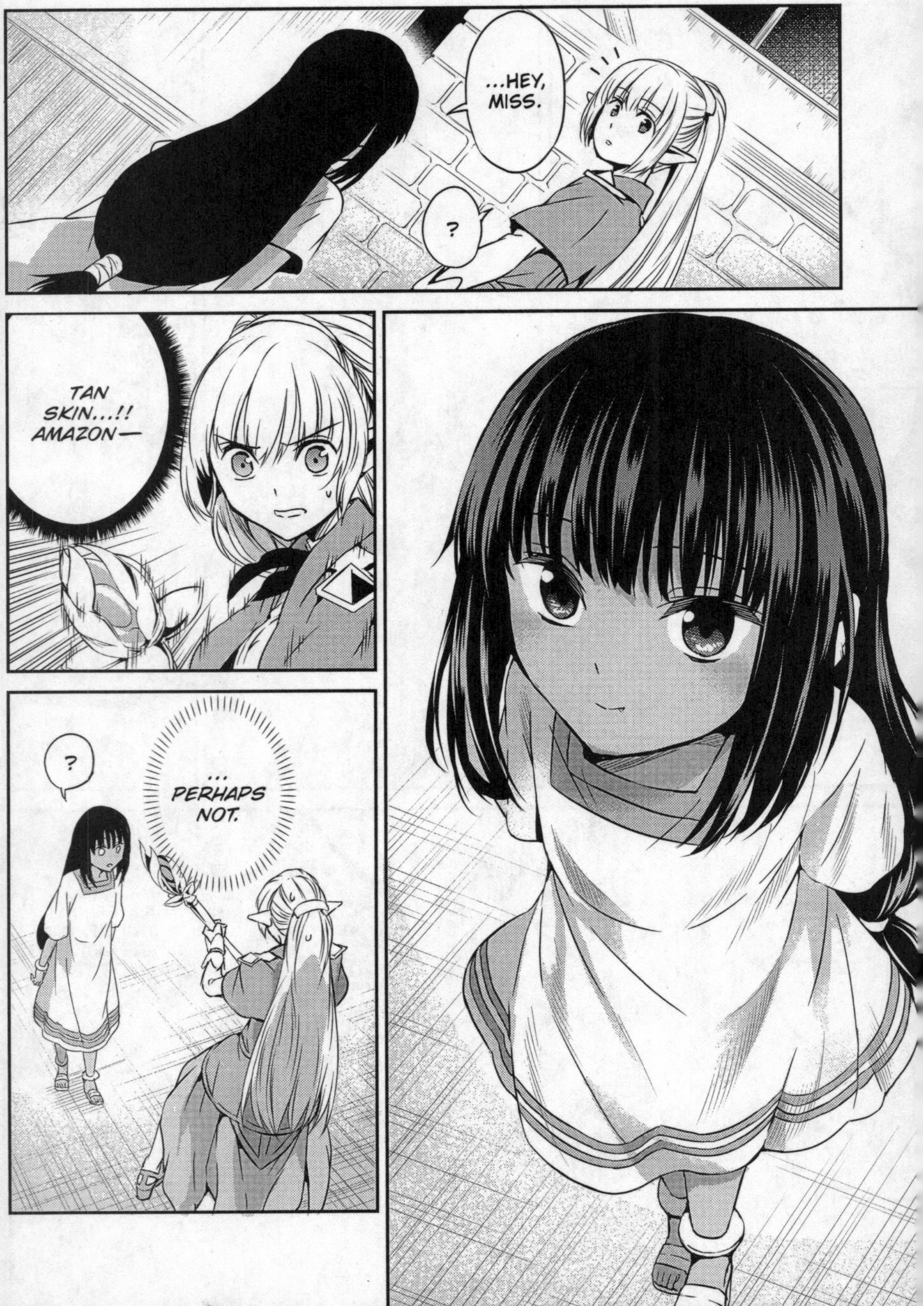
...HEY, MISS.
?
TAN SKIN...!! AMAZON—
...PERHAPS NOT.
?

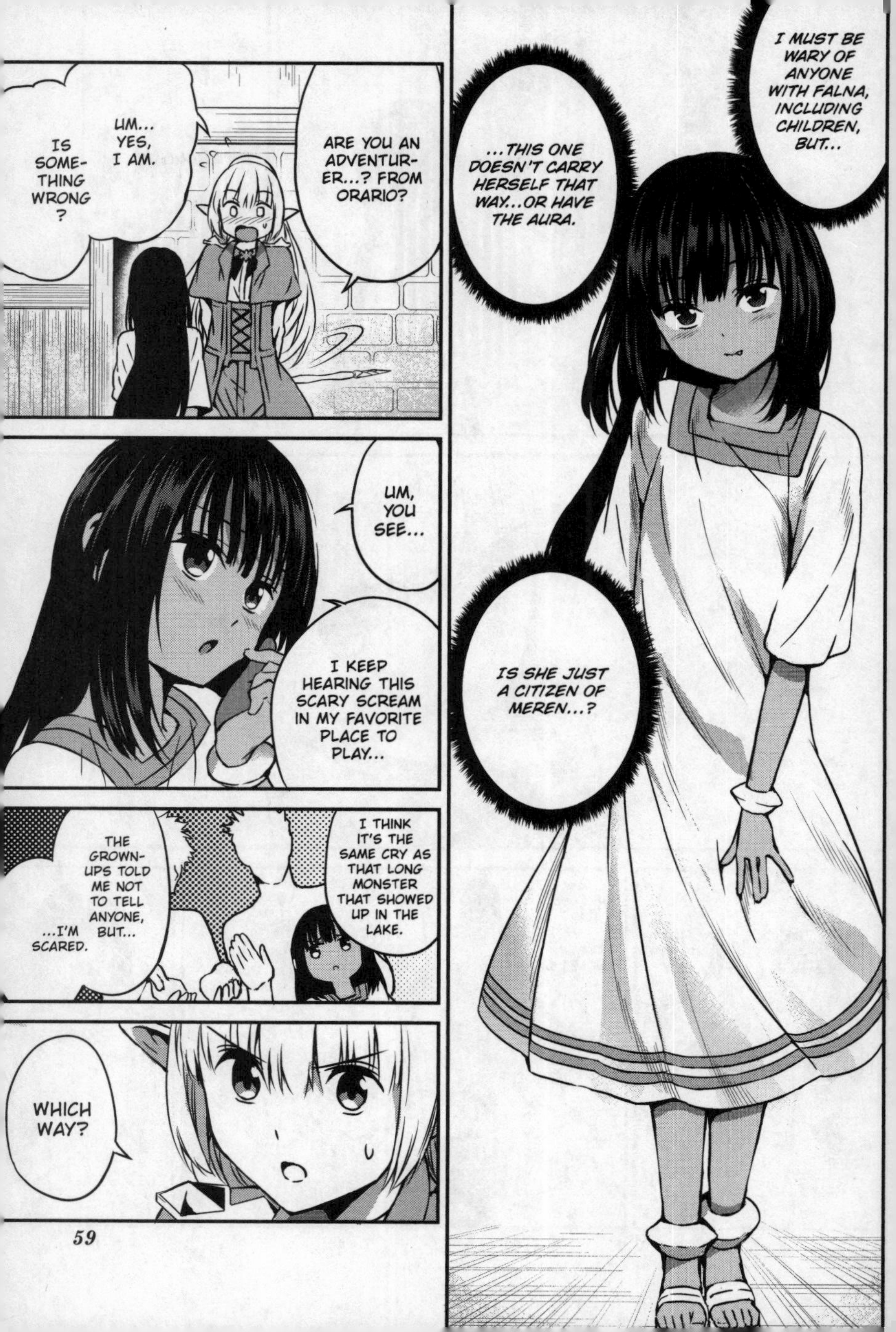
I MUST BE WARY OF ANYONE WITH FALNA, INCLUDING CHILDREN, BUT...
...THIS ONE DOESN'T CARRY HERSELF THAT WAY...OR HAVE THE AURA.
IS SHE JUST A CITIZEN OF MEREN...?
ARE YOU AN ADVENTURER...? FROM ORARIO?
UM... YES, I AM.
IS SOMETHING WRONG?
UM, YOU SEE...
I KEEP HEARING THIS SCARY SCREAM IN MY FAVORITE PLACE TO PLAY...
I THINK IT'S THE SAME CRY AS THAT LONG MONSTER THAT SHOWED UP IN THE LAKE.
THE GROWN-UPS TOLD ME NOT TO TELL ANYONE, BUT...
...I'M SCARED.
WHICH WAY?

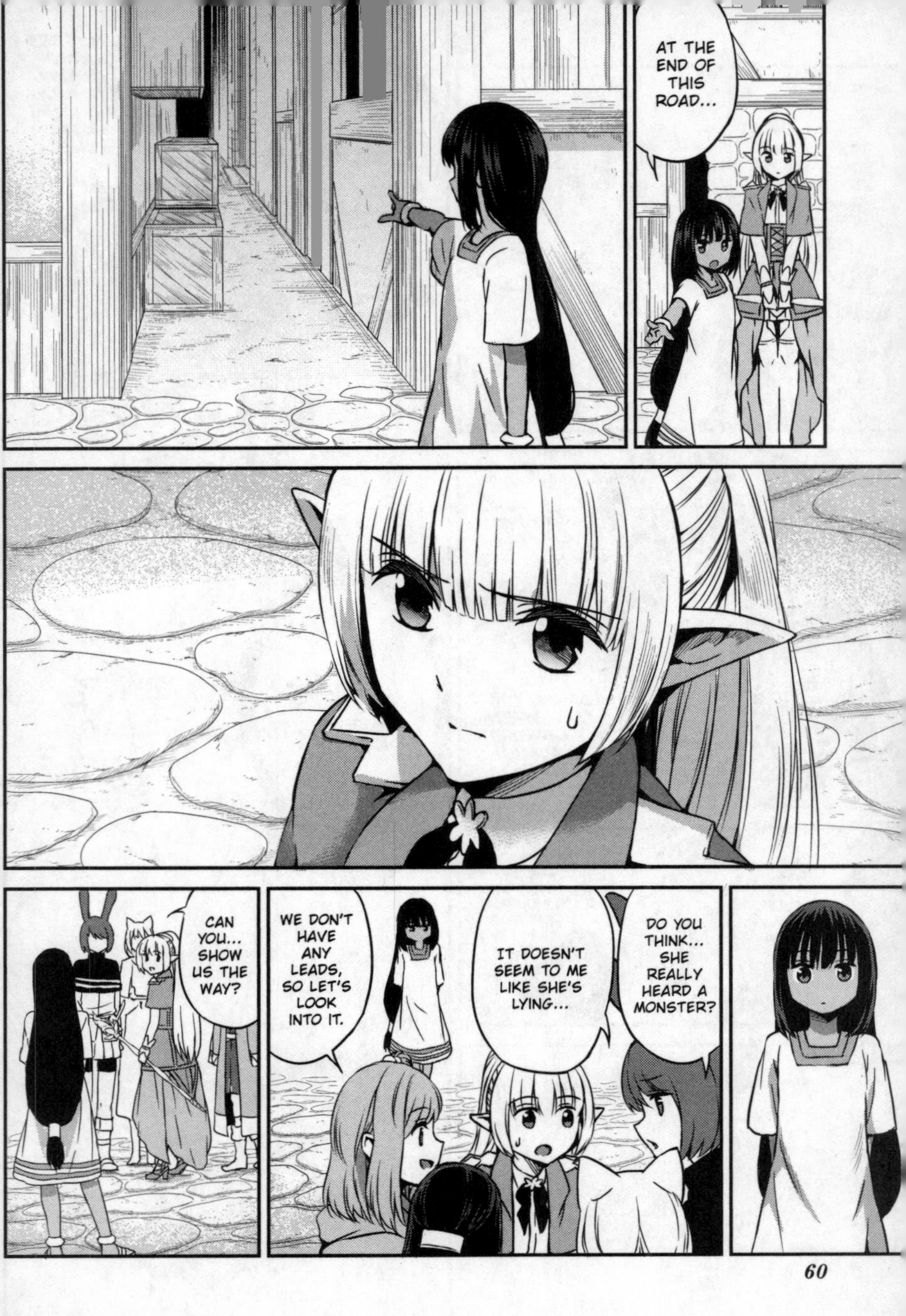
AT THE END OF THIS ROAD...
DO YOU THINK... SHE REALLY HEARD A MONSTER?
IT DOESN'T SEEM TO ME LIKE SHE'S LYING...
WE DON'T HAVE ANY LEADS, SO LET'S LOOK INTO IT.
CAN YOU... SHOW US THE WAY?

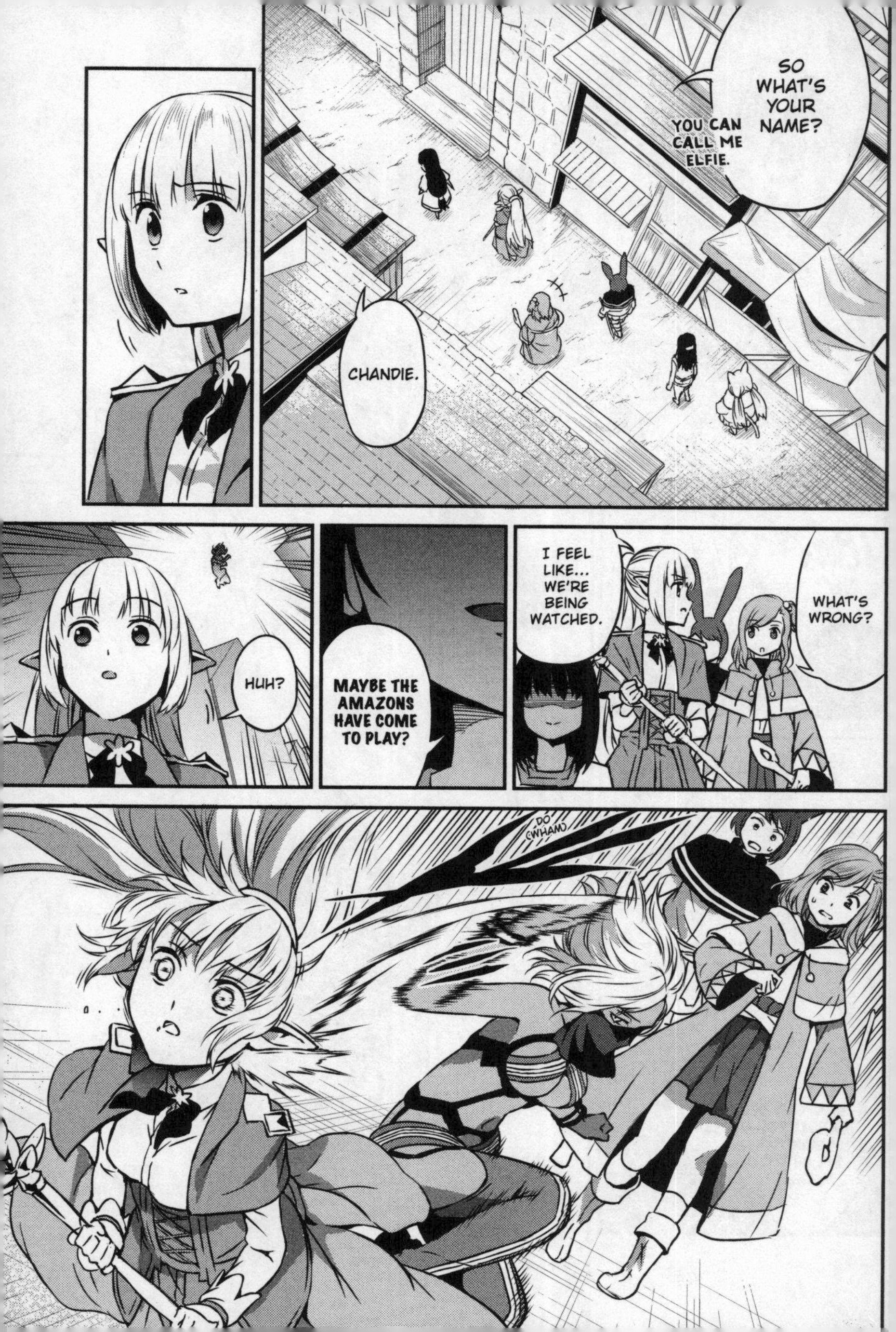
SO WHAT'S YOUR NAME?
YOU CAN CALL ME ELFIE.
CHANDIE.
WHAT'S WRONG?
I FEEL LIKE... WE'RE BEING WATCHED.
MAYBE THE AMAZONS HAVE COME TO PLAY?
HUH?
DO (WHAM)
...

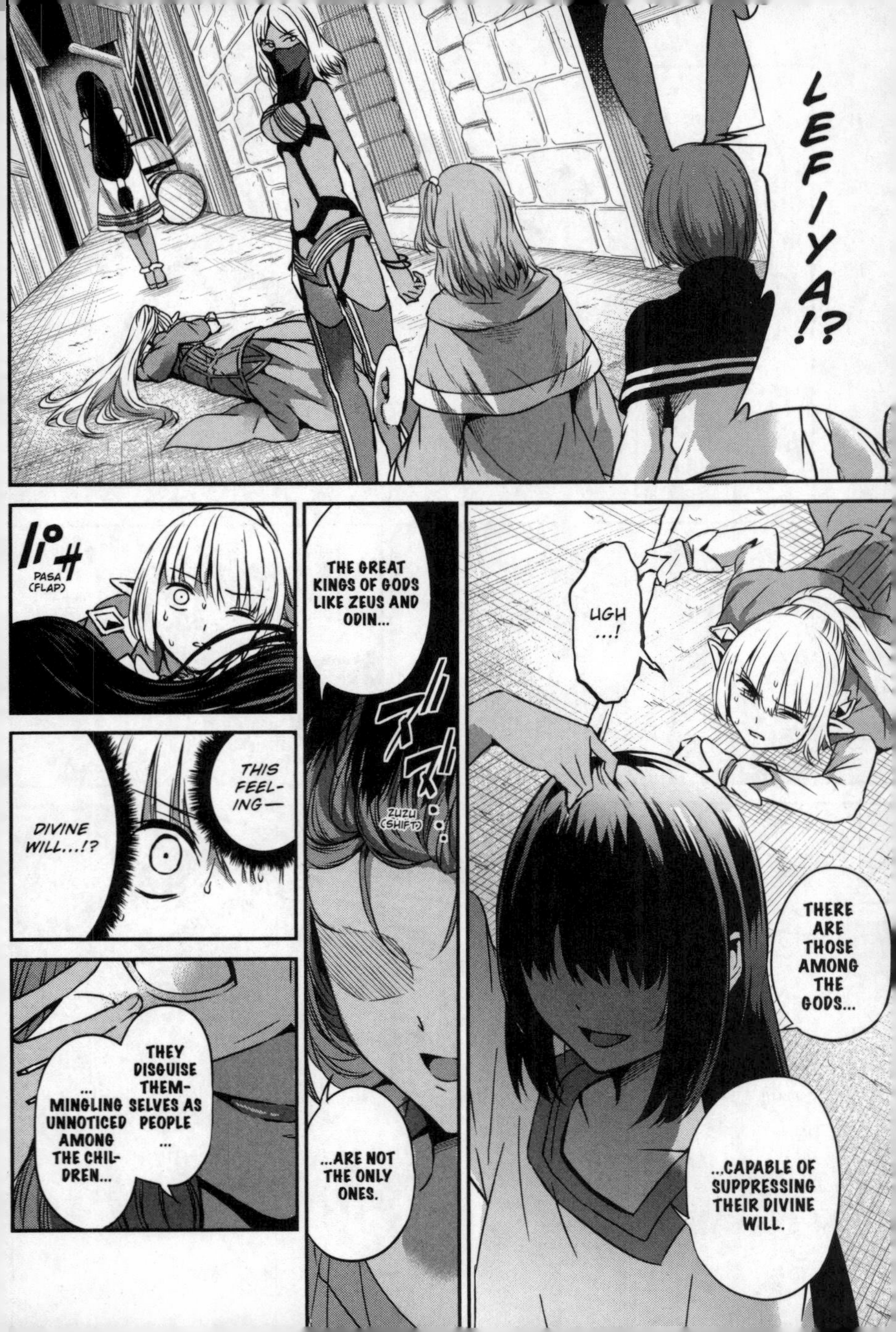
LEFIYA!?
UGH ...!
THERE ARE THOSE AMONG THE GODS...
...CAPABLE OF SUPPRESSING THEIR DIVINE WILL.
THE GREAT KINGS OF GODS LIKE ZEUS AND ODIN...
ズズ
ZUZU (SHIFT)
...ARE NOT THE ONLY ONES.
パサ
PASA (FLAP)
THIS FEEL-ING—
DIVINE WILL...!?
THEY DISGUISE THEM-SELVES AS PEOPLE ...
... MINGLING UNNOTICED AMONG THE CHIL-DREN...

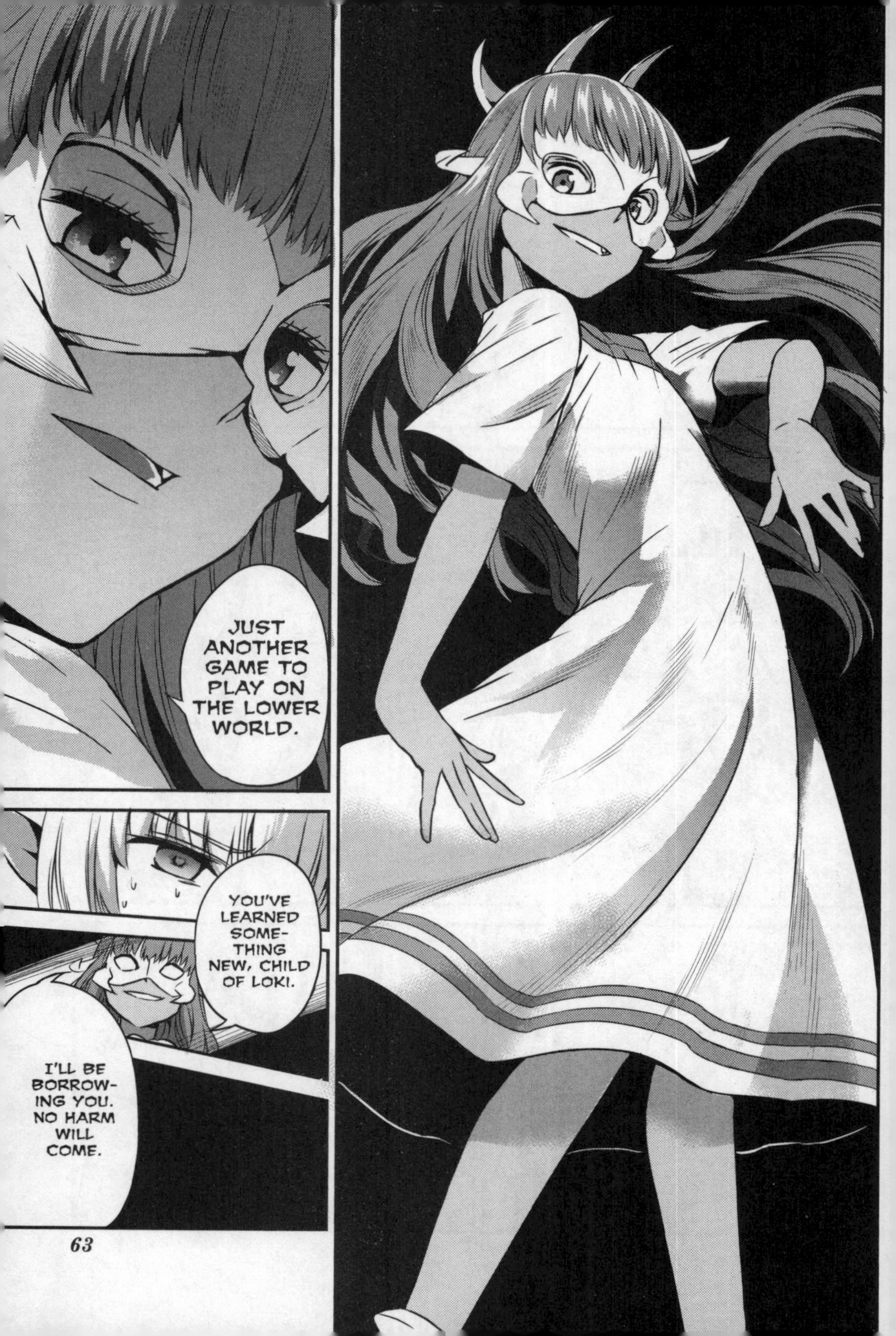
JUST ANOTHER GAME TO PLAY ON THE LOWER WORLD.
YOU'VE LEARNED SOME-THING NEW, CHILD OF LOKI.
I'LL BE BORROW-ING YOU. NO HARM WILL COME.

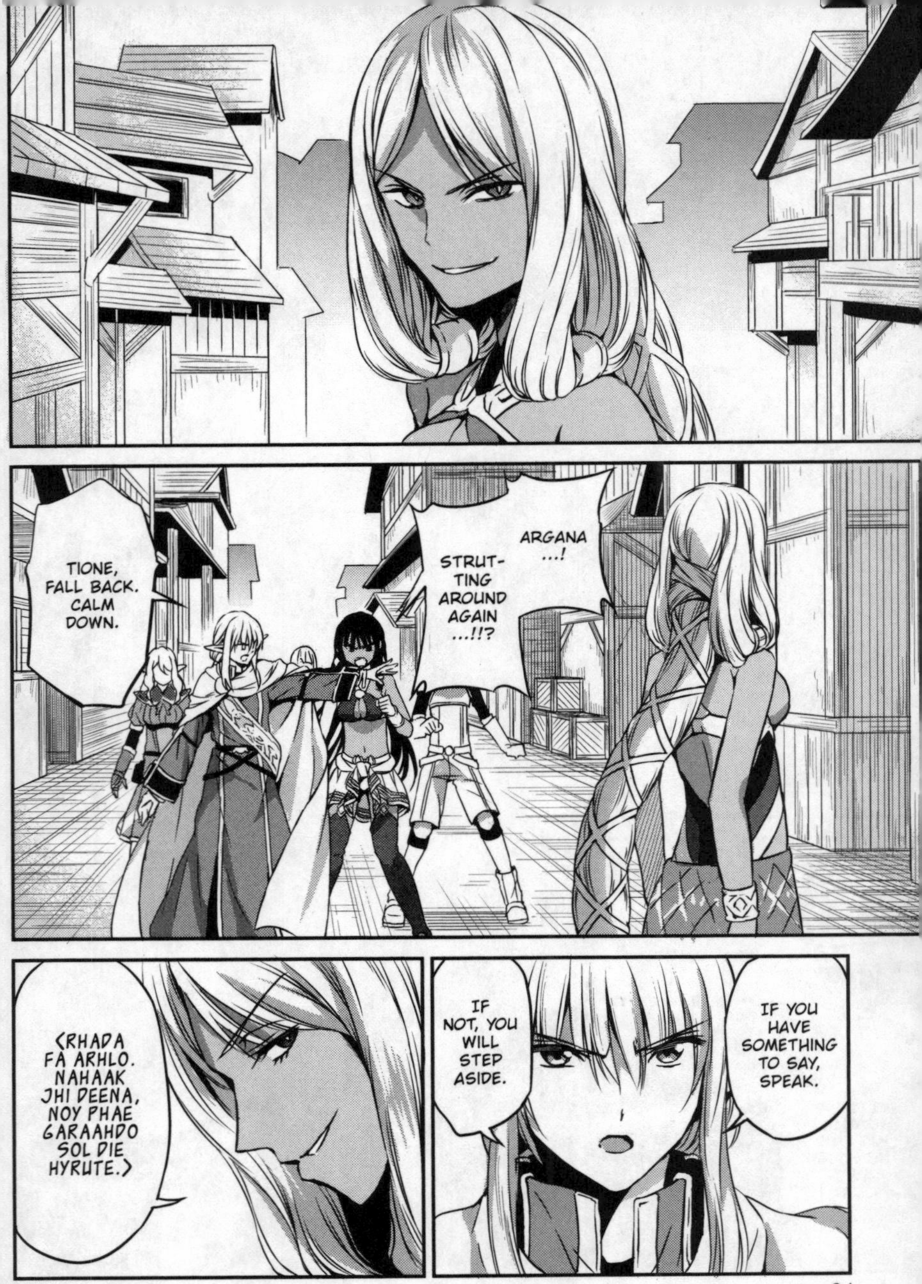
ARGANA ...!
STRUT-TING AROUND AGAIN ...!!?
TIONE, FALL BACK. CALM DOWN.
IF YOU HAVE SOMETHING TO SAY, SPEAK.
IF NOT, YOU WILL STEP ASIDE.
〈RHADA FA ARHLO. NAHAAK JHI DEENA, NOY PHAE GARAAHDO SOL DIE HYRUTE.〉

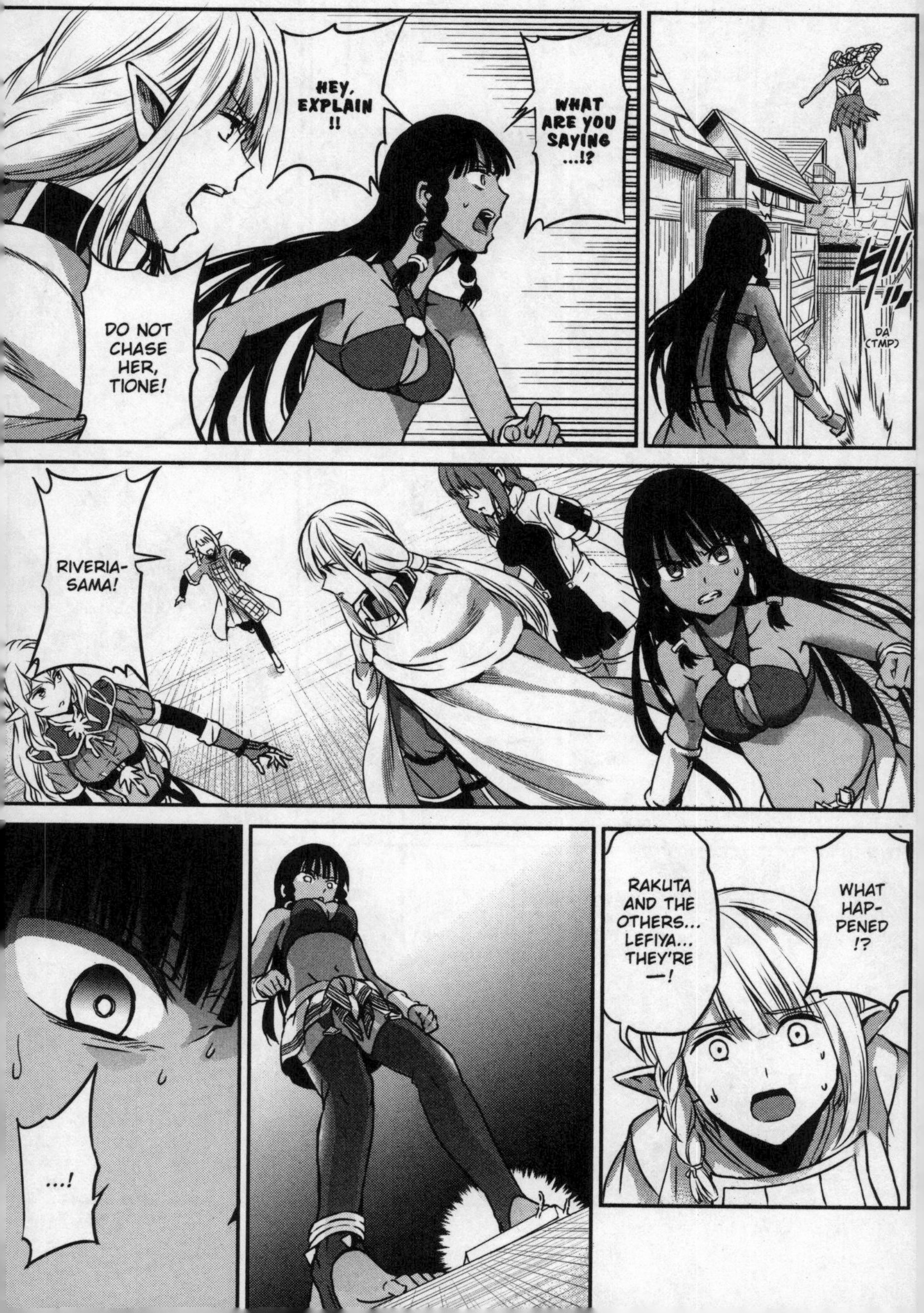
DA (TMP)
WHAT ARE YOU SAYING ...!?
HEY, EXPLAIN !!
DO NOT CHASE HER, TIONE!
RIVERIA-SAMA!
WHAT HAP-PENED !?
RAKUTA AND THE OTHERS... LEFIYA... THEY'RE—!
...!

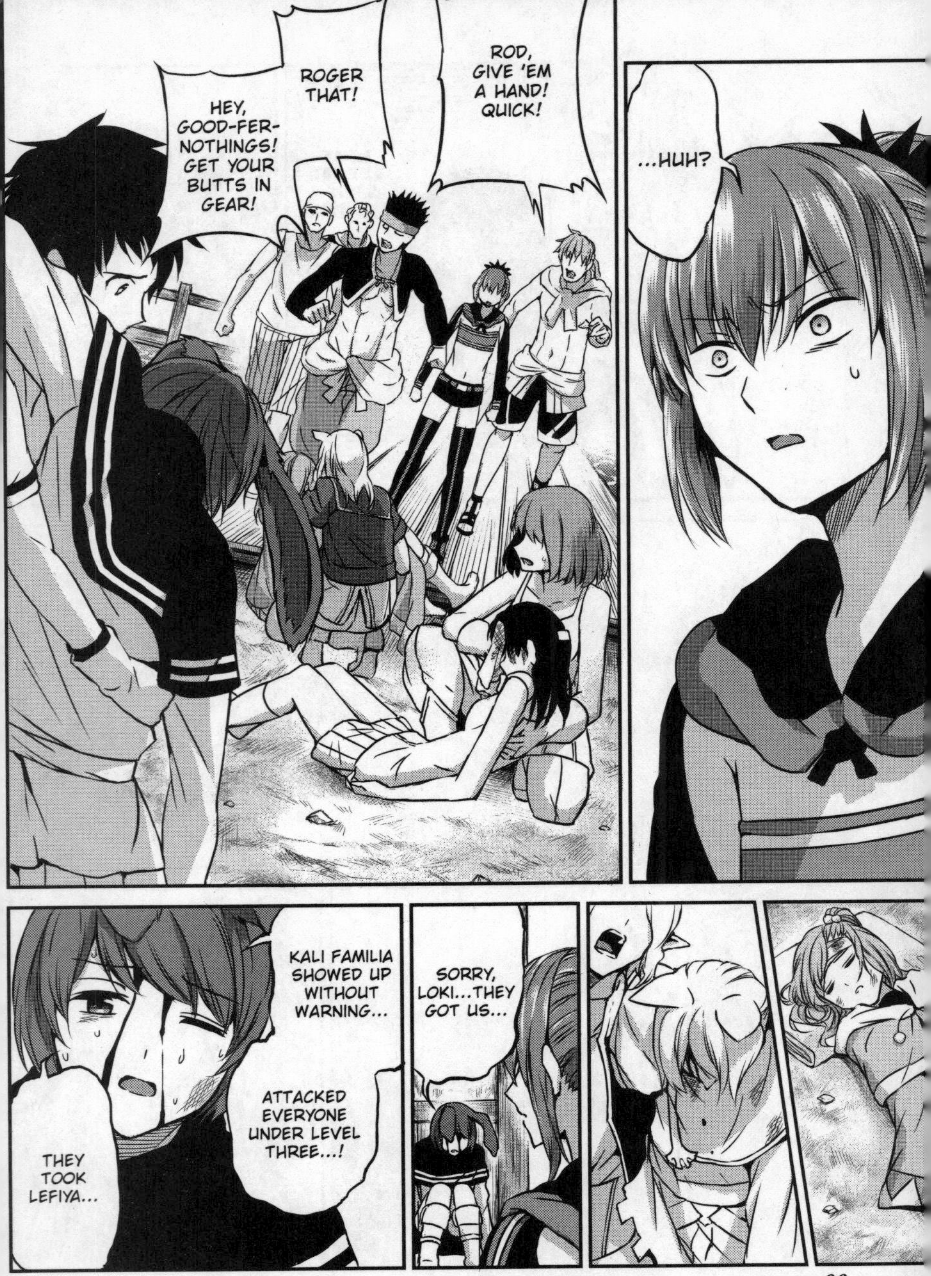
...HUH?
ROD, GIVE 'EM A HAND! QUICK!
ROGER THAT!
HEY, GOOD-FER-NOTHINGS! GET YOUR BUTTS IN GEAR!
SORRY, LOKI...THEY GOT US...
KALI FAMILIA SHOWED UP WITHOUT WARNING...
ATTACKED EVERYONE UNDER LEVEL THREE...!
THEY TOOK LEFIYA...

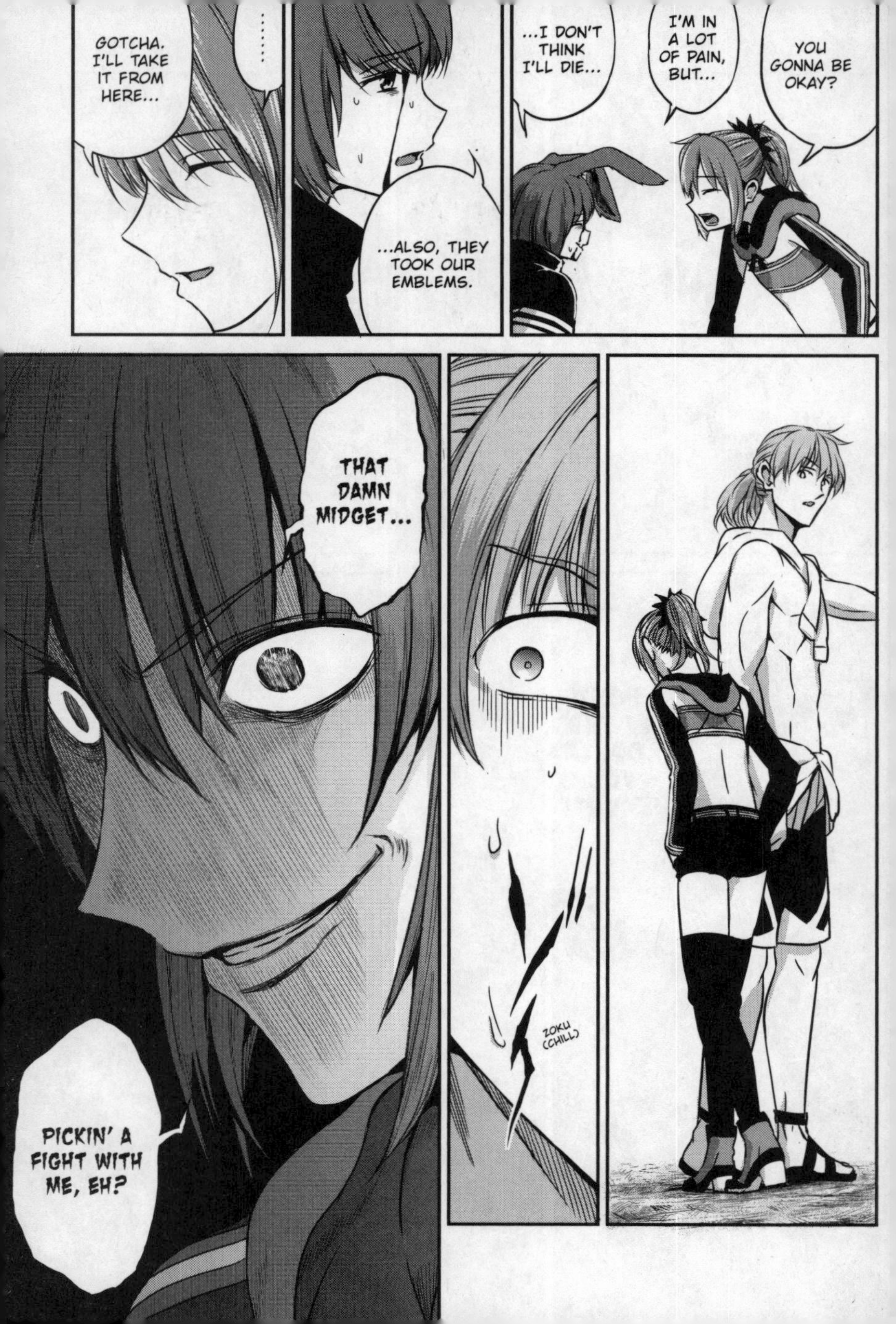
YOU GONNA BE OKAY?
I'M IN A LOT OF PAIN, BUT...
...I DON'T THINK I'LL DIE...
......
...ALSO, THEY TOOK OUR EMBLEMS.
GOTCHA. I'LL TAKE IT FROM HERE...
ZOKU (CHILL)
THAT DAMN MIDGET...
PICKIN' A FIGHT WITH ME, EH?

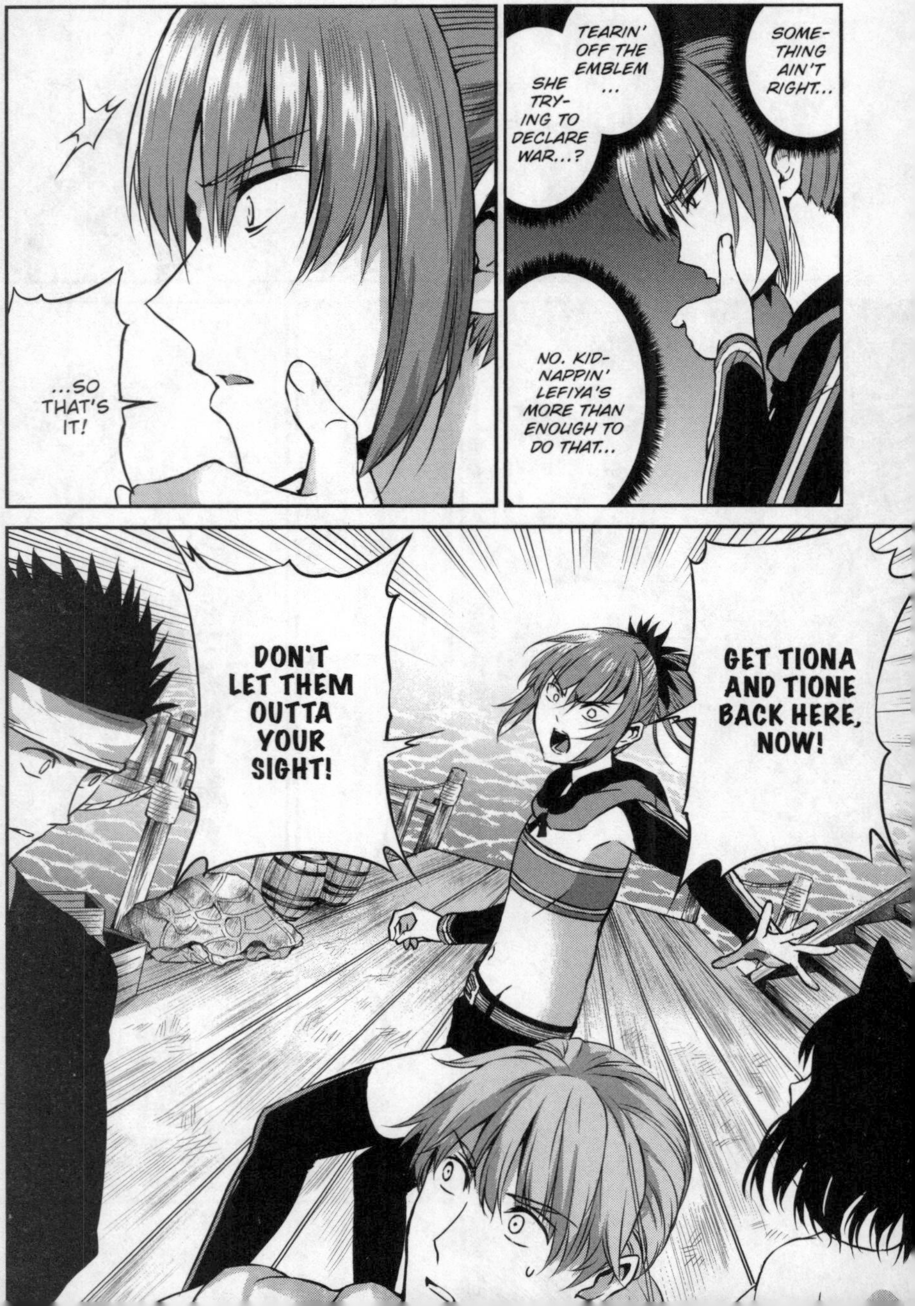
SOME-THING AIN'T RIGHT...
TEARIN' OFF THE EMBLEM...
SHE TRYING TO DECLARE WAR...?
NO. KIDNAPPIN' LEFIYA'S MORE THAN ENOUGH TO DO THAT...
...SO THAT'S IT!
GET TIONA AND TIONE BACK HERE, NOW!
DON'T LET THEM OUTTA YOUR SIGHT!

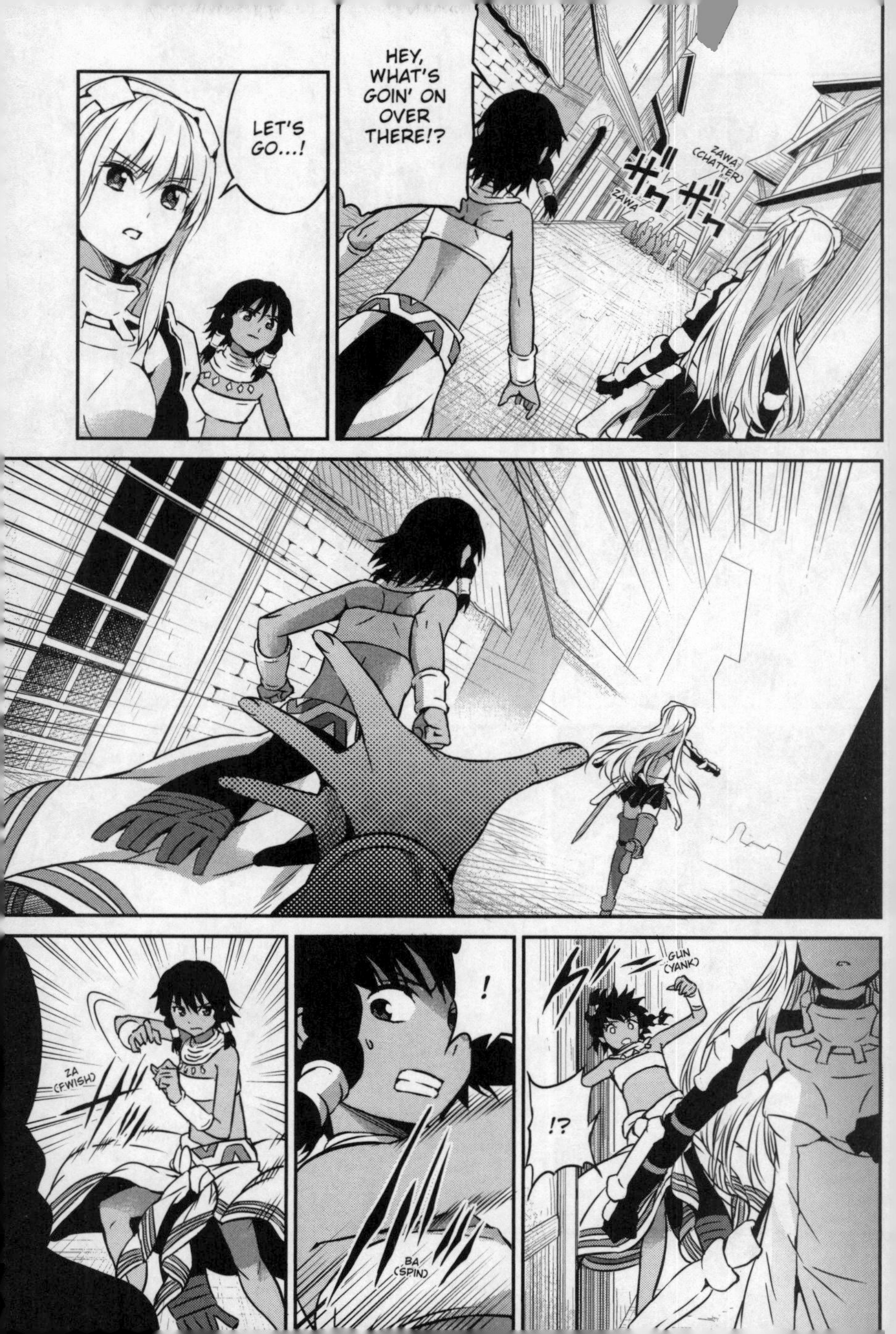
HEY, WHAT'S GOIN' ON OVER THERE!?
ZAWA (CHATTER)
ZAWA
LET'S GO...!
GUN (YANK)
!?
!
BA (SPIN)
ZA (FWISH)

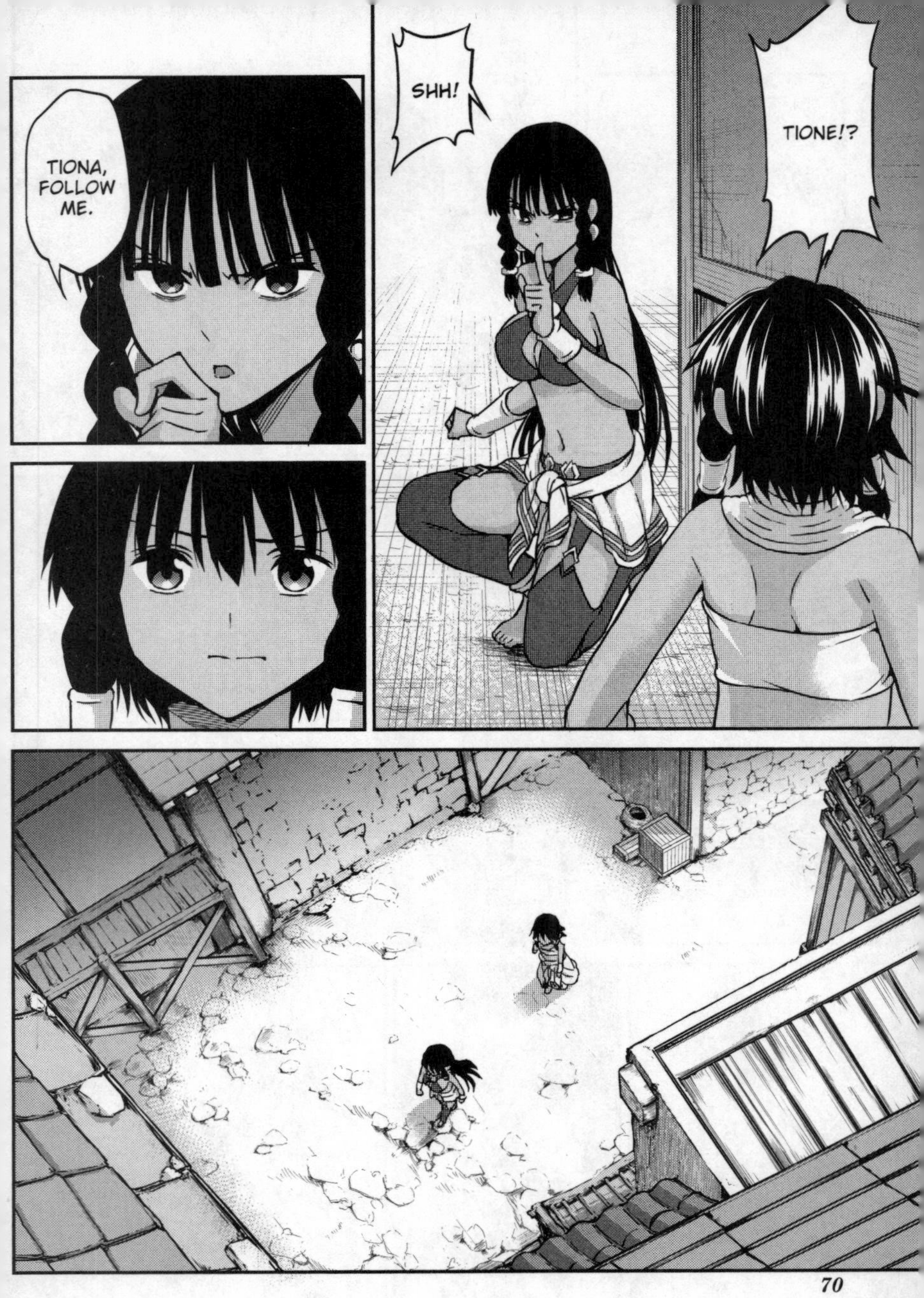
TIONE!?
SHH!
TIONA, FOLLOW ME.

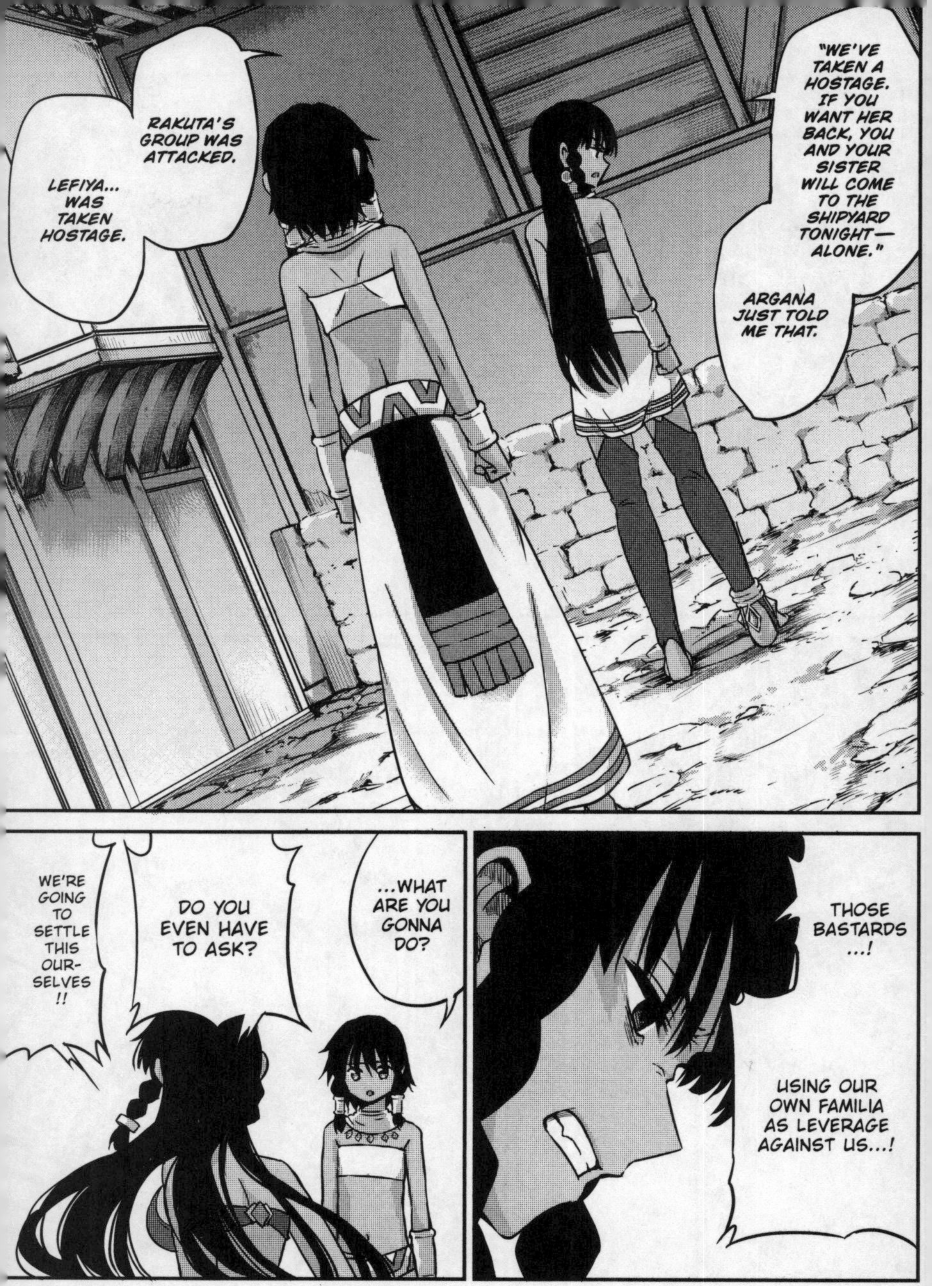
"WE'VE TAKEN A HOSTAGE. IF YOU WANT HER BACK, YOU AND YOUR SISTER WILL COME TO THE SHIPYARD TONIGHT—ALONE."
ARGANA JUST TOLD ME THAT.
RAKUTA'S GROUP WAS ATTACKED.
LEFIYA... WAS TAKEN HOSTAGE.
THOSE BASTARDS ...!
USING OUR OWN FAMILIA AS LEVERAGE AGAINST US...!
...WHAT ARE YOU GONNA DO?
DO YOU EVEN HAVE TO ASK?
WE'RE GOING TO SETTLE THIS OUR-SELVES !!

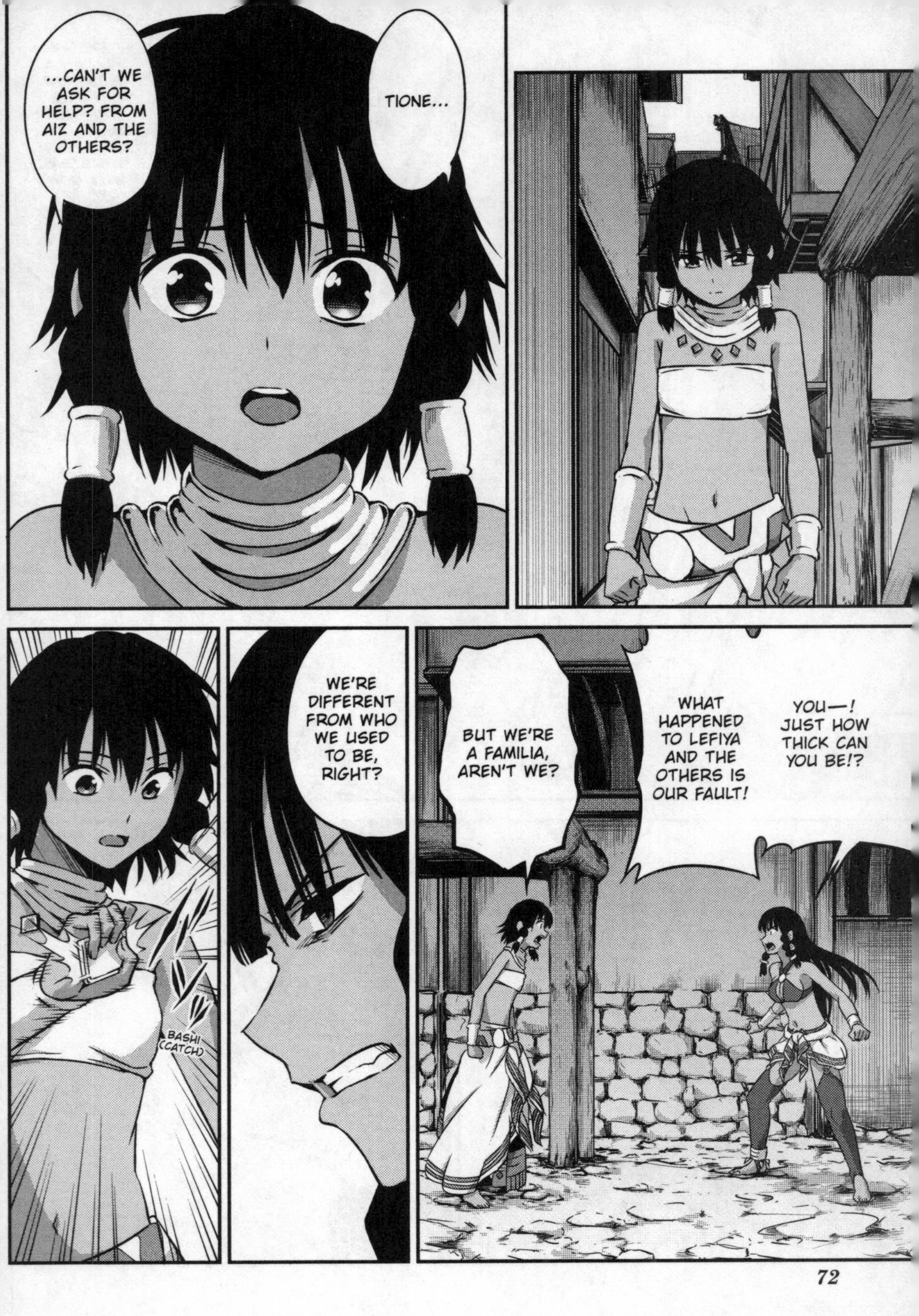
TIONE...
...CAN'T WE ASK FOR HELP? FROM AIZ AND THE OTHERS?
YOU—! JUST HOW THICK CAN YOU BE!?
WHAT HAPPENED TO LEFIYA AND THE OTHERS IS OUR FAULT!
BUT WE'RE A FAMILIA, AREN'T WE?
WE'RE DIFFERENT FROM WHO WE USED TO BE, RIGHT?
BASHI (CATCH)

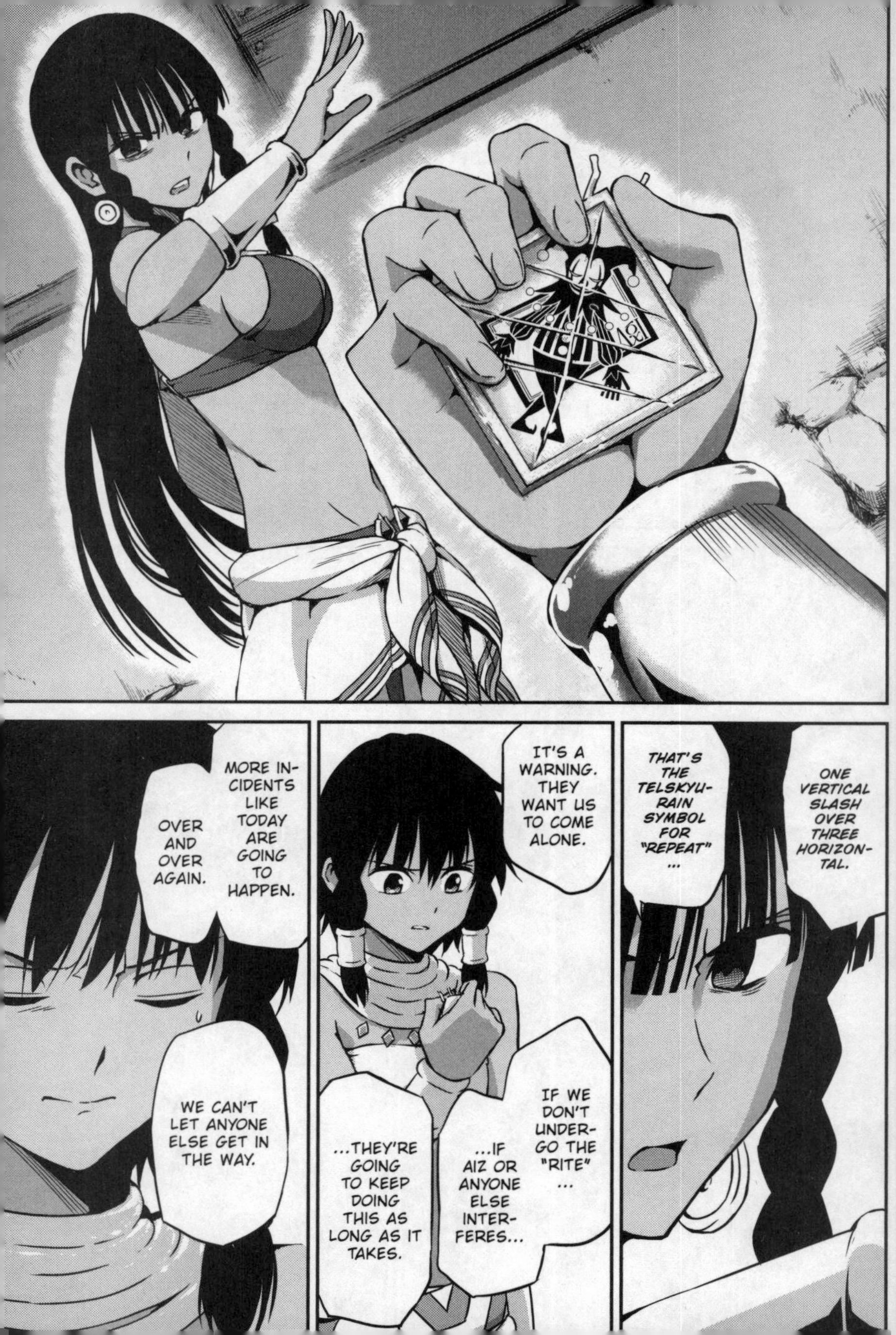
ONE VERTICAL SLASH OVER THREE HORIZONTAL.
THAT'S THE TELSKYURAIN SYMBOL FOR "REPEAT"...
IT'S A WARNING. THEY WANT US TO COME ALONE.
IF WE DON'T UNDERGO THE "RITE"...
...IF AIZ OR ANYONE ELSE INTERFERES...
...THEY'RE GOING TO KEEP DOING THIS AS LONG AS IT TAKES.
MORE INCIDENTS LIKE TODAY ARE GOING TO HAPPEN.
OVER AND OVER AGAIN.
WE CAN'T LET ANYONE ELSE GET IN THE WAY.

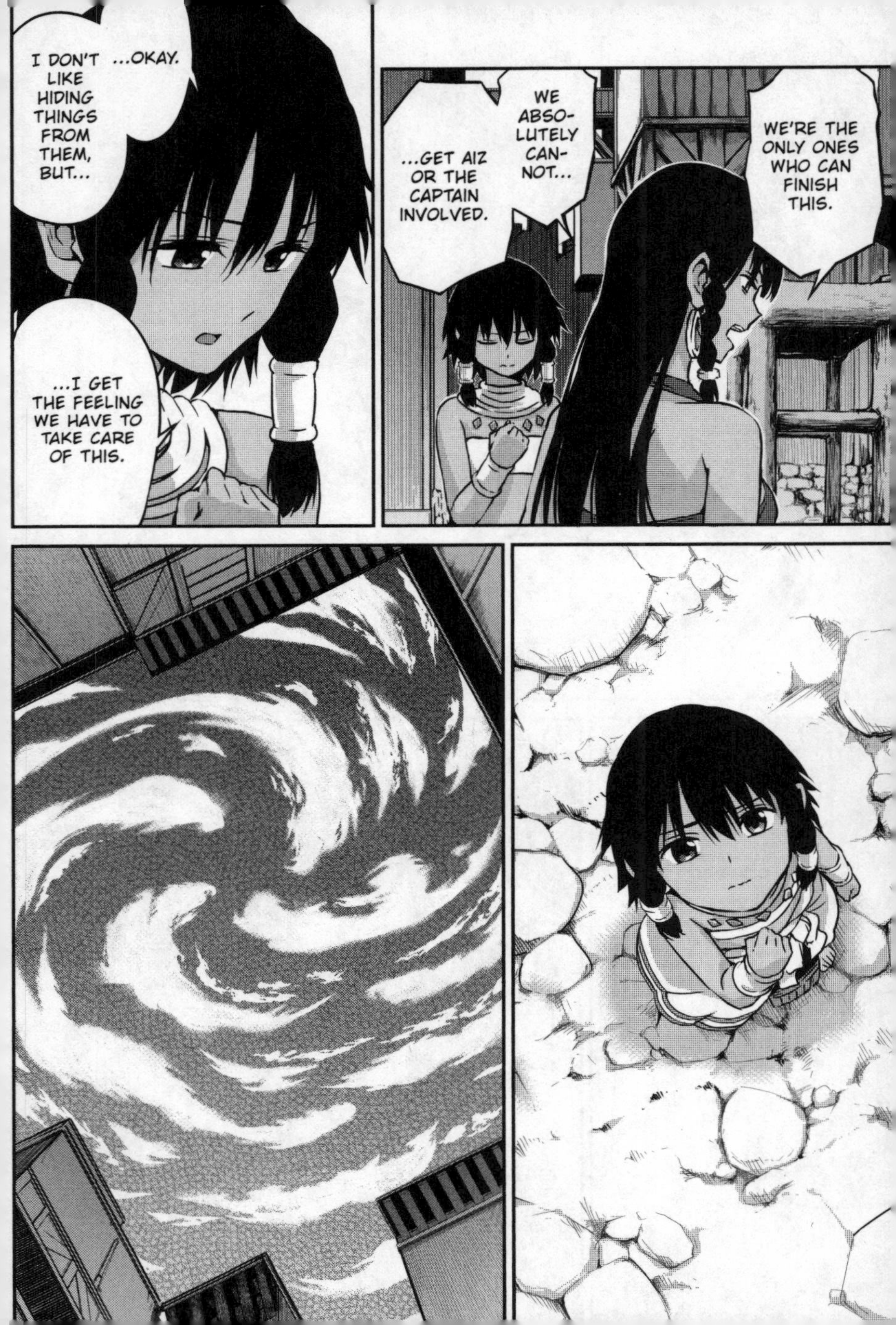
WE'RE THE ONLY ONES WHO CAN FINISH THIS.
WE ABSO-LUTELY CAN-NOT...
...GET AIZ OR THE CAPTAIN INVOLVED.
...OKAY.
I DON'T LIKE HIDING THINGS FROM THEM, BUT...
...I GET THE FEELING WE HAVE TO TAKE CARE OF THIS.

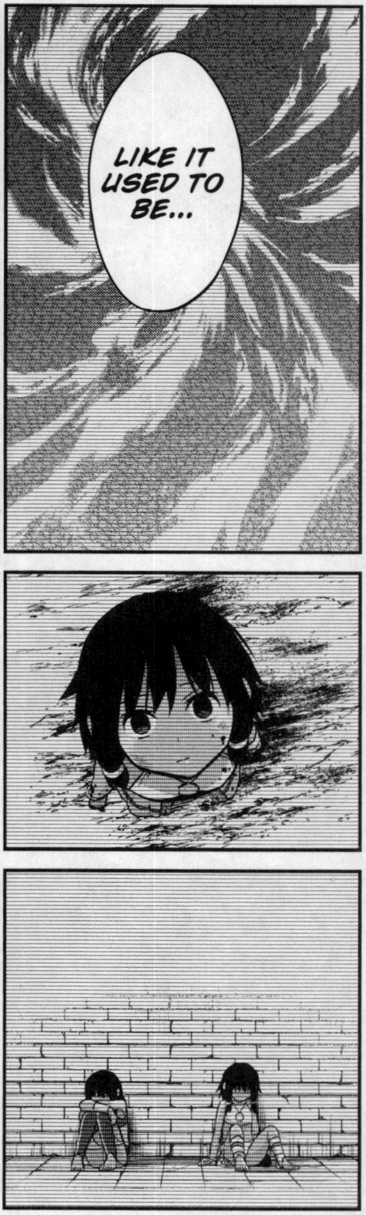
LIKE IT USED TO BE...
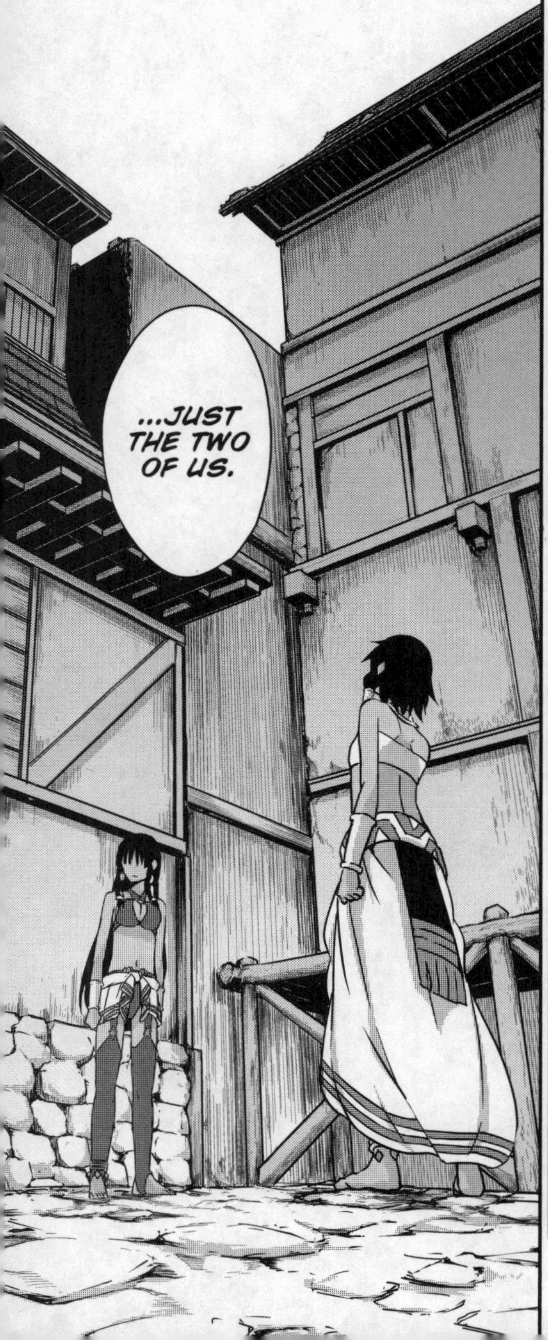
...JUST THE TWO OF US.

Is it WRONG to TRY to PICK UP GIRLS in a DUNGEON? ON THE SIDE

Sword Oratoria

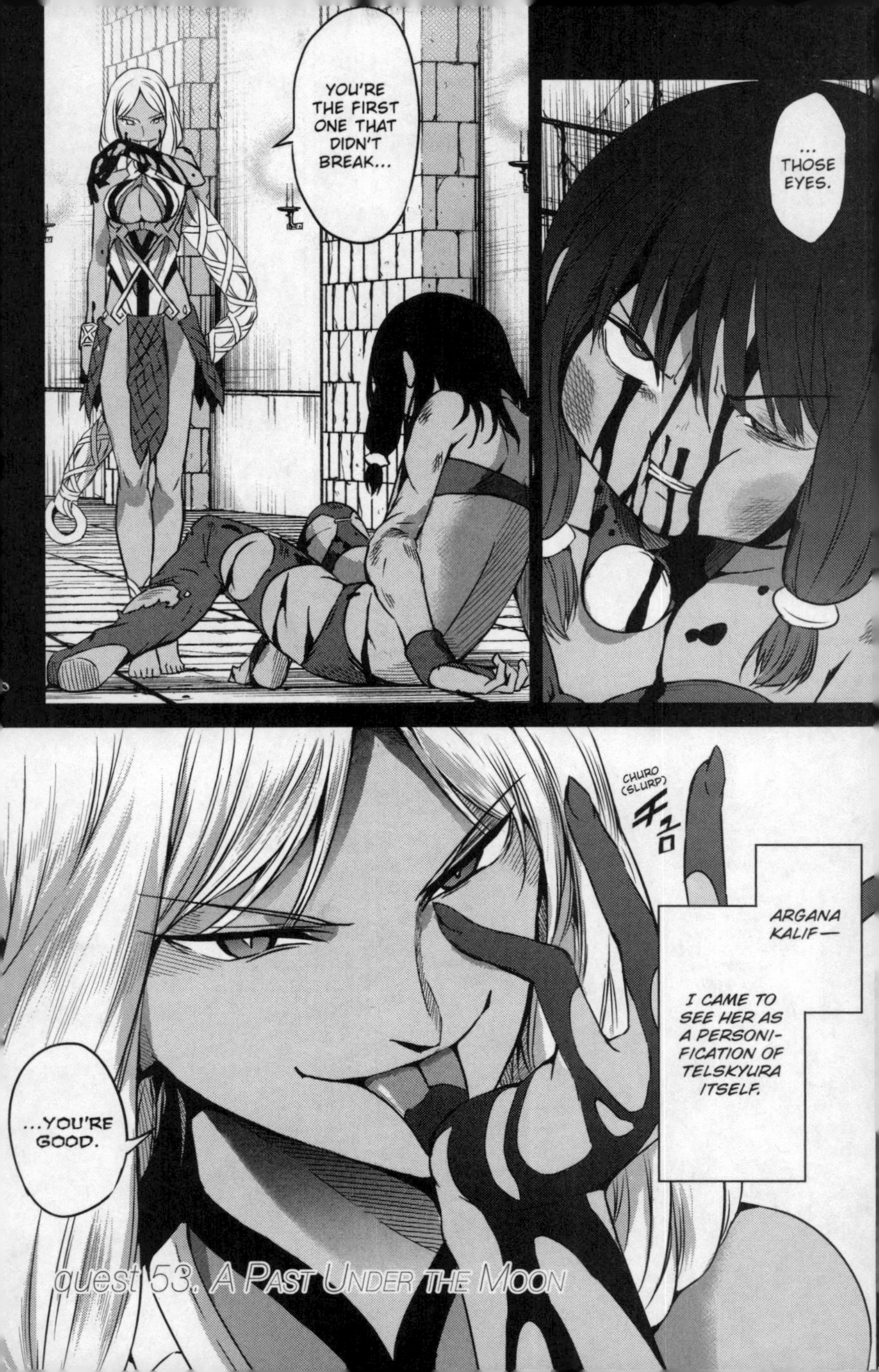
...THOSE EYES.
YOU'RE THE FIRST ONE THAT DIDN'T BREAK...
CHURO (SLURP)
ARGANA KALIF—
I CAME TO SEE HER AS A PERSONIFICATION OF TELSKYURA ITSELF.
...YOU'RE GOOD.
quest 53. A Past Under the Moon

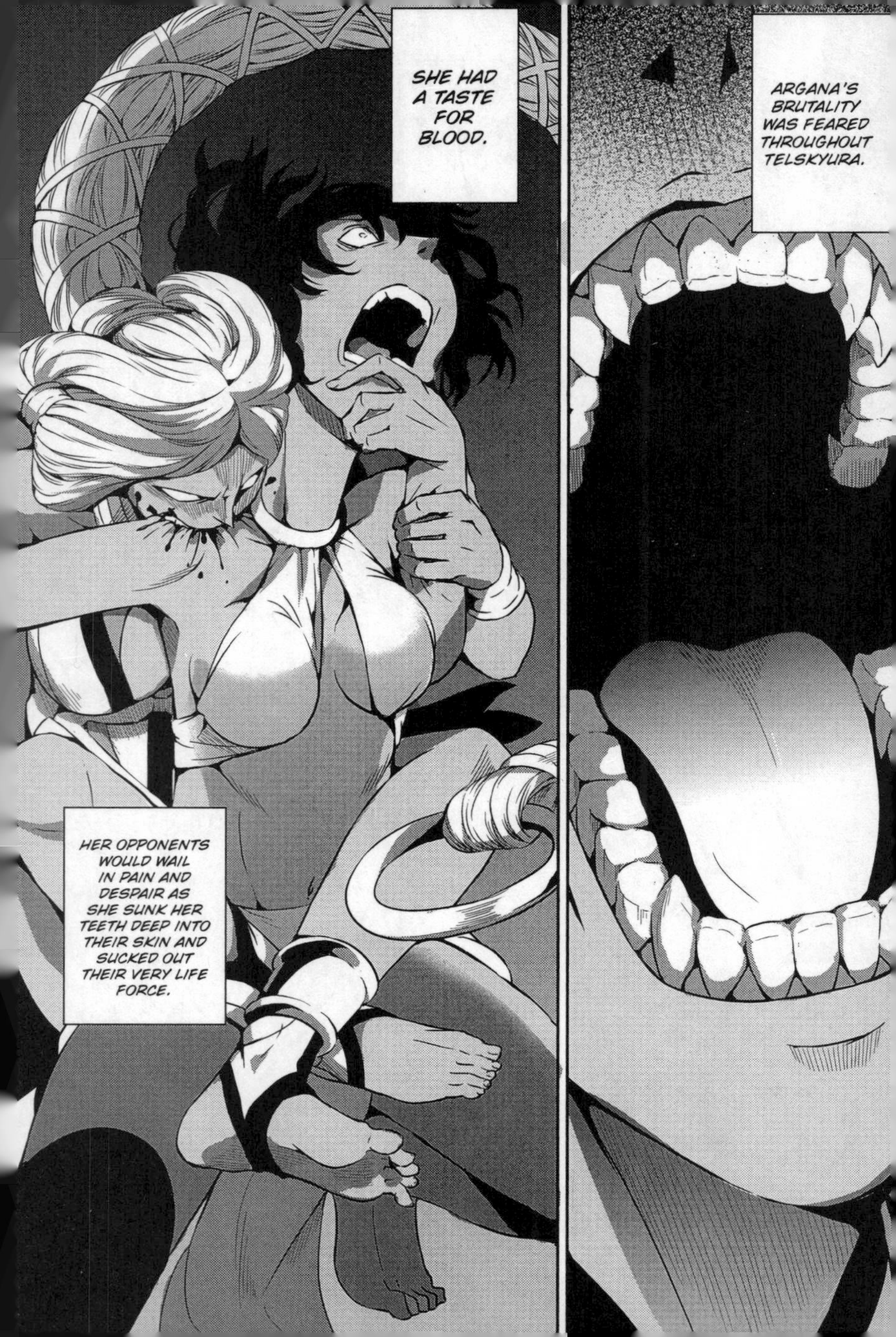
ARGANA'S BRUTALITY WAS FEARED THROUGHOUT TELSKYURA.
SHE HAD A TASTE FOR BLOOD.
HER OPPONENTS WOULD WAIL IN PAIN AND DESPAIR AS SHE SUNK HER TEETH DEEP INTO THEIR SKIN AND SUCKED OUT THEIR VERY LIFE FORCE.

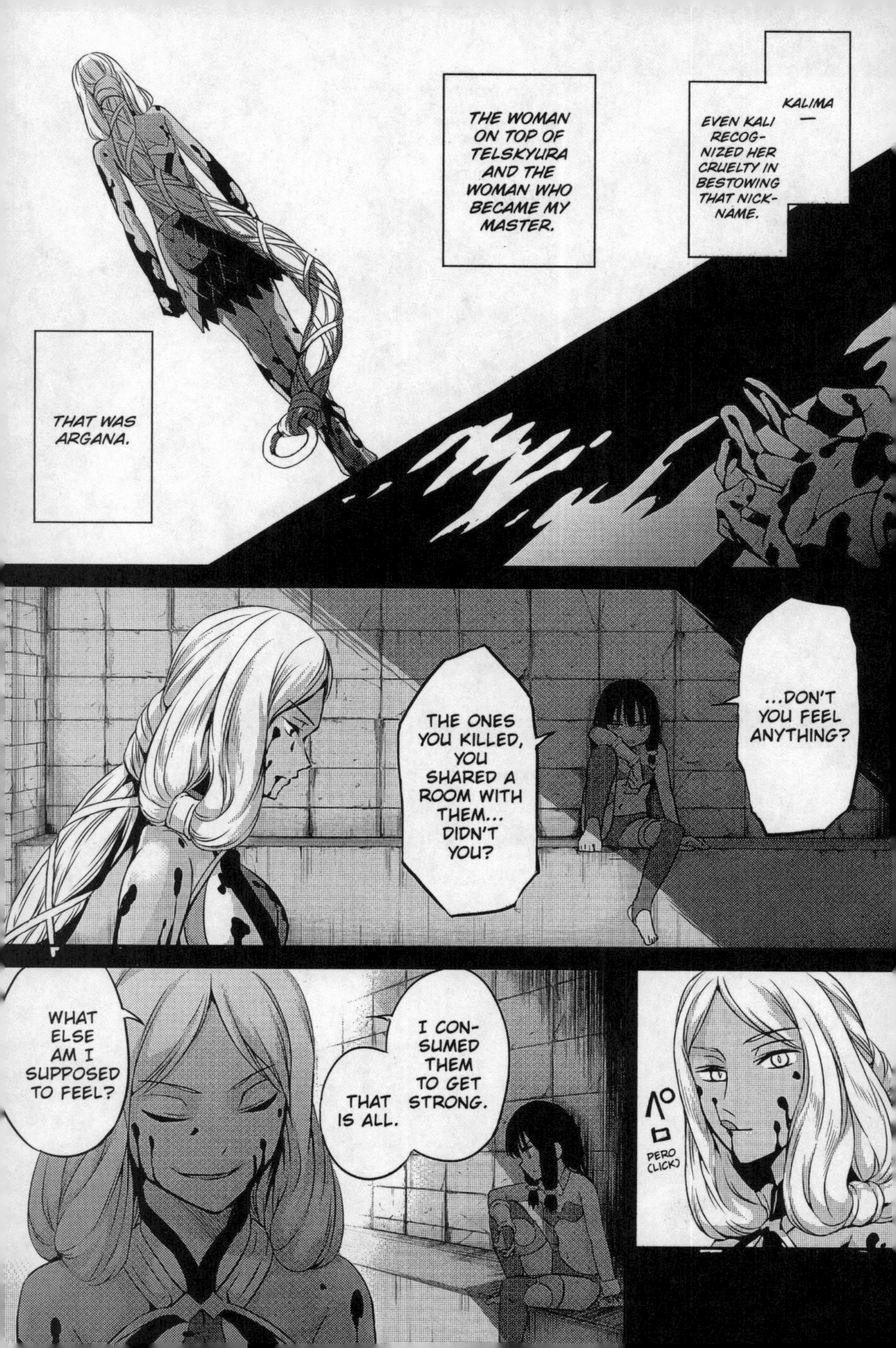
KALIMA —
EVEN KALI RECOGNIZED HER CRUELTY IN BESTOWING THAT NICKNAME.
THE WOMAN ON TOP OF TELSKYURA AND THE WOMAN WHO BECAME MY MASTER.
THAT WAS ARGANA.
...DON'T YOU FEEL ANYTHING?
THE ONES YOU KILLED, YOU SHARED A ROOM WITH THEM... DIDN'T YOU?
PERO (LICK)
I CONSUMED THEM TO GET STRONG.
THAT IS ALL.
WHAT ELSE AM I SUPPOSED TO FEEL?

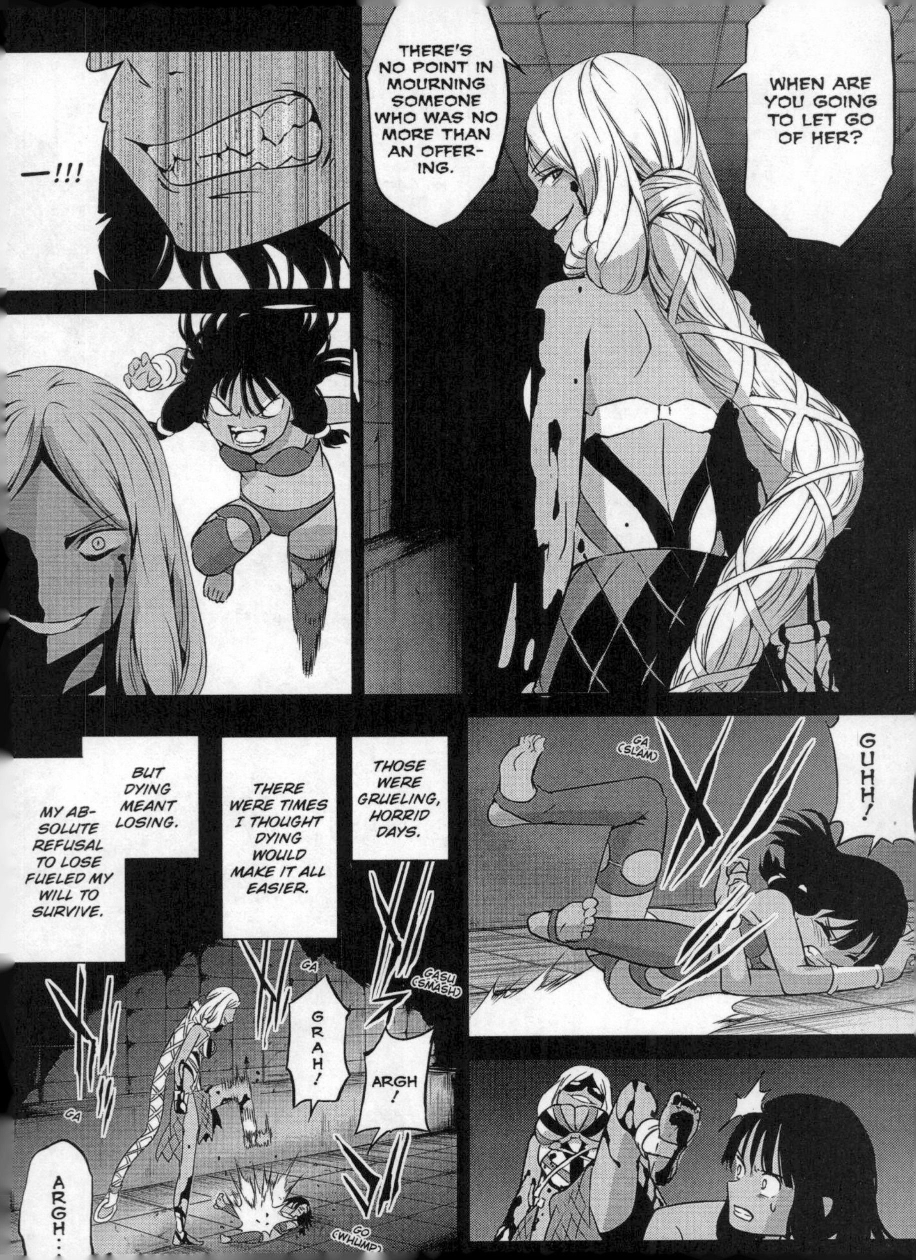
WHEN ARE YOU GOING TO LET GO OF HER?
THERE'S NO POINT IN MOURNING SOMEONE WHO WAS NO MORE THAN AN OFFER-ING.
—!!!
GUHH!
GA (SLAM)
THOSE WERE GRUELING, HORRID DAYS.
THERE WERE TIMES I THOUGHT DYING WOULD MAKE IT ALL EASIER.
BUT DYING MEANT LOSING.
MY AB-SOLUTE REFUSAL TO LOSE FUELED MY WILL TO SURVIVE.
GASU (SMASH)
GA
GRAH!
ARGH!
GA
ARGH...
GO (WHUMP)

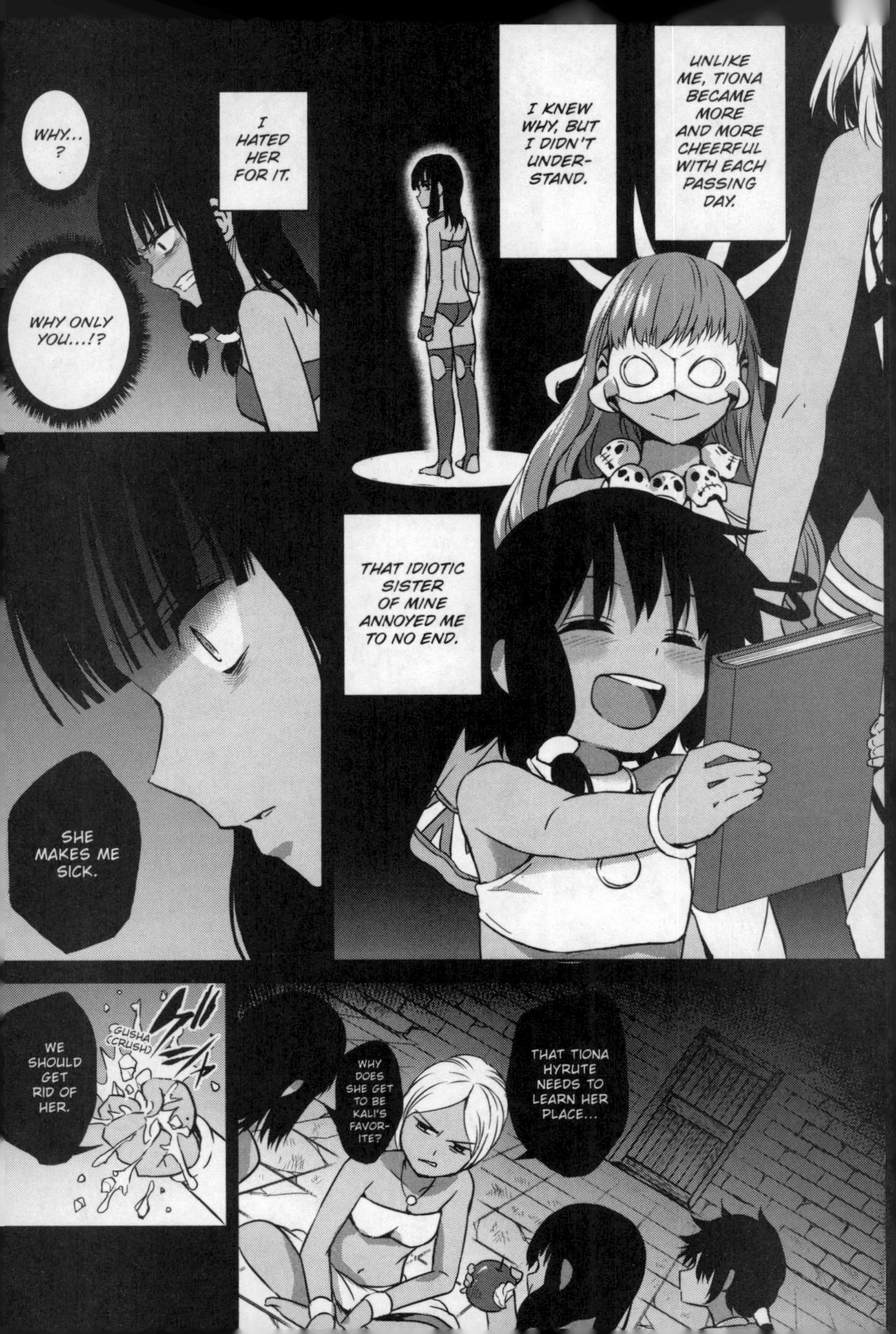
UNLIKE ME, TIONA BECAME MORE AND MORE CHEERFUL WITH EACH PASSING DAY.
I KNEW WHY, BUT I DIDN'T UNDER-STAND.
THAT IDIOTIC SISTER OF MINE ANNOYED ME TO NO END.
I HATED HER FOR IT.
WHY...?
WHY ONLY YOU...!?
SHE MAKES ME SICK.
THAT TIONA HYRUTE NEEDS TO LEARN HER PLACE...
WHY DOES SHE GET TO BE KALI'S FAVOR-ITE?
GUSHA (CRUSH)
WE SHOULD GET RID OF HER.

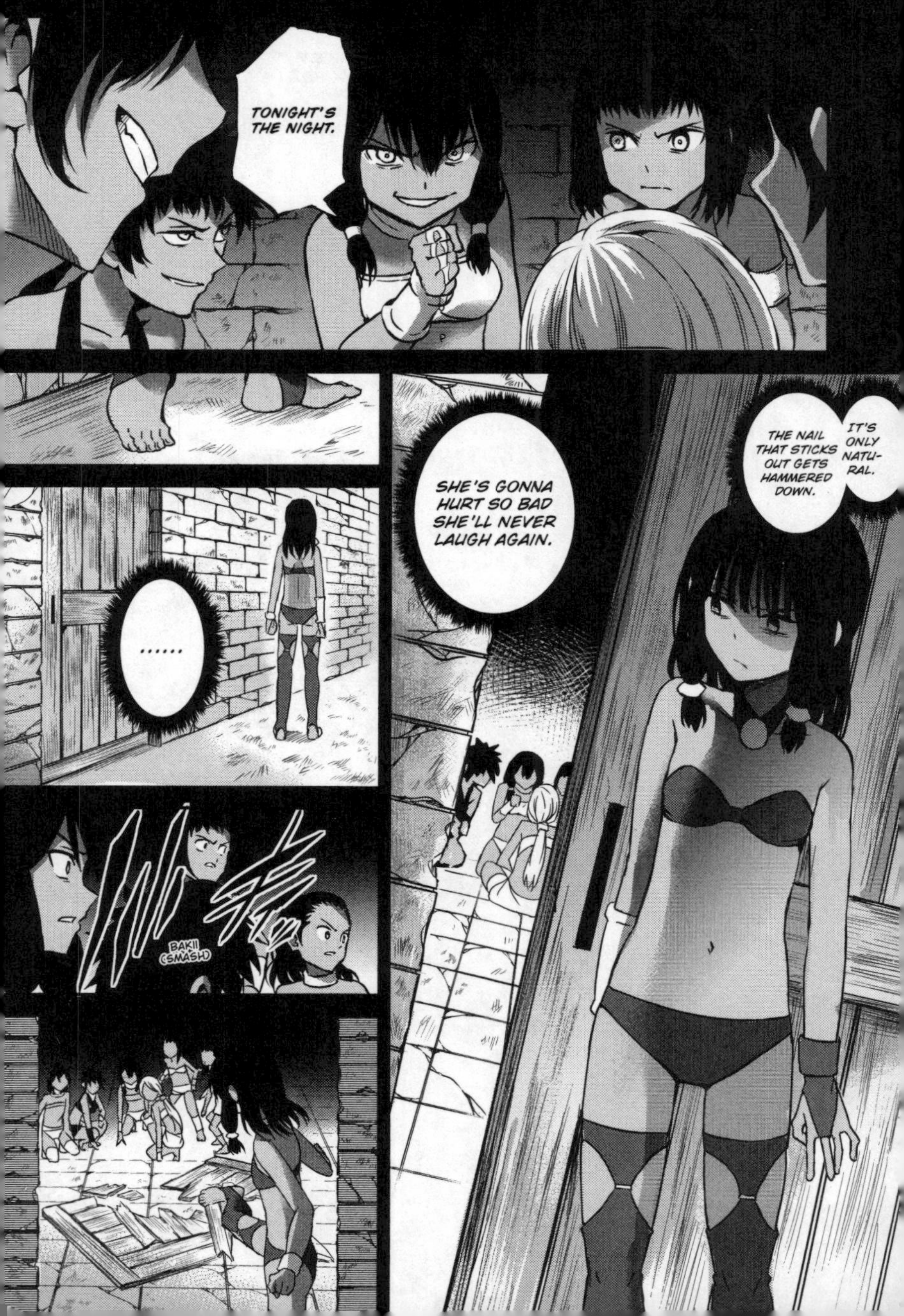
TONIGHT'S THE NIGHT.
IT'S ONLY NATURAL.
THE NAIL THAT STICKS OUT GETS HAMMERED DOWN.
SHE'S GONNA HURT SO BAD SHE'LL NEVER LAUGH AGAIN.
......
BAKII (SMASH)

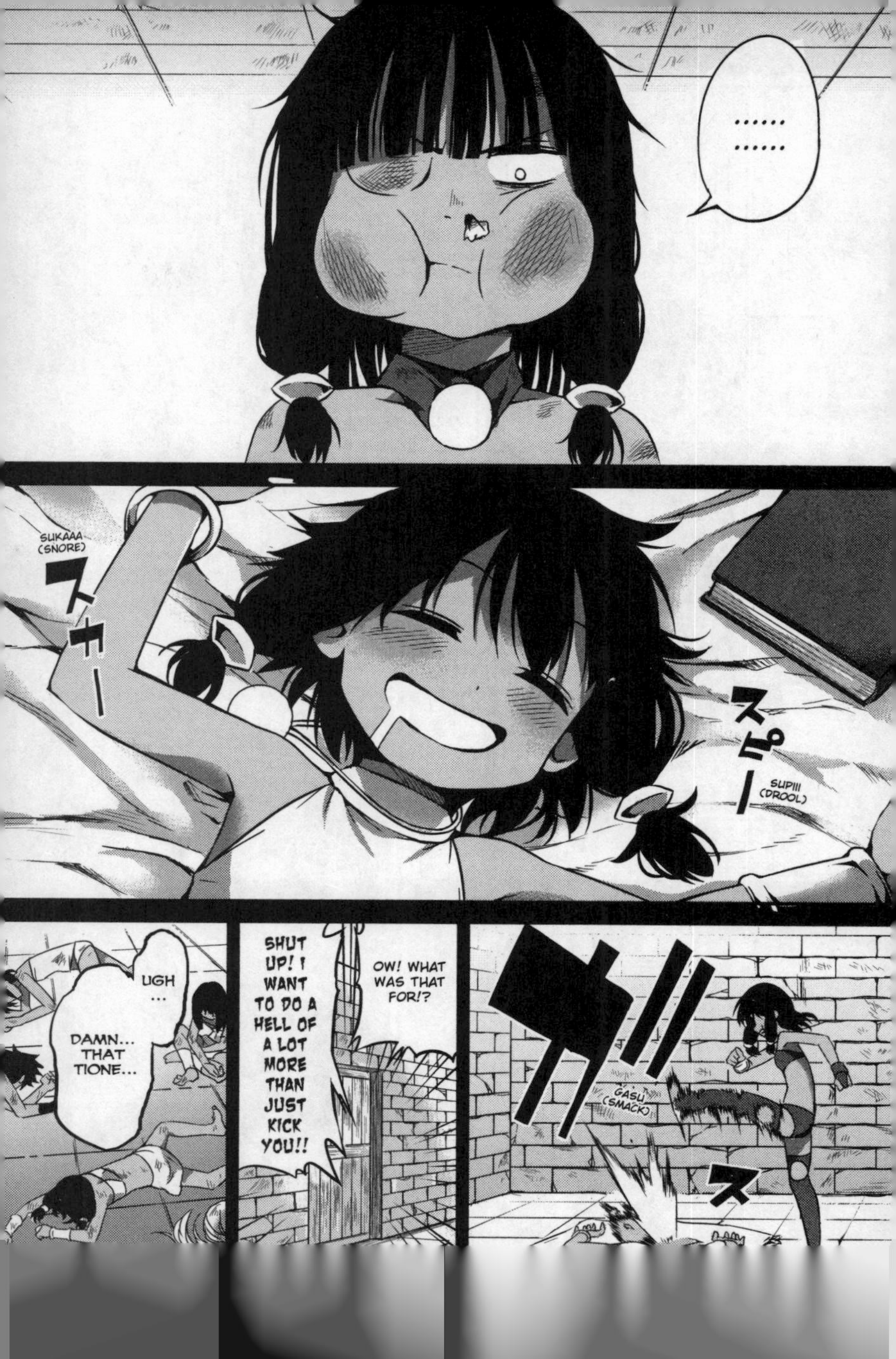
......
......
スカー
SUKAAA (SNORE)
スピー
SUPIII (DROOL)
ガッ
GASU (SMACK)
OW! WHAT WAS THAT FOR!?
SHUT UP! I WANT TO DO A HELL OF A LOT MORE THAN JUST KICK YOU!!
UGH ...
DAMN... THAT TIONE...

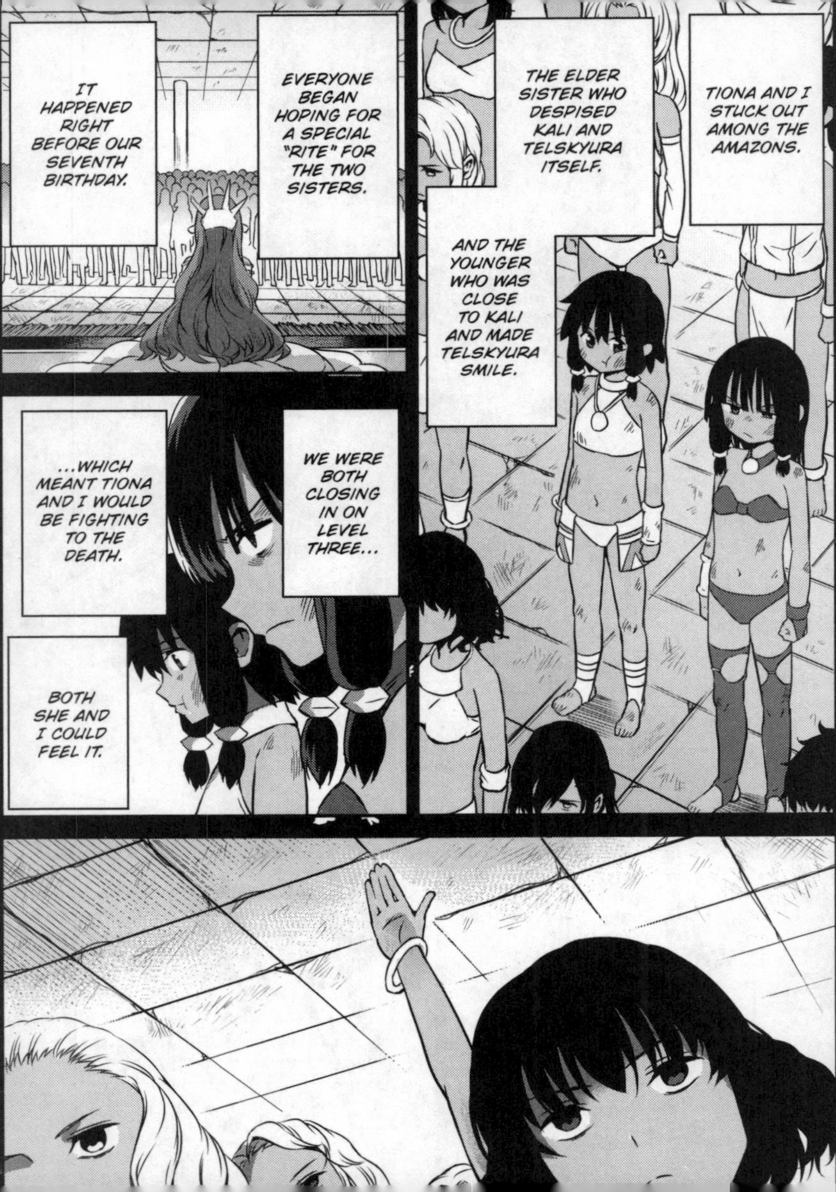
TIONA AND I STUCK OUT AMONG THE AMAZONS.
THE ELDER SISTER WHO DESPISED KALI AND TELSKYURA ITSELF.
AND THE YOUNGER WHO WAS CLOSE TO KALI AND MADE TELSKYURA SMILE.
EVERYONE BEGAN HOPING FOR A SPECIAL "RITE" FOR THE TWO SISTERS.
IT HAPPENED RIGHT BEFORE OUR SEVENTH BIRTHDAY.
WE WERE BOTH CLOSING IN ON LEVEL THREE...
...WHICH MEANT TIONA AND I WOULD BE FIGHTING TO THE DEATH.
BOTH SHE AND I COULD FEEL IT.

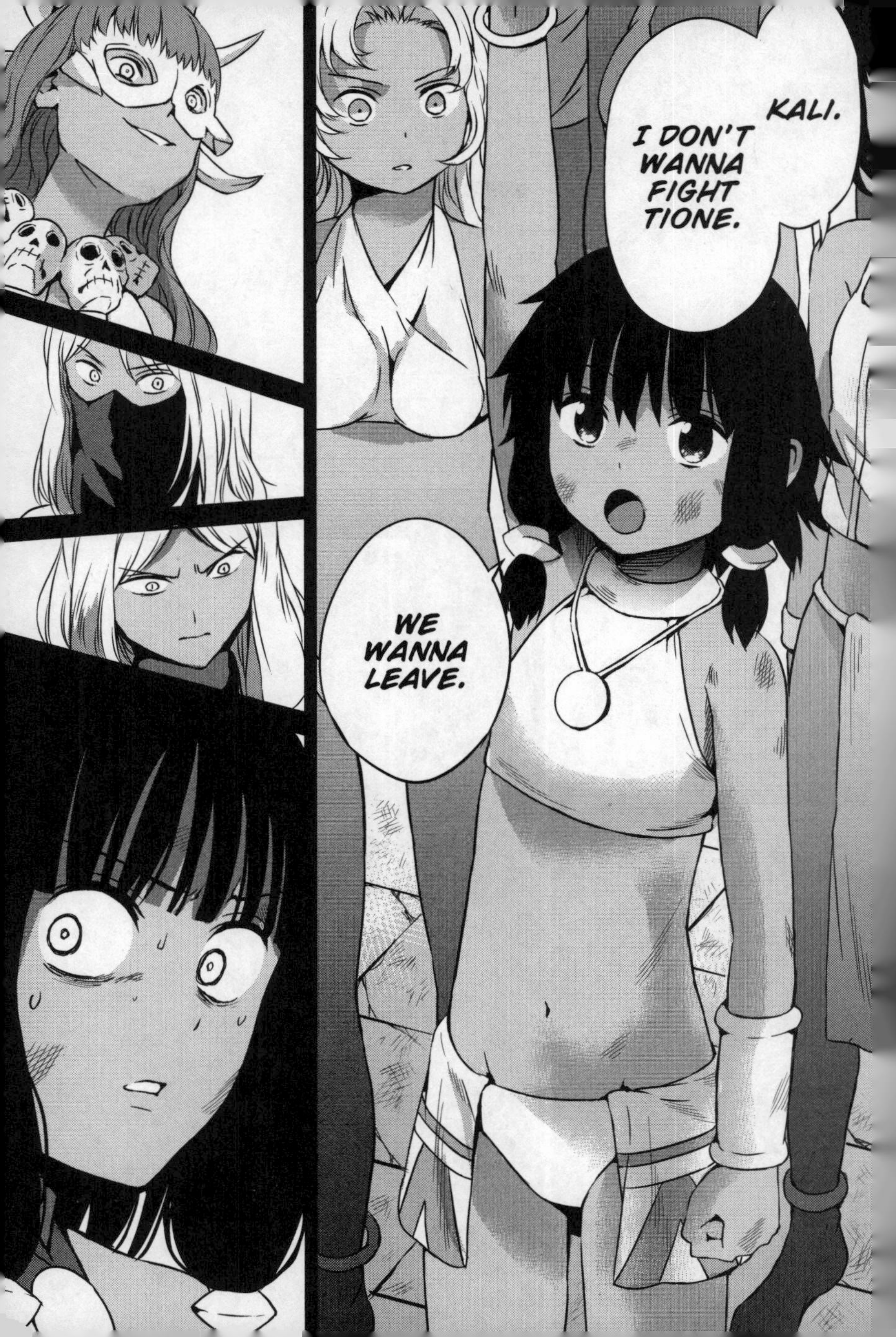
KALI.
I DON'T WANNA FIGHT TIONE.
WE WANNA LEAVE.

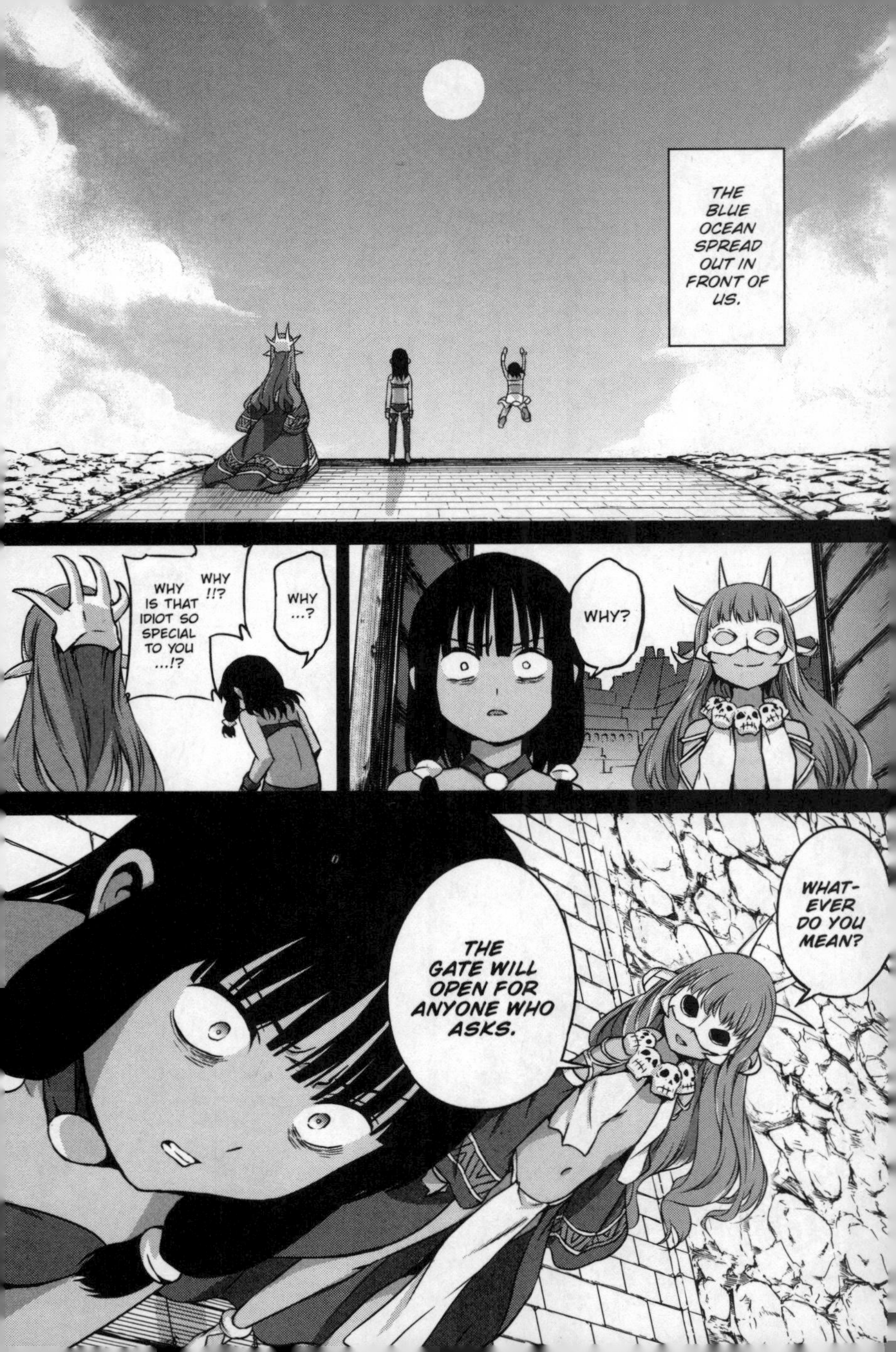
THE BLUE OCEAN SPREAD OUT IN FRONT OF US.
WHY?
WHY ...?
WHY !!?
WHY IS THAT IDIOT SO SPECIAL TO YOU ...!?
WHAT-EVER DO YOU MEAN?
THE GATE WILL OPEN FOR ANYONE WHO ASKS.

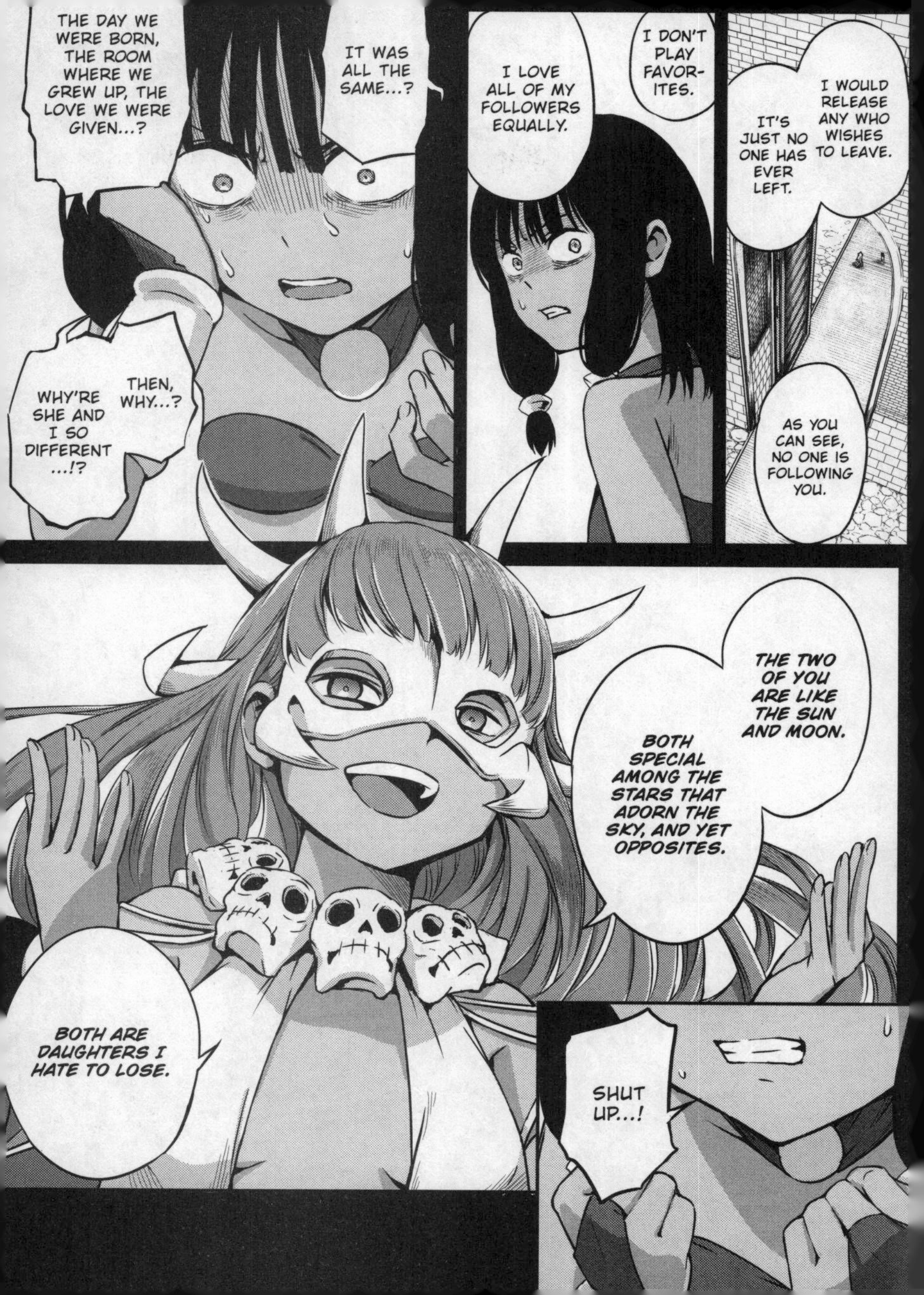
I WOULD RELEASE ANY WHO WISHES TO LEAVE.
IT'S JUST NO ONE HAS EVER LEFT.
AS YOU CAN SEE, NO ONE IS FOLLOWING YOU.
I DON'T PLAY FAVOR-ITES.
I LOVE ALL OF MY FOLLOWERS EQUALLY.
IT WAS ALL THE SAME...?
THE DAY WE WERE BORN, THE ROOM WHERE WE GREW UP, THE LOVE WE WERE GIVEN...?
THEN, WHY...?
WHY'RE SHE AND I SO DIFFERENT ...!?
THE TWO OF YOU ARE LIKE THE SUN AND MOON.
BOTH SPECIAL AMONG THE STARS THAT ADORN THE SKY, AND YET OPPOSITES.
BOTH ARE DAUGHTERS I HATE TO LOSE.
SHUT UP...!

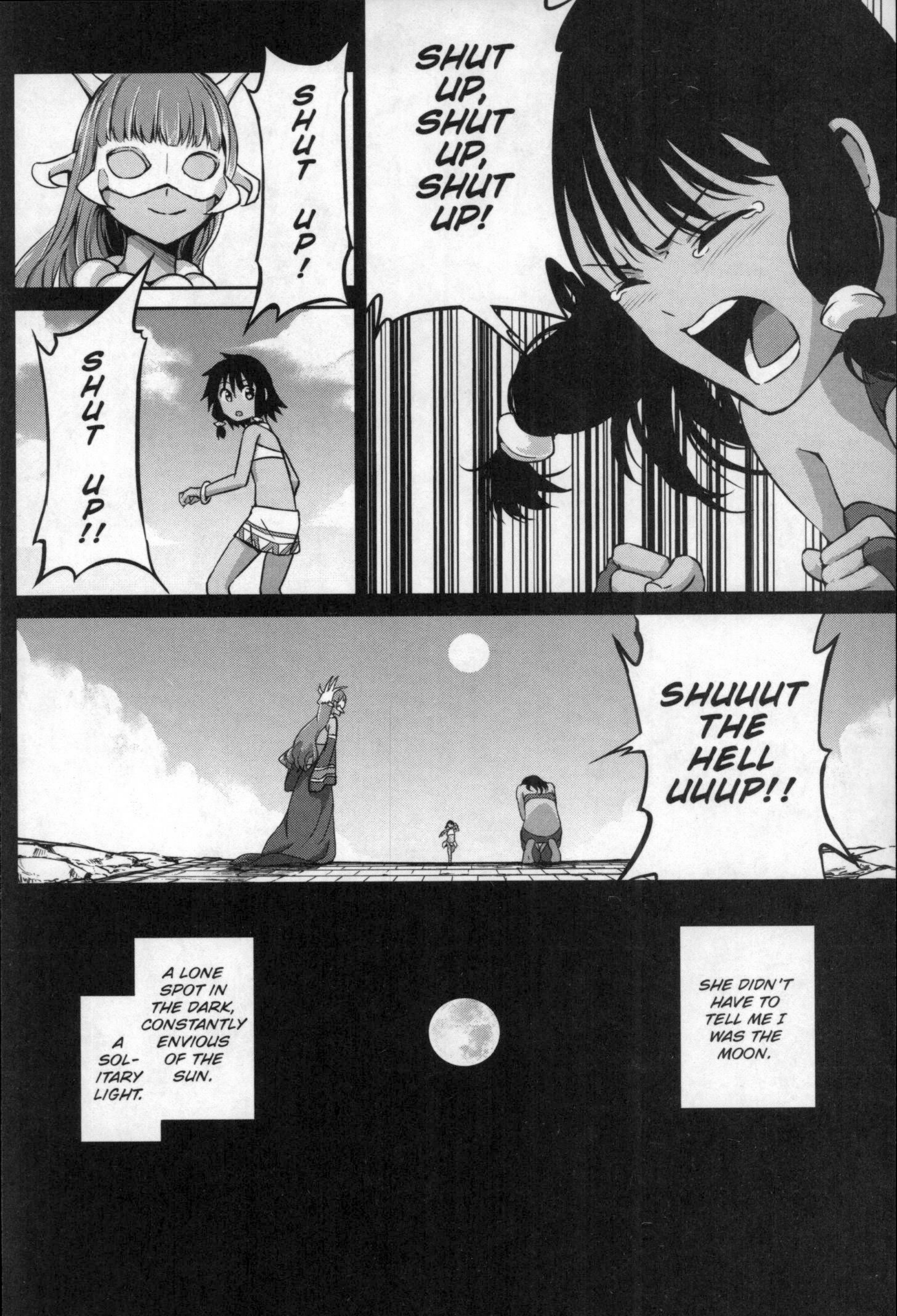
SHUT UP, SHUT UP, SHUT UP!
SHUT UP!
SHUT UP!!
SHUUUT THE HELL UUUP!!
SHE DIDN'T HAVE TO TELL ME I WAS THE MOON.
A LONE SPOT IN THE DARK, CONSTANTLY ENVIOUS OF THE SUN.
A SOL-ITARY LIGHT.

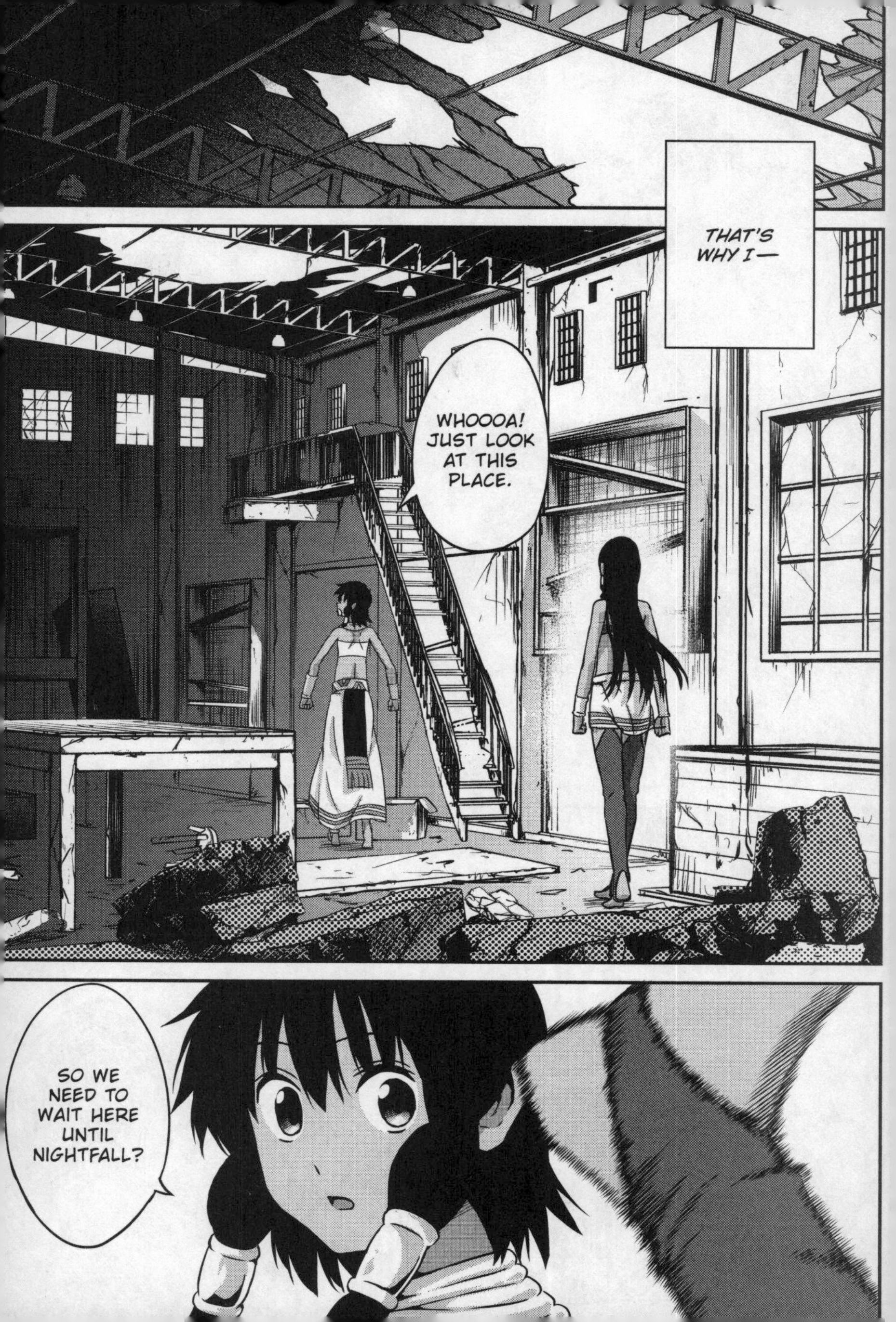
THAT'S WHY I—
WHOOOA! JUST LOOK AT THIS PLACE.
SO WE NEED TO WAIT HERE UNTIL NIGHTFALL?

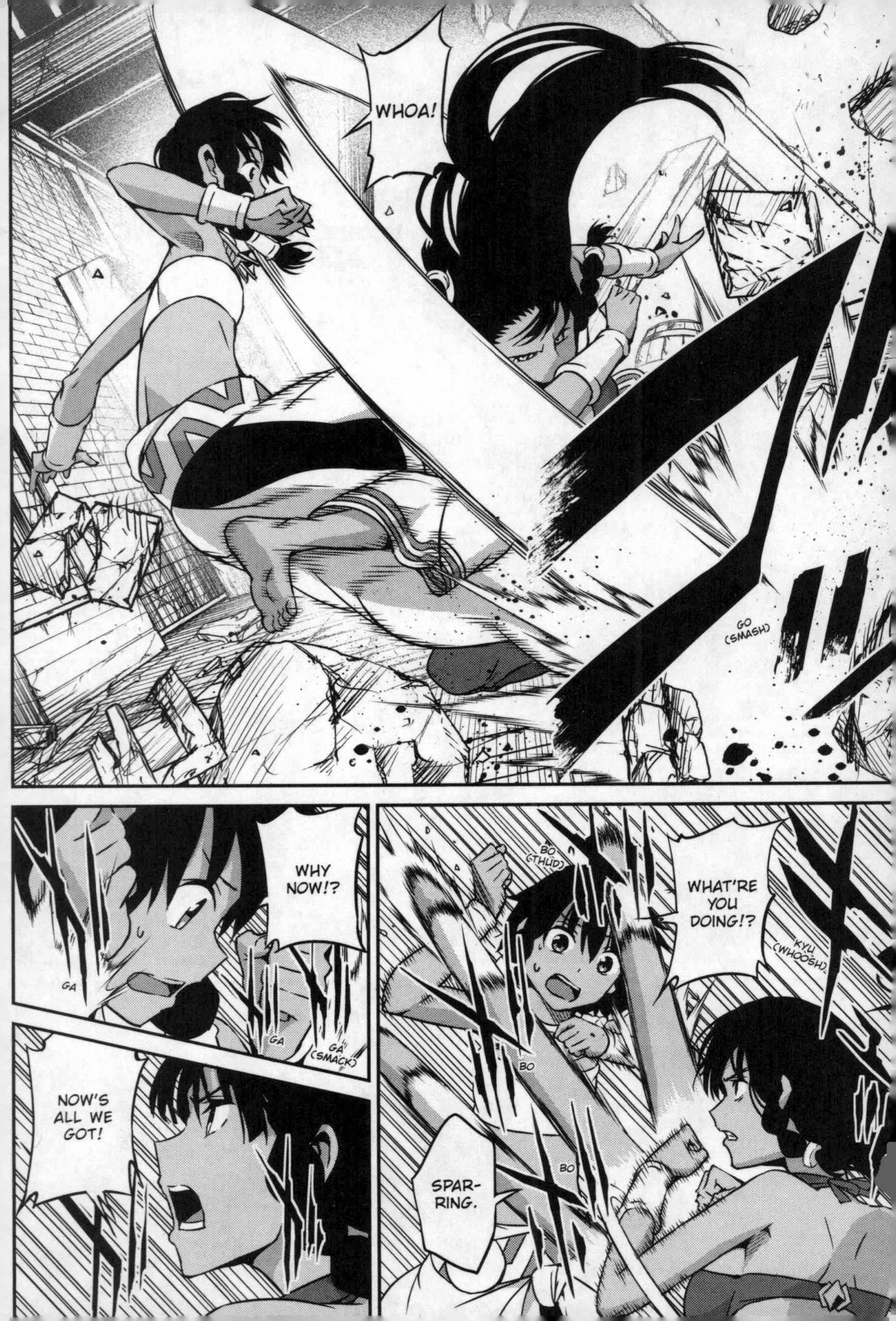
WHOA!
GO (SMASH)
WHAT'RE YOU DOING!?
KYU (WHOOSH)
BO (THUD)
BO
BO
SPAR-RING.
WHY NOW!?
GA
GA
GA (SMACK)
NOW'S ALL WE GOT!

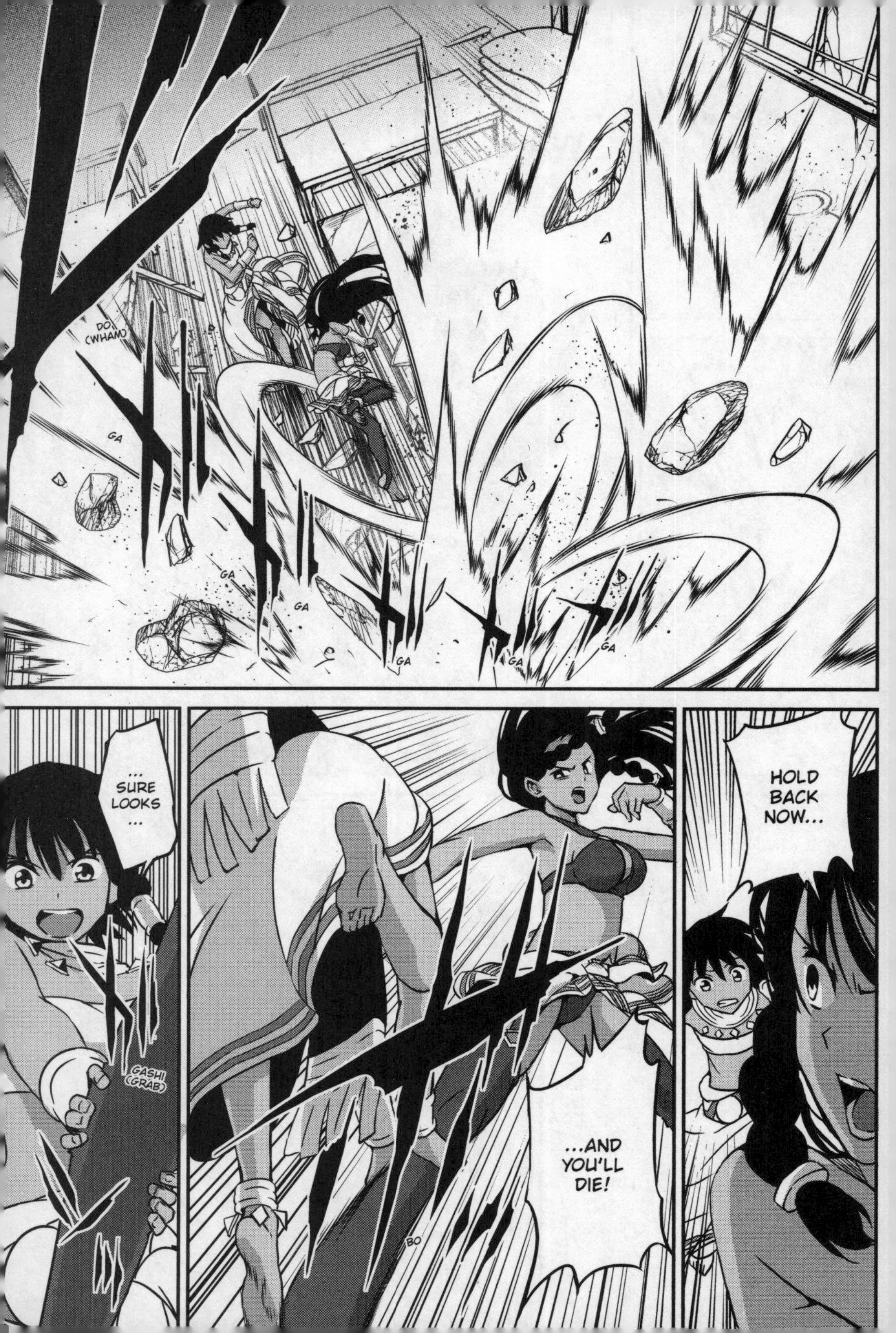
DO (WHAM)
GA
GA
GA
GA
GA
GA
HOLD BACK NOW...
...AND YOU'LL DIE!
BO
... SURE LOOKS ...
GASHI (GRAB)

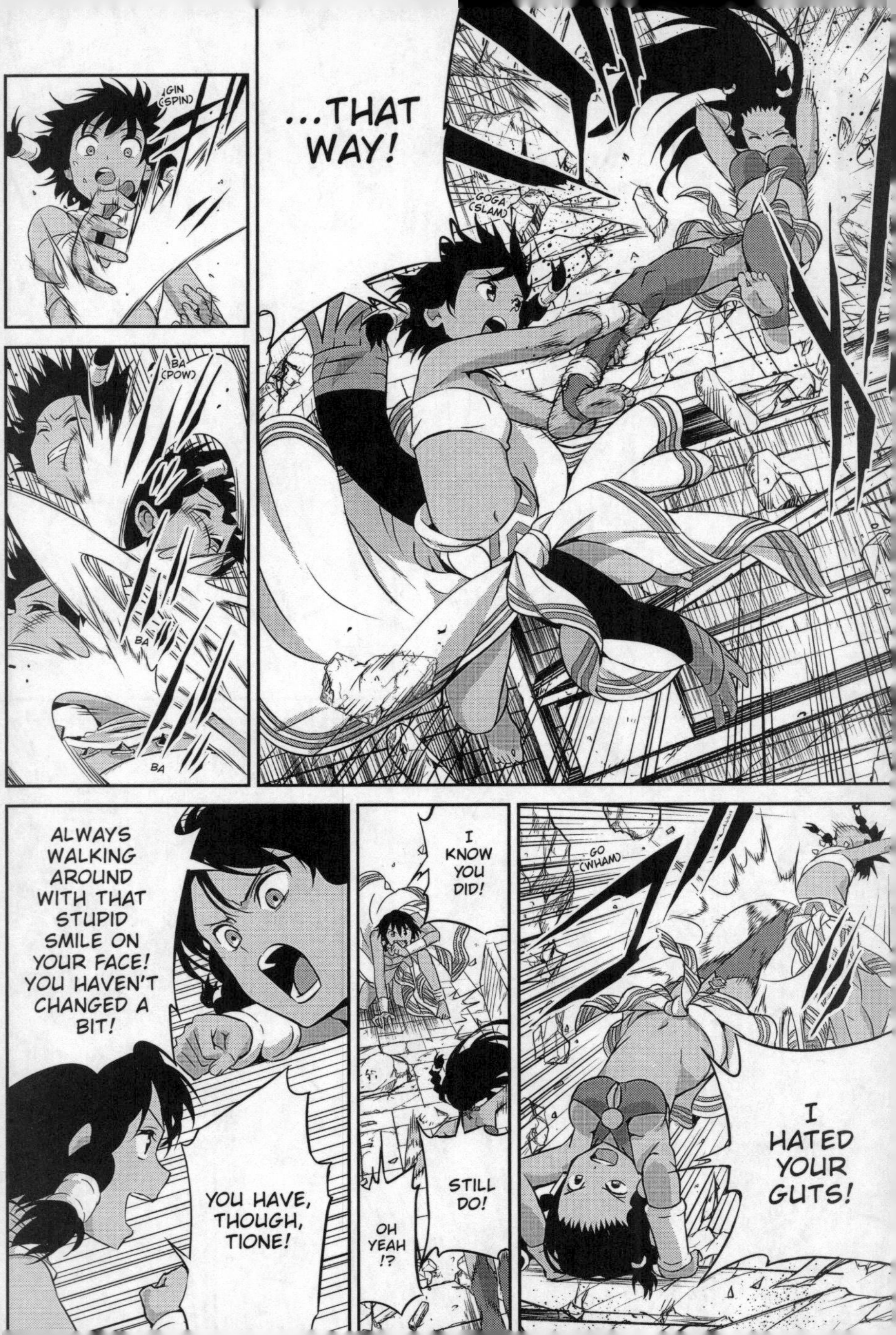
...THAT WAY!
GOGA (SLAM)
GIN (SPIN)
BA (POW)
BA
BA
GO (WHAM)
I HATED YOUR GUTS!
I KNOW YOU DID!
STILL DO!
OH YEAH!?
ALWAYS WALKING AROUND WITH THAT STUPID SMILE ON YOUR FACE! YOU HAVEN'T CHANGED A BIT!
YOU HAVE, THOUGH, TIONE!

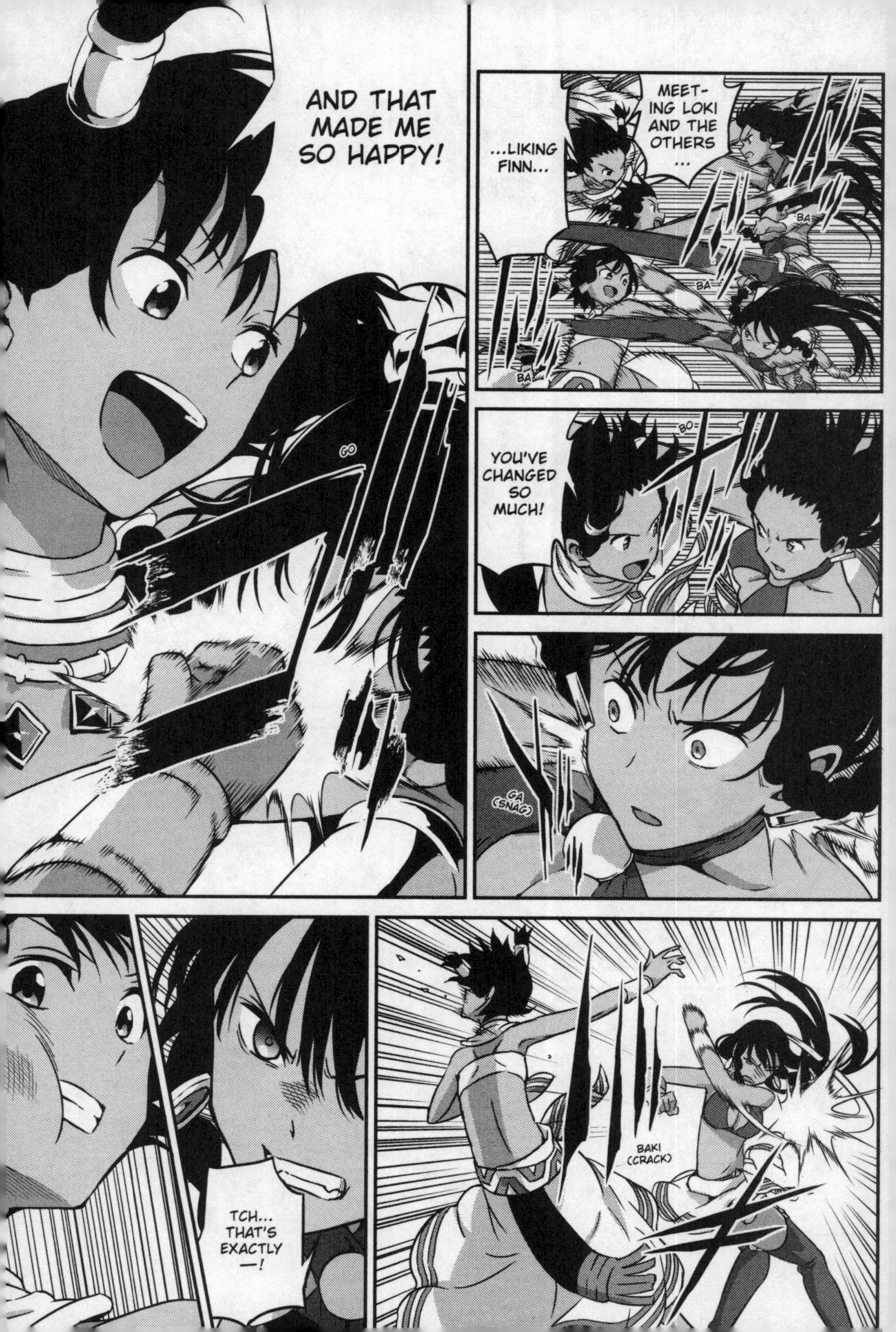
MEET-ING LOKI AND THE OTHERS ...
...LIKING FINN...
BA
BA
BA
BO
YOU'VE CHANGED SO MUCH!
GA (SNAG)
AND THAT MADE ME SO HAPPY!
GO
BAKI (CRACK)
TCH... THAT'S EXACTLY —!

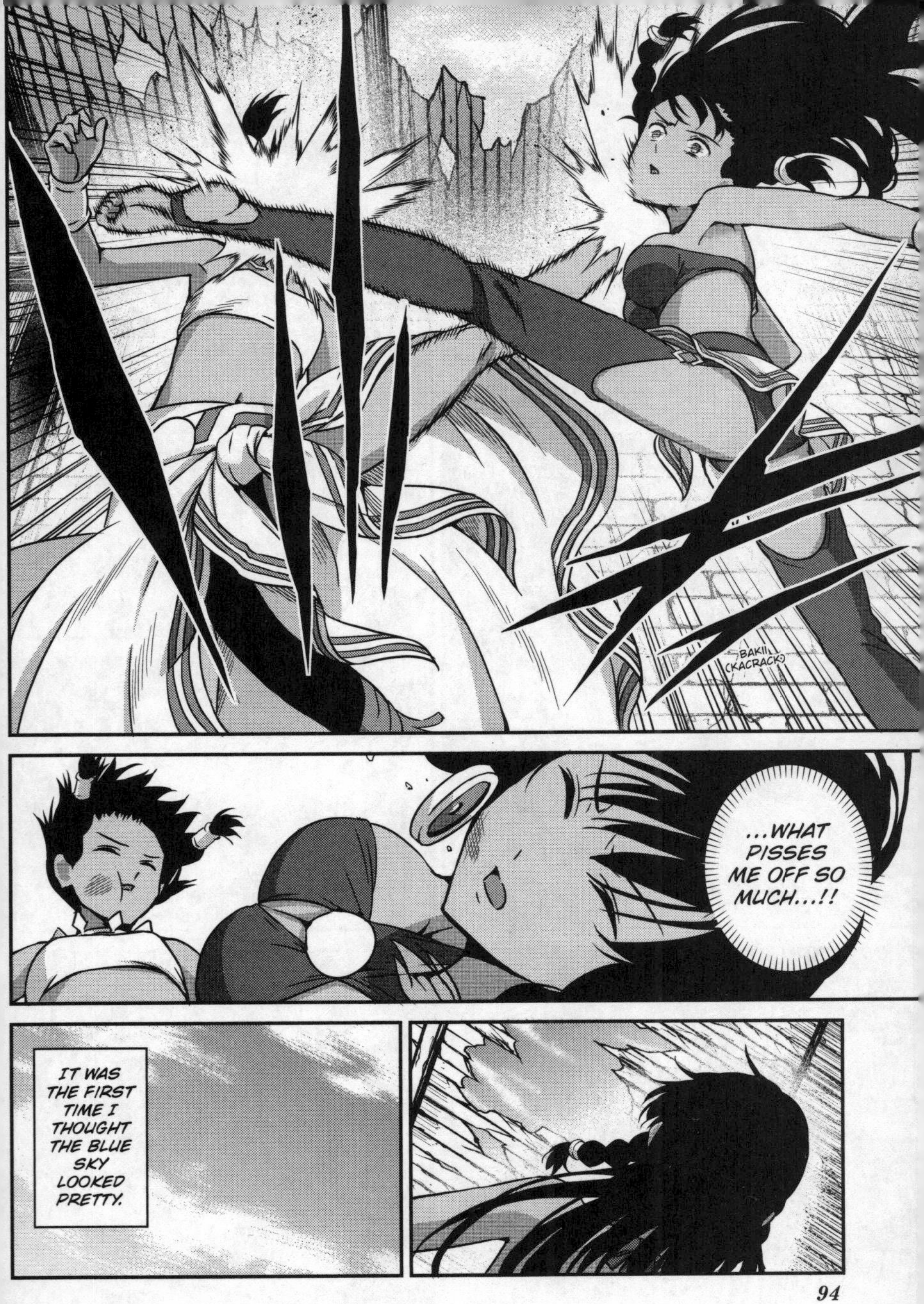
BAKII (KACRACK)
...WHAT PISSES ME OFF SO MUCH...!!
IT WAS THE FIRST TIME I THOUGHT THE BLUE SKY LOOKED PRETTY.

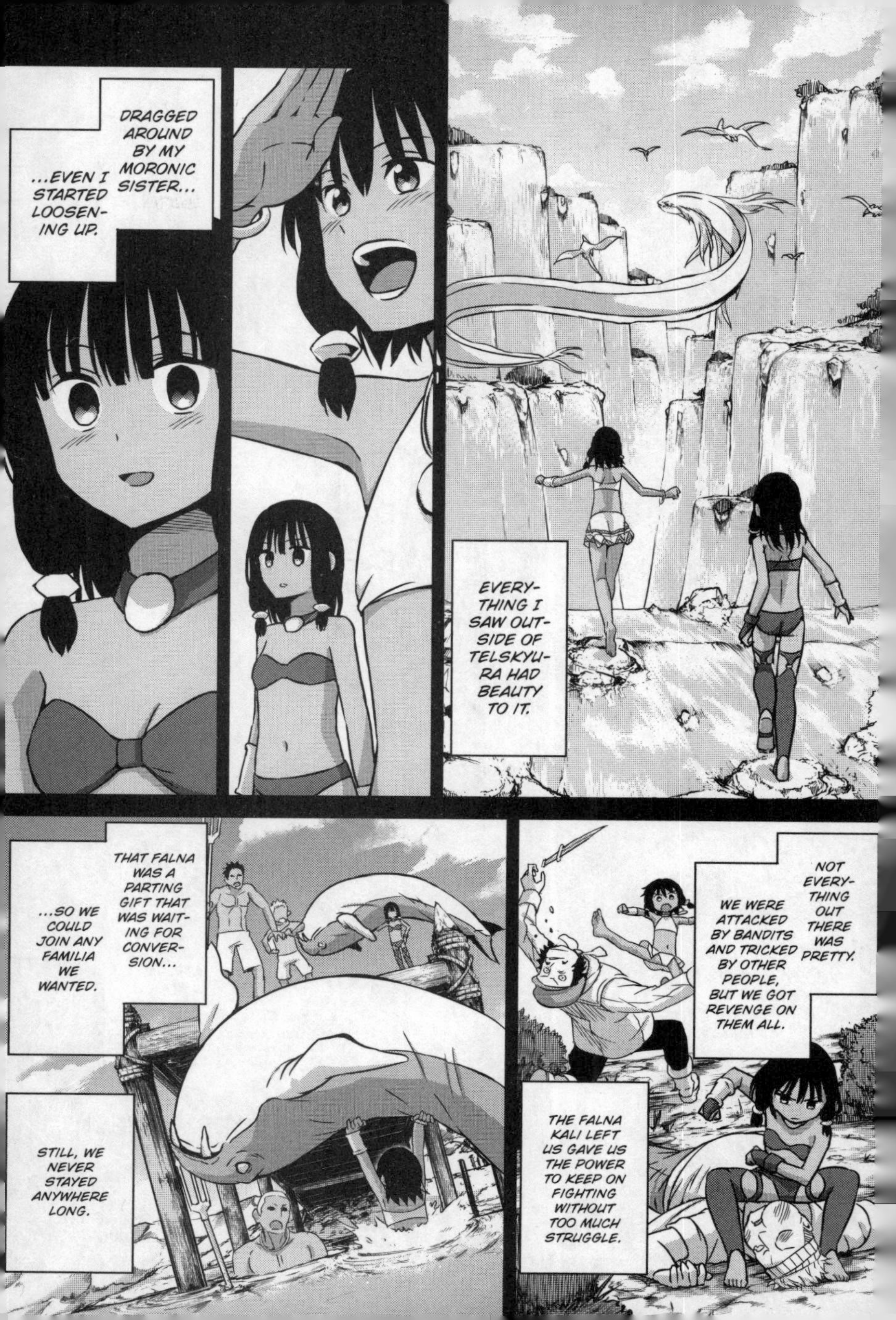
EVERYTHING I SAW OUTSIDE OF TELSKYURA HAD BEAUTY TO IT.
DRAGGED AROUND BY MY MORONIC SISTER...
...EVEN I STARTED LOOSENING UP.
NOT EVERYTHING OUT THERE WAS PRETTY.
WE WERE ATTACKED BY BANDITS AND TRICKED BY OTHER PEOPLE, BUT WE GOT REVENGE ON THEM ALL.
THE FALNA KALI LEFT US GAVE US THE POWER TO KEEP ON FIGHTING WITHOUT TOO MUCH STRUGGLE.
THAT FALNA WAS A PARTING GIFT THAT WAS WAITING FOR CONVERSION...
...SO WE COULD JOIN ANY FAMILIA WE WANTED.
STILL, WE NEVER STAYED ANYWHERE LONG.

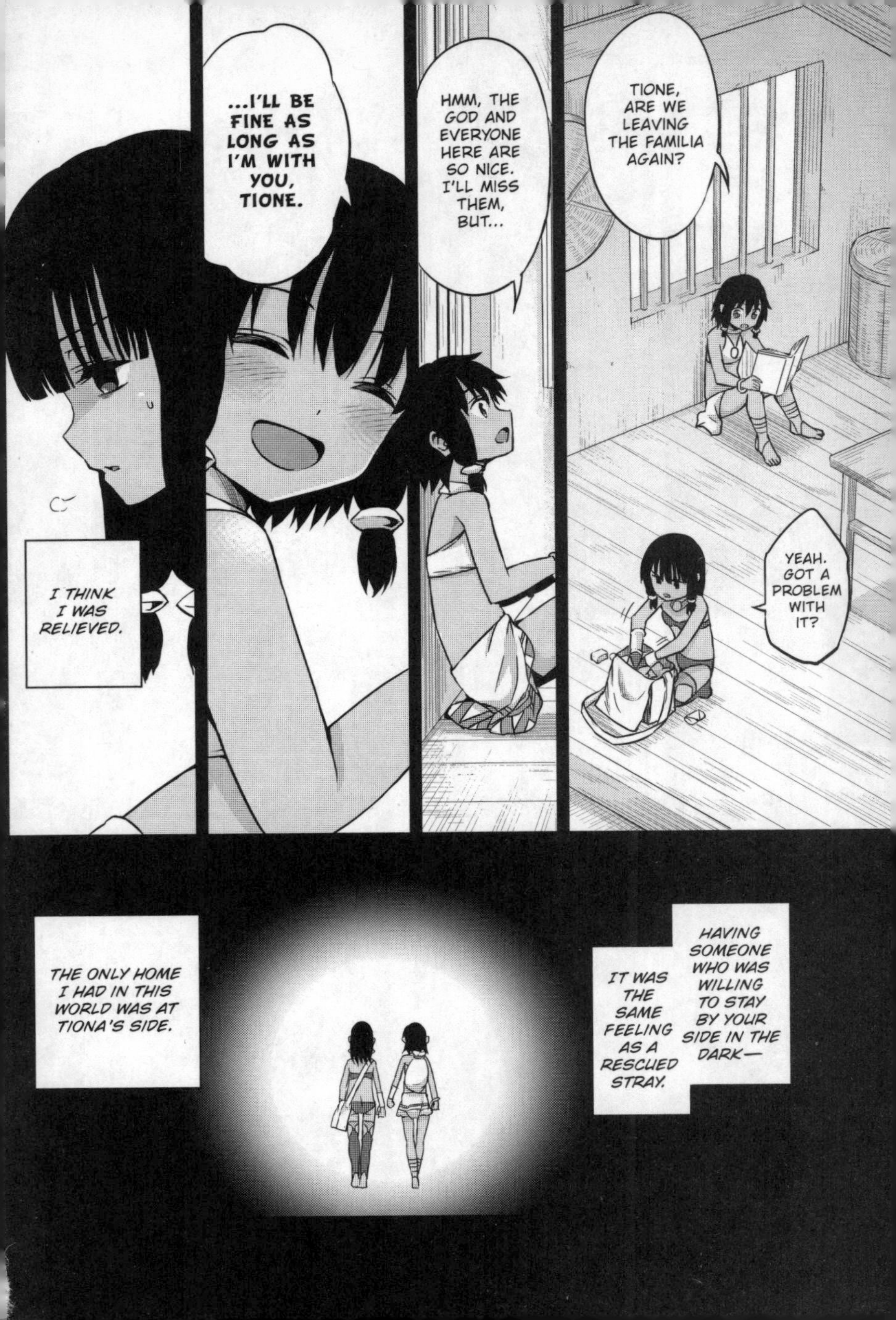
TIONE, ARE WE LEAVING THE FAMILIA AGAIN?
YEAH. GOT A PROBLEM WITH IT?
HMM, THE GOD AND EVERYONE HERE ARE SO NICE. I'LL MISS THEM, BUT...
...I'LL BE FINE AS LONG AS I'M WITH YOU, TIONE.
I THINK I WAS RELIEVED.
HAVING SOMEONE WHO WAS WILLING TO STAY BY YOUR SIDE IN THE DARK—
IT WAS THE SAME FEELING AS A RESCUED STRAY.
THE ONLY HOME I HAD IN THIS WORLD WAS AT TIONA'S SIDE.

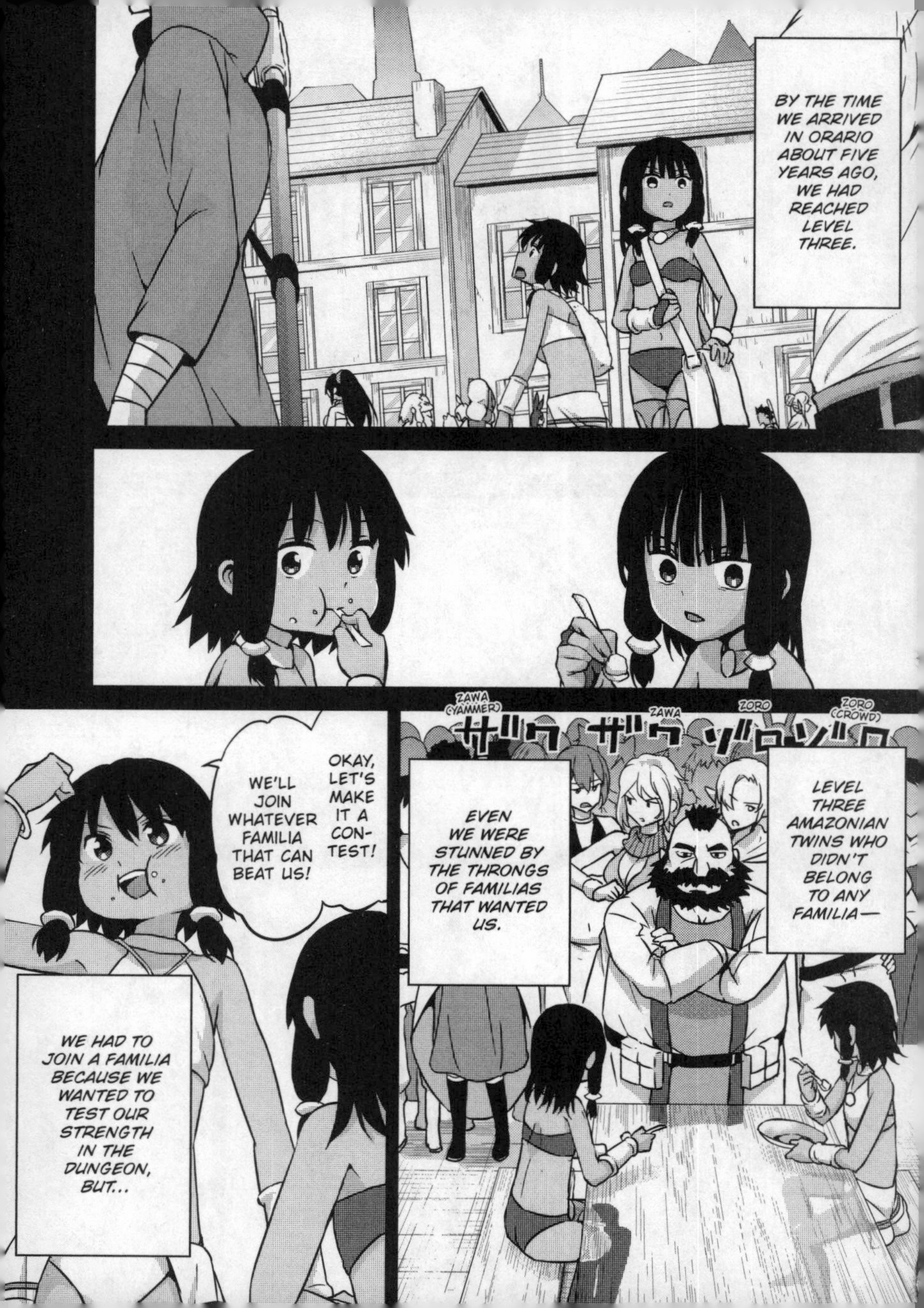
BY THE TIME WE ARRIVED IN ORARIO ABOUT FIVE YEARS AGO, WE HAD REACHED LEVEL THREE.
ZAWA (YAMMER) ZAWA ZORO ZORO (CROWD)
LEVEL THREE AMAZONIAN TWINS WHO DIDN'T BELONG TO ANY FAMILIA—
EVEN WE WERE STUNNED BY THE THRONGS OF FAMILIAS THAT WANTED US.
OKAY, LET'S MAKE IT A CONTEST!
WE'LL JOIN WHATEVER FAMILIA THAT CAN BEAT US!
WE HAD TO JOIN A FAMILIA BECAUSE WE WANTED TO TEST OUR STRENGTH IN THE DUNGEON, BUT...

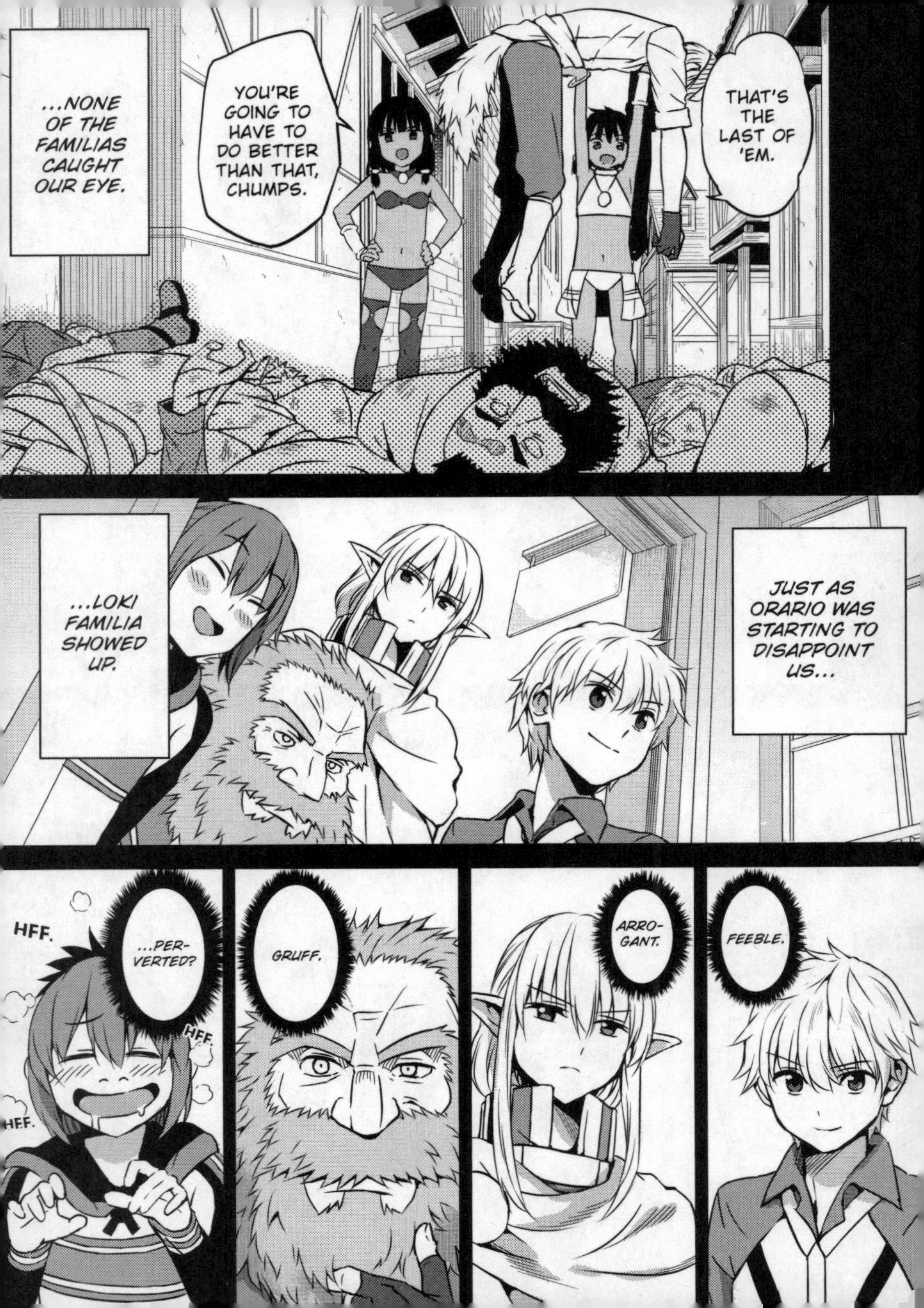
THAT'S THE LAST OF 'EM.
YOU'RE GOING TO HAVE TO DO BETTER THAN THAT, CHUMPS.
...NONE OF THE FAMILIAS CAUGHT OUR EYE.
JUST AS ORARIO WAS STARTING TO DISAPPOINT US...
...LOKI FAMILIA SHOWED UP.
FEEBLE.
ARRO-GANT.
GRUFF.
...PER-VERTED?
HFF.
HFF.
HFF.

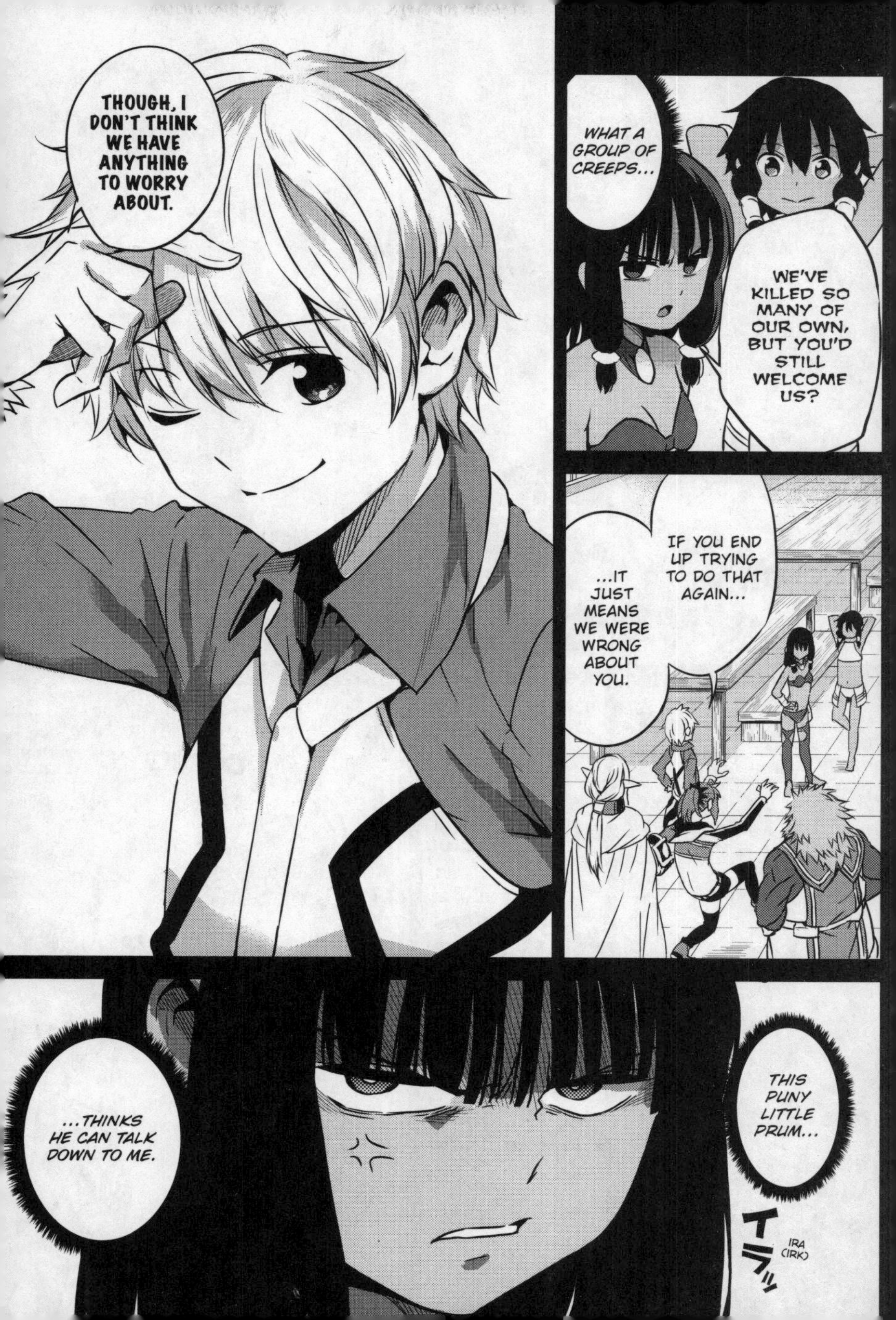
WHAT A GROUP OF CREEPS...
WE'VE KILLED SO MANY OF OUR OWN, BUT YOU'D STILL WELCOME US?
IF YOU END UP TRYING TO DO THAT AGAIN...
...IT JUST MEANS WE WERE WRONG ABOUT YOU.
THOUGH, I DON'T THINK WE HAVE ANYTHING TO WORRY ABOUT.
THIS PUNY LITTLE PRUM...
...THINKS HE CAN TALK DOWN TO ME.
IRA (IRK)

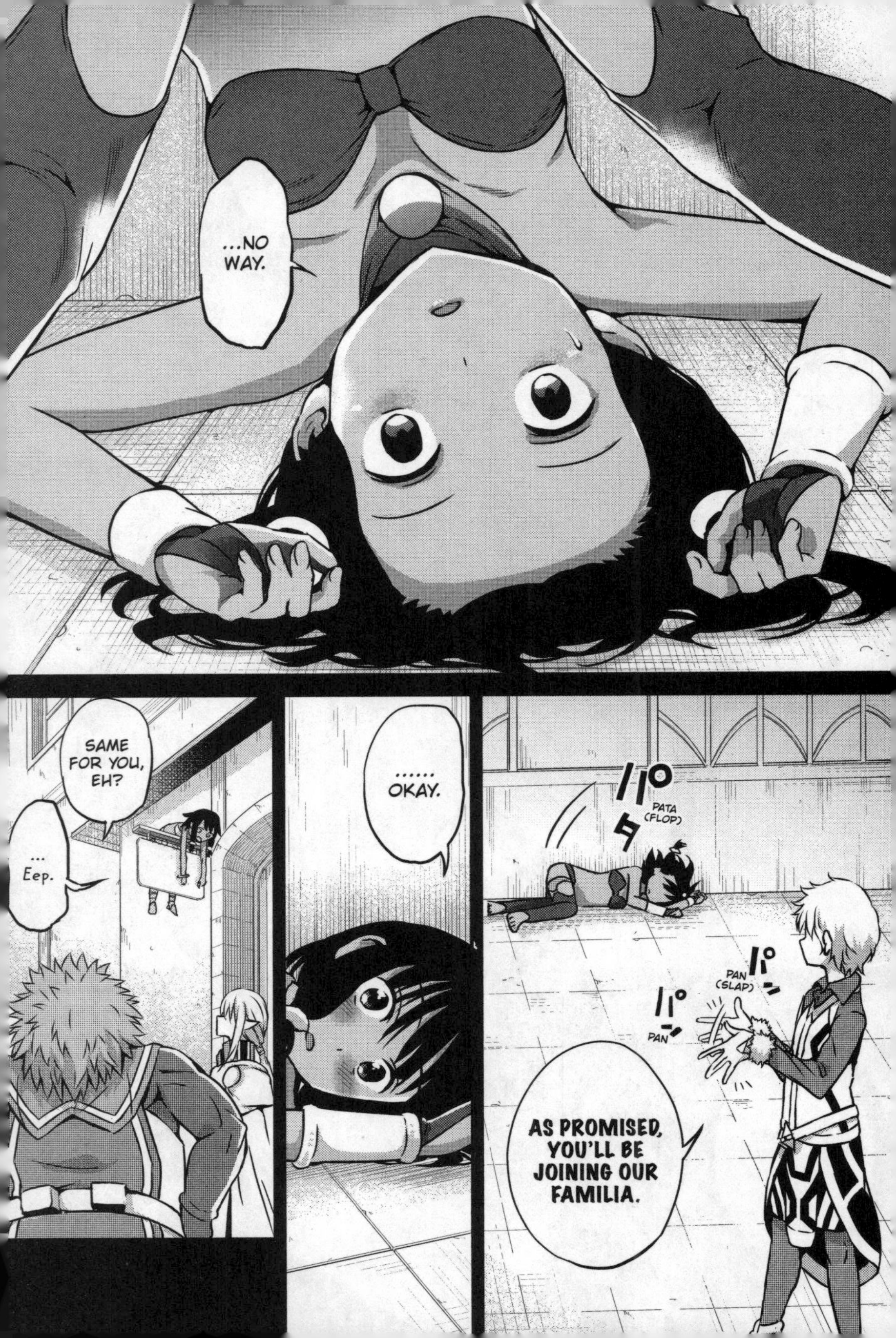
...NO WAY.
パタ
PATA (FLOP)
パン
PAN (SLAP)
パン
PAN
AS PROMISED, YOU'LL BE JOINING OUR FAMILIA.
......OKAY.
SAME FOR YOU, EH?
... Eep.

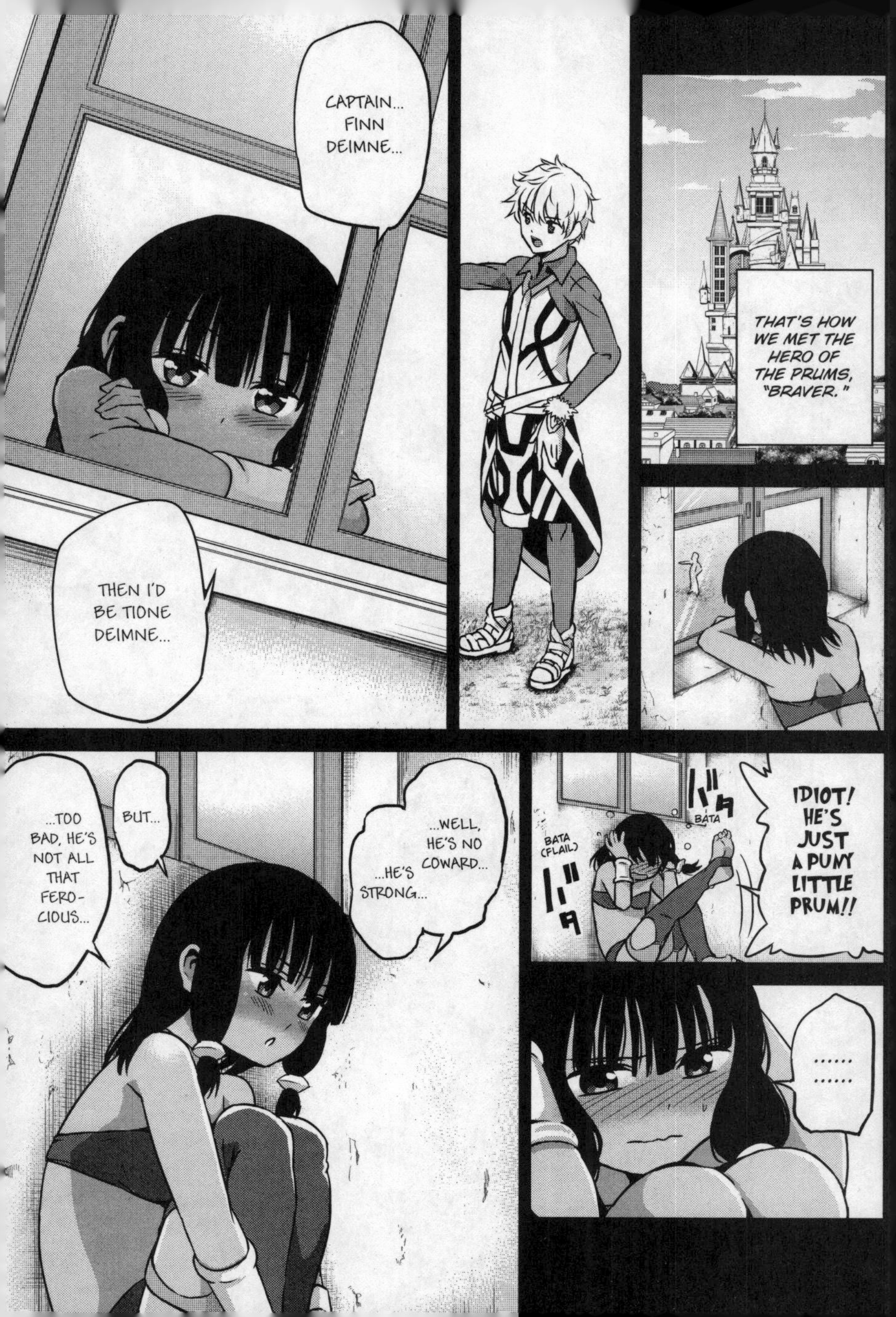
THAT'S HOW WE MET THE HERO OF THE PRUMS, "BRAVER."
CAPTAIN... FINN DEIMNE...
THEN I'D BE TIONE DEIMNE...
IDIOT! HE'S JUST A PUNY LITTLE PRUM!!
BATA
BATA (FLAIL)
......
......
...WELL, HE'S NO COWARD...
...HE'S STRONG...
BUT...
...TOO BAD, HE'S NOT ALL THAT FERO-CIOUS...

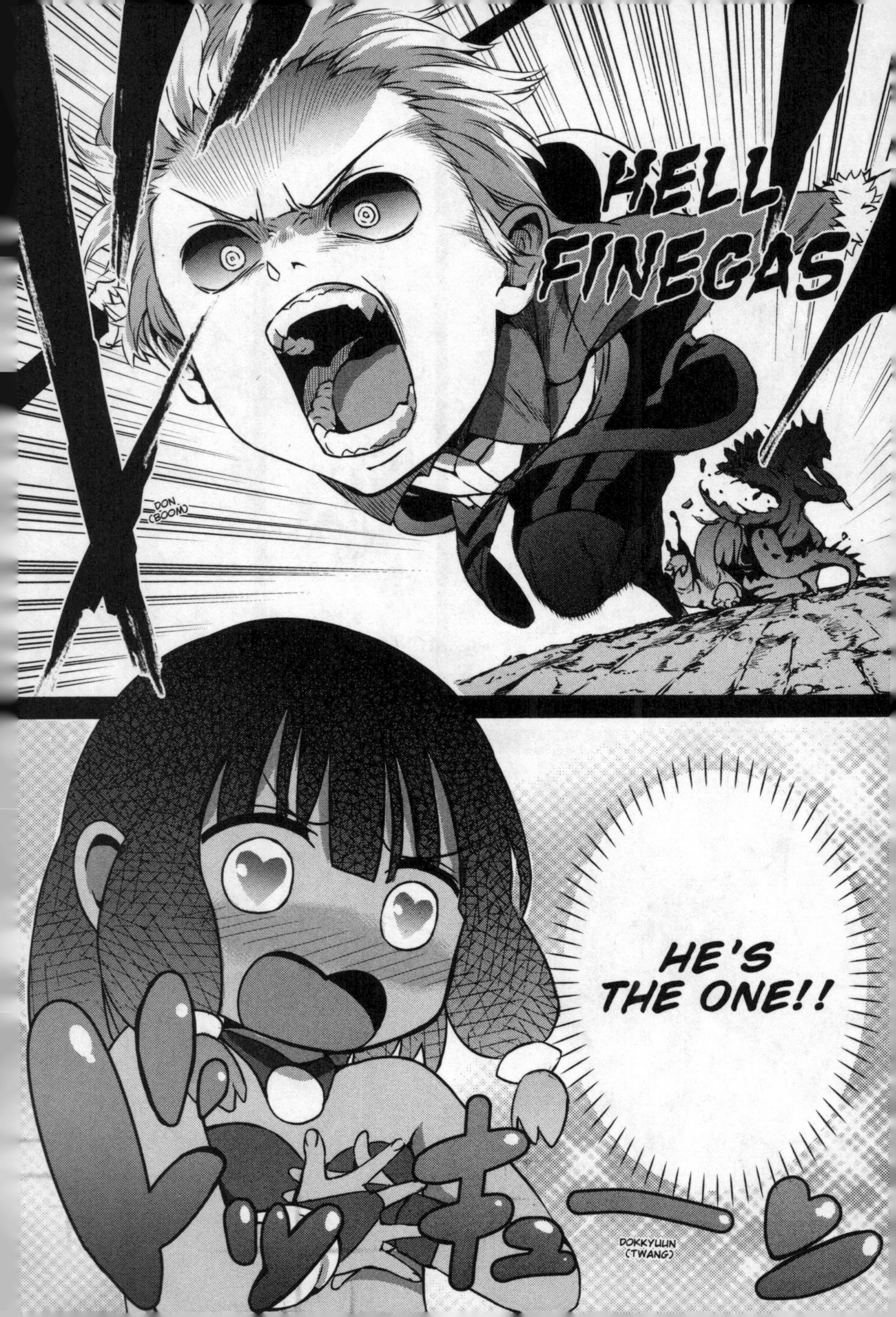
HELL FINEGAS
DON (BOOM)
HE'S THE ONE!!
DOKKYUUN (TWANG)

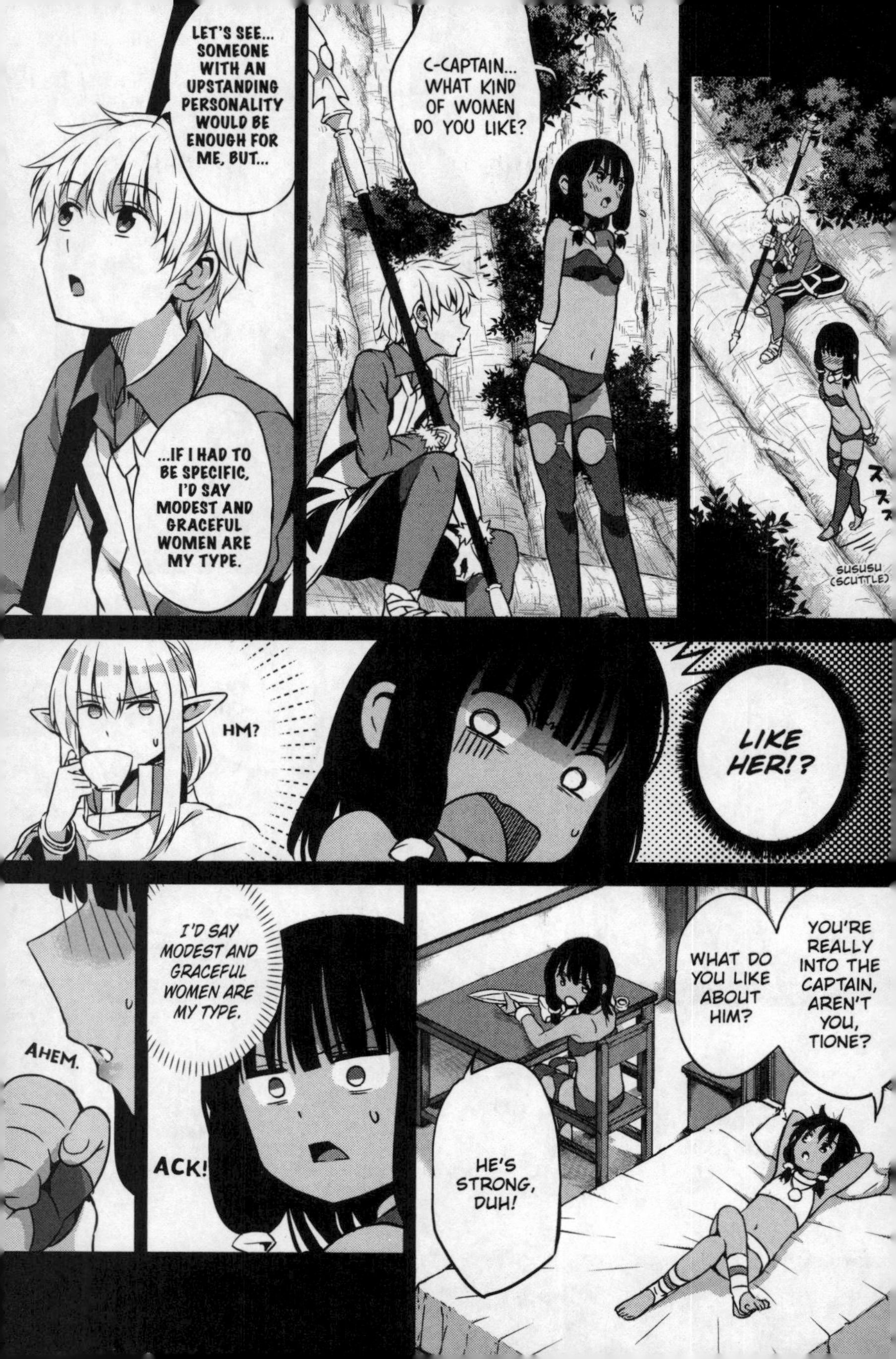
ススス
SUSUSU (SCUTTLE)
C-CAPTAIN... WHAT KIND OF WOMEN DO YOU LIKE?
LET'S SEE... SOMEONE WITH AN UPSTANDING PERSONALITY WOULD BE ENOUGH FOR ME, BUT...
...IF I HAD TO BE SPECIFIC, I'D SAY MODEST AND GRACEFUL WOMEN ARE MY TYPE.
LIKE HER!?
HM?
YOU'RE REALLY INTO THE CAPTAIN, AREN'T YOU, TIONE?
WHAT DO YOU LIKE ABOUT HIM?
HE'S STRONG, DUH!
I'D SAY MODEST AND GRACEFUL WOMEN ARE MY TYPE.
ACK!
AHEM.

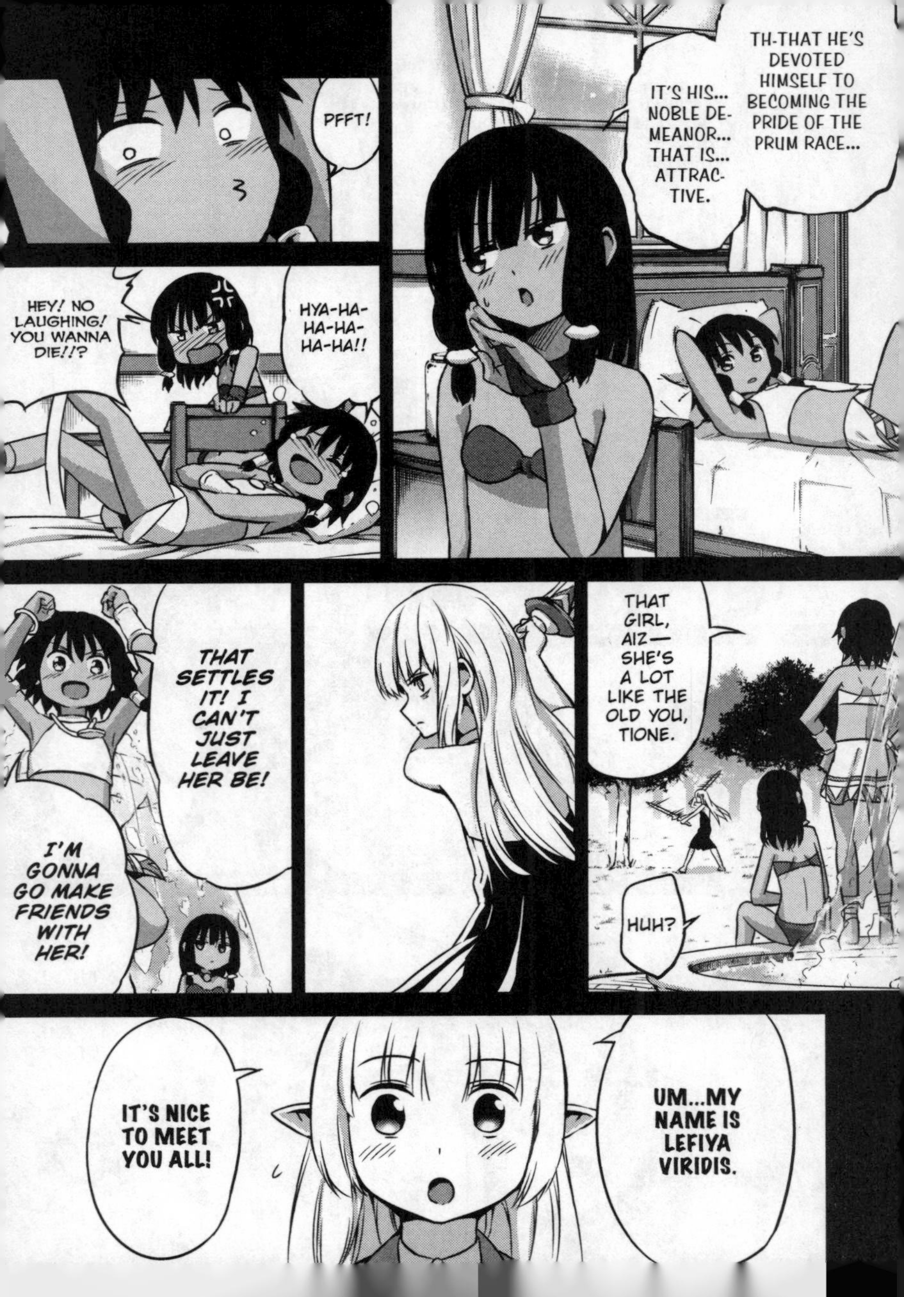
TH-THAT HE'S DEVOTED HIMSELF TO BECOMING THE PRIDE OF THE PRUM RACE...
IT'S HIS... NOBLE DE-MEANOR... THAT IS... ATTRAC-TIVE.
PFFT!
HYA-HA-HA-HA-HA-HA!!
HEY! NO LAUGHING! YOU WANNA DIE!!?
THAT GIRL, AIZ—SHE'S A LOT LIKE THE OLD YOU, TIONE.
HUH?
THAT SETTLES IT! I CAN'T JUST LEAVE HER BE!
I'M GONNA GO MAKE FRIENDS WITH HER!
UM...MY NAME IS LEFIYA VIRIDIS.
IT'S NICE TO MEET YOU ALL!

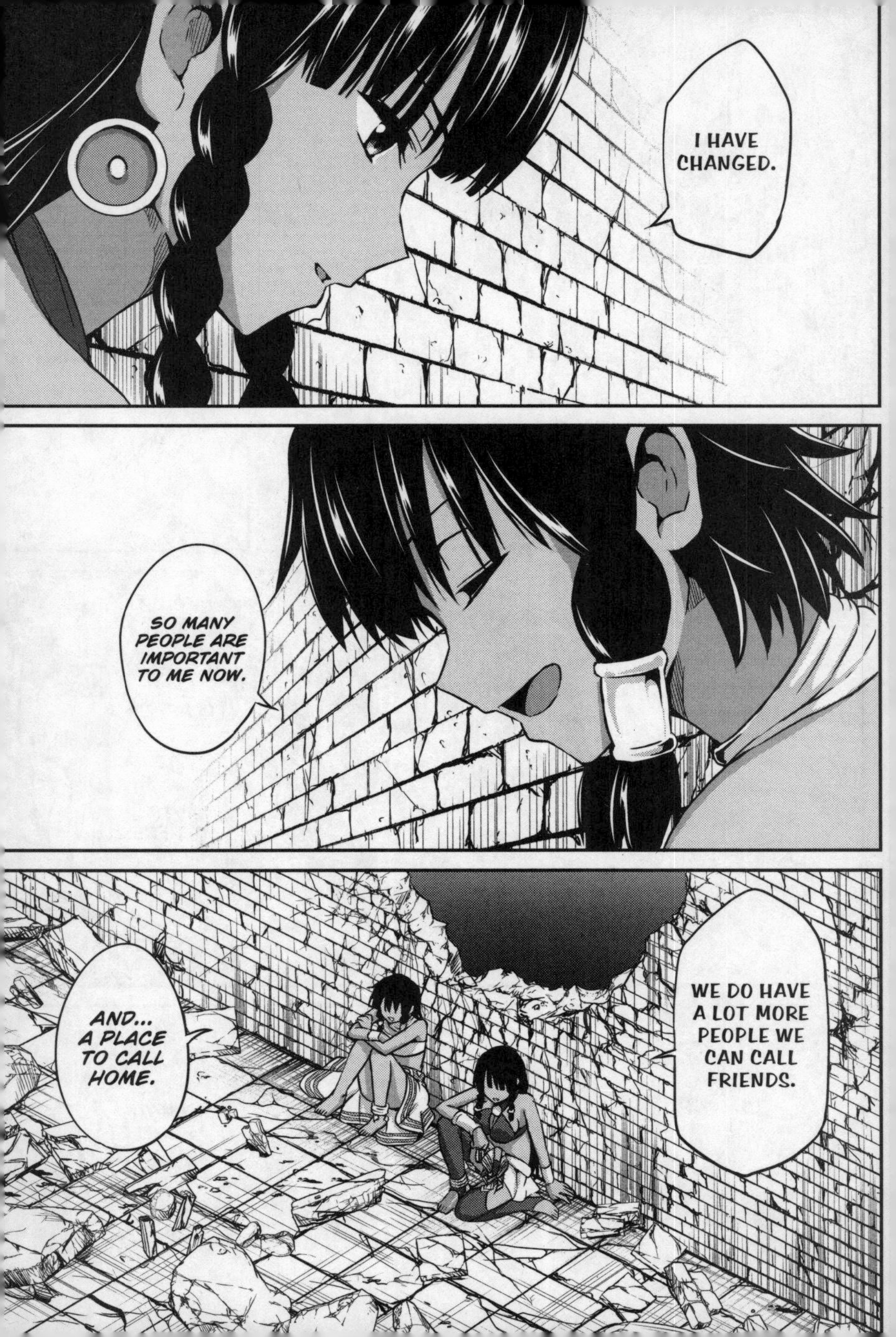
I HAVE CHANGED.
SO MANY PEOPLE ARE IMPORTANT TO ME NOW.
WE DO HAVE A LOT MORE PEOPLE WE CAN CALL FRIENDS.
AND... A PLACE TO CALL HOME.

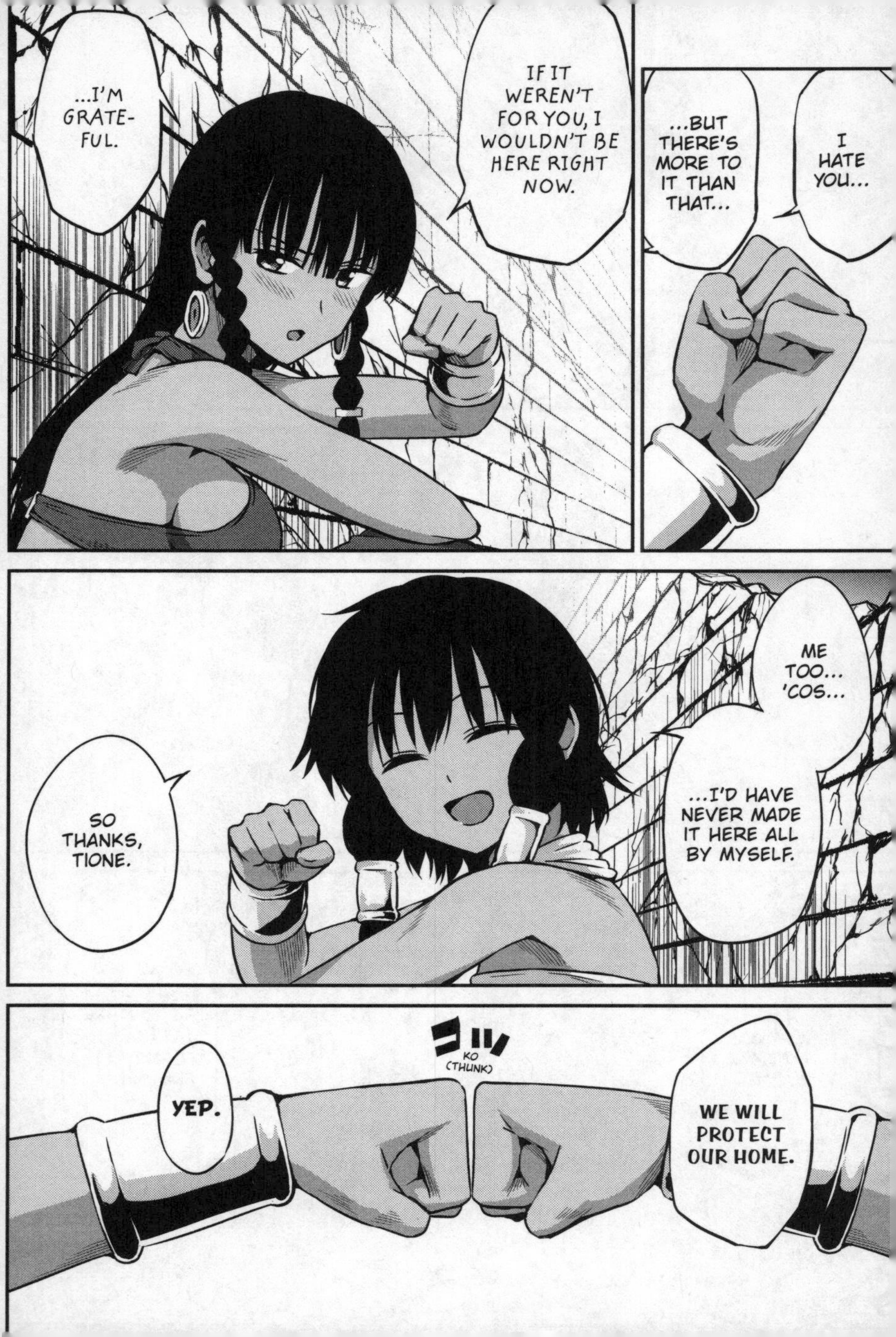
I HATE YOU...
...BUT THERE'S MORE TO IT THAN THAT...
IF IT WEREN'T FOR YOU, I WOULDN'T BE HERE RIGHT NOW.
...I'M GRATE-FUL.
ME TOO... 'COS...
...I'D HAVE NEVER MADE IT HERE ALL BY MYSELF.
SO THANKS, TIONE.
WE WILL PROTECT OUR HOME.
コツ
KO (THUNK)
YEP.

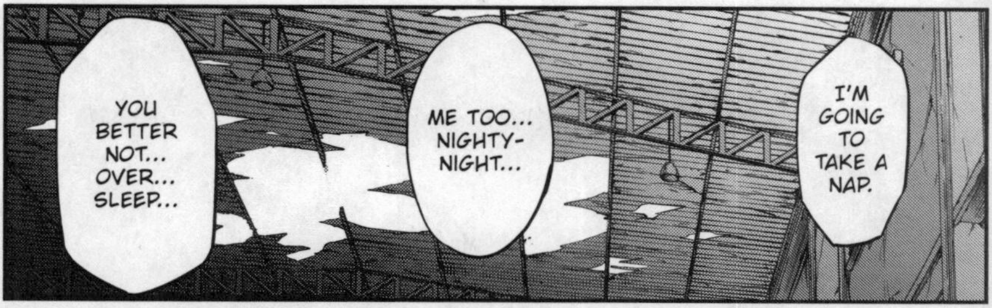
I'M GOING TO TAKE A NAP.
ME TOO... NIGHTY-NIGHT...
YOU BETTER NOT... OVER... SLEEP...

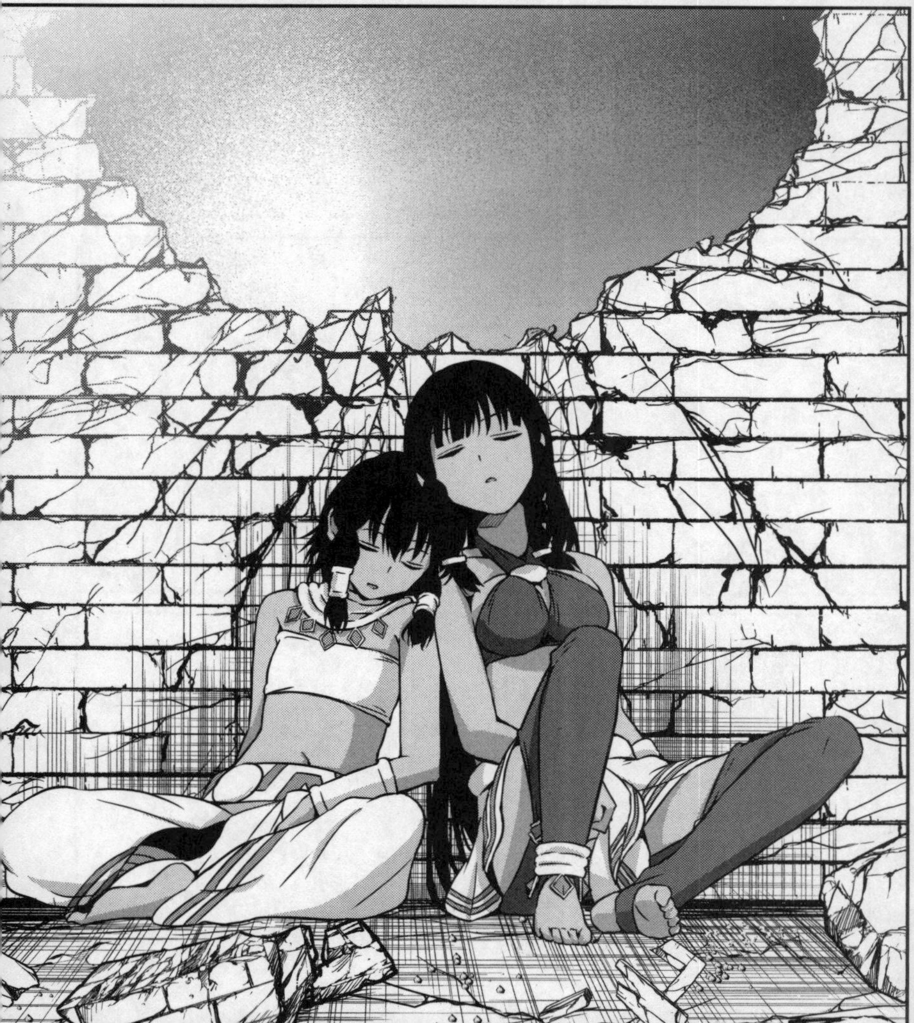

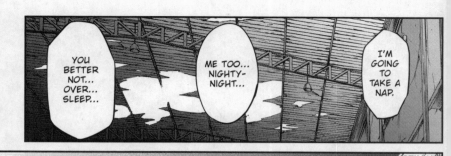

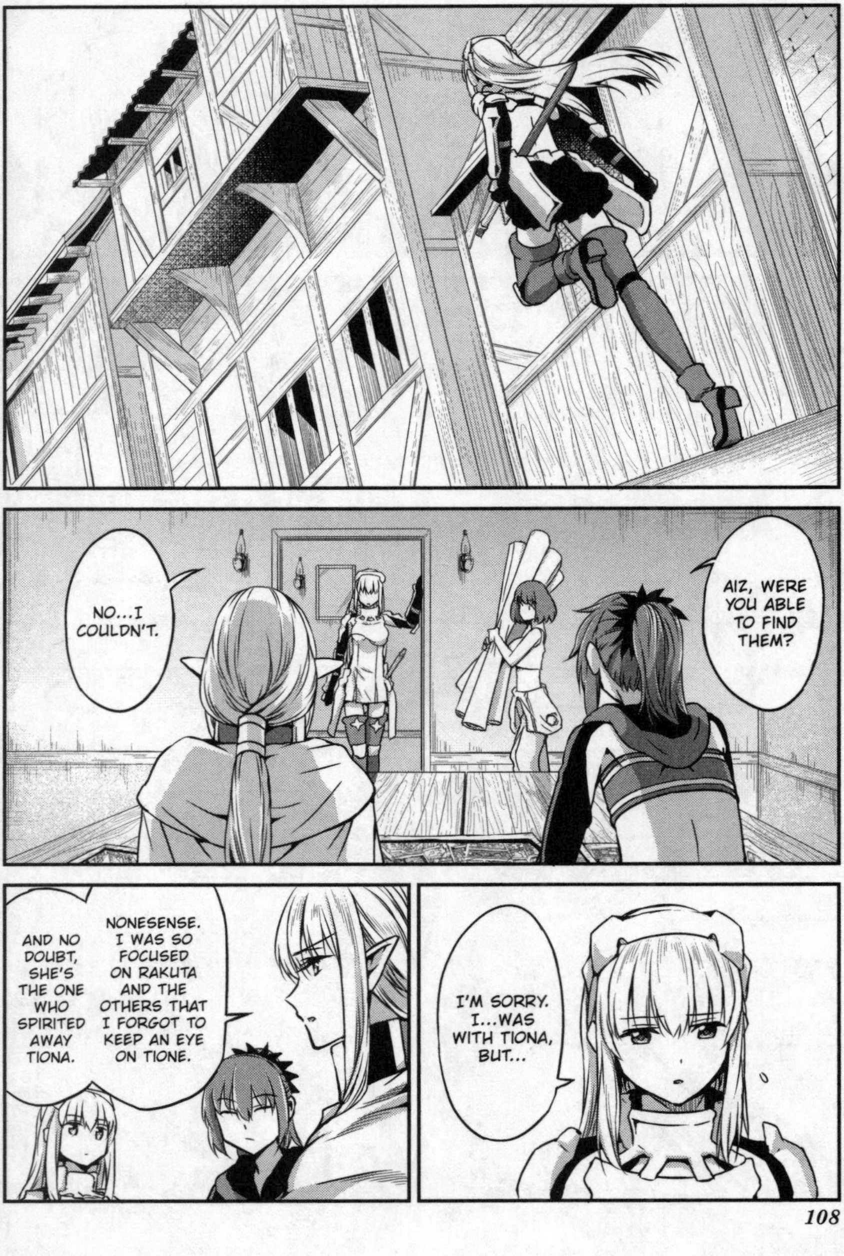
AIZ, WERE YOU ABLE TO FIND THEM?
NO...I COULDN'T.
I'M SORRY. I...WAS WITH TIONA, BUT...
NONESENSE. I WAS SO FOCUSED ON RAKUTA AND THE OTHERS THAT I FORGOT TO KEEP AN EYE ON TIONE.
AND NO DOUBT, SHE'S THE ONE WHO SPIRITED AWAY TIONA.

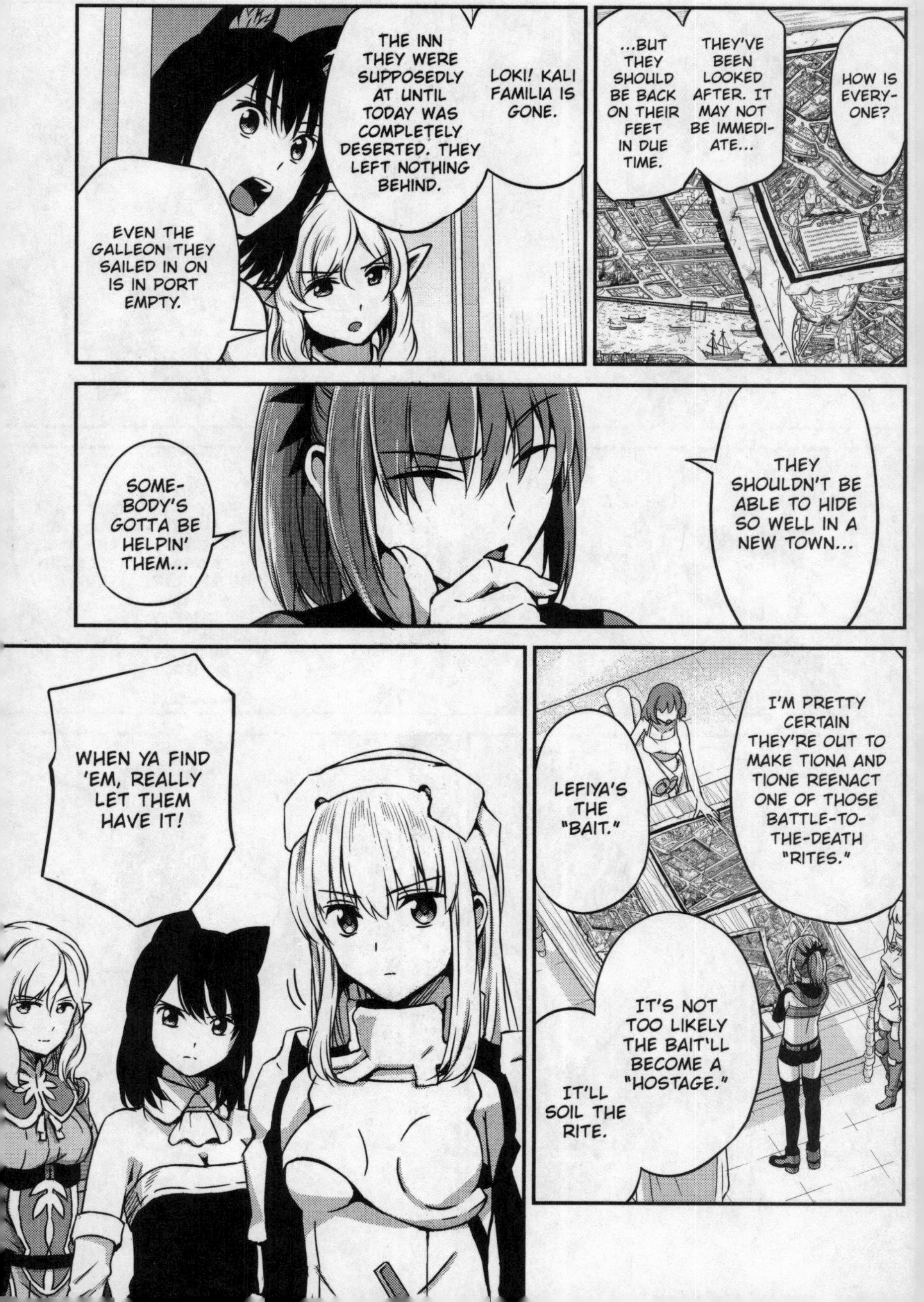
HOW IS EVERYONE?
THEY'VE BEEN LOOKED AFTER. IT MAY NOT BE IMMEDIATE...
...BUT THEY SHOULD BE BACK ON THEIR FEET IN DUE TIME.
LOKI! KALI FAMILIA IS GONE.
THE INN THEY WERE SUPPOSEDLY AT UNTIL TODAY WAS COMPLETELY DESERTED. THEY LEFT NOTHING BEHIND.
EVEN THE GALLEON THEY SAILED IN ON IS IN PORT EMPTY.
THEY SHOULDN'T BE ABLE TO HIDE SO WELL IN A NEW TOWN...
SOMEBODY'S GOTTA BE HELPIN' THEM...
I'M PRETTY CERTAIN THEY'RE OUT TO MAKE TIONA AND TIONE REENACT ONE OF THOSE BATTLE-TO-THE-DEATH "RITES."
LEFIYA'S THE "BAIT."
IT'S NOT TOO LIKELY THE BAIT'LL BECOME A "HOSTAGE."
IT'LL SOIL THE RITE.
WHEN YA FIND 'EM, REALLY LET THEM HAVE IT!

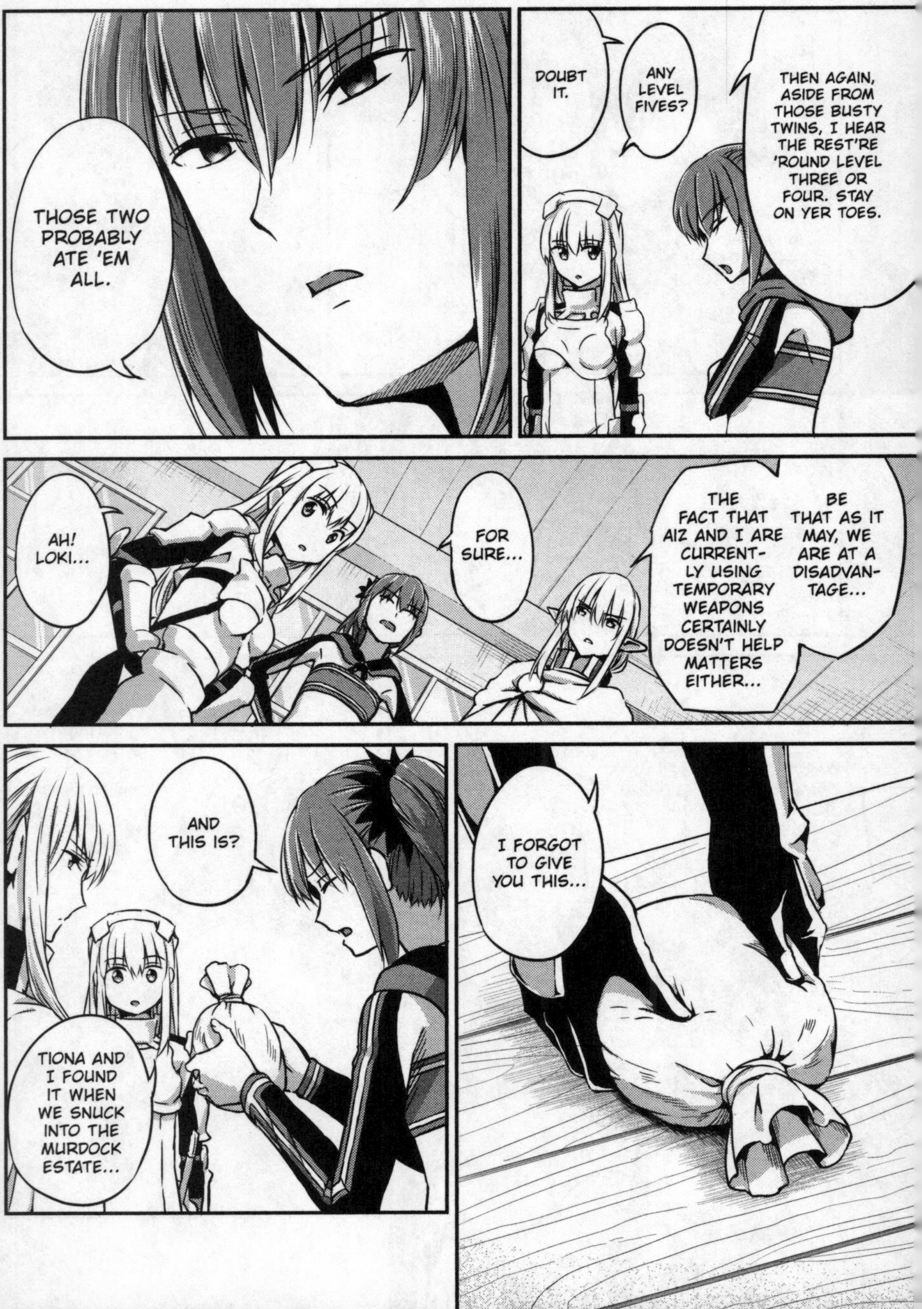
THEN AGAIN, ASIDE FROM THOSE BUSTY TWINS, I HEAR THE REST'RE 'ROUND LEVEL THREE OR FOUR. STAY ON YER TOES.
ANY LEVEL FIVES?
DOUBT IT.
THOSE TWO PROBABLY ATE 'EM ALL.
BE THAT AS IT MAY, WE ARE AT A DISADVANTAGE...
THE FACT THAT AIZ AND I ARE CURRENTLY USING TEMPORARY WEAPONS CERTAINLY DOESN'T HELP MATTERS EITHER...
FOR SURE...
AH! LOKI...
I FORGOT TO GIVE YOU THIS...
AND THIS IS?
TIONA AND I FOUND IT WHEN WE SNUCK INTO THE MURDOCK ESTATE...

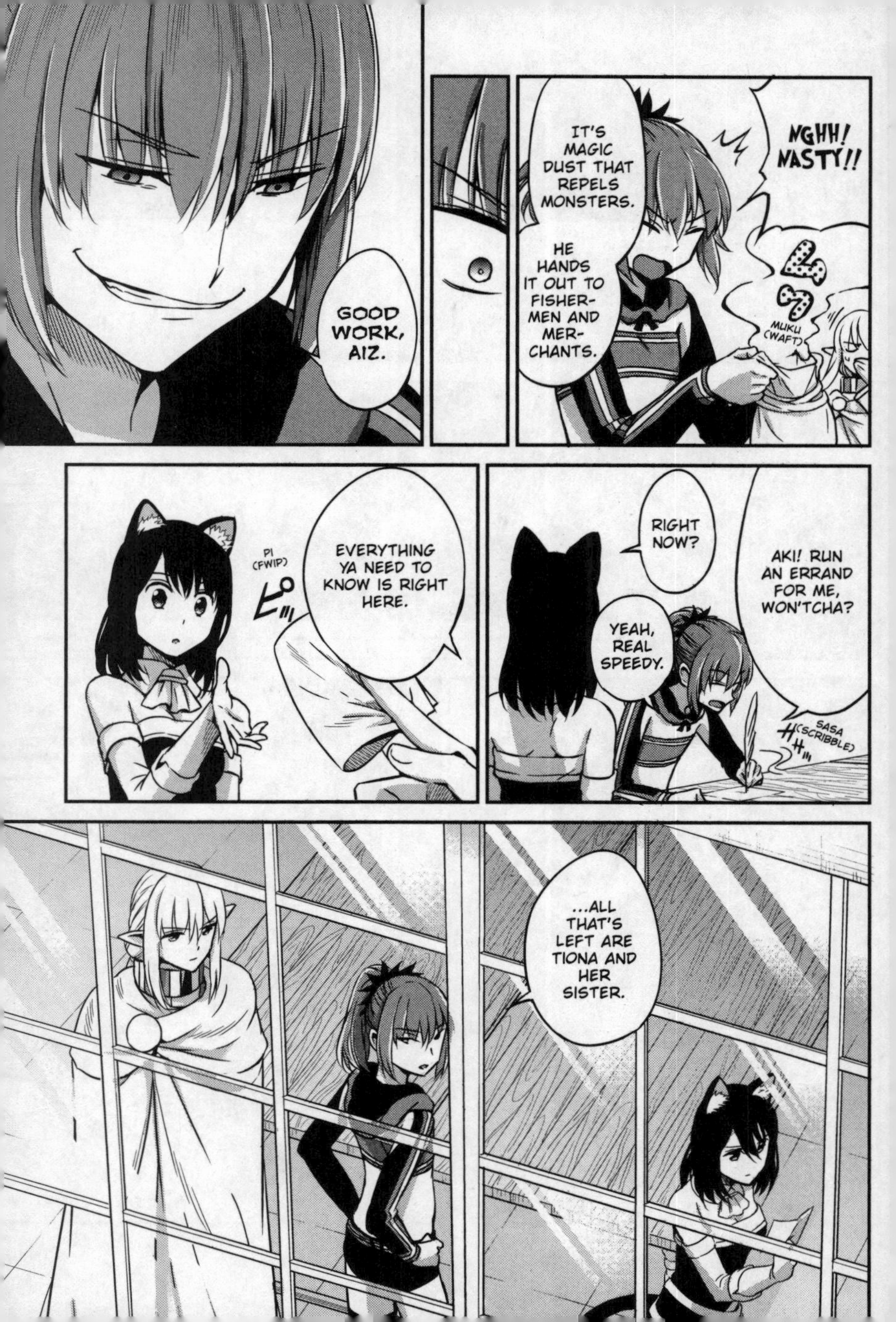
NGHH! NASTY!!
IT'S MAGIC DUST THAT REPELS MONSTERS.
HE HANDS IT OUT TO FISHERMEN AND MERCHANTS.
MUKU (WAFT)
GOOD WORK, AIZ.
AKI! RUN AN ERRAND FOR ME, WON'TCHA?
RIGHT NOW?
YEAH, REAL SPEEDY.
SASA (SCRIBBLE)
EVERYTHING YA NEED TO KNOW IS RIGHT HERE.
PI (FWIP)
...ALL THAT'S LEFT ARE TIONA AND HER SISTER.

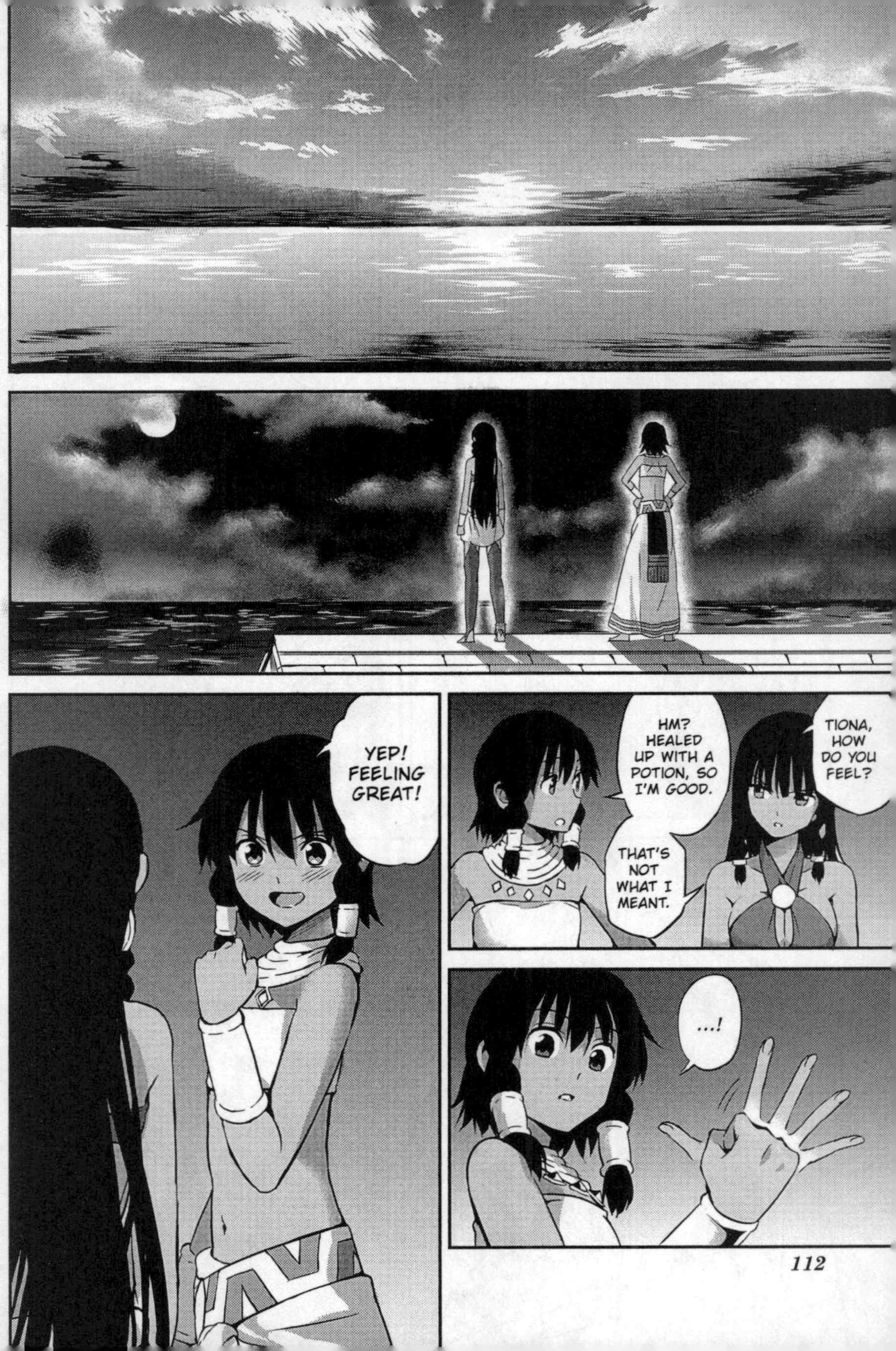
TIONA, HOW DO YOU FEEL?
HM? HEALED UP WITH A POTION, SO I'M GOOD.
THAT'S NOT WHAT I MEANT.
...!
YEP! FEELING GREAT!

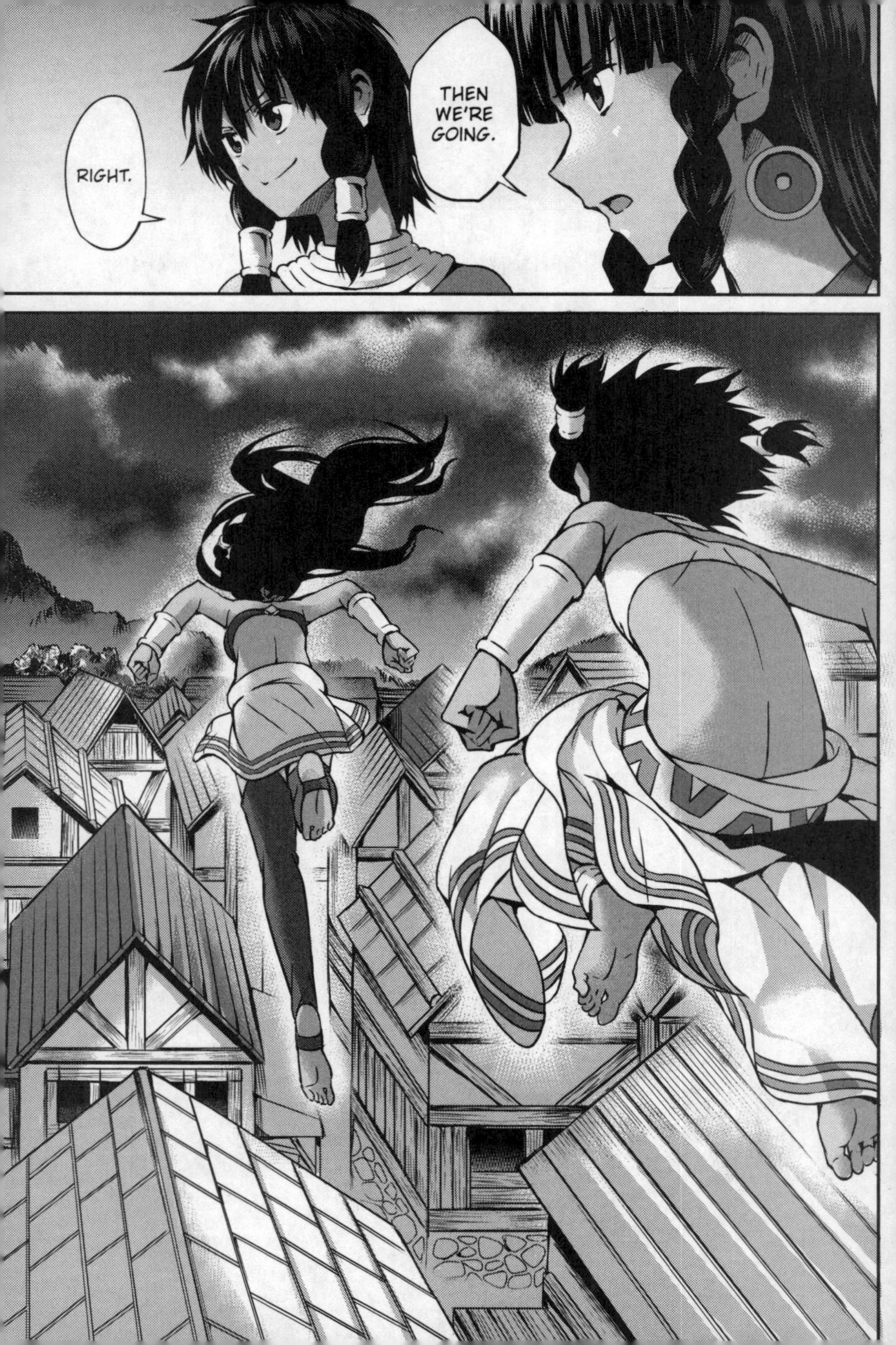
THEN WE'RE GOING.
RIGHT.

IS IT WRONG TO TRY TO PICK UP GIRLS IN A DUNGEON? ON THE SIDE

Sword Oratoria

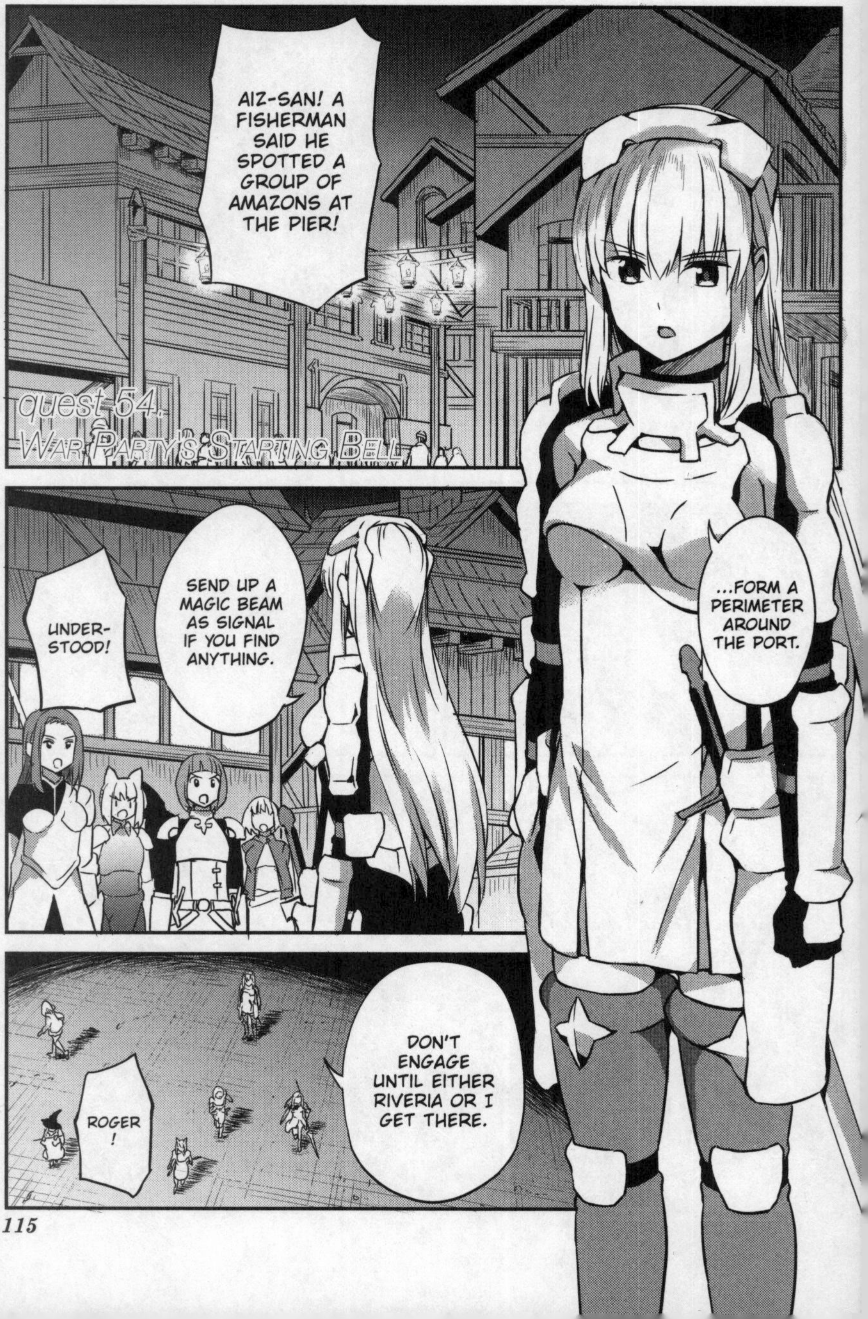
AIZ-SAN! A FISHERMAN SAID HE SPOTTED A GROUP OF AMAZONS AT THE PIER!
quest 54. War Party's Starting Bell
...FORM A PERIMETER AROUND THE PORT.
SEND UP A MAGIC BEAM AS SIGNAL IF YOU FIND ANYTHING.
UNDER-STOOD!
DON'T ENGAGE UNTIL EITHER RIVERIA OR I GET THERE.
ROGER!

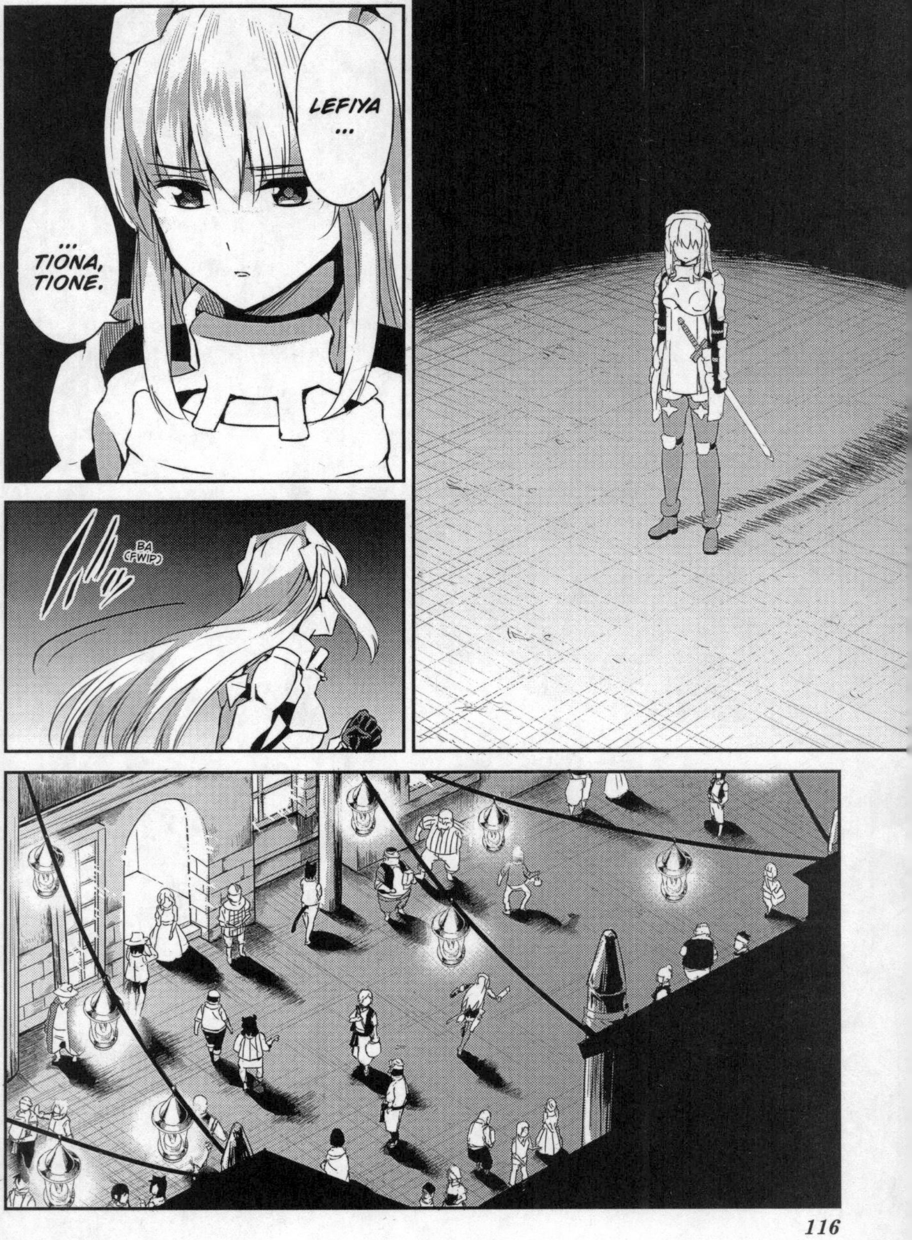
LEFIYA ...
... TIONA, TIONE.
BA (FWIP)

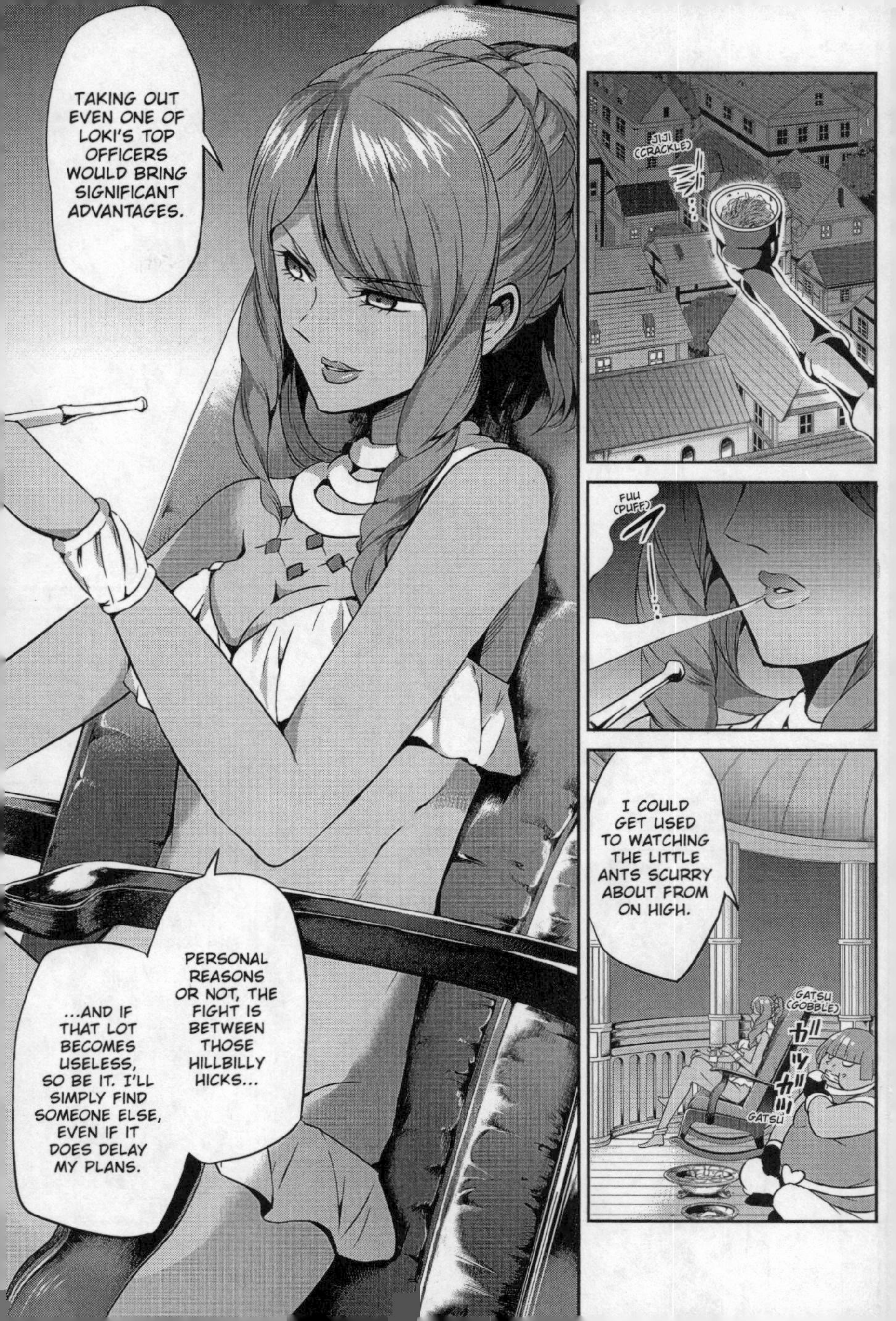
JIJI (CRACKLE)
FUU (PUFF)
I COULD GET USED TO WATCHING THE LITTLE ANTS SCURRY ABOUT FROM ON HIGH.
GATSU (GOBBLE)
GATSU
TAKING OUT EVEN ONE OF LOKI'S TOP OFFICERS WOULD BRING SIGNIFICANT ADVANTAGES.
PERSONAL REASONS OR NOT, THE FIGHT IS BETWEEN THOSE HILLBILLY HICKS...
...AND IF THAT LOT BECOMES USELESS, SO BE IT. I'LL SIMPLY FIND SOMEONE ELSE, EVEN IF IT DOES DELAY MY PLANS.

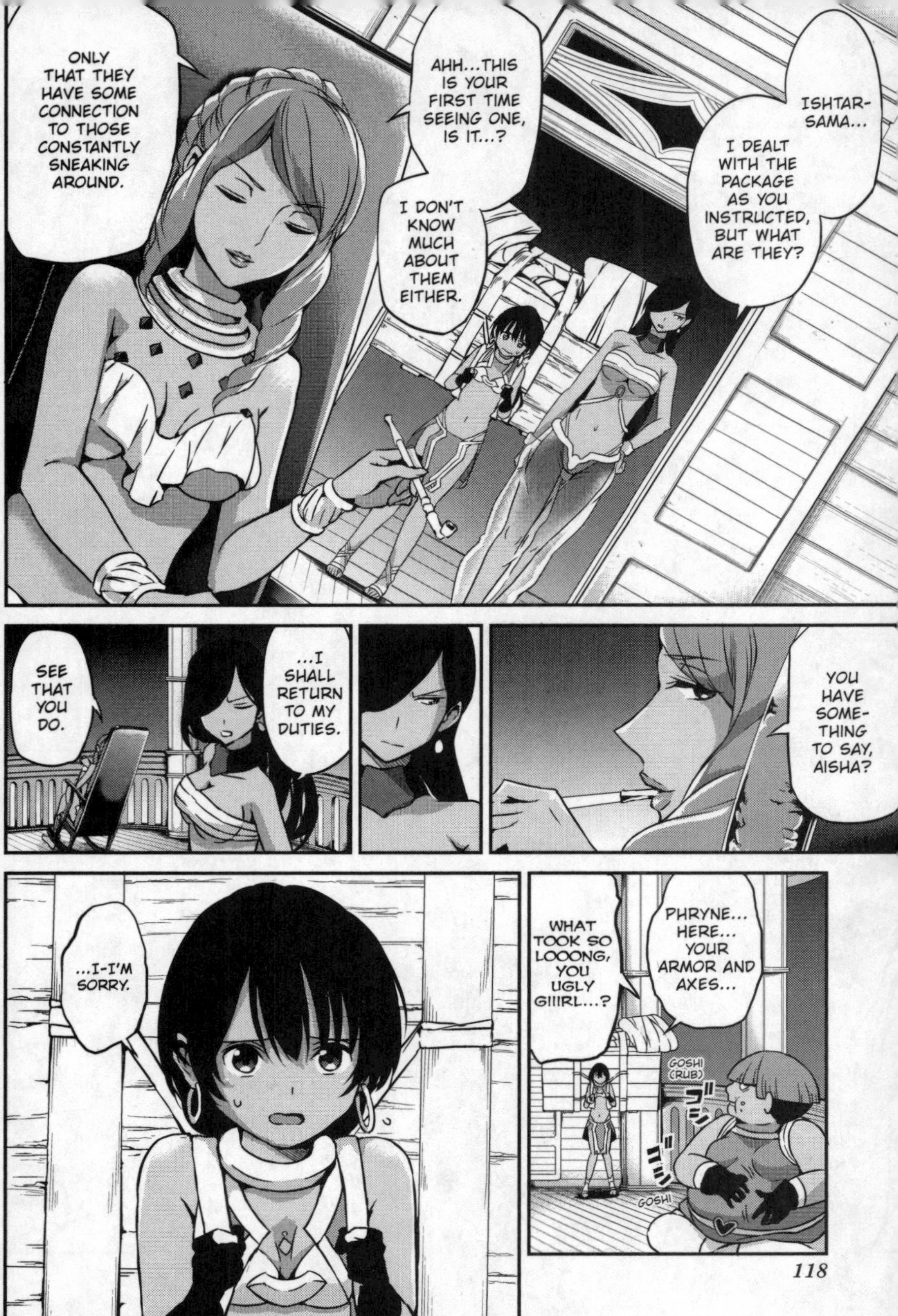
ISHTAR-SAMA...
I DEALT WITH THE PACKAGE AS YOU INSTRUCTED, BUT WHAT ARE THEY?
AHH...THIS IS YOUR FIRST TIME SEEING ONE, IS IT...?
I DON'T KNOW MUCH ABOUT THEM EITHER.
ONLY THAT THEY HAVE SOME CONNECTION TO THOSE CONSTANTLY SNEAKING AROUND.
YOU HAVE SOME-THING TO SAY, AISHA?
...I SHALL RETURN TO MY DUTIES.
SEE THAT YOU DO.
PHRYNE... HERE... YOUR ARMOR AND AXES...
WHAT TOOK SO LOOONG, YOU UGLY GIIIRL...?
GOSHI (RUB)
GOSHI
...I-I'M SORRY.

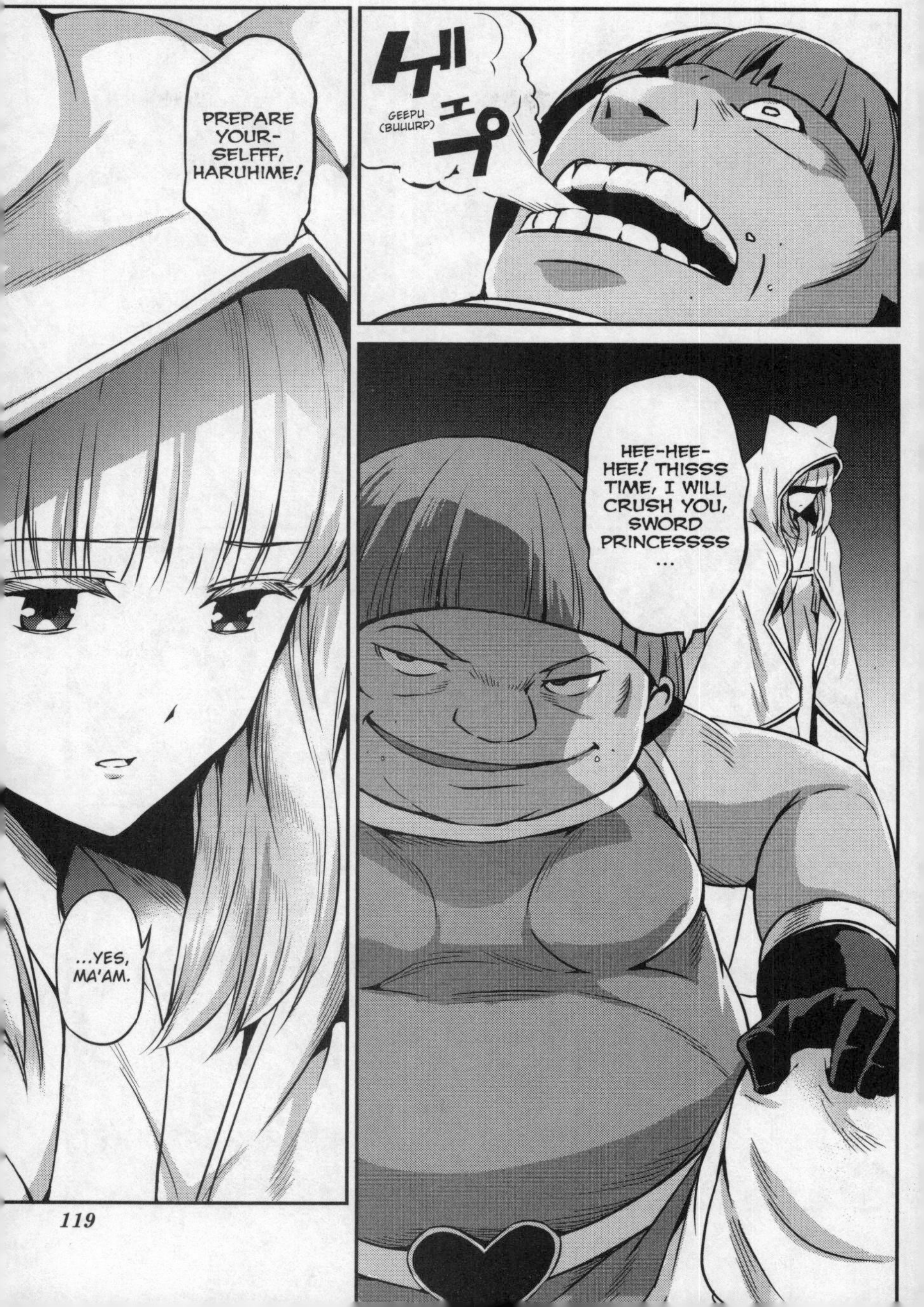
ゲェプ
GEEPU (BUUURP)
HEE-HEE-HEE! THISSS TIME, I WILL CRUSH YOU, SWORD PRINCESSSS ...
PREPARE YOUR-SELFFF, HARUHIME!
...YES, MA'AM.

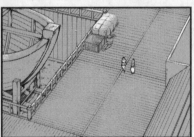

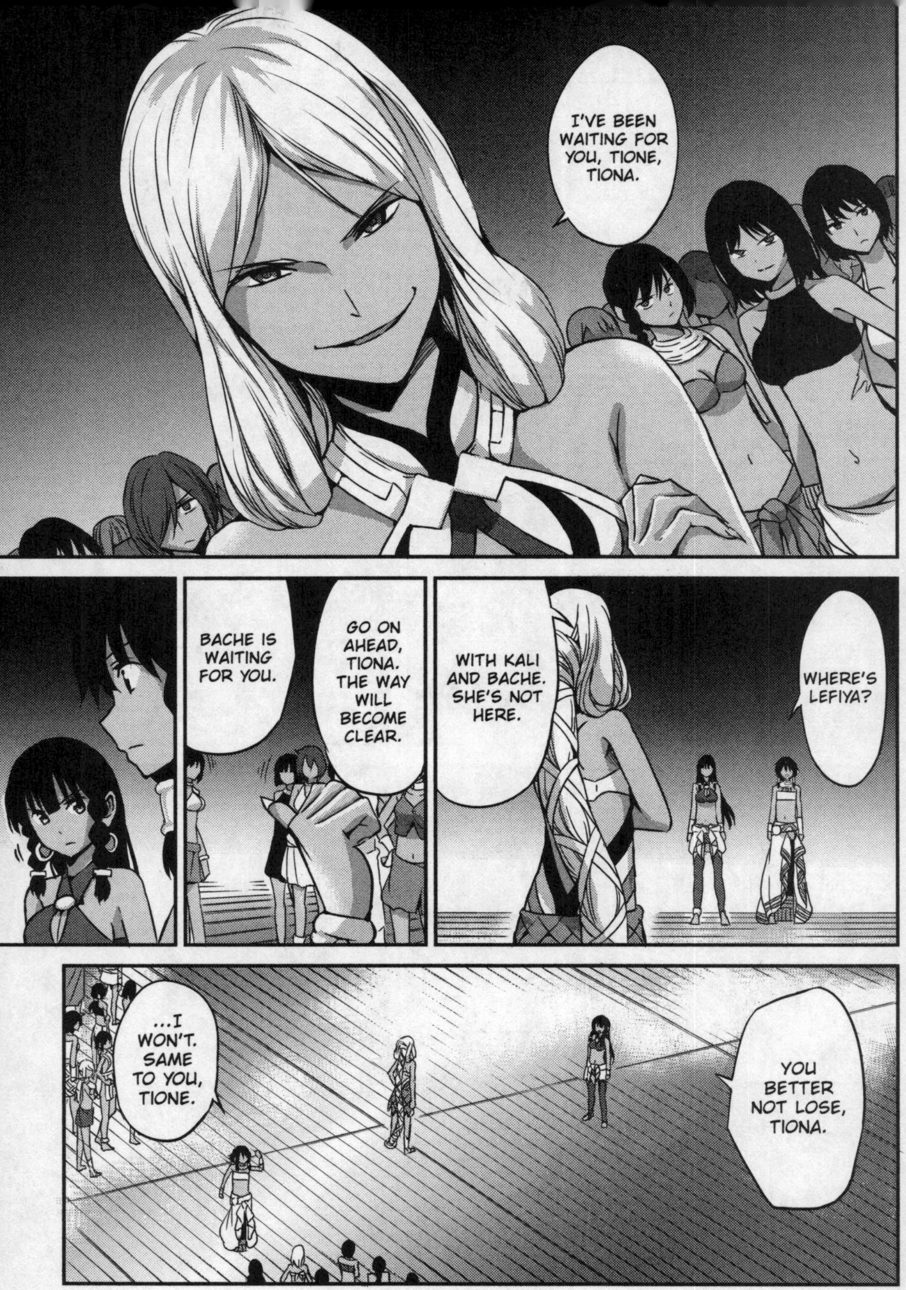
I'VE BEEN WAITING FOR YOU, TIONE, TIONA.
WHERE'S LEFIYA?
WITH KALI AND BACHE. SHE'S NOT HERE.
GO ON AHEAD, TIONA. THE WAY WILL BECOME CLEAR.
BACHE IS WAITING FOR YOU.
YOU BETTER NOT LOSE, TIONA.
...I WON'T. SAME TO YOU, TIONE.

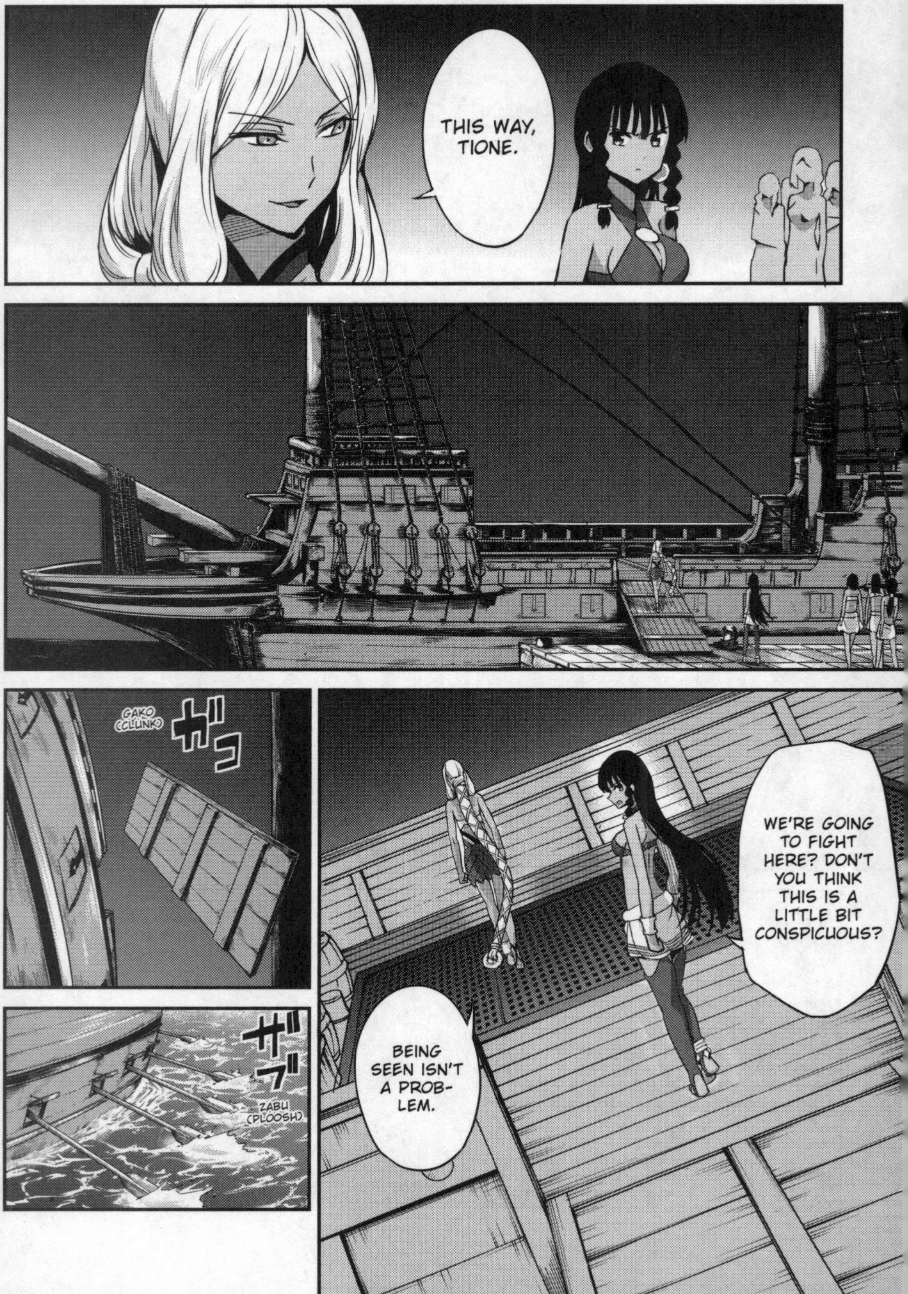
THIS WAY, TIONE.
WE'RE GOING TO FIGHT HERE? DON'T YOU THINK THIS IS A LITTLE BIT CONSPICUOUS?
BEING SEEN ISN'T A PROB-LEM.
ガコ
GAKO (CLUNK)
ザブ
ZABU (PLOOSH)

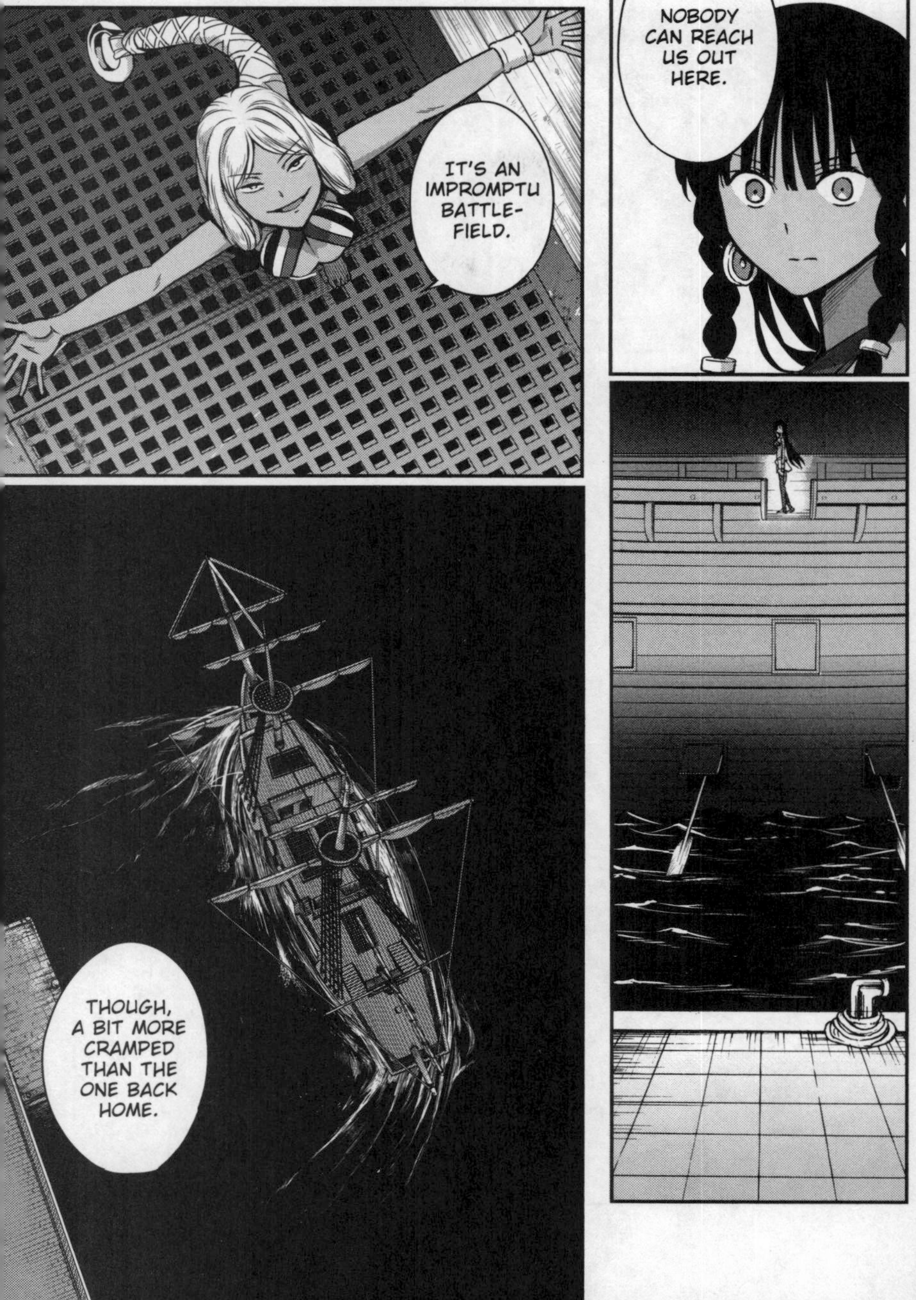
NOBODY CAN REACH US OUT HERE.
IT'S AN IMPROMPTU BATTLE-FIELD.
THOUGH, A BIT MORE CRAMPED THAN THE ONE BACK HOME.

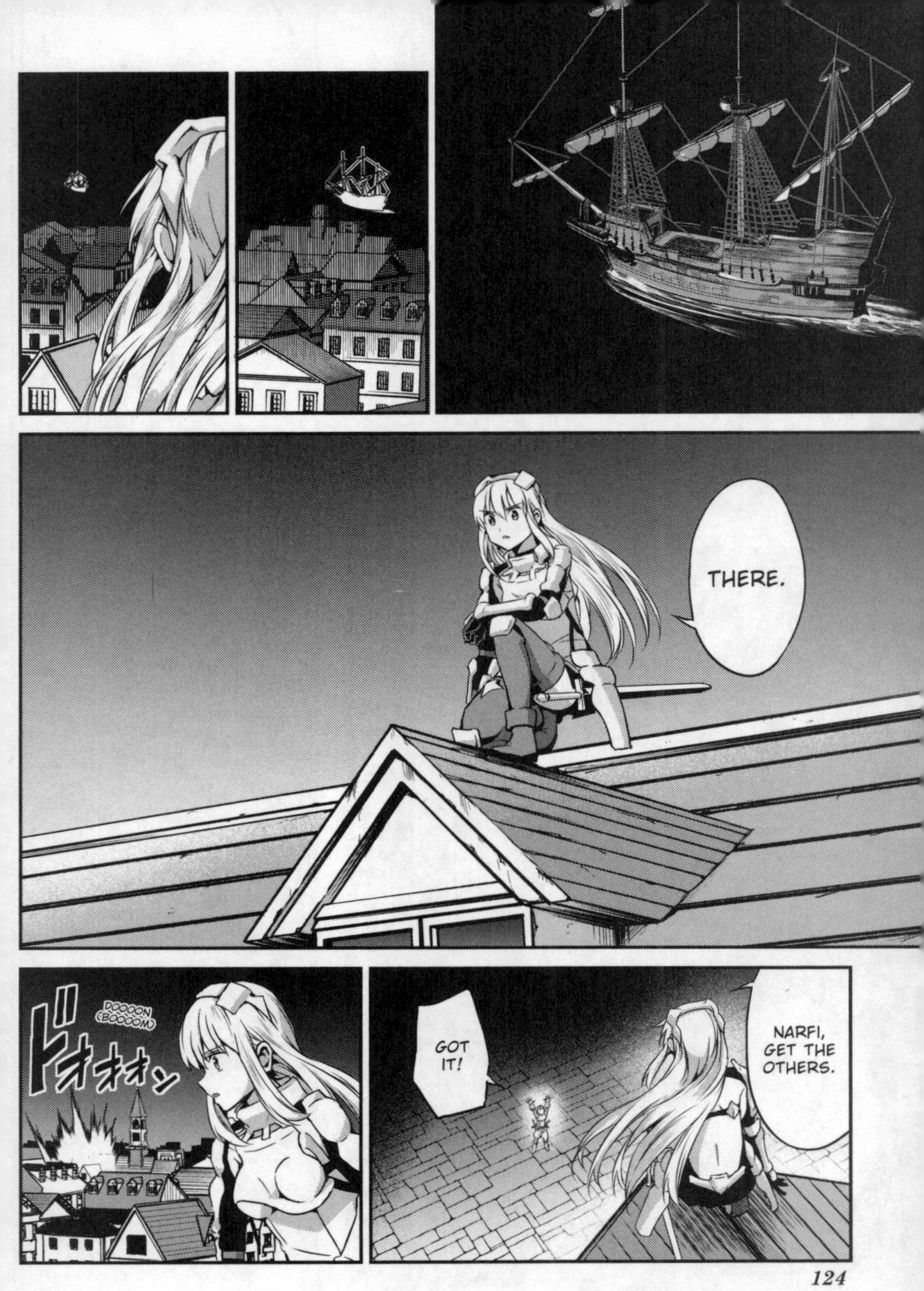
THERE.
NARFI, GET THE OTHERS.
GOT IT!
ドオオオン
DOOOON (BOOOOM)

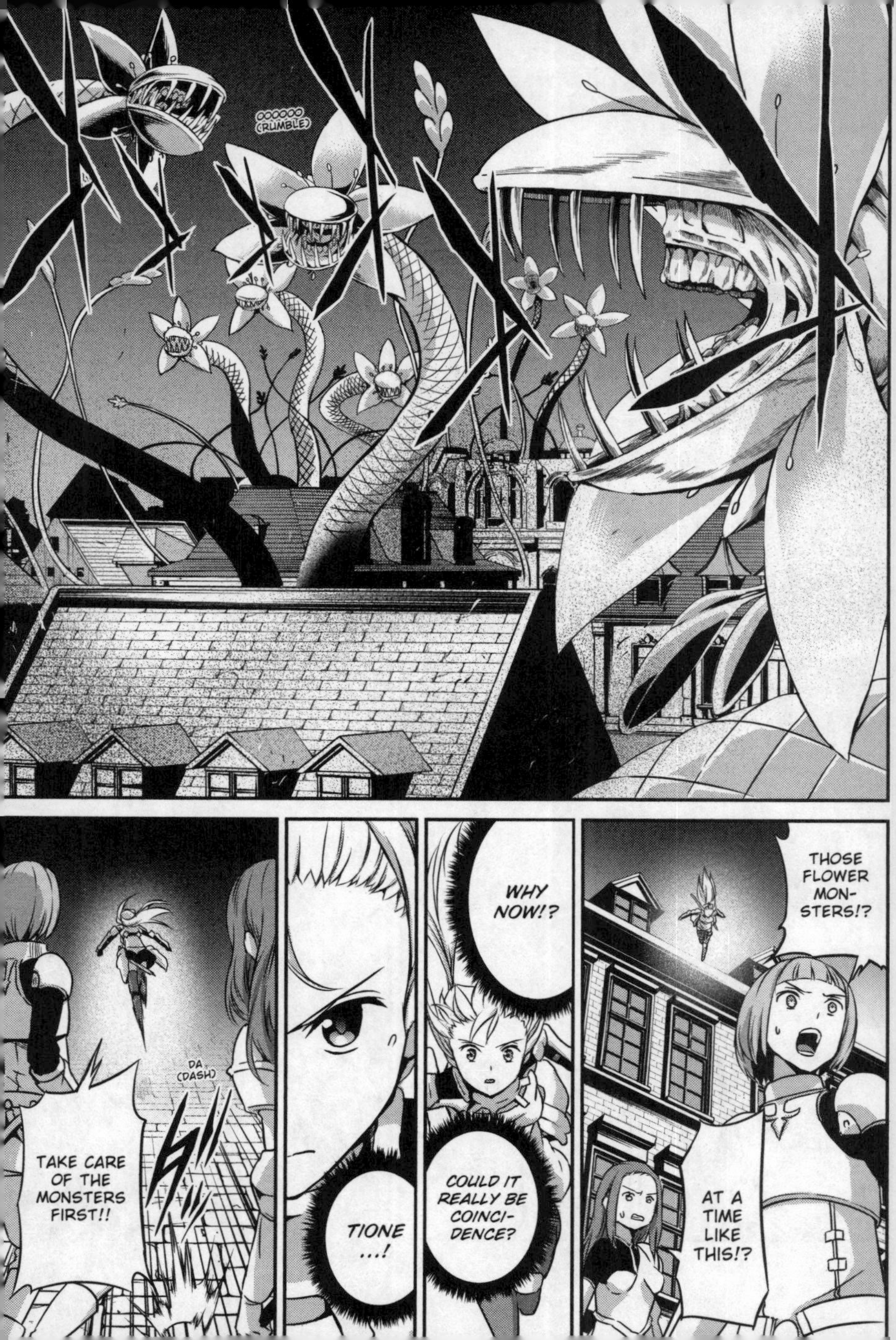
OOOOOO (RUMBLE)
THOSE FLOWER MON-STERS!?
AT A TIME LIKE THIS!?
WHY NOW!?
COULD IT REALLY BE COINCI-DENCE?
TIONE ...!
DA (DASH)
TAKE CARE OF THE MONSTERS FIRST!!

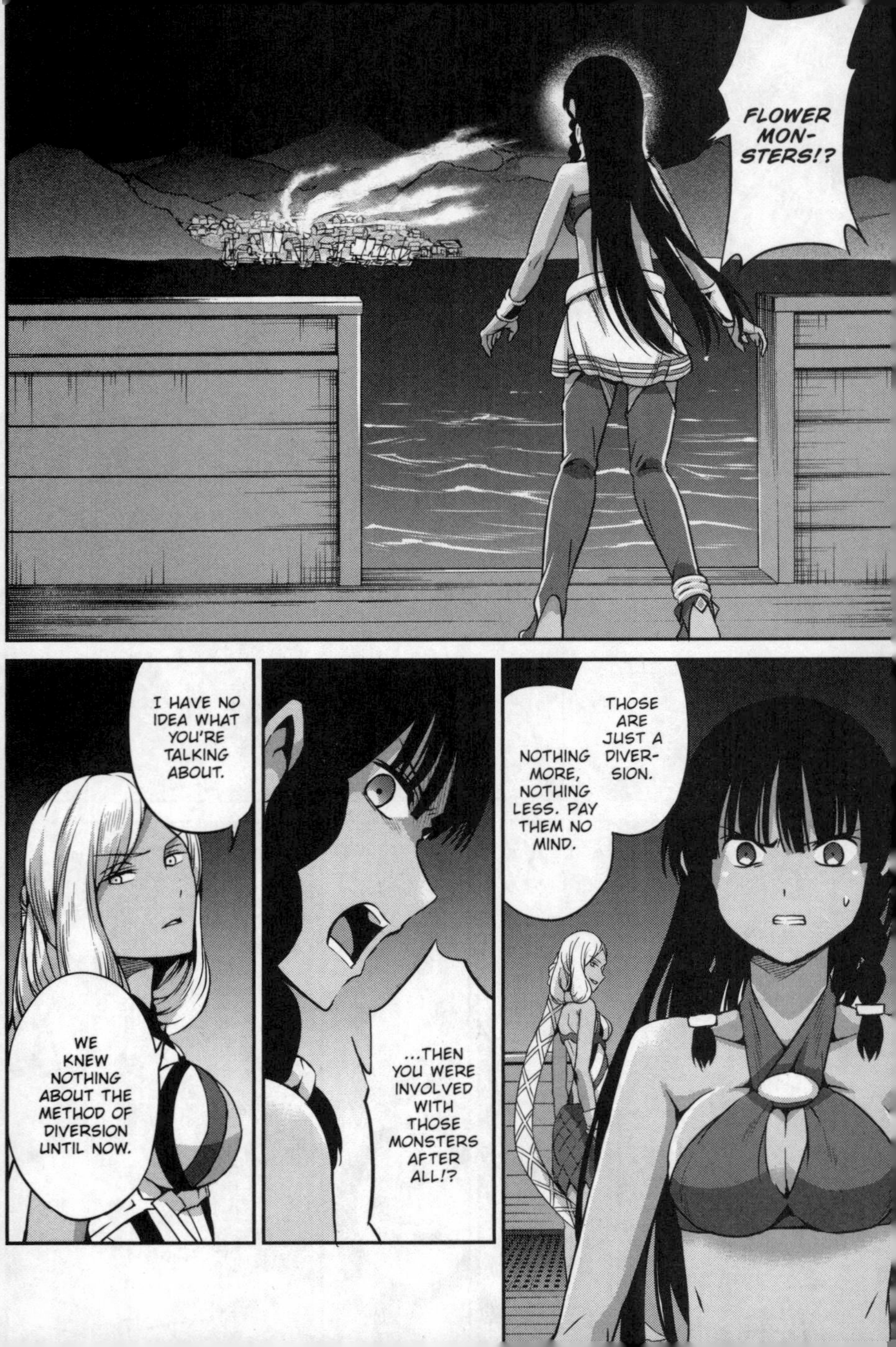
FLOWER MONSTERS!?
THOSE ARE JUST A DIVERSION.
NOTHING MORE, NOTHING LESS. PAY THEM NO MIND.
...THEN YOU WERE INVOLVED WITH THOSE MONSTERS AFTER ALL!?
I HAVE NO IDEA WHAT YOU'RE TALKING ABOUT.
WE KNEW NOTHING ABOUT THE METHOD OF DIVERSION UNTIL NOW.

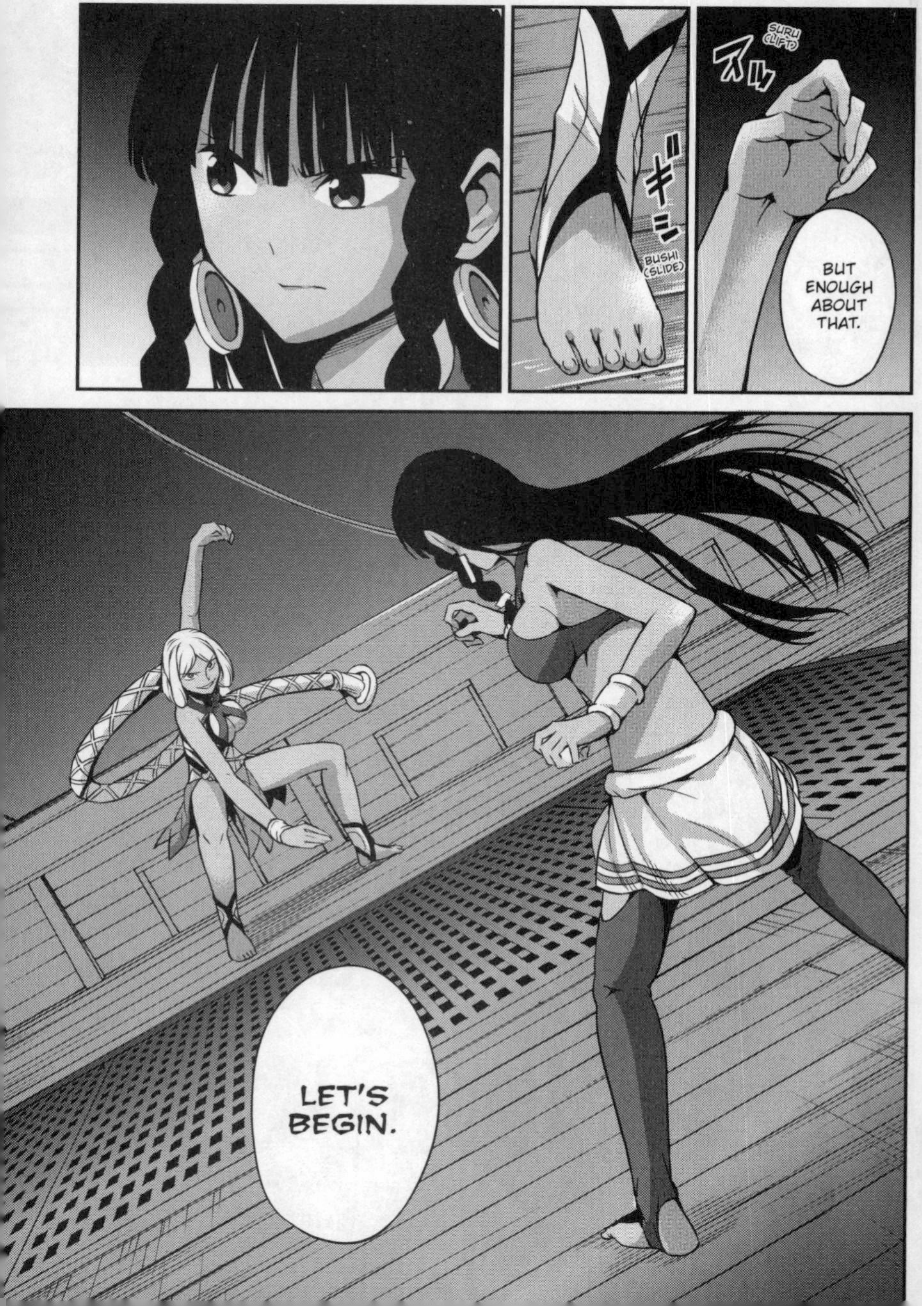
スル
SURU (LIFT)
BUT ENOUGH ABOUT THAT.
ギシ
BUSHI (SLIDE)
LET'S BEGIN.

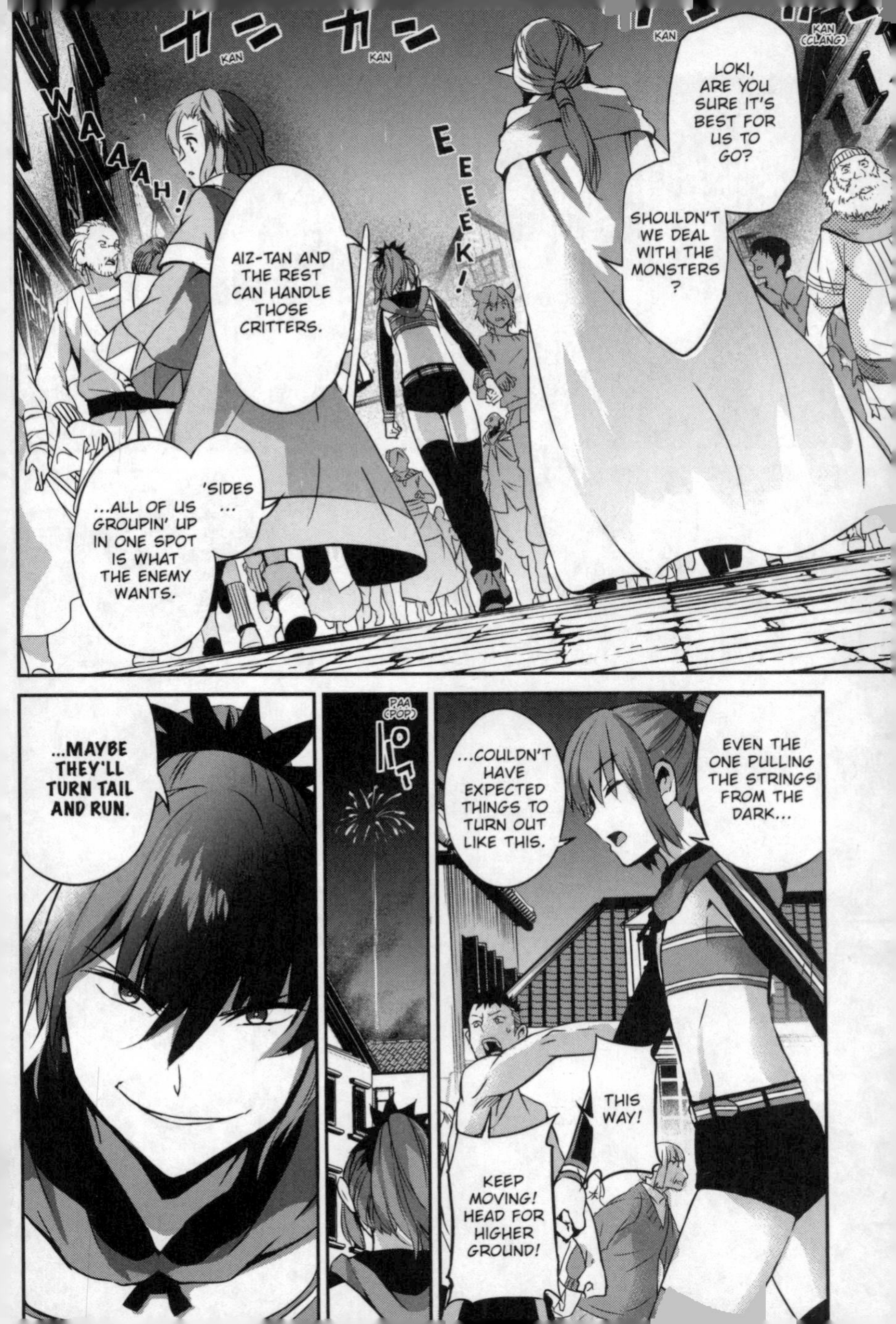
KAN (CLANG)
KAN
KAN
KAN
LOKI, ARE YOU SURE IT'S BEST FOR US TO GO?
SHOULDN'T WE DEAL WITH THE MONSTERS?
EEEEK!
AIZ-TAN AND THE REST CAN HANDLE THOSE CRITTERS.
WAAAAH!
'SIDES...
...ALL OF US GROUPIN' UP IN ONE SPOT IS WHAT THE ENEMY WANTS.
EVEN THE ONE PULLING THE STRINGS FROM THE DARK...
...COULDN'T HAVE EXPECTED THINGS TO TURN OUT LIKE THIS.
THIS WAY!
KEEP MOVING! HEAD FOR HIGHER GROUND!
PAA (POP)
...MAYBE THEY'LL TURN TAIL AND RUN.

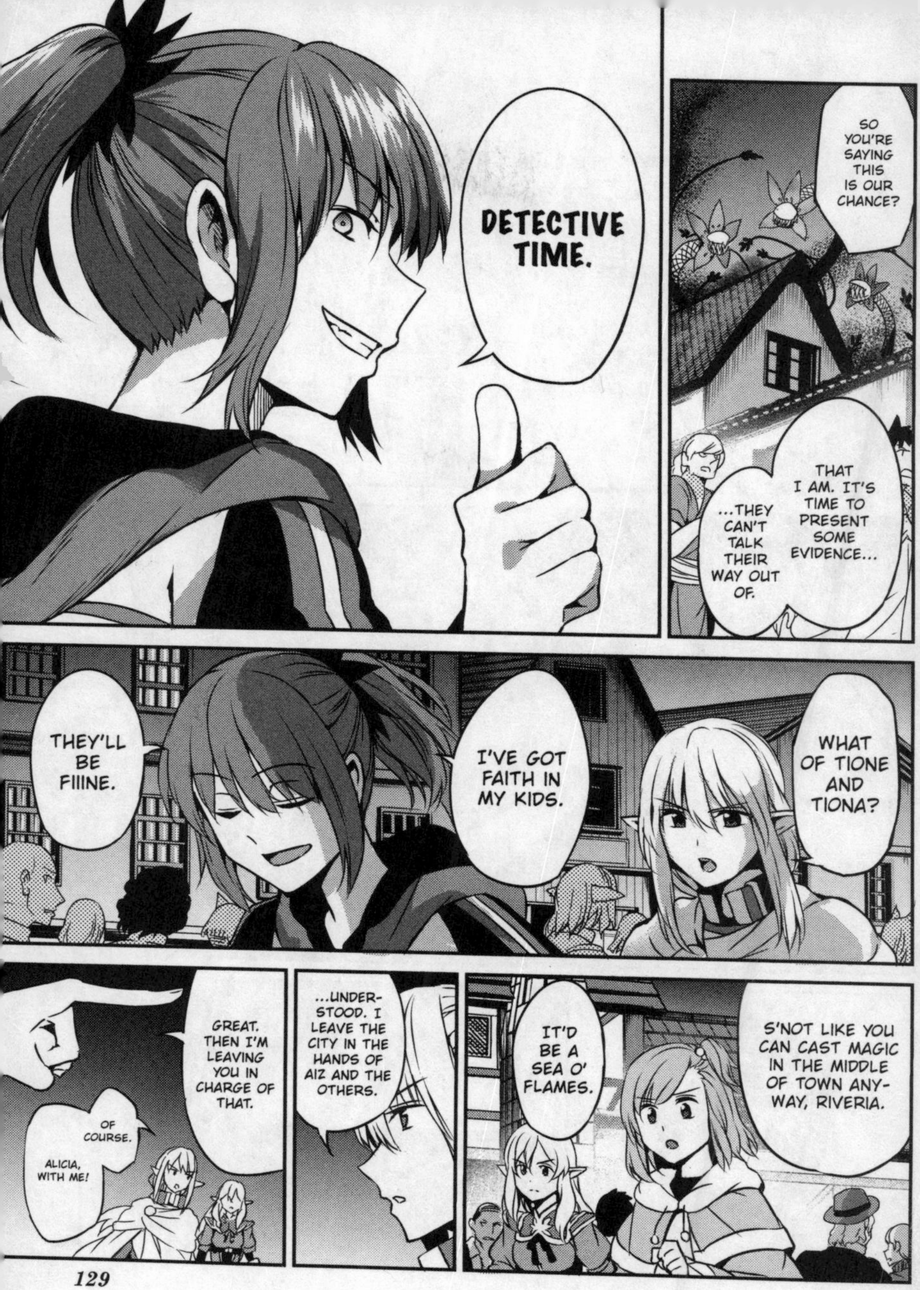
SO YOU'RE SAYING THIS IS OUR CHANCE?
THAT I AM. IT'S TIME TO PRESENT SOME EVIDENCE...
...THEY CAN'T TALK THEIR WAY OUT OF.
DETECTIVE TIME.
WHAT OF TIONE AND TIONA?
I'VE GOT FAITH IN MY KIDS.
THEY'LL BE FIIINE.
S'NOT LIKE YOU CAN CAST MAGIC IN THE MIDDLE OF TOWN ANY-WAY, RIVERIA.
IT'D BE A SEA O' FLAMES.
...UNDER-STOOD. I LEAVE THE CITY IN THE HANDS OF AIZ AND THE OTHERS.
GREAT. THEN I'M LEAVING YOU IN CHARGE OF THAT.
OF COURSE.
ALICIA, WITH ME!

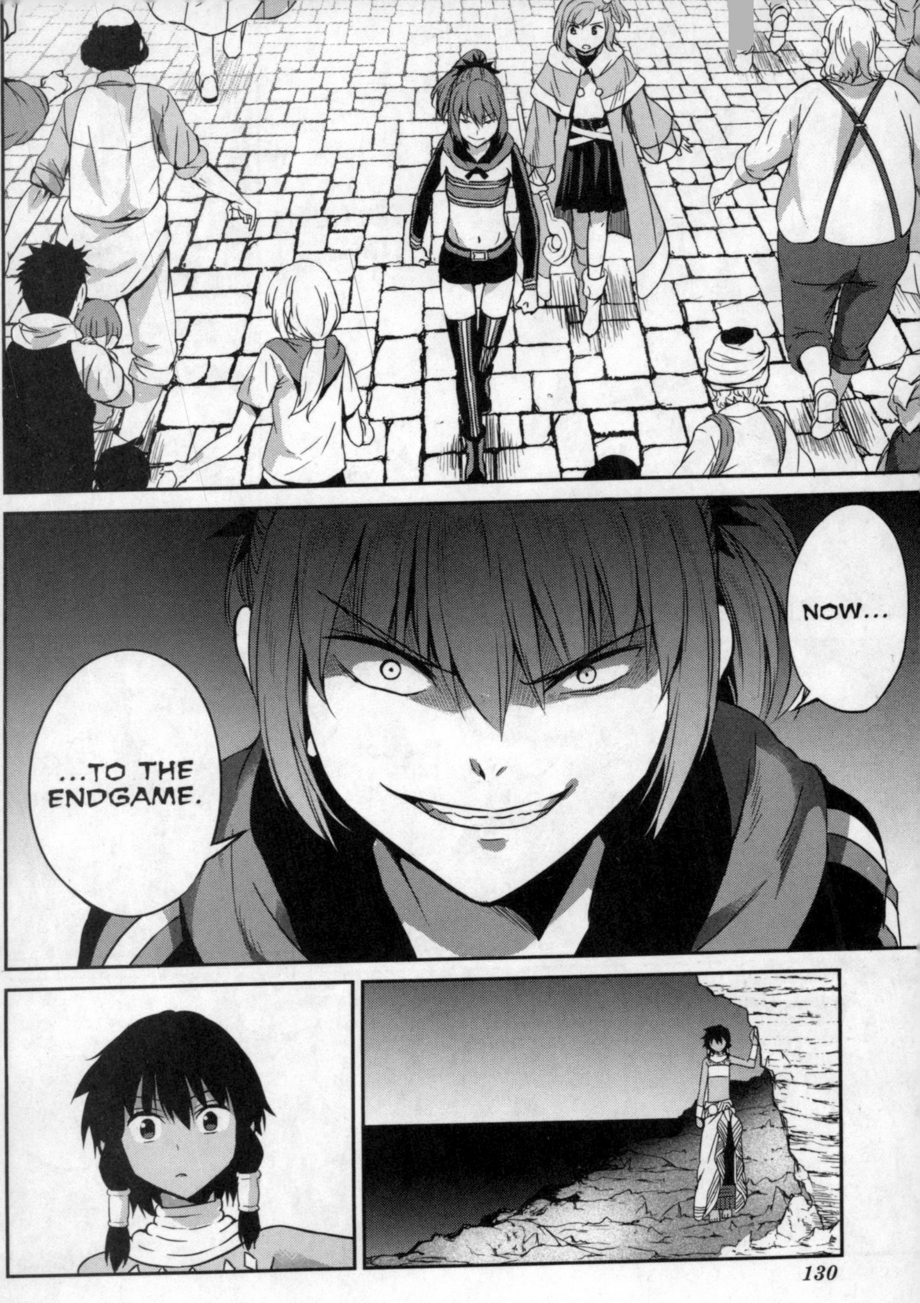
NOW...
...TO THE ENDGAME.

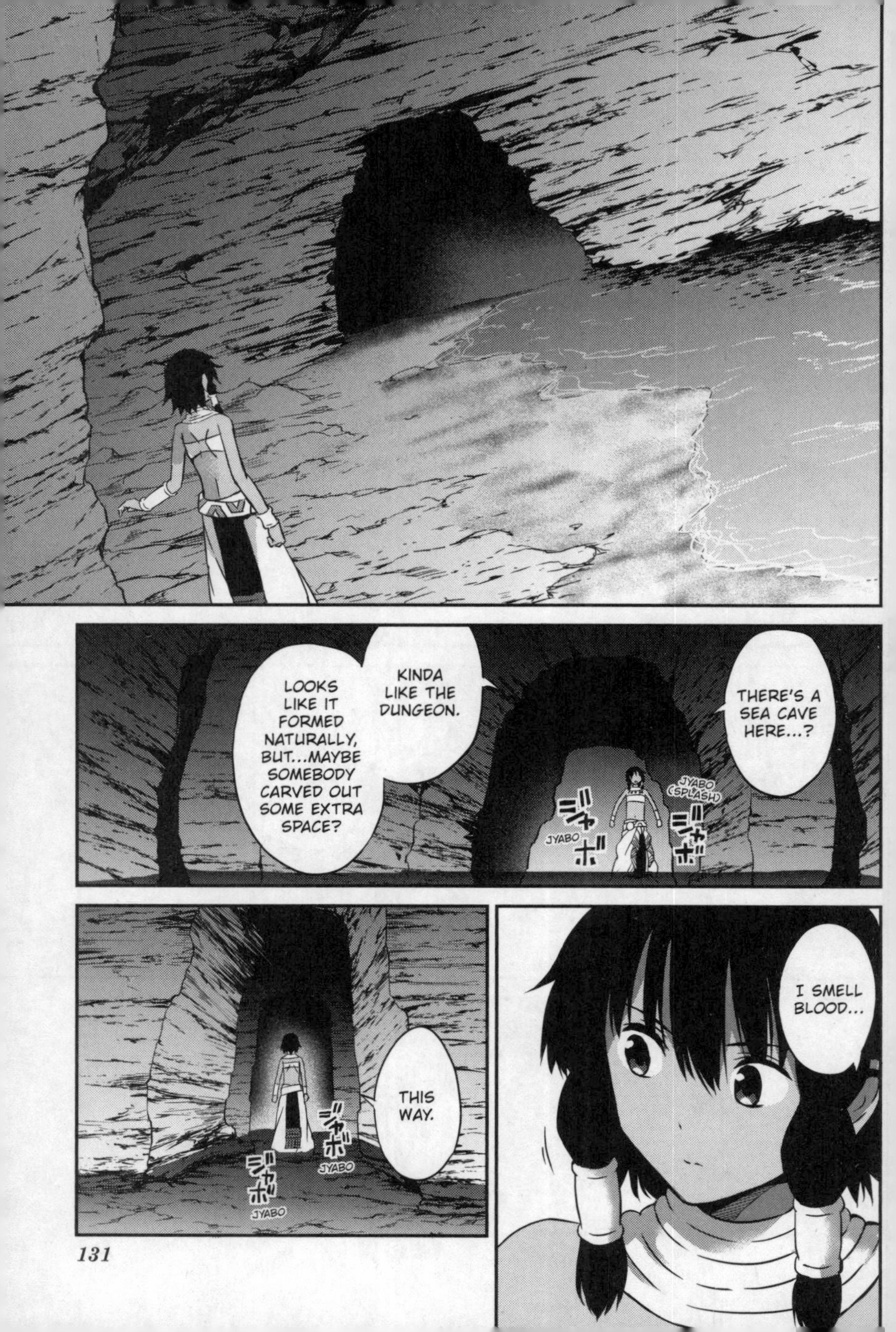

THERE'S A SEA CAVE HERE...?
ジャボ
JYABO (SPLASH)
ジャボ
JYABO
KINDA LIKE THE DUNGEON.
LOOKS LIKE IT FORMED NATURALLY, BUT...MAYBE SOMEBODY CARVED OUT SOME EXTRA SPACE?
I SMELL BLOOD...
THIS WAY.
ジャボ
JYABO
ジャボ
JYABO

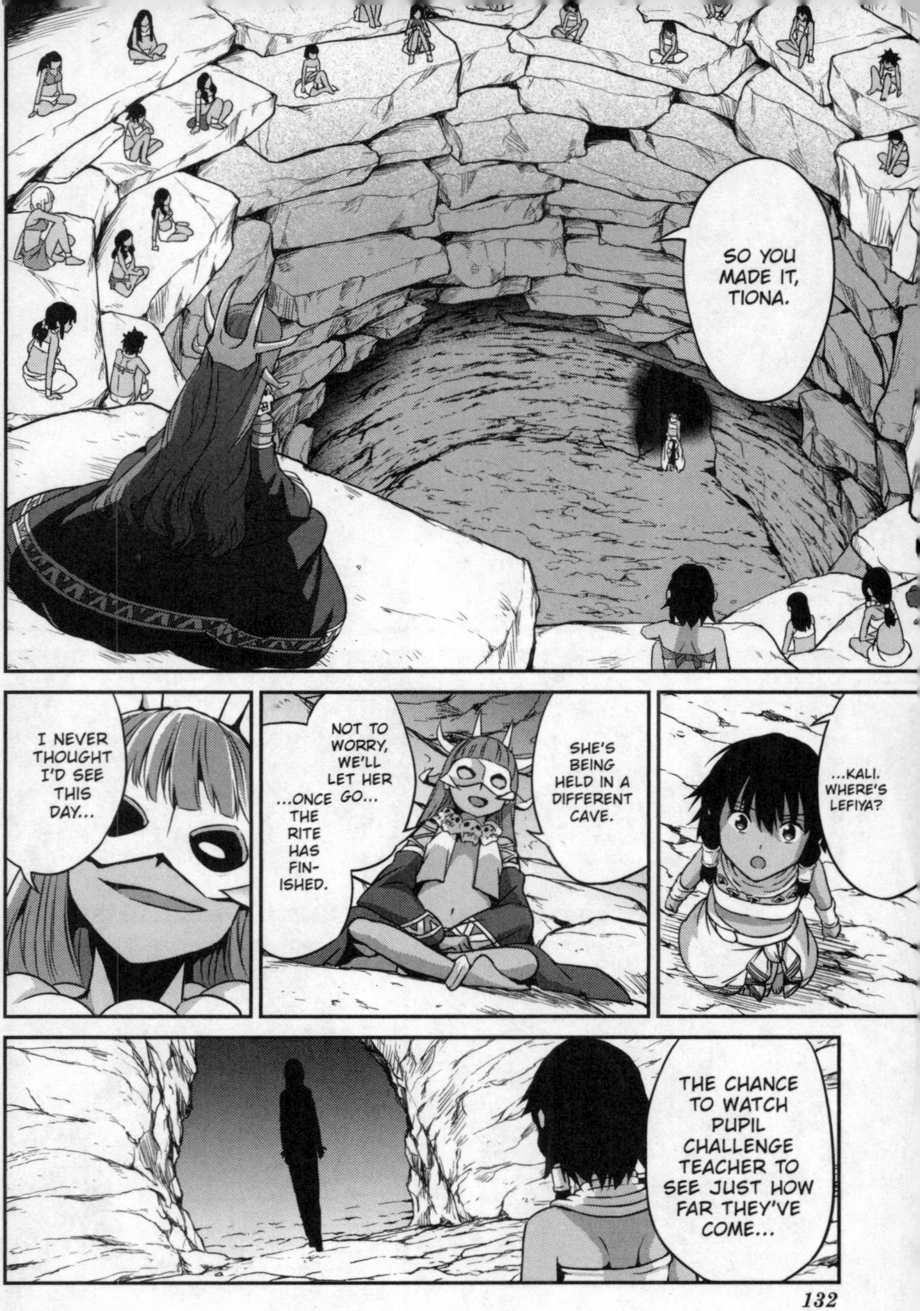
SO YOU MADE IT, TIONA.
...KALI. WHERE'S LEFIYA?
SHE'S BEING HELD IN A DIFFERENT CAVE.
NOT TO WORRY, WE'LL LET HER GO...
...ONCE THE RITE HAS FINISHED.
I NEVER THOUGHT I'D SEE THIS DAY...
THE CHANCE TO WATCH PUPIL CHALLENGE TEACHER TO SEE JUST HOW FAR THEY'VE COME...

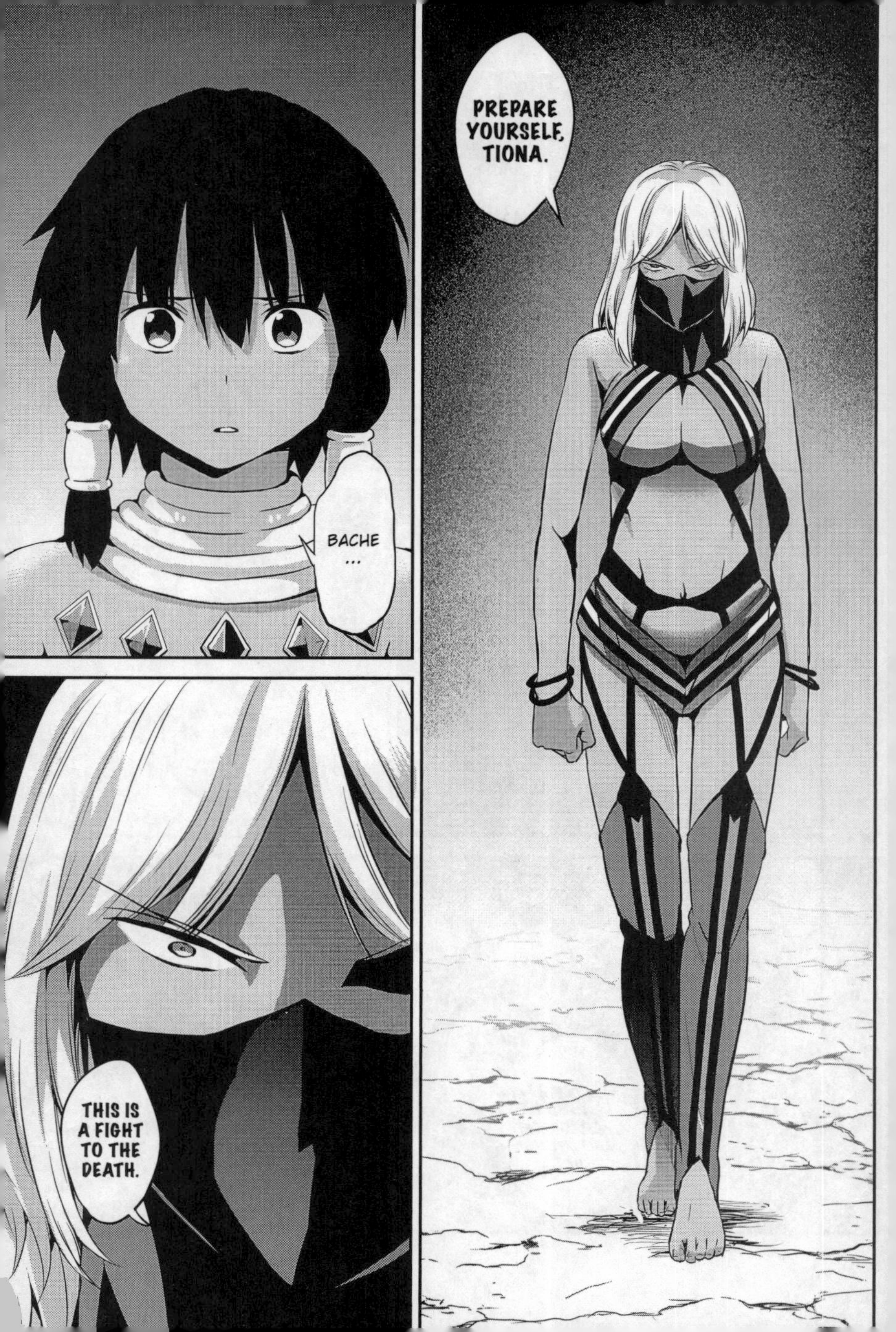
PREPARE YOURSELF, TIONA.
BACHE ...
THIS IS A FIGHT TO THE DEATH.

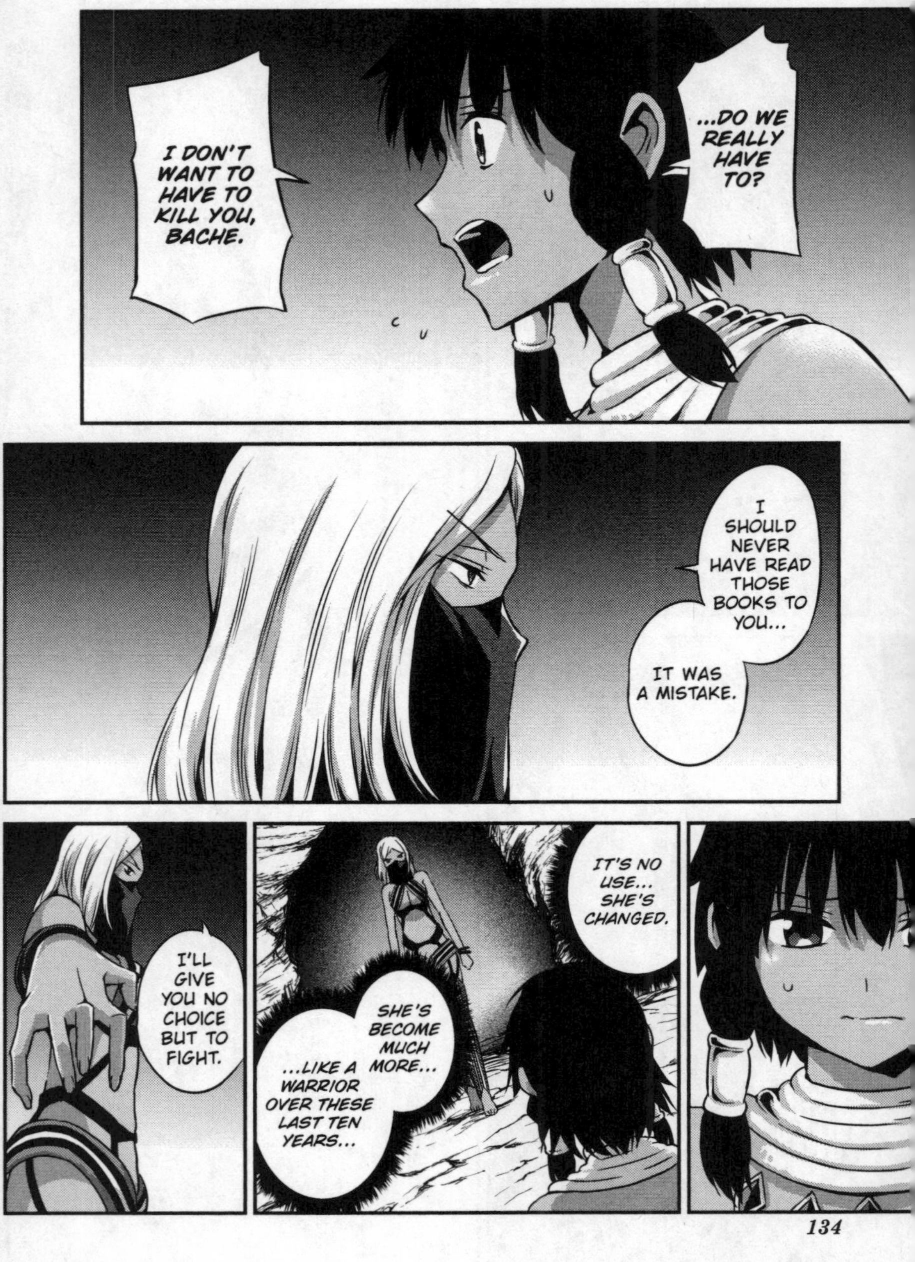
...DO WE REALLY HAVE TO?
I DON'T WANT TO HAVE TO KILL YOU, BACHE.
I SHOULD NEVER HAVE READ THOSE BOOKS TO YOU...
IT WAS A MISTAKE.
IT'S NO USE... SHE'S CHANGED.
SHE'S BECOME MUCH MORE...
...LIKE A WARRIOR OVER THESE LAST TEN YEARS...
I'LL GIVE YOU NO CHOICE BUT TO FIGHT.

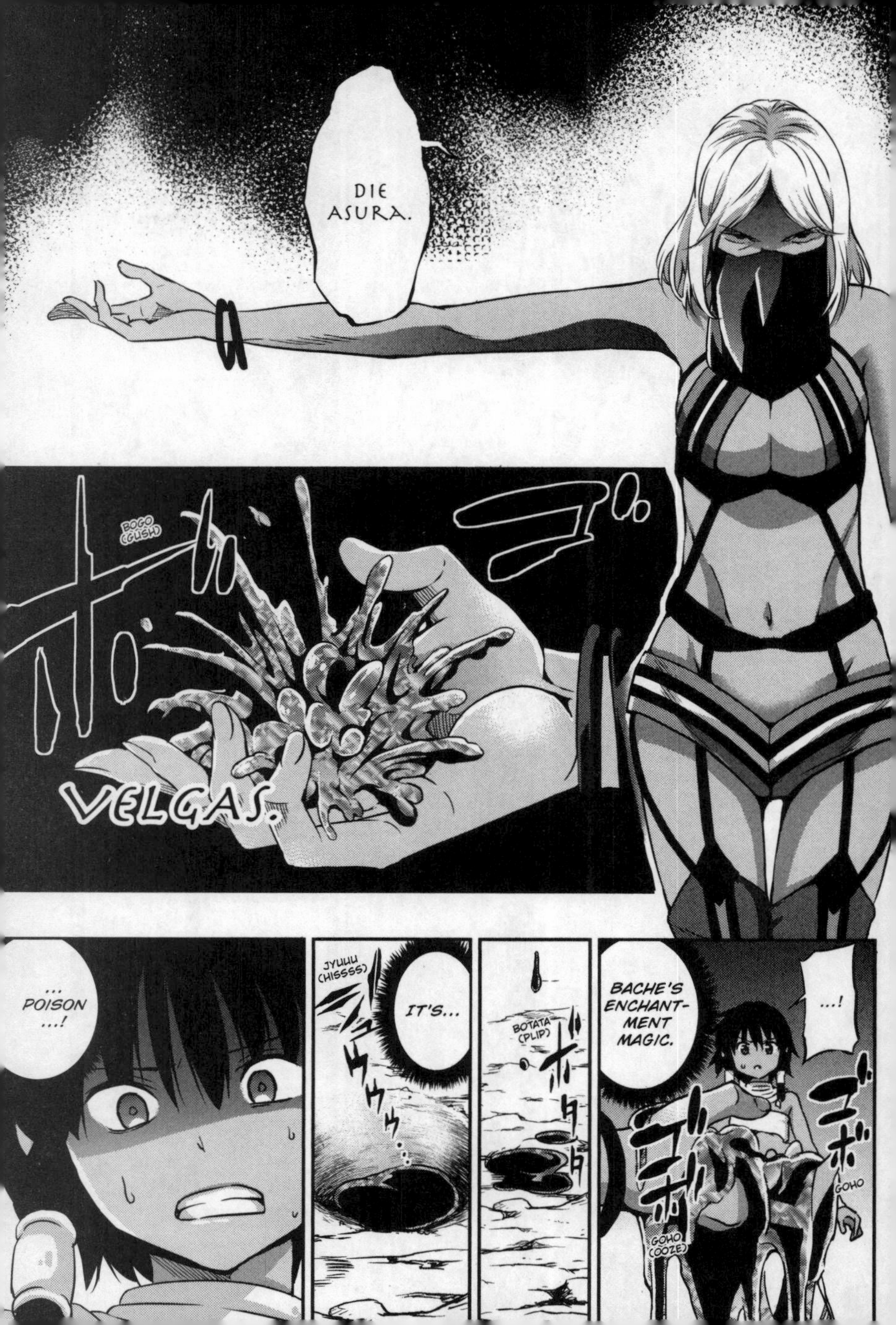
DIE ASURA.
BOGO (GUSH)
VELGAS.
...!
BACHE'S ENCHANTMENT MAGIC.
GOHO
GOHO (OOZE)
BOTATA (PLIP)
JYUUU (HISSSS)
IT'S...
...POISON ...!

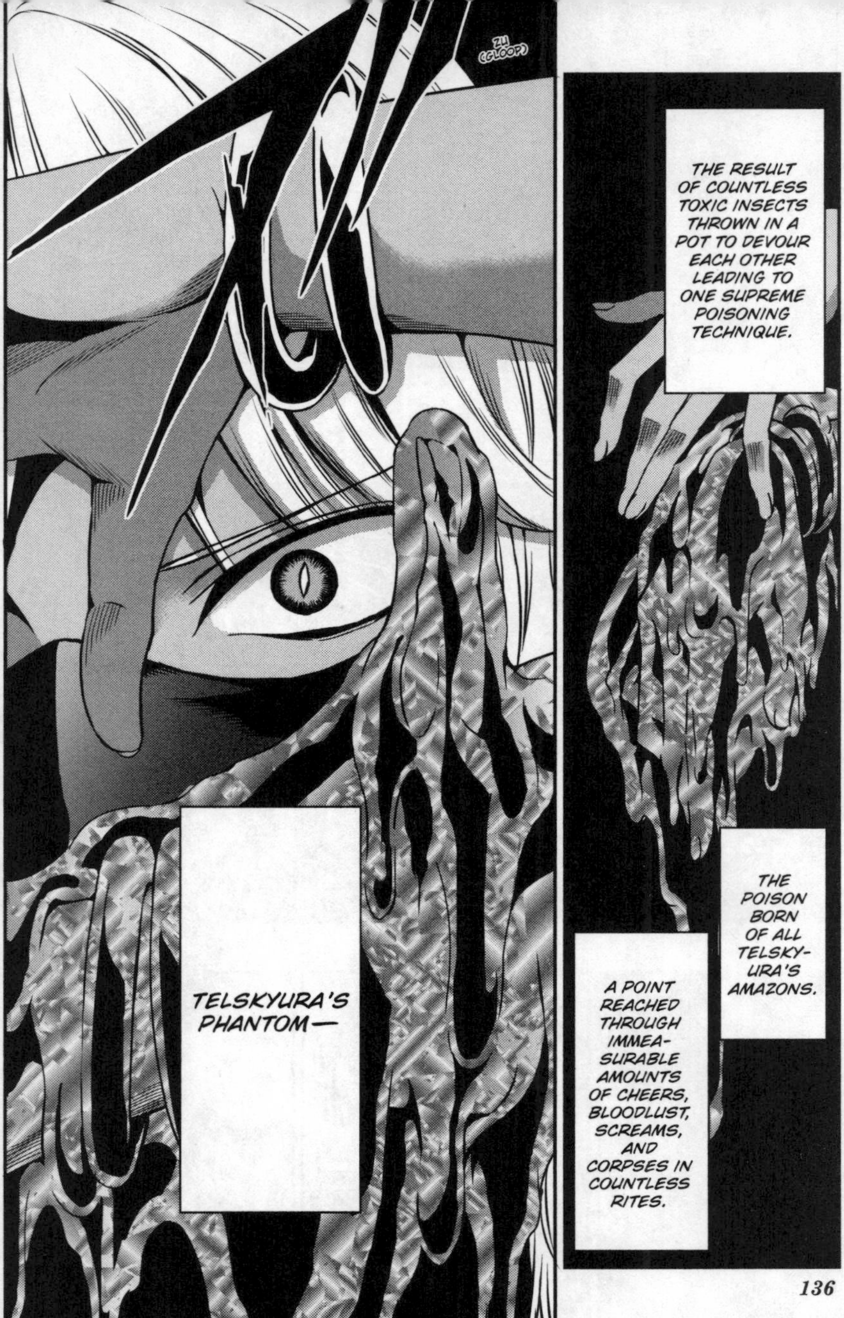
THE RESULT OF COUNTLESS TOXIC INSECTS THROWN IN A POT TO DEVOUR EACH OTHER LEADING TO ONE SUPREME POISONING TECHNIQUE.
THE POISON BORN OF ALL TELSKY-URA'S AMAZONS.
A POINT REACHED THROUGH IMMEA-SURABLE AMOUNTS OF CHEERS, BLOODLUST, SCREAMS, AND CORPSES IN COUNTLESS RITES.
ZU (GLOOP)
TELSKYURA'S PHANTOM—

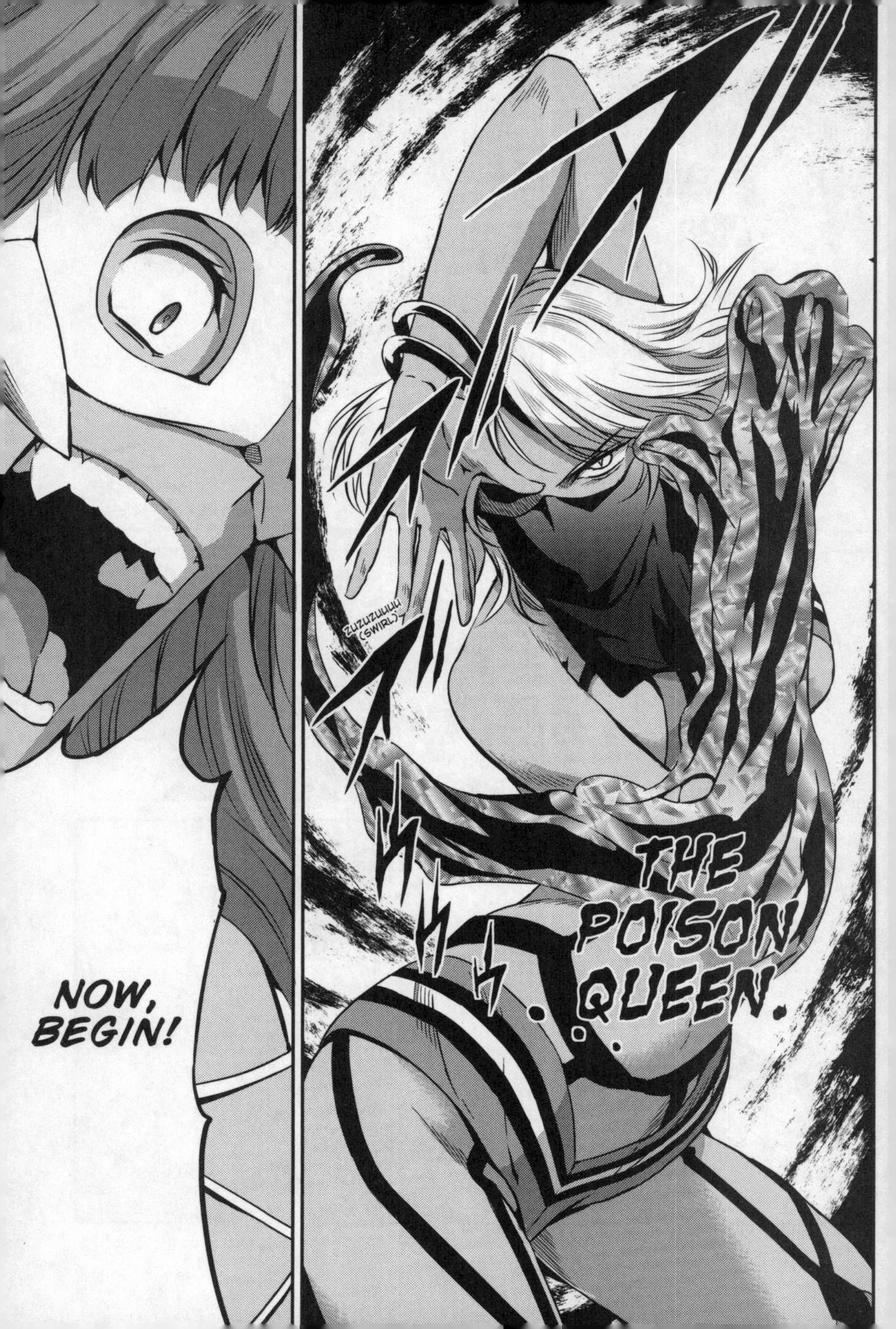
ZUZUZUUUU (SWIRL)
THE POISON QUEEN...
NOW, BEGIN!

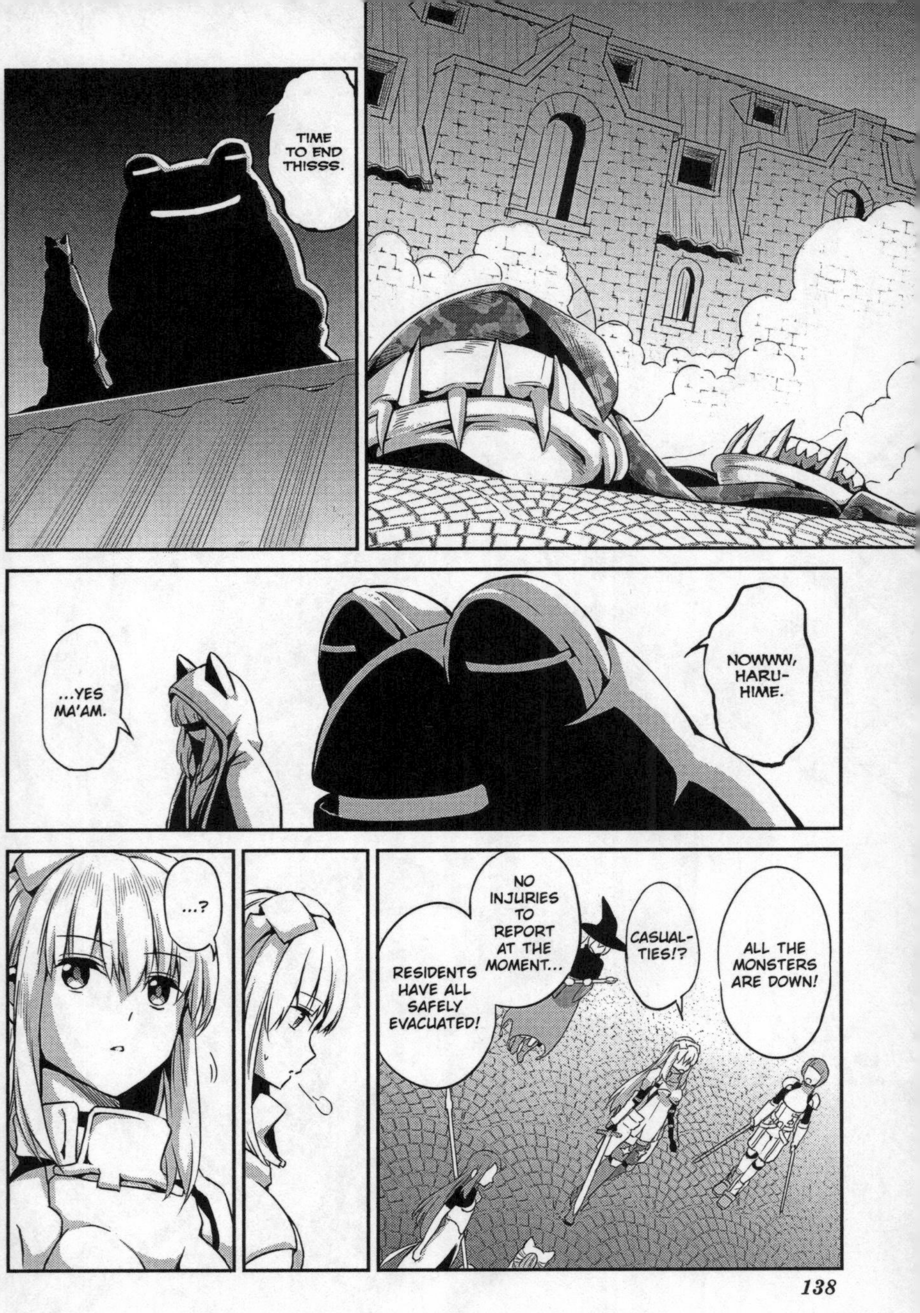
TIME TO END THISSS.
NOWWW, HARU-HIME.
...YES MA'AM.
ALL THE MONSTERS ARE DOWN!
CASUAL-TIES!?
NO INJURIES TO REPORT AT THE MOMENT...
RESIDENTS HAVE ALL SAFELY EVACUATED!
...?

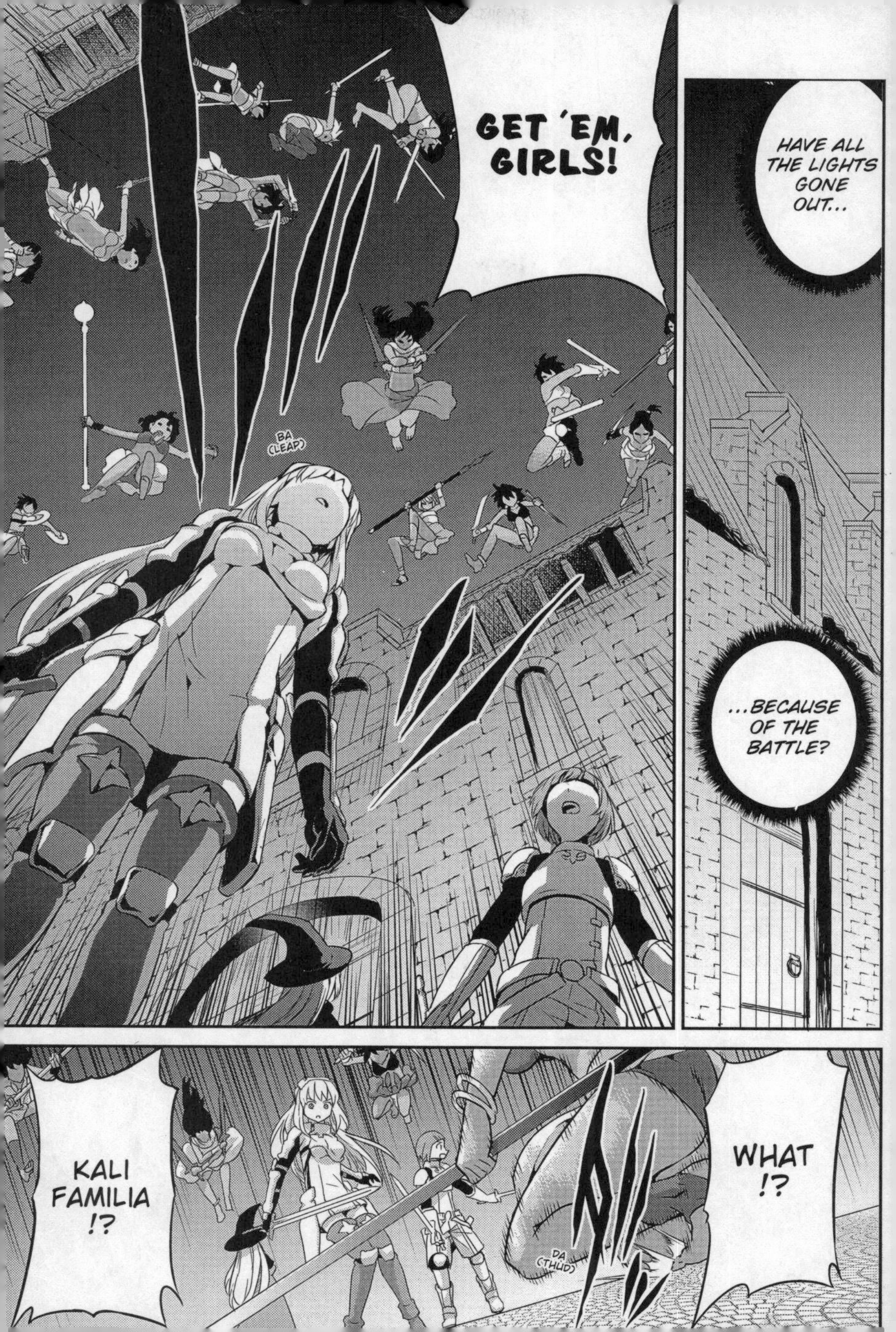
HAVE ALL THE LIGHTS GONE OUT...
...BECAUSE OF THE BATTLE?
GET 'EM, GIRLS!
BA (LEAP)
WHAT!?
KALI FAMILIA!?
DA (THUD)

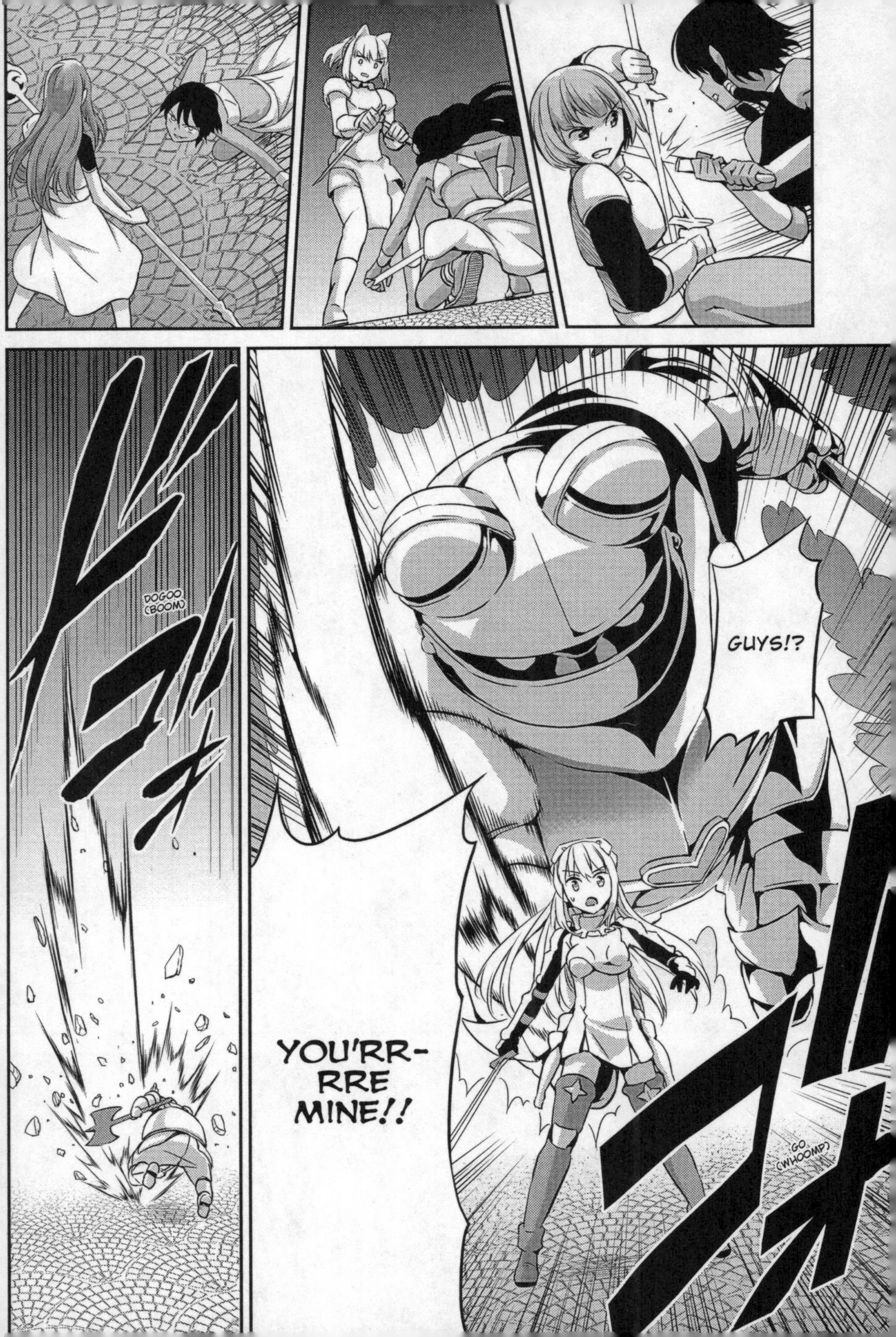
GUYS!?
YOU'RR-RRE MINE!!
GO (WHOOMP)
DOGOO (BOOM)

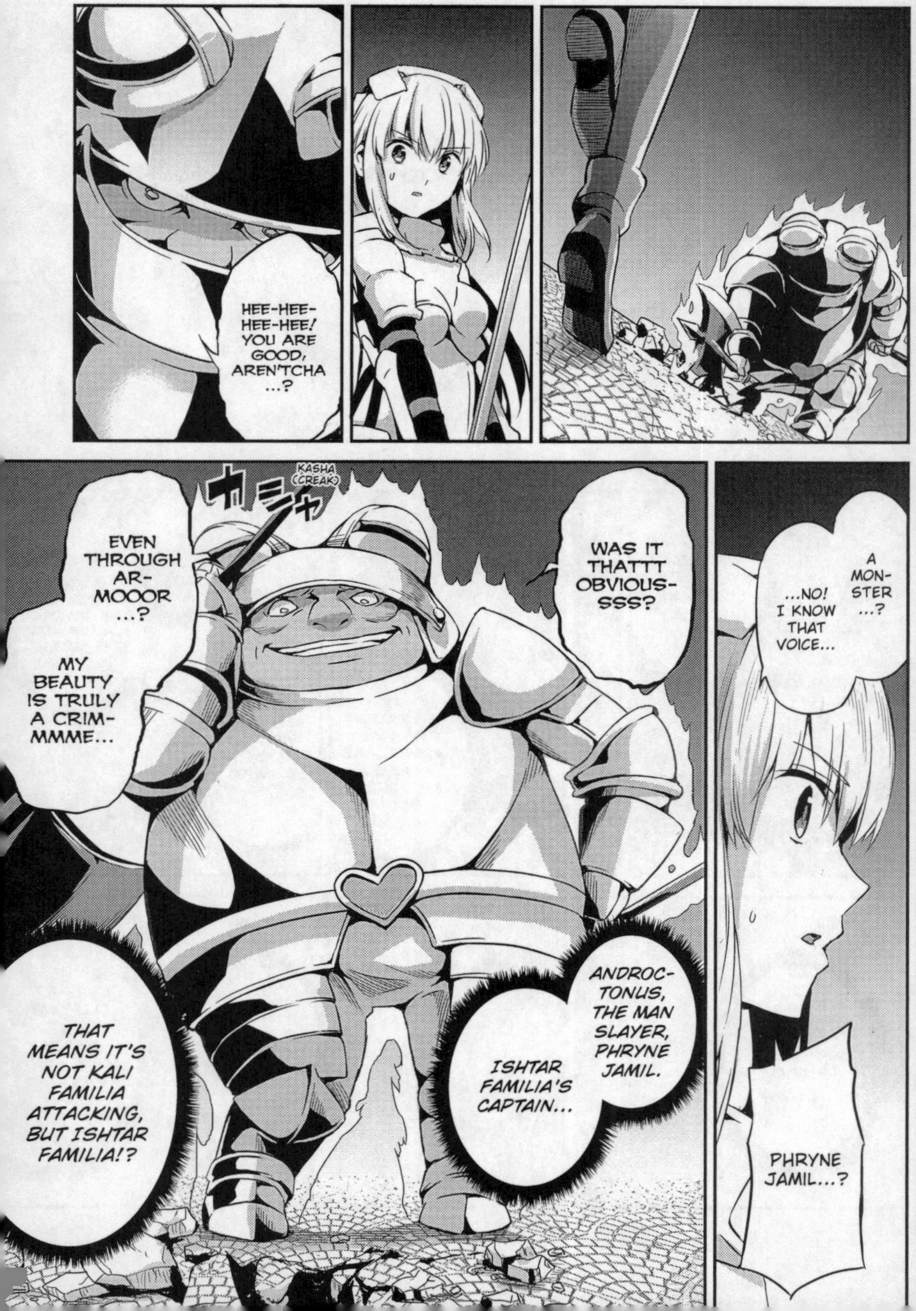
HEE-HEE-HEE-HEE! YOU ARE GOOD, AREN'TCHA ...?
A MONSTER ...?
...NO! I KNOW THAT VOICE...
PHRYNE JAMIL...?
KASHA (CREAK)
WAS IT THATTT OBVIOUSSS?
EVEN THROUGH AR-MOOOR ...?
MY BEAUTY IS TRULY A CRIM-MMME...
ANDROC-TONUS, THE MAN SLAYER, PHRYNE JAMIL.
ISHTAR FAMILIA'S CAPTAIN...
THAT MEANS IT'S NOT KALI FAMILIA ATTACKING, BUT ISHTAR FAMILIA!?

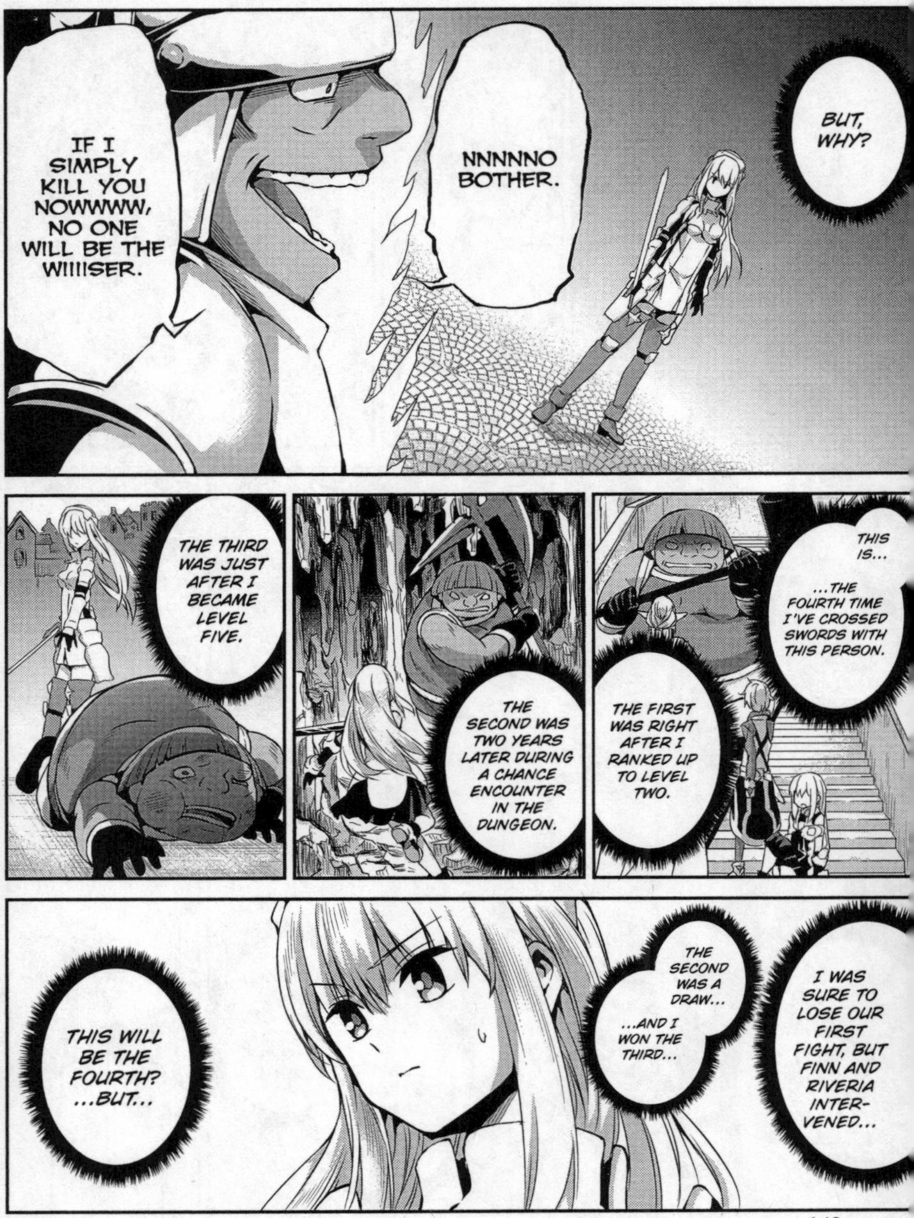
BUT, WHY?
NNNNNO BOTHER.
IF I SIMPLY KILL YOU NOWWWW, NO ONE WILL BE THE WIIIISER.
THIS IS...
...THE FOURTH TIME I'VE CROSSED SWORDS WITH THIS PERSON.
THE FIRST WAS RIGHT AFTER I RANKED UP TO LEVEL TWO.
THE SECOND WAS TWO YEARS LATER DURING A CHANCE ENCOUNTER IN THE DUNGEON.
THE THIRD WAS JUST AFTER I BECAME LEVEL FIVE.
I WAS SURE TO LOSE OUR FIRST FIGHT, BUT FINN AND RIVERIA INTER-VENED...
THE SECOND WAS A DRAW...
...AND I WON THE THIRD...
THIS WILL BE THE FOURTH? ...BUT...

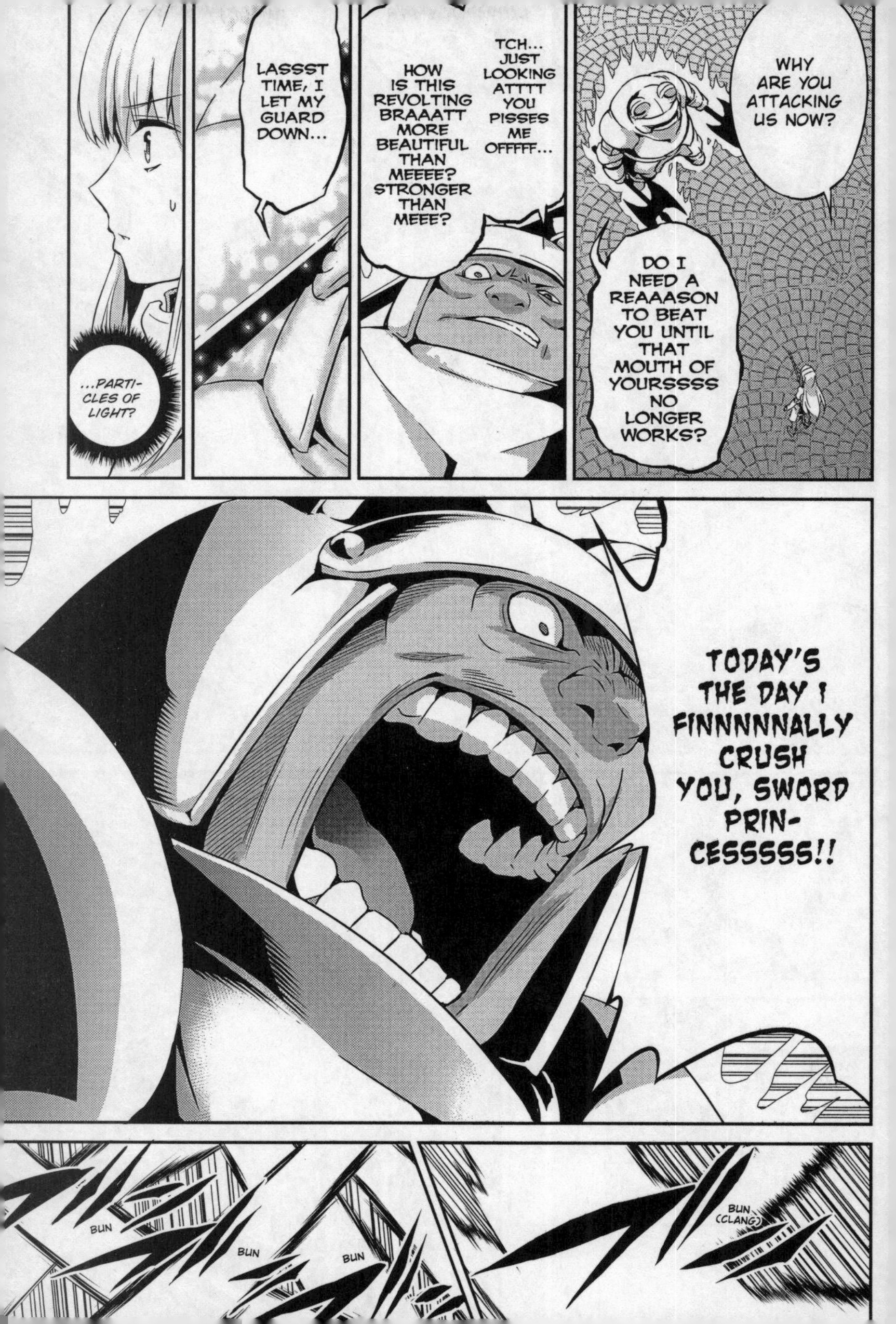
WHY ARE YOU ATTACKING US NOW?
DO I NEED A REAAAASON TO BEAT YOU UNTIL THAT MOUTH OF YOURSSSS NO LONGER WORKS?
TCH... JUST LOOKING ATTTT YOU PISSES ME OFFFFF...
HOW IS THIS REVOLTING BRAAATT MORE BEAUTIFUL THAN MEEEE? STRONGER THAN MEEE?
LASSST TIME, I LET MY GUARD DOWN...
...PARTI-CLES OF LIGHT?
TODAY'S THE DAY I FINNNNNALLY CRUSH YOU, SWORD PRIN-CESSSSS!!
BUN (CLANG)
BUN
BUN
BUN

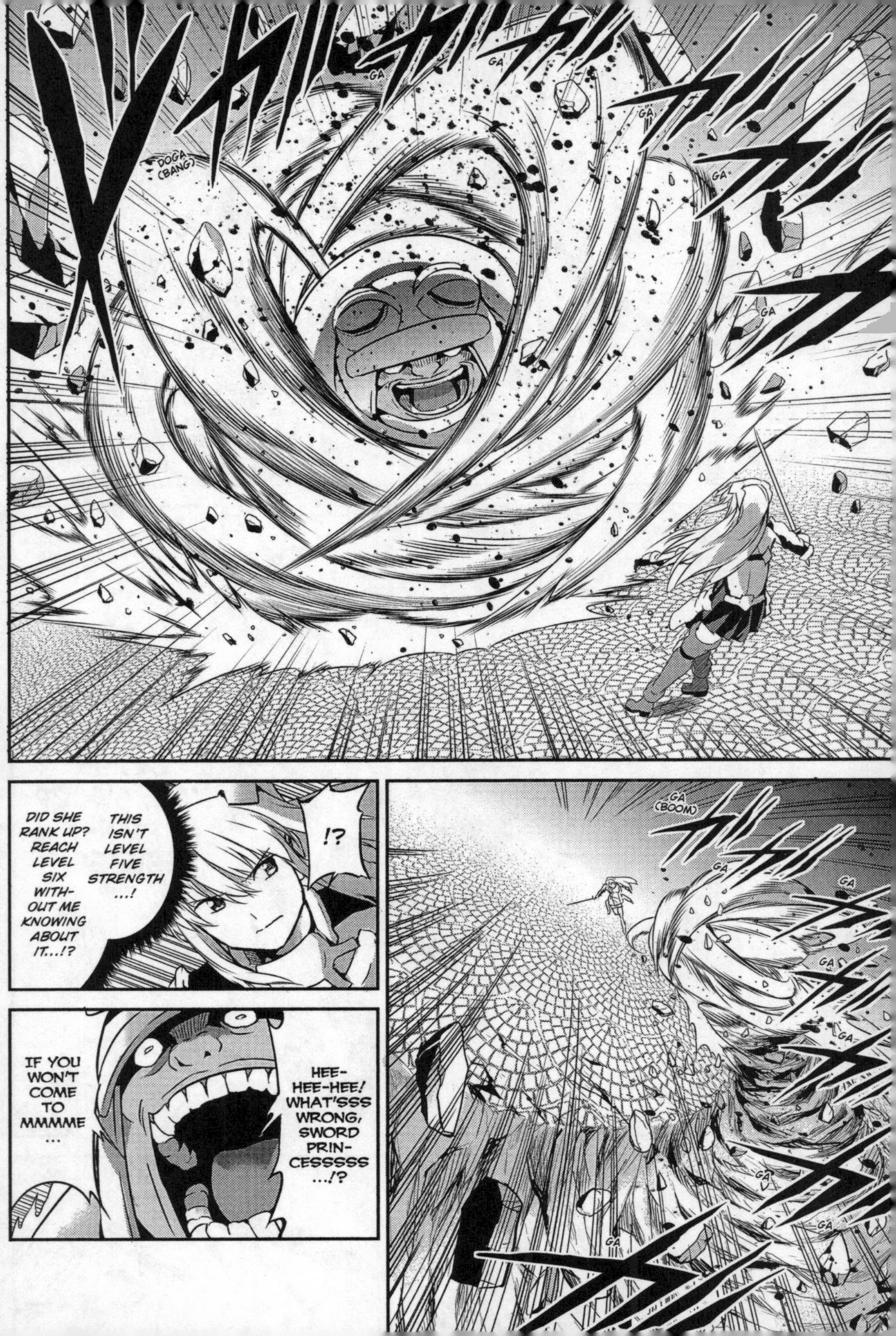
GA
GA
GA
GA
GA
DOGA (BANG)
GA (BOOM)
GA
GA
GA
GA
GA
GA
!?
THIS ISN'T LEVEL FIVE STRENGTH ...!
DID SHE RANK UP? REACH LEVEL SIX WITH-OUT ME KNOWING ABOUT IT...!?
HEE-HEE-HEE! WHAT'SSS WRONG, SWORD PRIN-CESSSSS ...!?
IF YOU WON'T COME TO MMMME ...

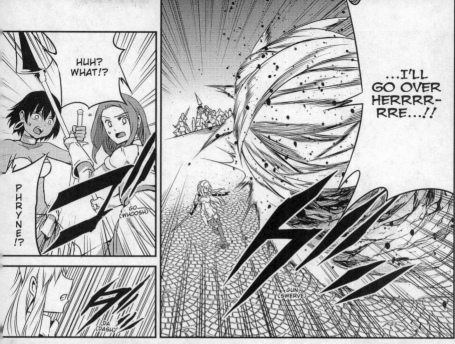

HUH? WHAT!?

PHRYNE!?

GO (WHOOSH)

...I'LL GO OVER HERRRR- RRE...!!

GUN (SWERVE)

DA (DASH)

GI (CLANG)

GI

GI

GI

GI

GA

NOWWW, SHARAY! DO IT NOWW- WW!!

PIK! (CRACK)

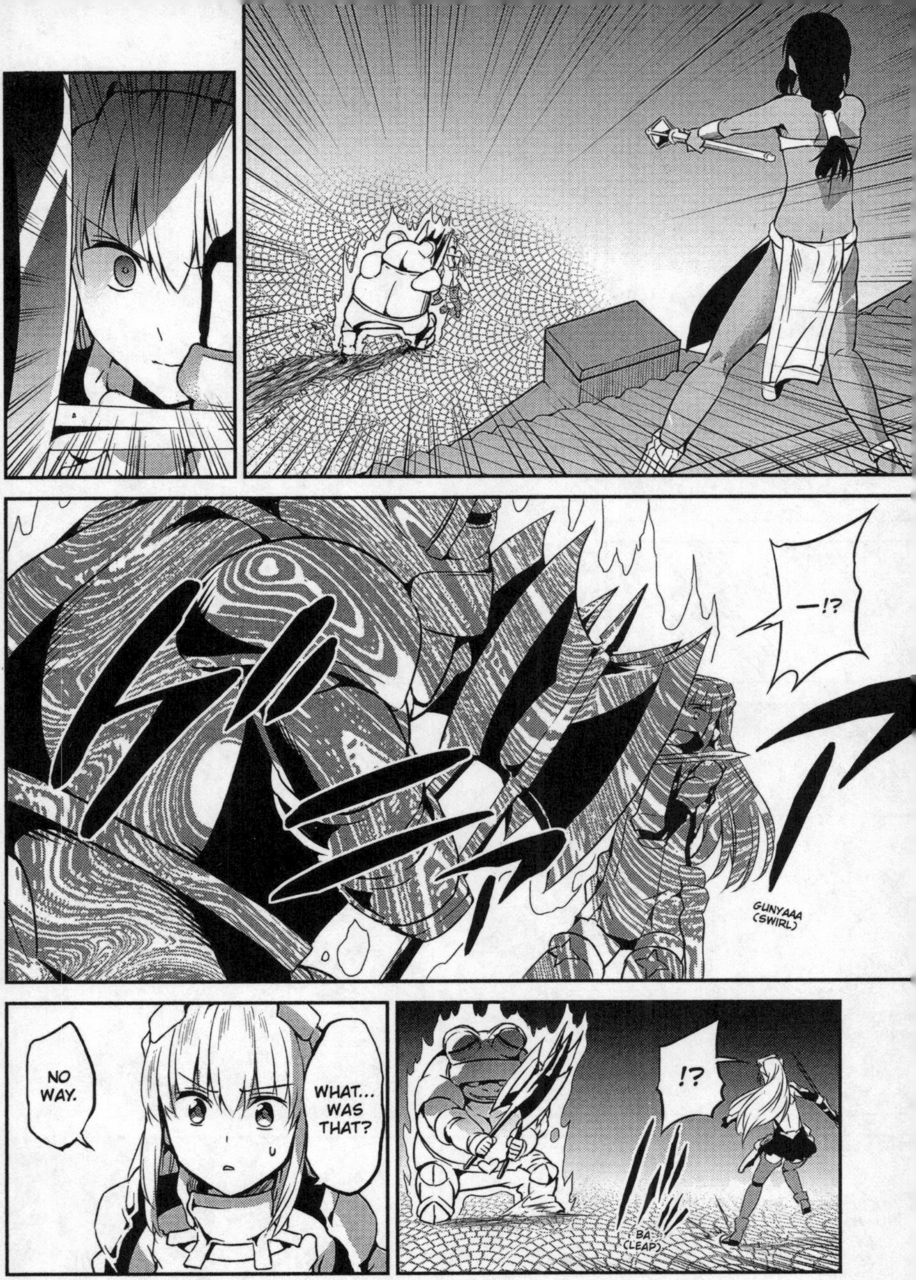
—!?
GUNYAAA (SWIRL)
!?
BA (LEAP)
WHAT... WAS THAT?
NO WAY.

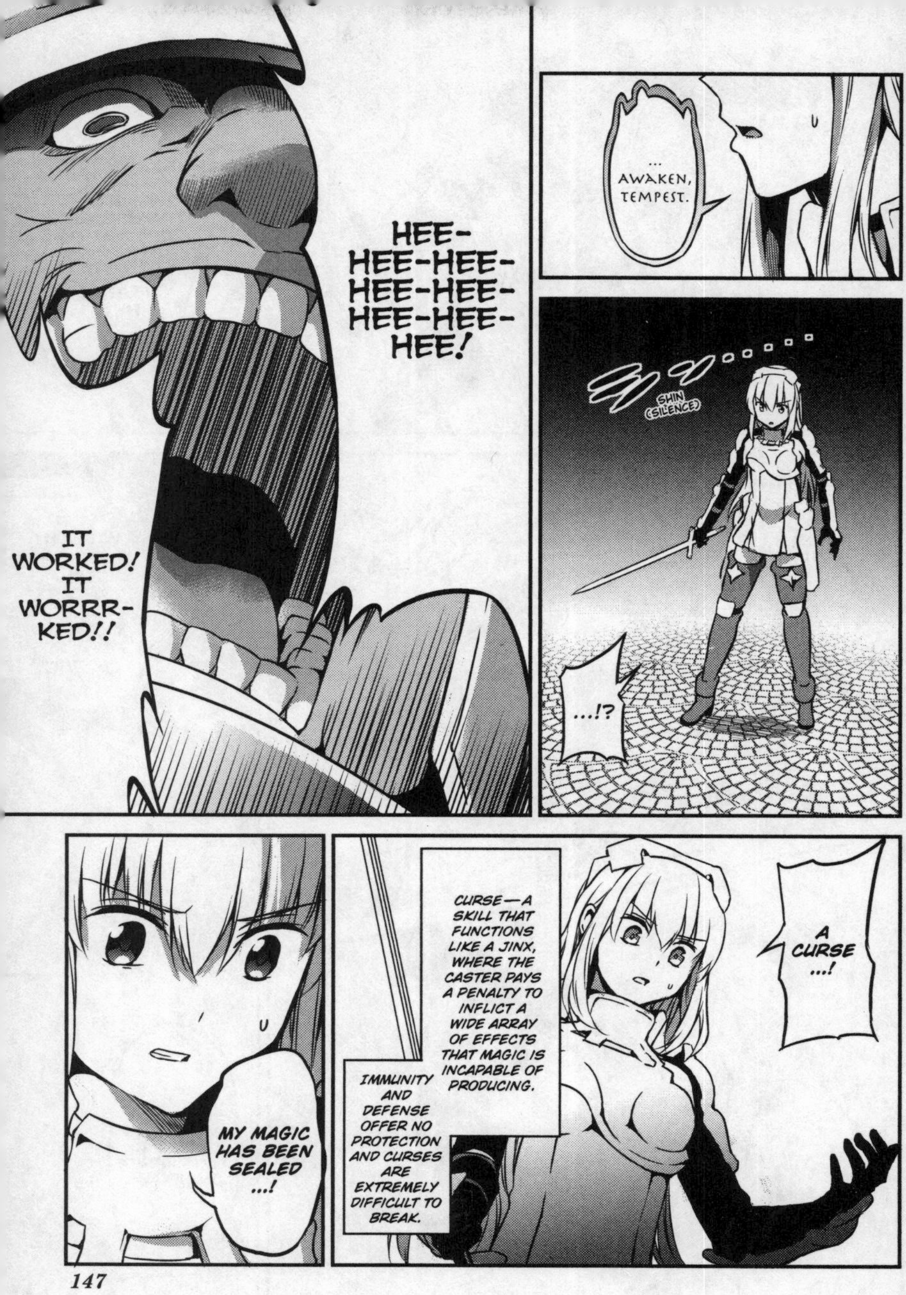
... AWAKEN, TEMPEST.
SHIN (SILENCE)
...!?
HEE-HEE-HEE-HEE-HEE-HEE-HEE!
IT WORKED! IT WORRRKED!!
A CURSE ...!
CURSE—A SKILL THAT FUNCTIONS LIKE A JINX, WHERE THE CASTER PAYS A PENALTY TO INFLICT A WIDE ARRAY OF EFFECTS THAT MAGIC IS INCAPABLE OF PRODUCING.
IMMUNITY AND DEFENSE OFFER NO PROTECTION AND CURSES ARE EXTREMELY DIFFICULT TO BREAK.
MY MAGIC HAS BEEN SEALED ...!

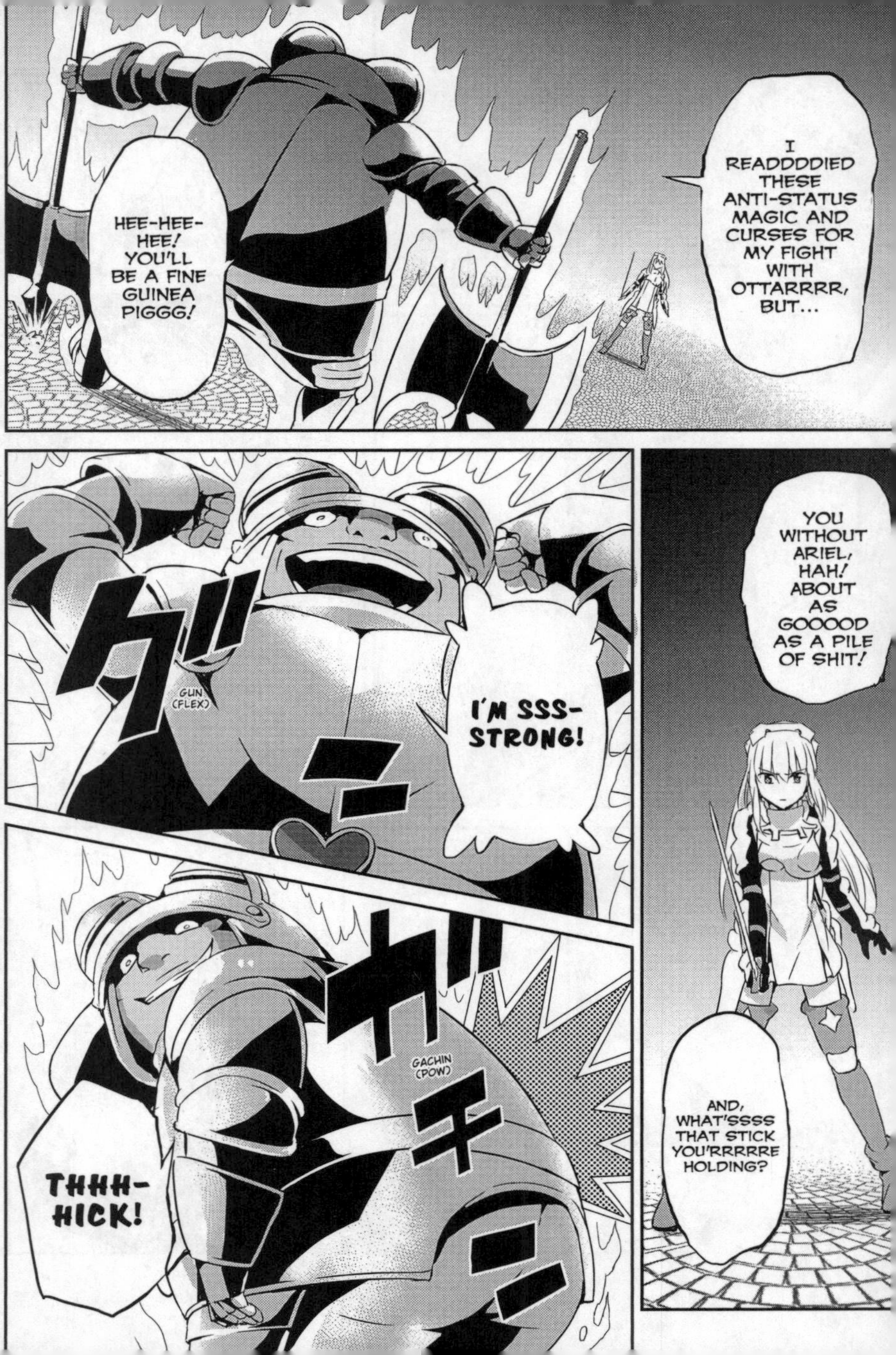
I READDDDIED THESE ANTI-STATUS MAGIC AND CURSES FOR MY FIGHT WITH OTTARRRR, BUT...
HEE-HEE-HEE! YOU'LL BE A FINE GUINEA PIGGG!
YOU WITHOUT ARIEL, HAH! ABOUT AS GOOOOD AS A PILE OF SHIT!
AND, WHAT'SSSS THAT STICK YOU'RRRRRE HOLDING?
I'M SSS-STRONG!
GUN (FLEX)
GACHIN (POW)
THHH-HICK!

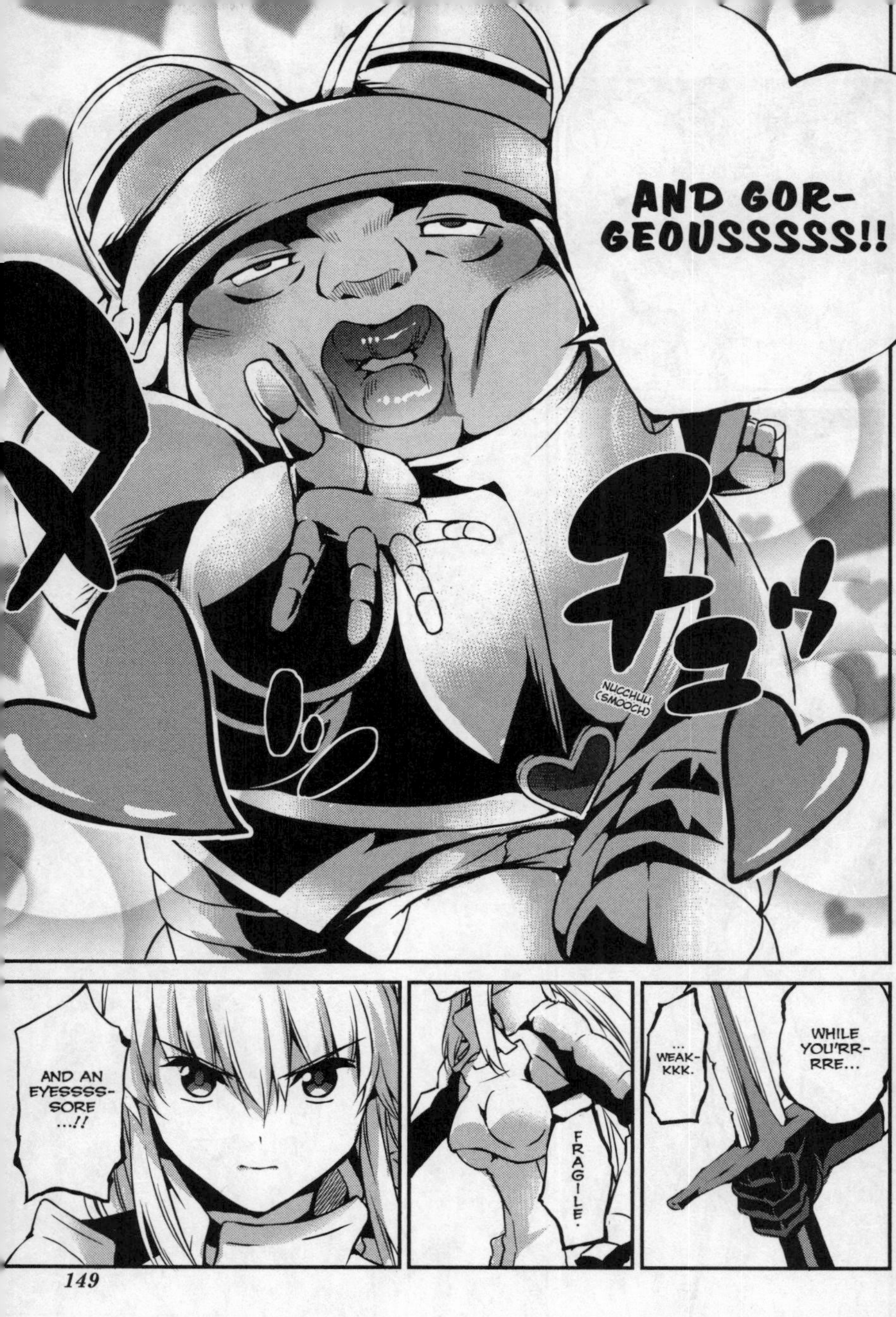
AND GOR-
GEOUSSSSS!!
NUCCHUU
(SMOOCH)
WHILE YOU'RRRRE...
...WEAKKKK.
FRAGILE.
AND AN EYESSSS-SORE ...!!

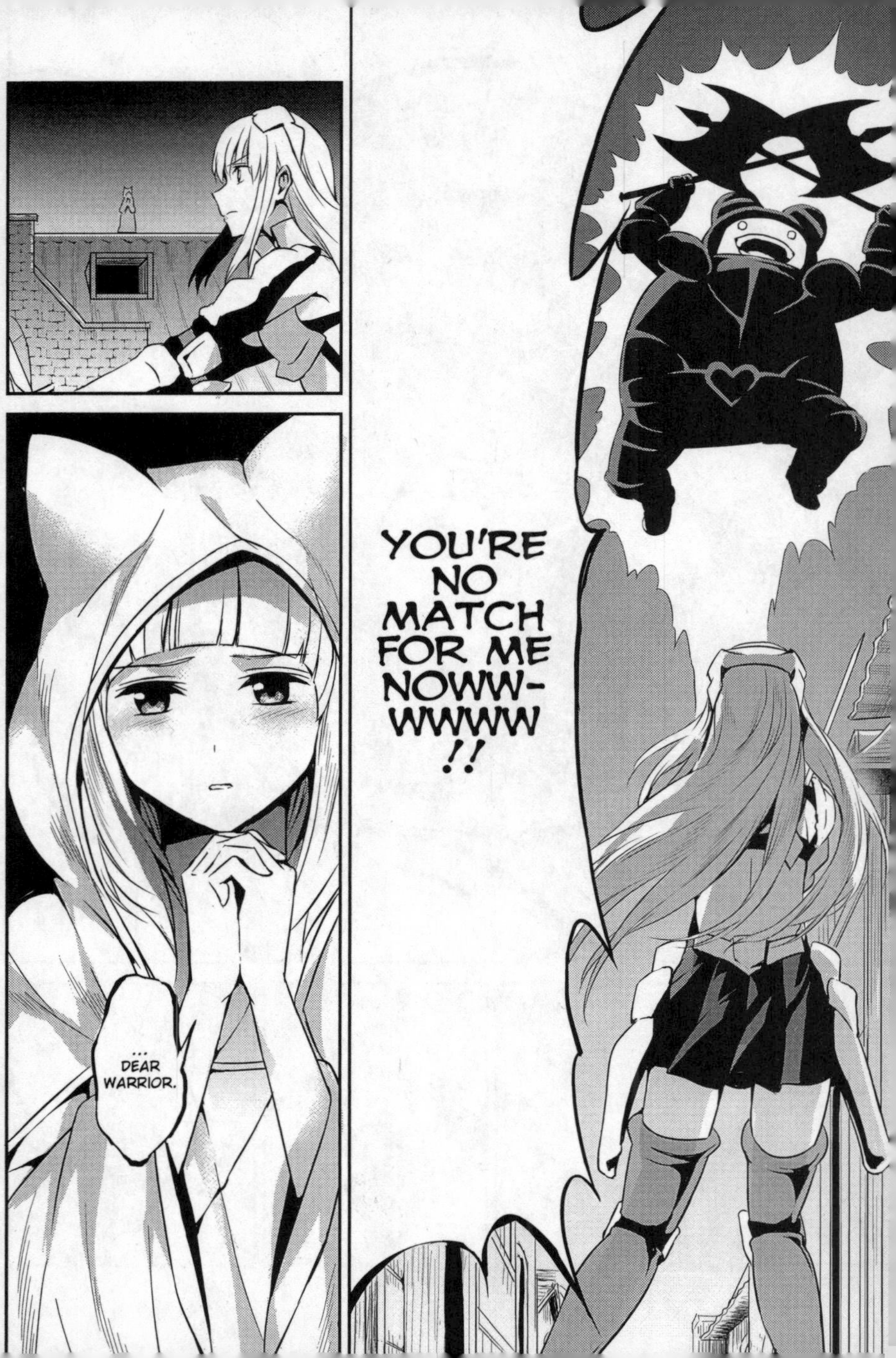
YOU'RE NO MATCH FOR ME NOWW-WWWW!!
... DEAR WARRIOR.

Is it WRONG to TRY to PICK UP GIRLS IN A DUNGEON? ON THE SIDE

Sword Oratoria

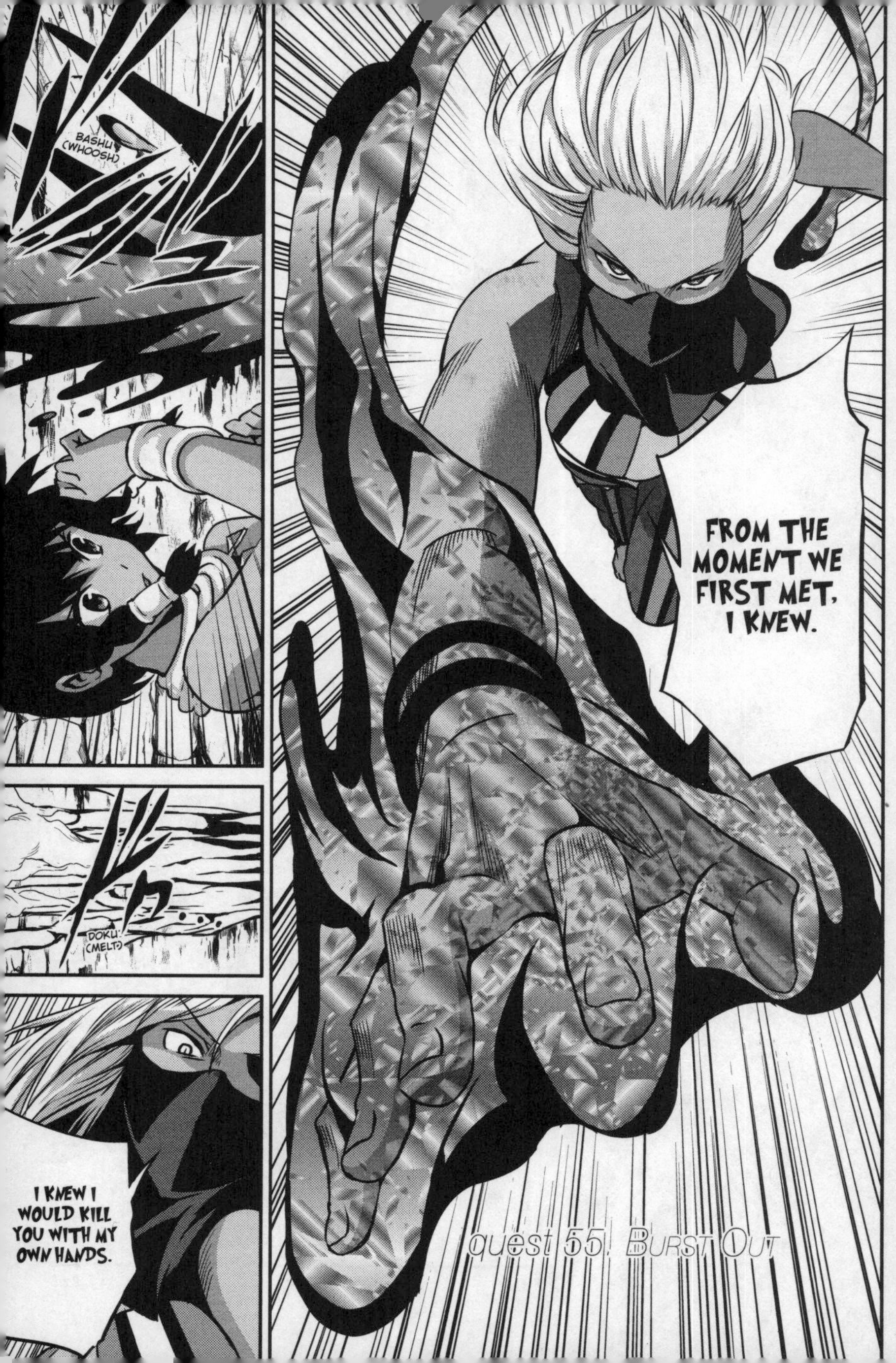
FROM THE MOMENT WE FIRST MET, I KNEW.
quest 55: Burst Out
BASHU (WHOOSH)
DOKU (MELT)
I KNEW I WOULD KILL YOU WITH MY OWN HANDS.

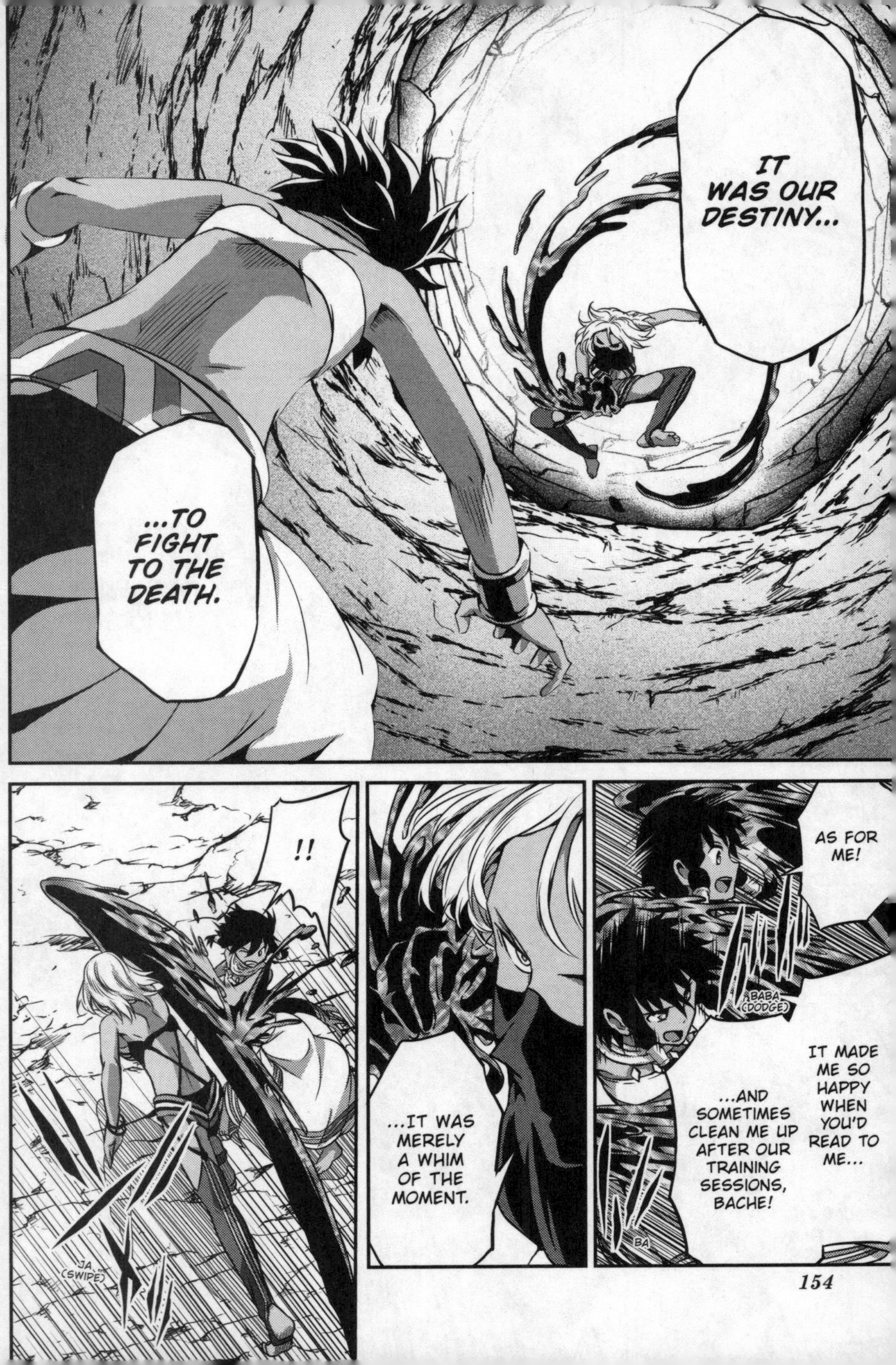
IT WAS OUR DESTINY...
...TO FIGHT TO THE DEATH.
AS FOR ME!
BABA (DODGE)
IT MADE ME SO HAPPY WHEN YOU'D READ TO ME...
...AND SOMETIMES CLEAN ME UP AFTER OUR TRAINING SESSIONS, BACHE!
BA
...IT WAS MERELY A WHIM OF THE MOMENT.
!!
JA (SWIPE)

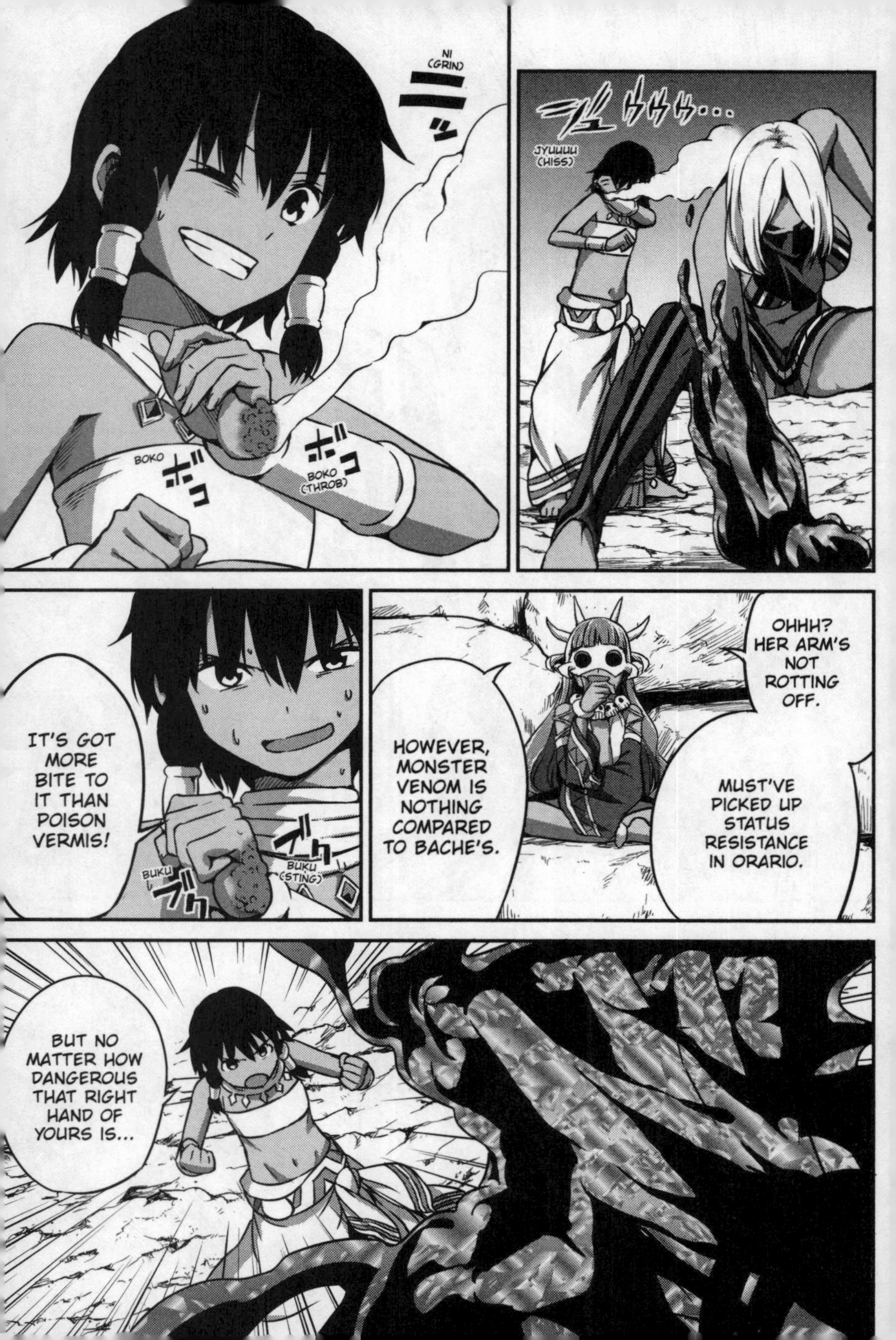
ジュゥゥゥ…
JYUUUU (HISS)
NI (GRIN)
BOKO
BOKO (THROB)
OHHH? HER ARM'S NOT ROTTING OFF.
MUST'VE PICKED UP STATUS RESISTANCE IN ORARIO.
HOWEVER, MONSTER VENOM IS NOTHING COMPARED TO BACHE'S.
IT'S GOT MORE BITE TO IT THAN POISON VERMIS!
BUKU (STING)
BUKU
BUT NO MATTER HOW DANGEROUS THAT RIGHT HAND OF YOURS IS...

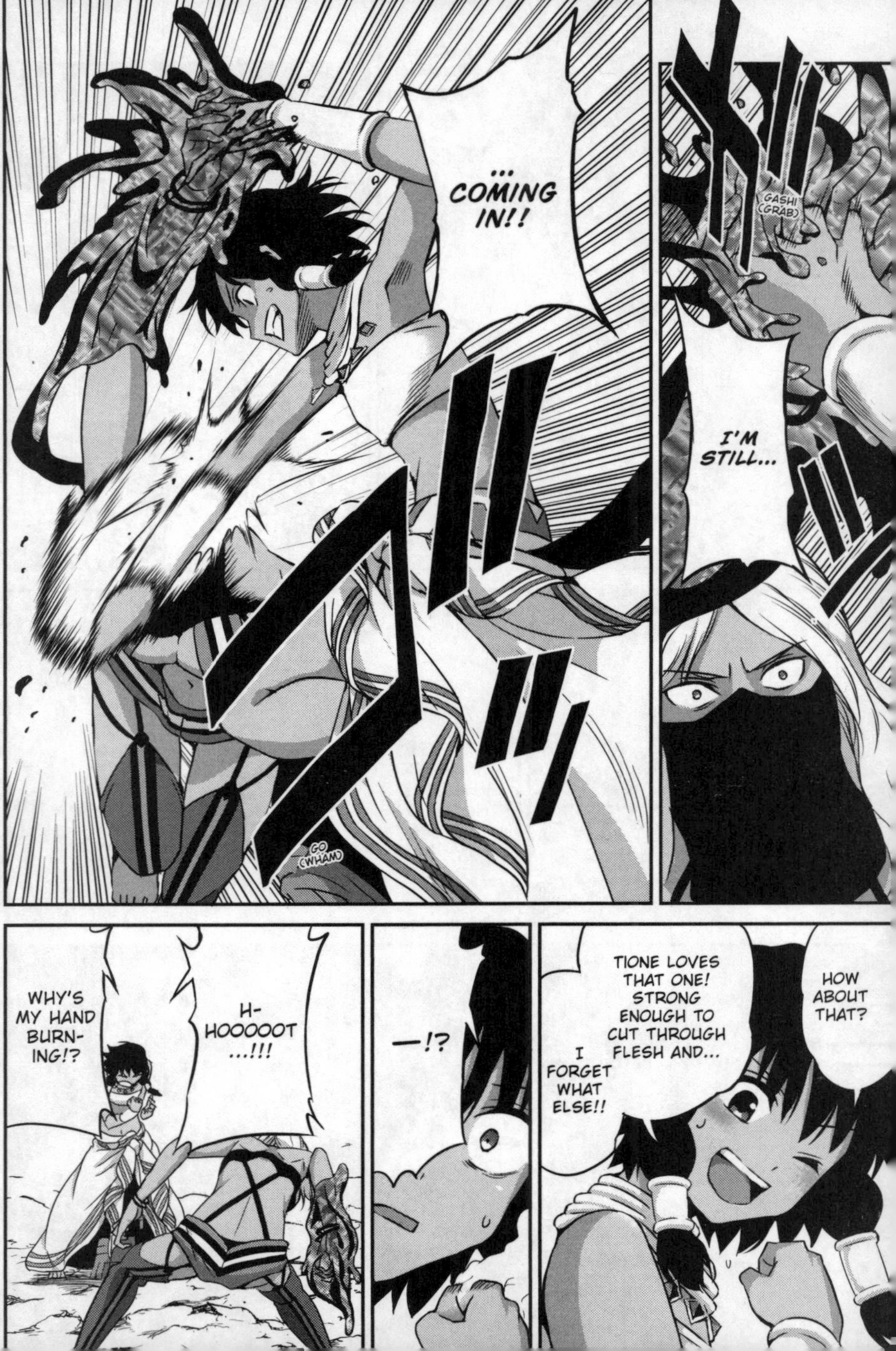
GASHI (GRAB)
I'M STILL...
... COMING IN!!
GO (WHAM)
HOW ABOUT THAT?
TIONE LOVES THAT ONE! STRONG ENOUGH TO CUT THROUGH FLESH AND...
I FORGET WHAT ELSE!!
—!?
H-HOOOOOT ...!!!
WHY'S MY HAND BURNING!?

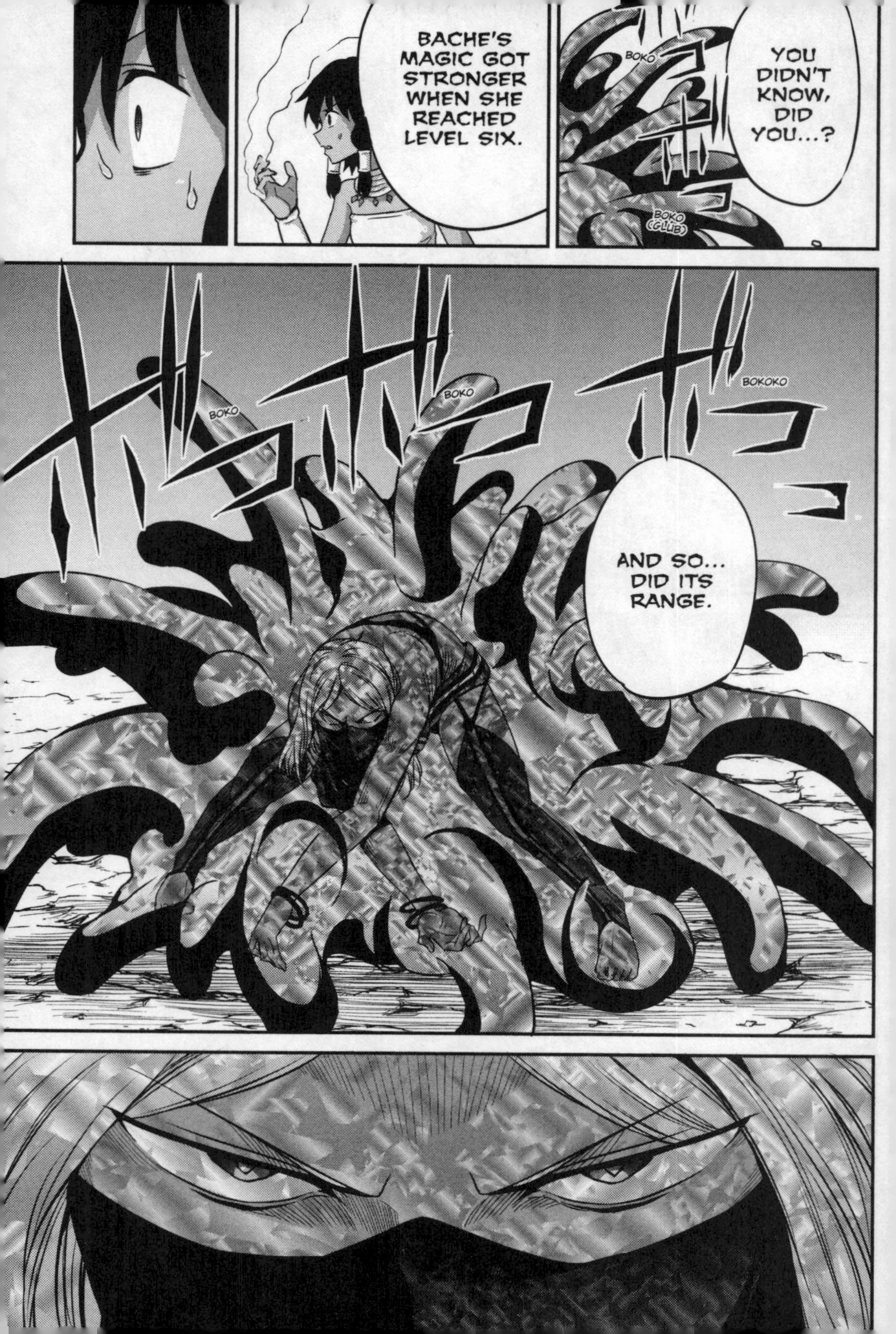
BOKO
YOU DIDN'T KNOW, DID YOU...?
BOKO (GLUB)
BACHE'S MAGIC GOT STRONGER WHEN SHE REACHED LEVEL SIX.
BOKOKO
BOKO
BOKO
AND SO... DID ITS RANGE.

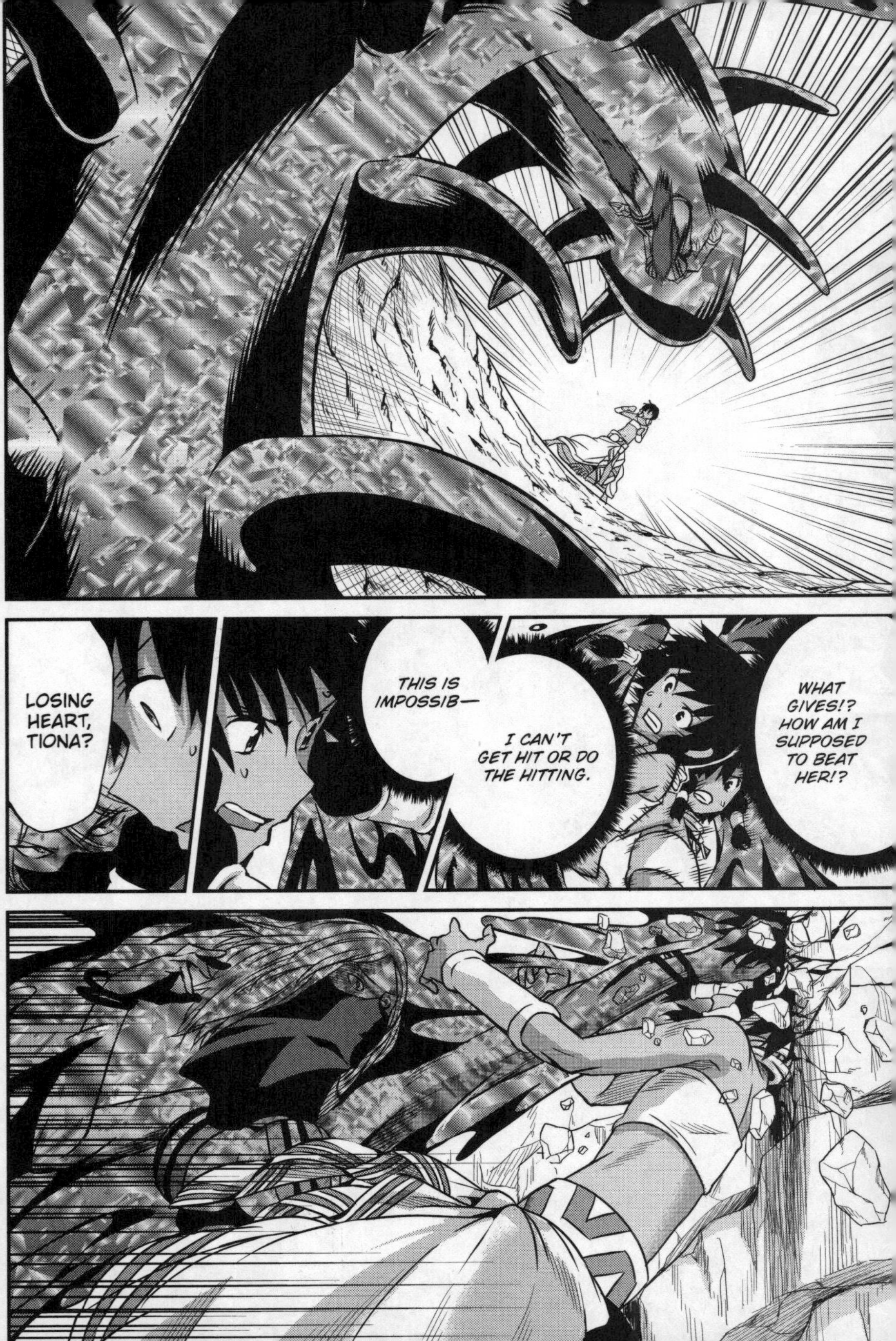
WHAT GIVES!? HOW AM I SUPPOSED TO BEAT HER!?
THIS IS IMPOSSIB—
I CAN'T GET HIT OR DO THE HITTING.
LOSING HEART, TIONA?

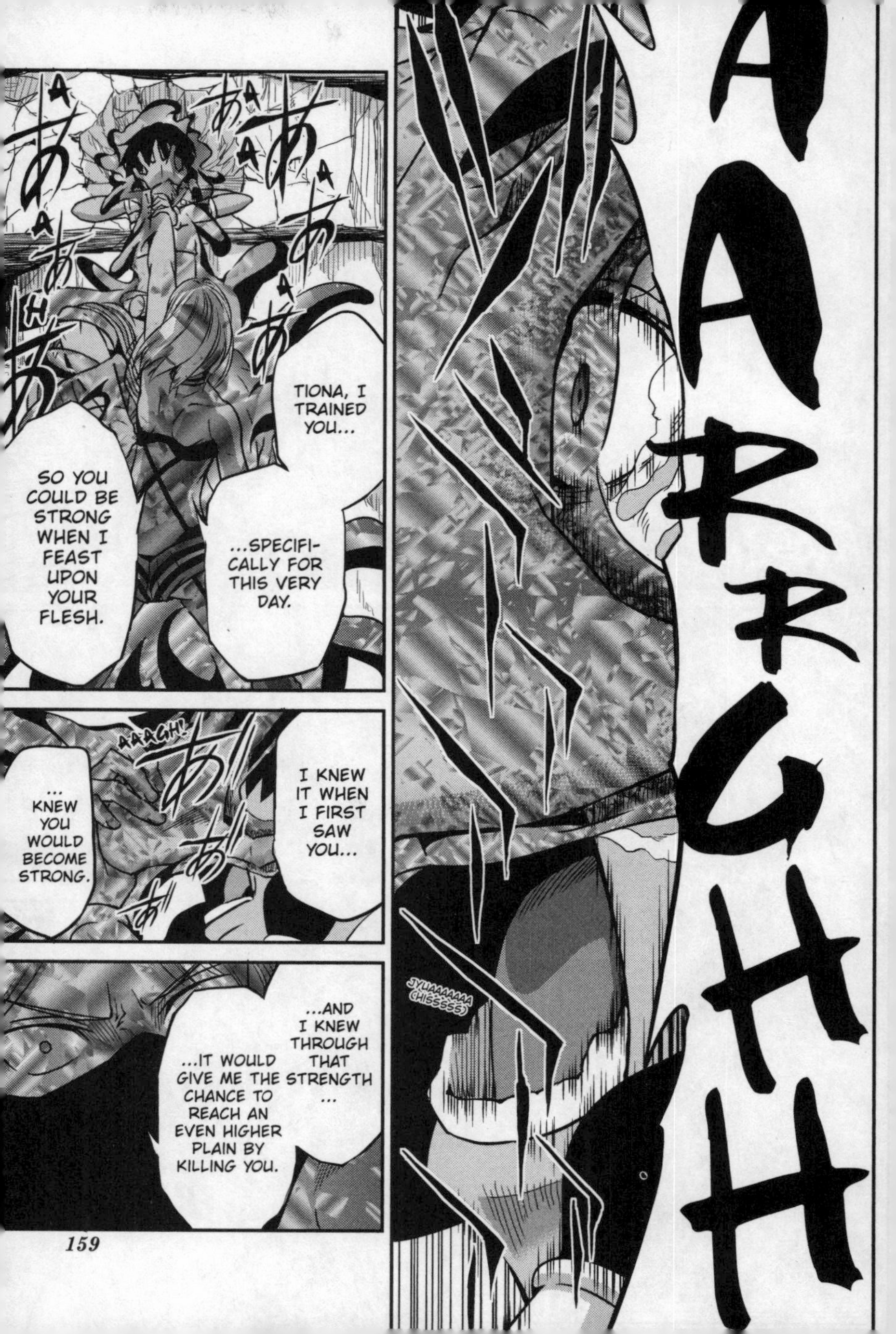
AAARRGHHH
JYUAAAAAAA (HISSSSSS)
TIONA, I TRAINED YOU...
...SPECIFICALLY FOR THIS VERY DAY.
SO YOU COULD BE STRONG WHEN I FEAST UPON YOUR FLESH.
AAAGH!
I KNEW IT WHEN I FIRST SAW YOU...
...KNEW YOU WOULD BECOME STRONG.
...AND I KNEW THROUGH THAT STRENGTH...
...IT WOULD GIVE ME THE CHANCE TO REACH AN EVEN HIGHER PLAIN BY KILLING YOU.

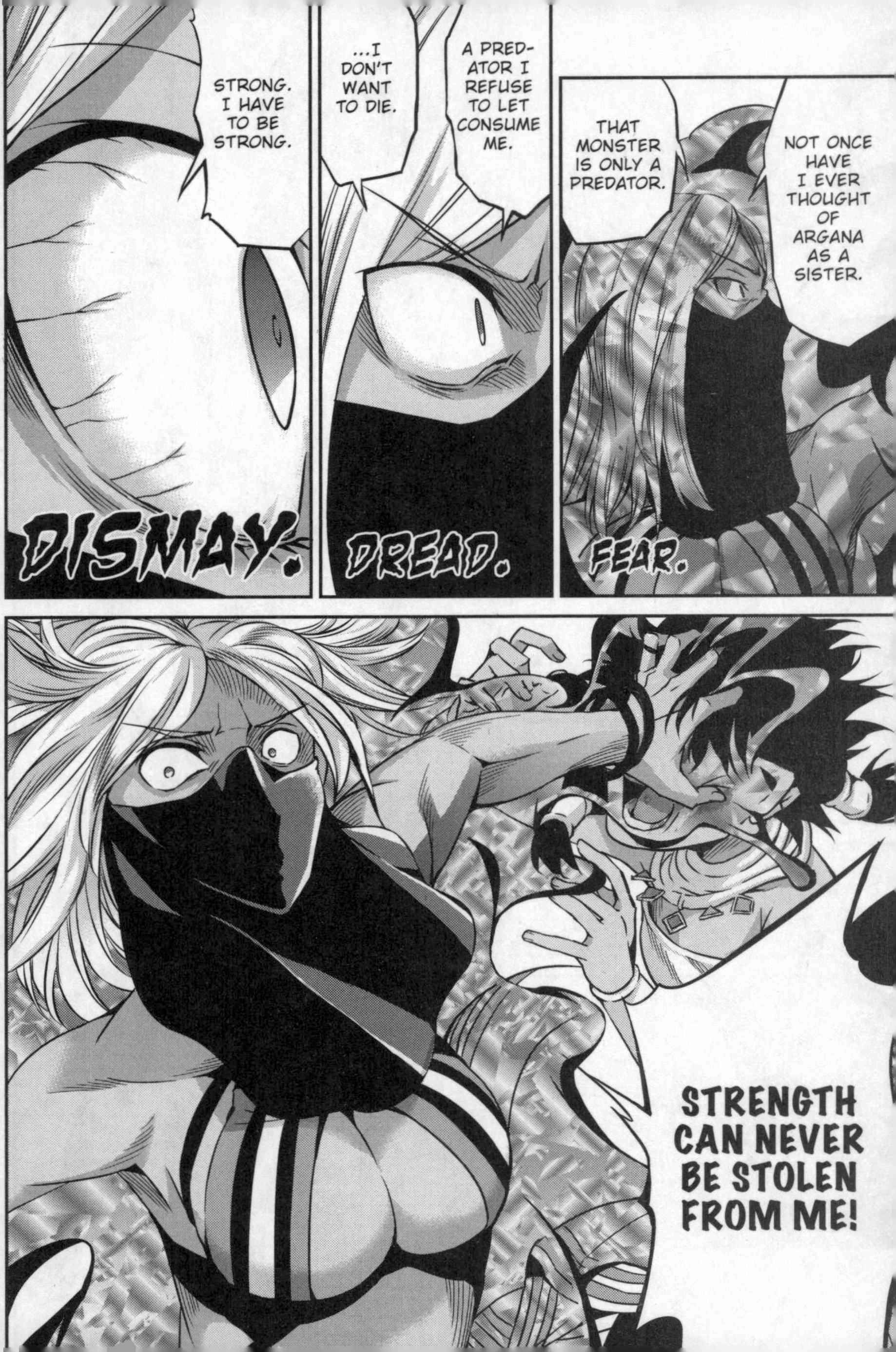
NOT ONCE HAVE I EVER THOUGHT OF ARGANA AS A SISTER.
THAT MONSTER IS ONLY A PREDATOR.
FEAR.
A PRED-ATOR I REFUSE TO LET CONSUME ME.
...I DON'T WANT TO DIE.
DREAD.
STRONG. I HAVE TO BE STRONG.
DISMAY.
STRENGTH CAN NEVER BE STOLEN FROM ME!

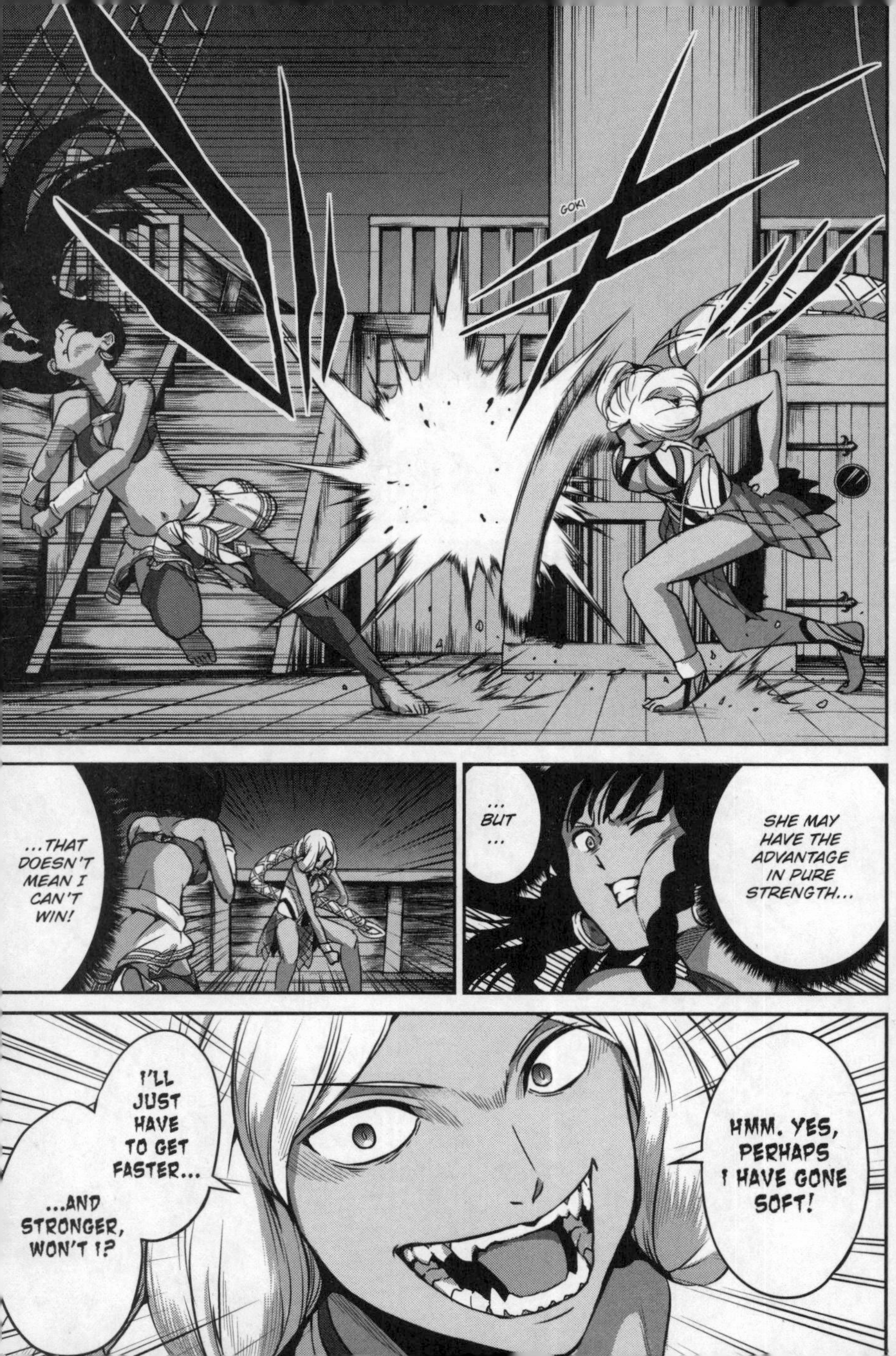
GOKI
SHE MAY HAVE THE ADVANTAGE IN PURE STRENGTH...
...BUT...
...THAT DOESN'T MEAN I CAN'T WIN!
HMM. YES, PERHAPS I HAVE GONE SOFT!
I'LL JUST HAVE TO GET FASTER...
...AND STRONGER, WON'T I?

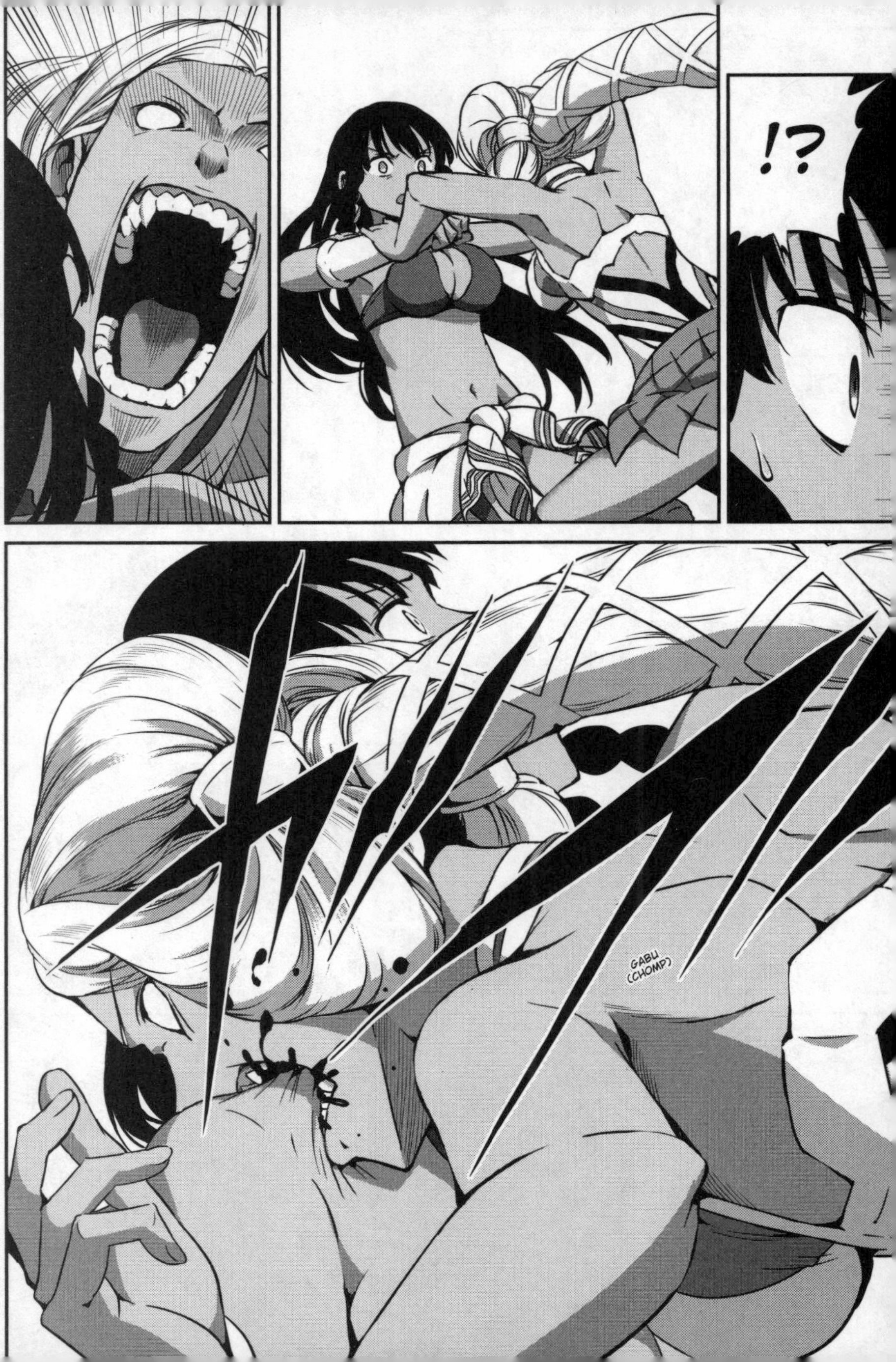
!?
GABU
(CHOMP)

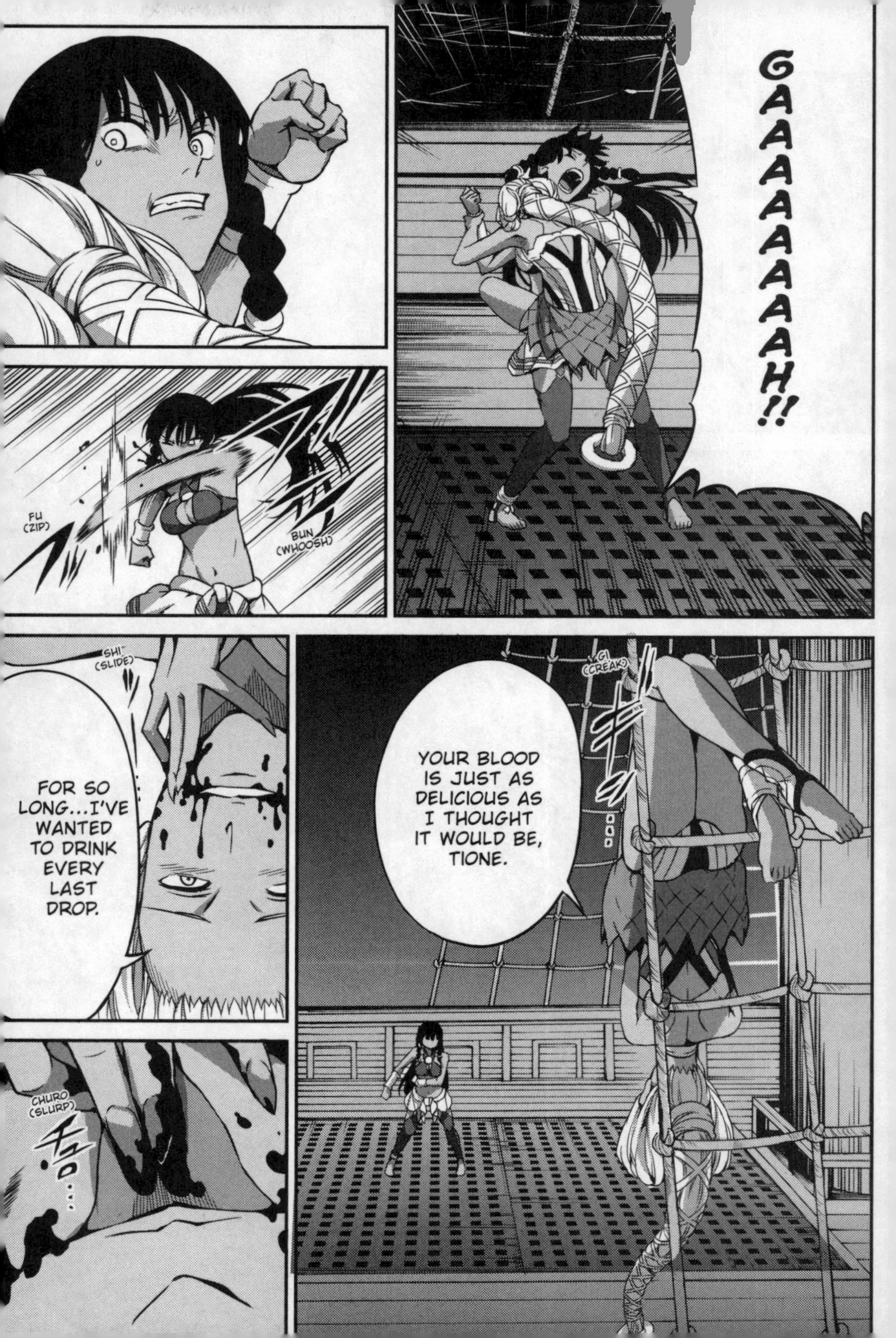
GAAAAAAAAAH!!
BUN (WHOOSH)
FU (ZIP)
GI (CREAK)
YOUR BLOOD IS JUST AS DELICIOUS AS I THOUGHT IT WOULD BE, TIONE.
SHI (SLIDE)
FOR SO LONG...I'VE WANTED TO DRINK EVERY LAST DROP.
CHURO (SLURP)

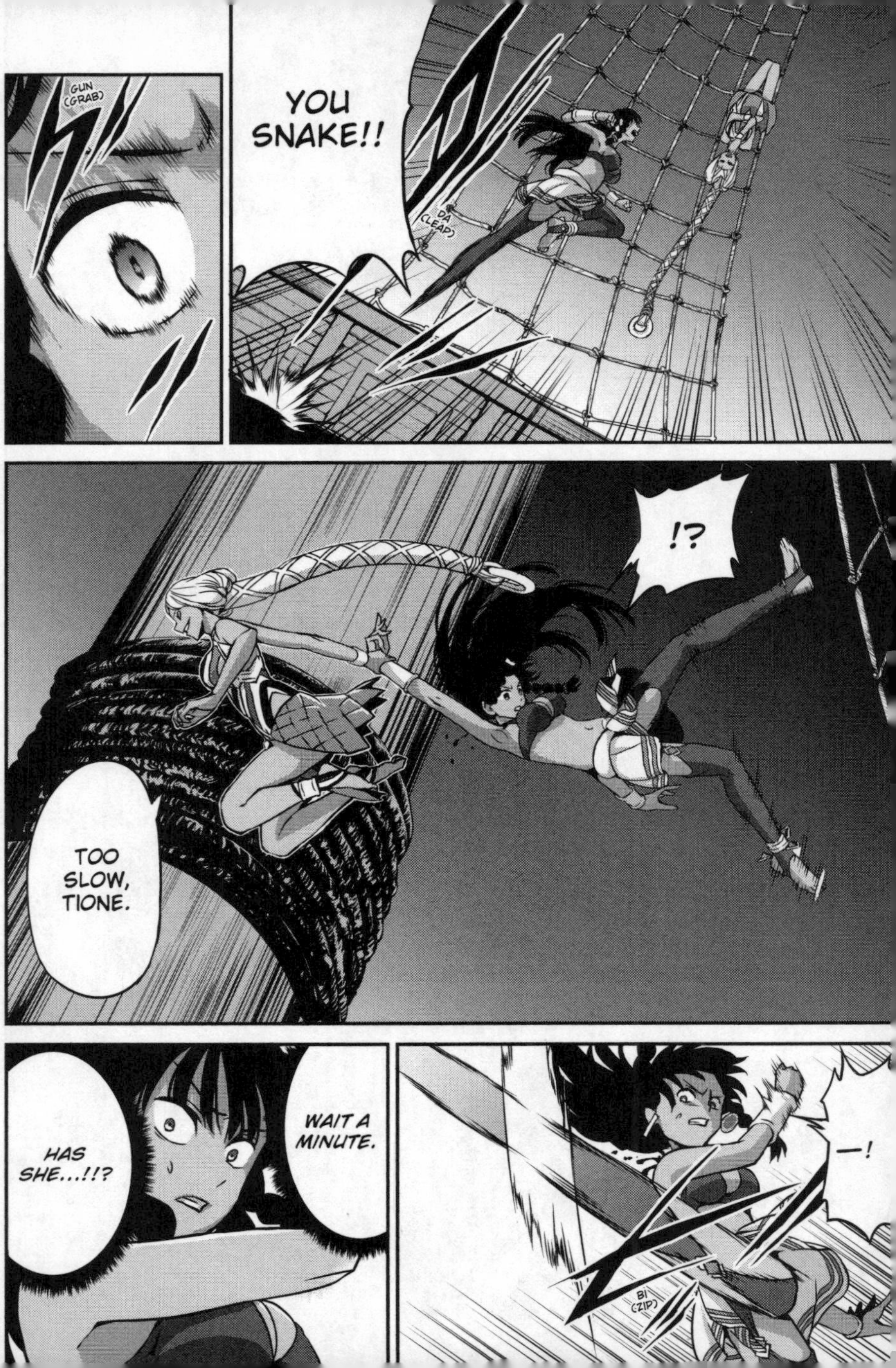
YOU SNAKE!!
DA (LEAP)
GUN (GRAB)
!?
TOO SLOW, TIONE.
—!
BI (ZIP)
WAIT A MINUTE.
HAS SHE...!!?

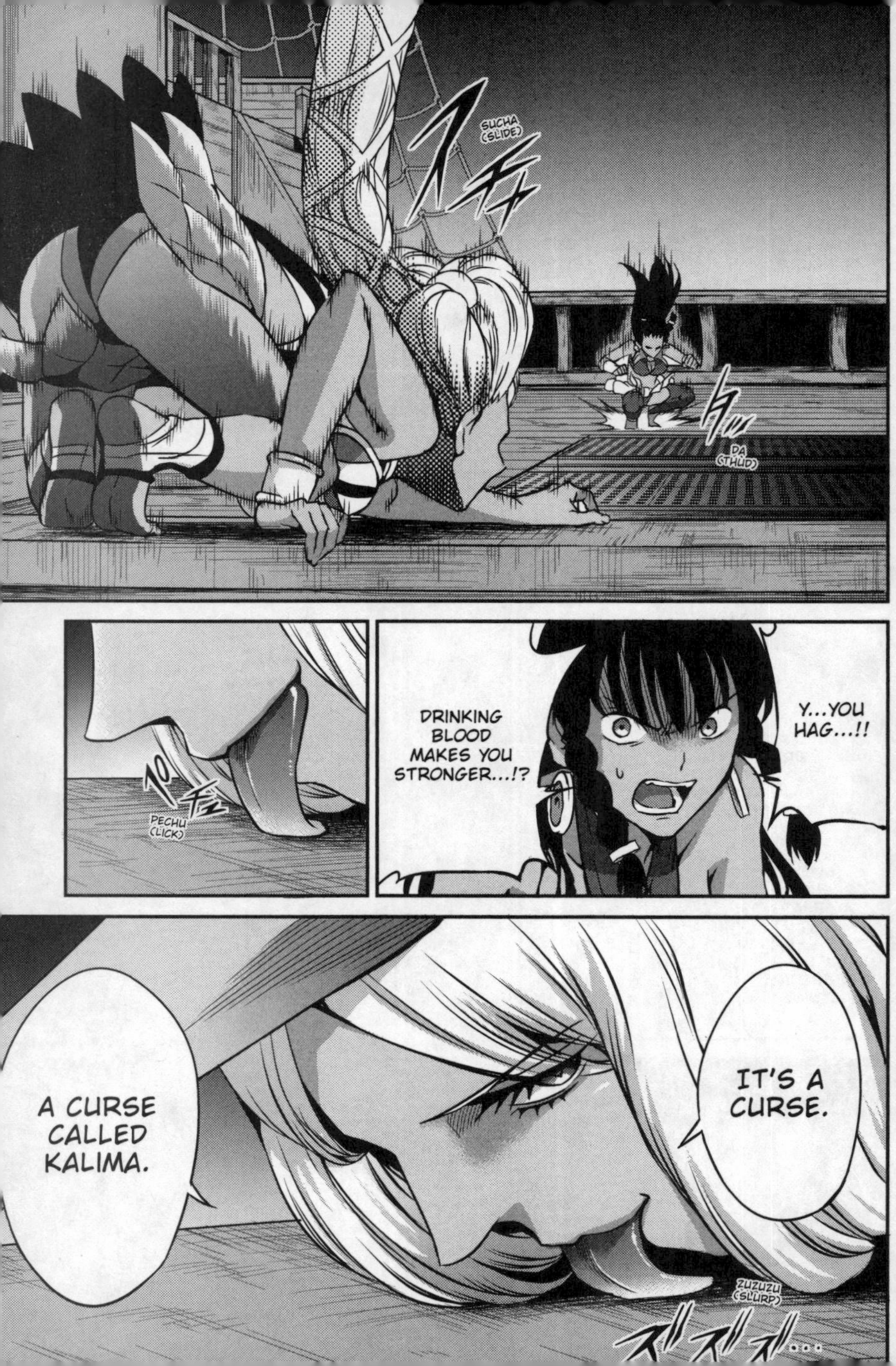
SUCHA (SLIDE)
DA (THUD)
Y...YOU HAG...!!
DRINKING BLOOD MAKES YOU STRONGER...!?
PECHU (LICK)
IT'S A CURSE.
A CURSE CALLED KALIMA.
ZUZUZU (SLURP)
...

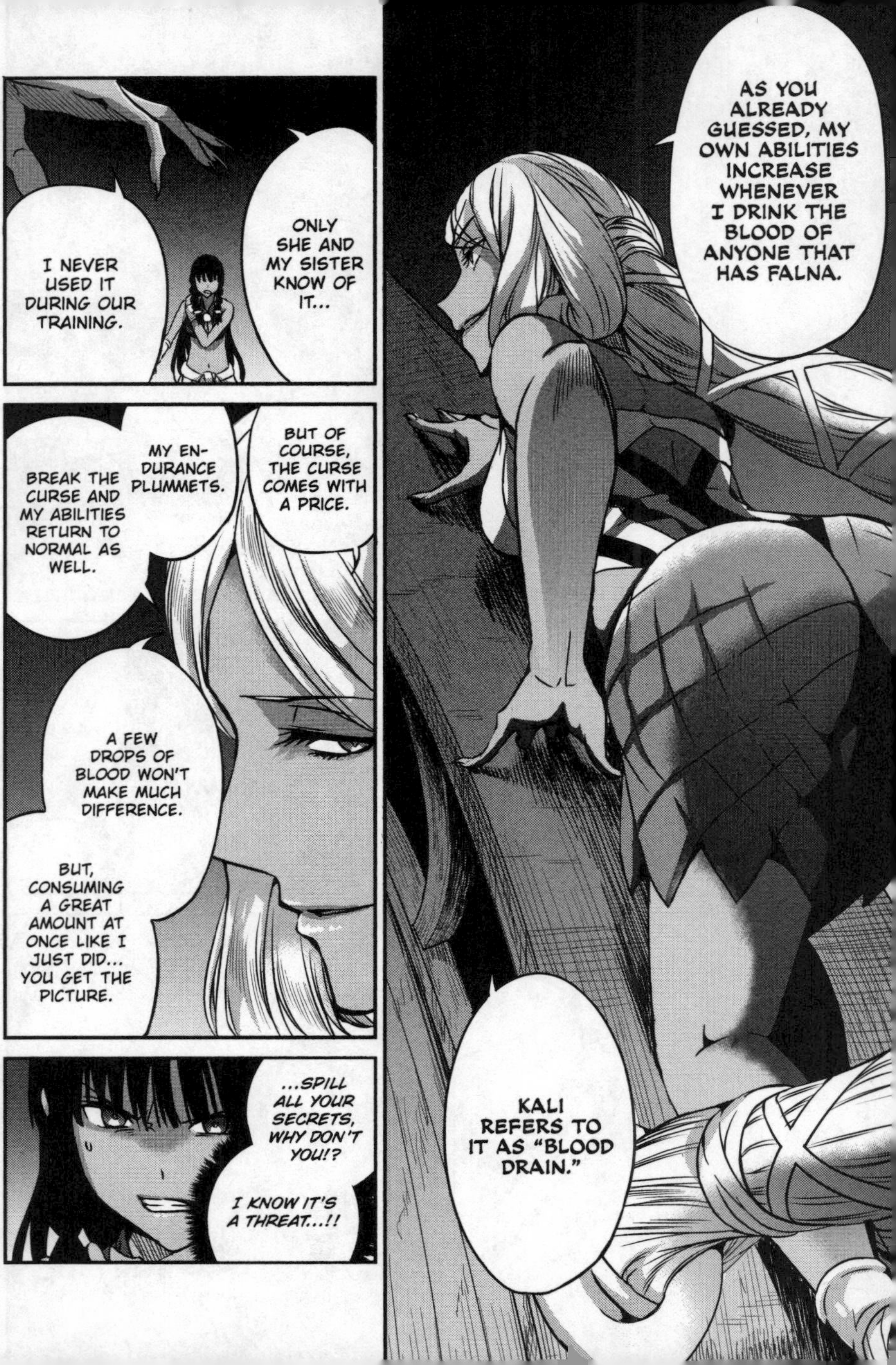
AS YOU ALREADY GUESSED, MY OWN ABILITIES INCREASE WHENEVER I DRINK THE BLOOD OF ANYONE THAT HAS FALNA.
KALI REFERS TO IT AS "BLOOD DRAIN."
ONLY SHE AND MY SISTER KNOW OF IT...
I NEVER USED IT DURING OUR TRAINING.
BUT OF COURSE, THE CURSE COMES WITH A PRICE.
MY EN-DURANCE PLUMMETS.
BREAK THE CURSE AND MY ABILITIES RETURN TO NORMAL AS WELL.
A FEW DROPS OF BLOOD WON'T MAKE MUCH DIFFERENCE.
BUT, CONSUMING A GREAT AMOUNT AT ONCE LIKE I JUST DID... YOU GET THE PICTURE.
...SPILL ALL YOUR SECRETS, WHY DON'T YOU!?
I KNOW IT'S A THREAT...!!

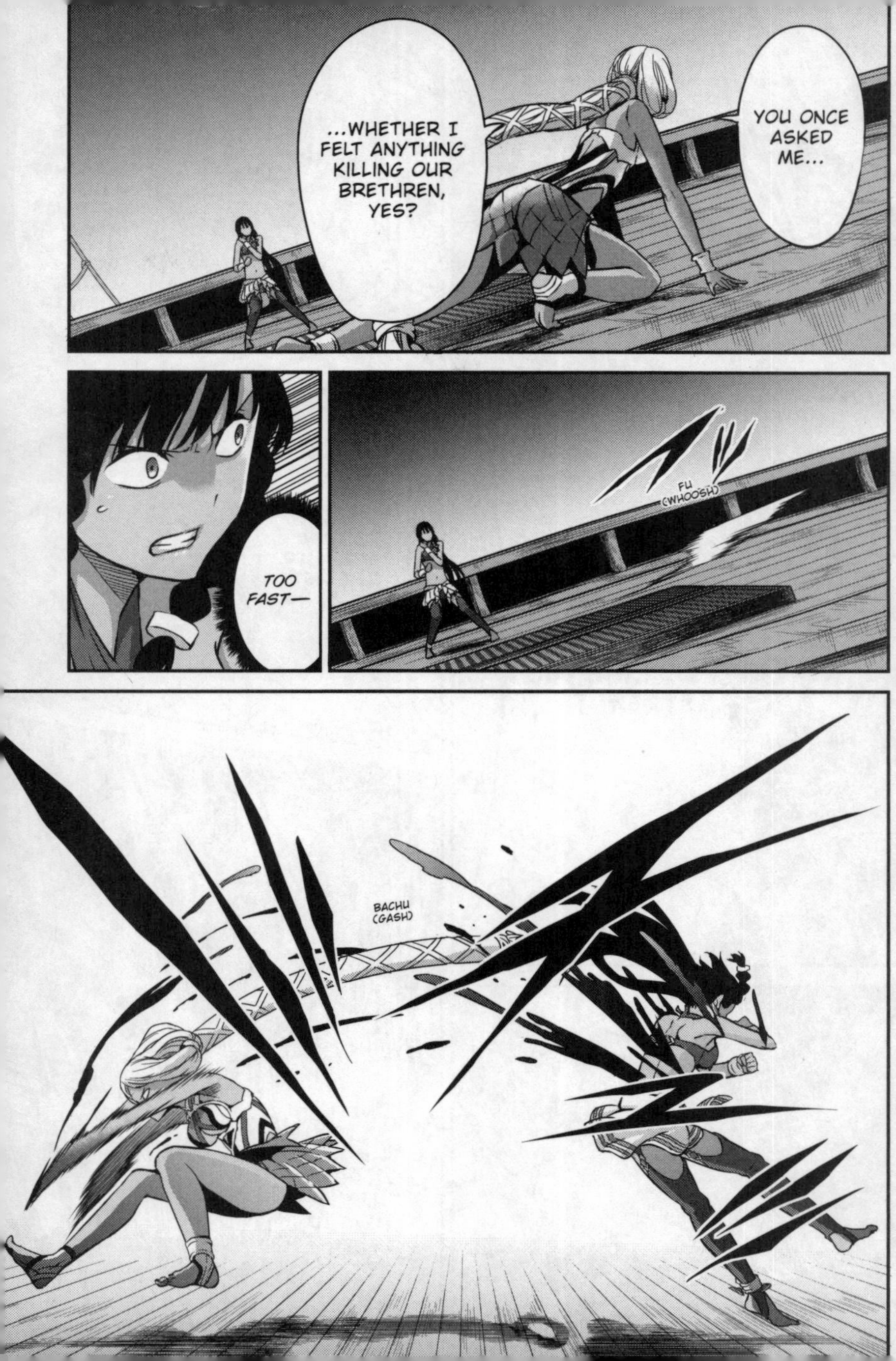
YOU ONCE ASKED ME...
...WHETHER I FELT ANYTHING KILLING OUR BRETHREN, YES?
FU (WHOOSH)
TOO FAST—
BACHU (GASH)

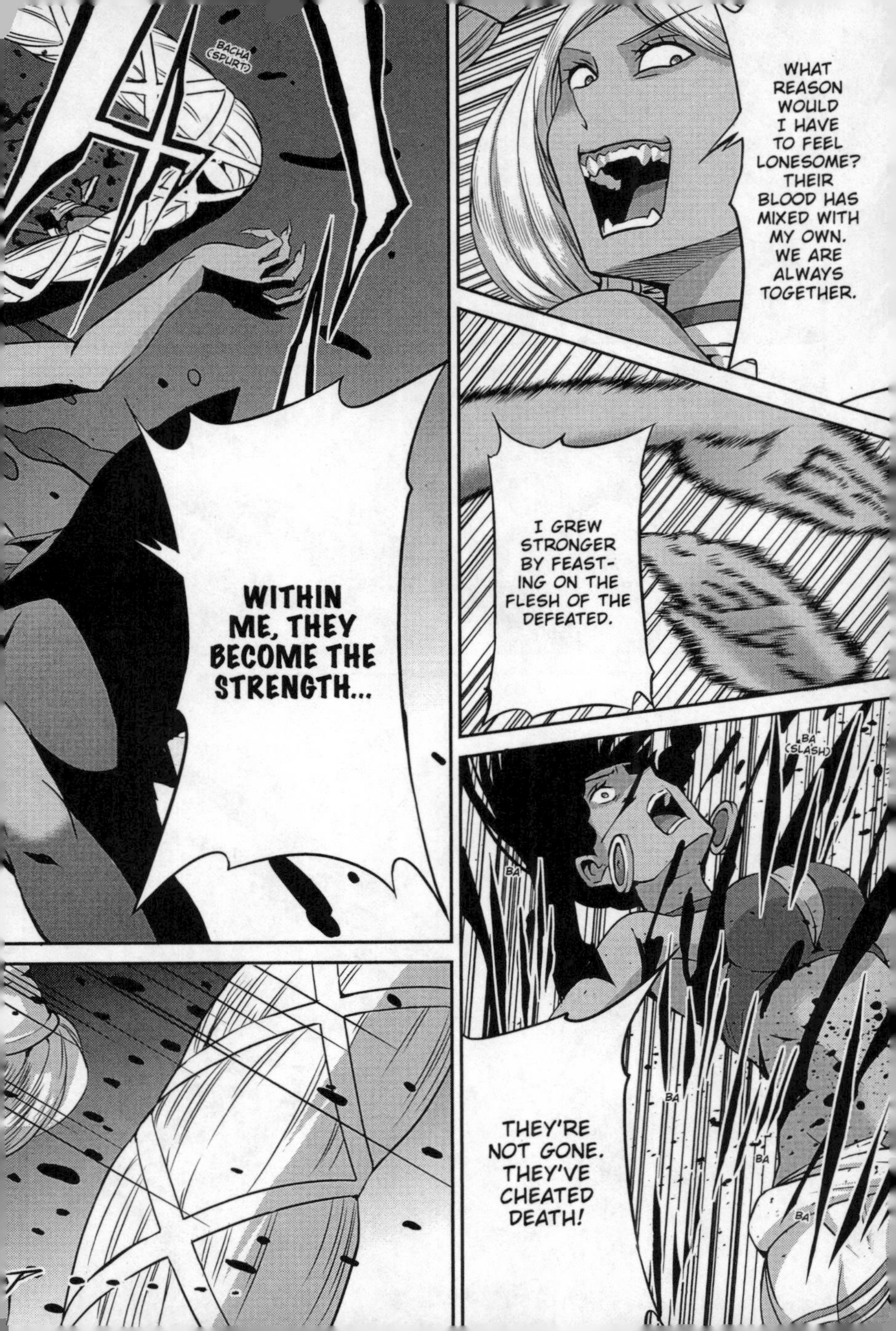
WHAT REASON WOULD I HAVE TO FEEL LONESOME? THEIR BLOOD HAS MIXED WITH MY OWN. WE ARE ALWAYS TOGETHER.
I GREW STRONGER BY FEAST-ING ON THE FLESH OF THE DEFEATED.
BA (SLASH)
BA
BA
BA
BA
THEY'RE NOT GONE. THEY'VE CHEATED DEATH!
BACHA (SPURT)
WITHIN ME, THEY BECOME THE STRENGTH...

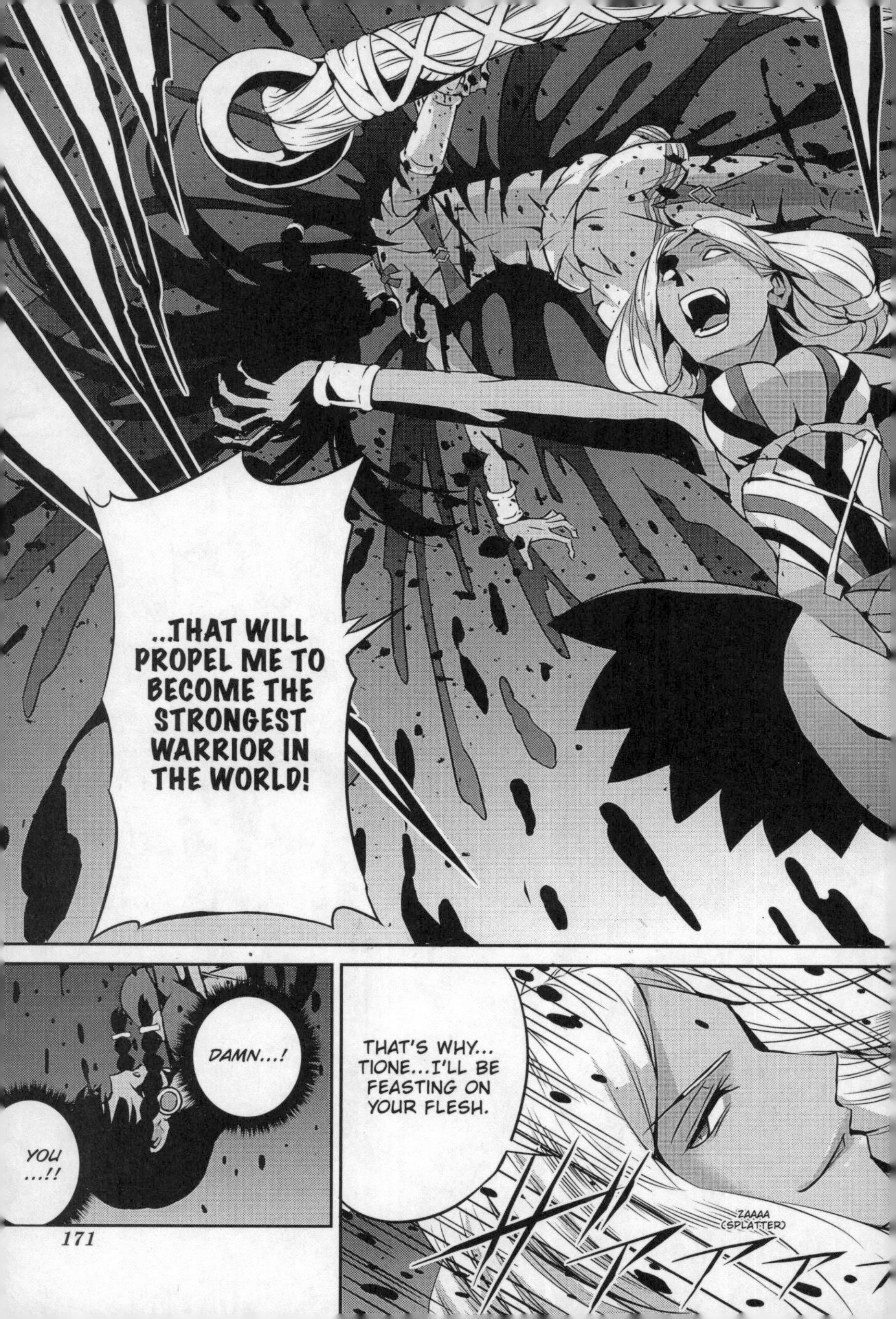
...THAT WILL PROPEL ME TO BECOME THE STRONGEST WARRIOR IN THE WORLD!
THAT'S WHY... TIONE...I'LL BE FEASTING ON YOUR FLESH.
ZAAAA (SPLATTER)
DAMN...!
YOU ...!!

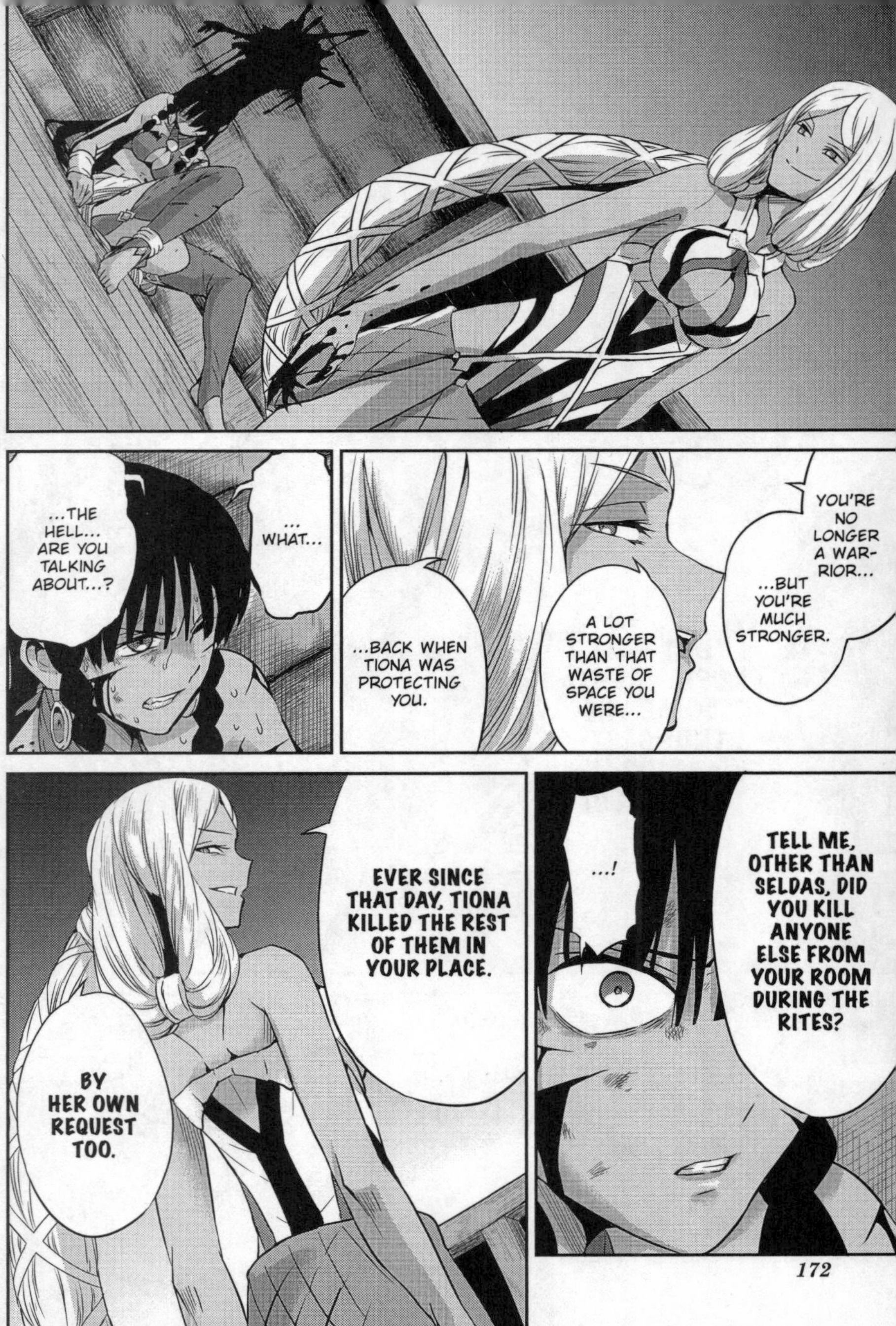
YOU'RE NO LONGER A WARRIOR...
...BUT YOU'RE MUCH STRONGER.
A LOT STRONGER THAN THAT WASTE OF SPACE YOU WERE...
...BACK WHEN TIONA WAS PROTECTING YOU.
... WHAT...
...THE HELL... ARE YOU TALKING ABOUT...?
TELL ME, OTHER THAN SELDAS, DID YOU KILL ANYONE ELSE FROM YOUR ROOM DURING THE RITES?
...!
EVER SINCE THAT DAY, TIONA KILLED THE REST OF THEM IN YOUR PLACE.
BY HER OWN REQUEST TOO.

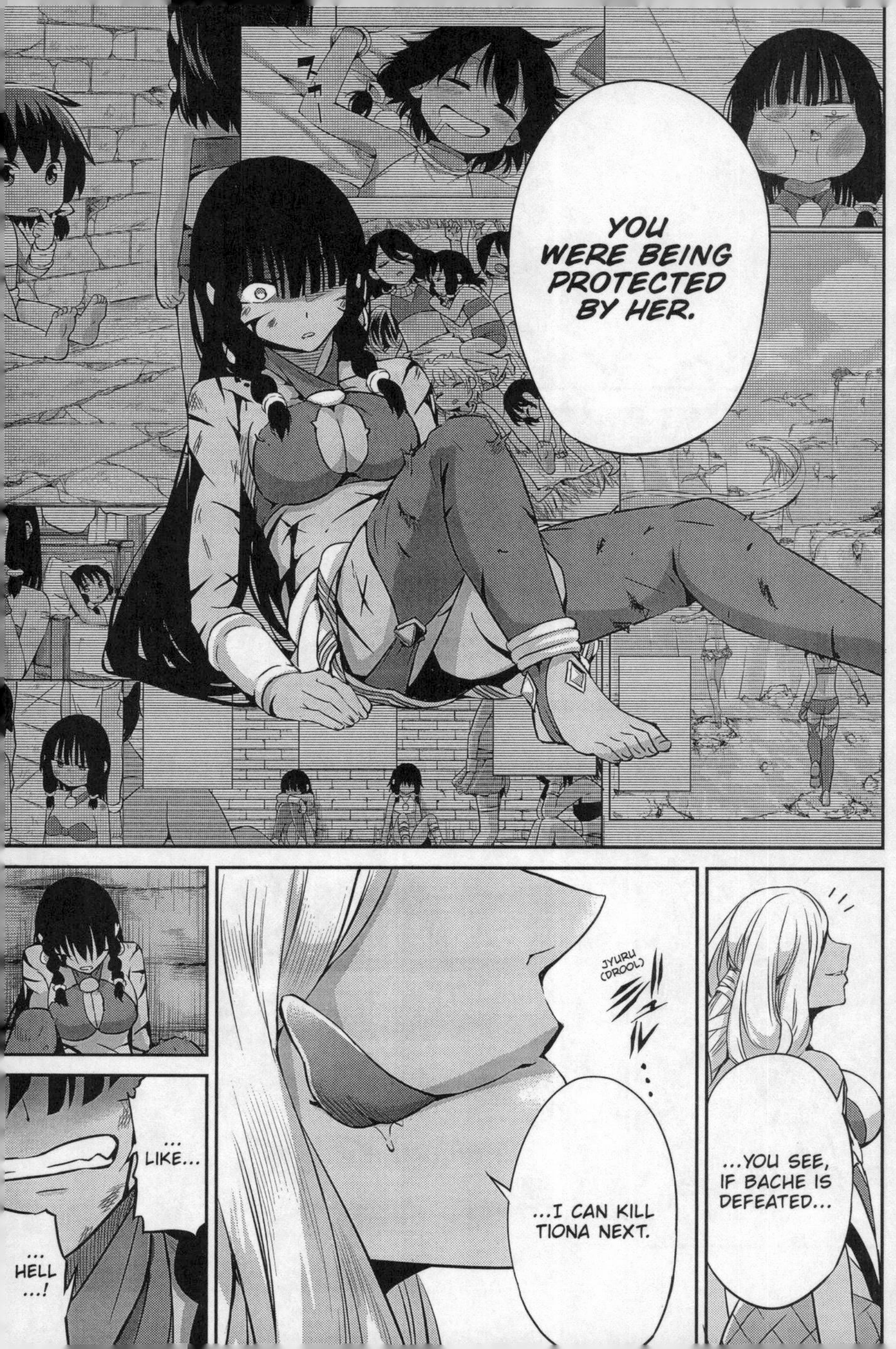
YOU WERE BEING PROTECTED BY HER.
...YOU SEE, IF BACHE IS DEFEATED...
JYURU (DROOL)
...I CAN KILL TIONA NEXT.
... LIKE...
... HELL ...!

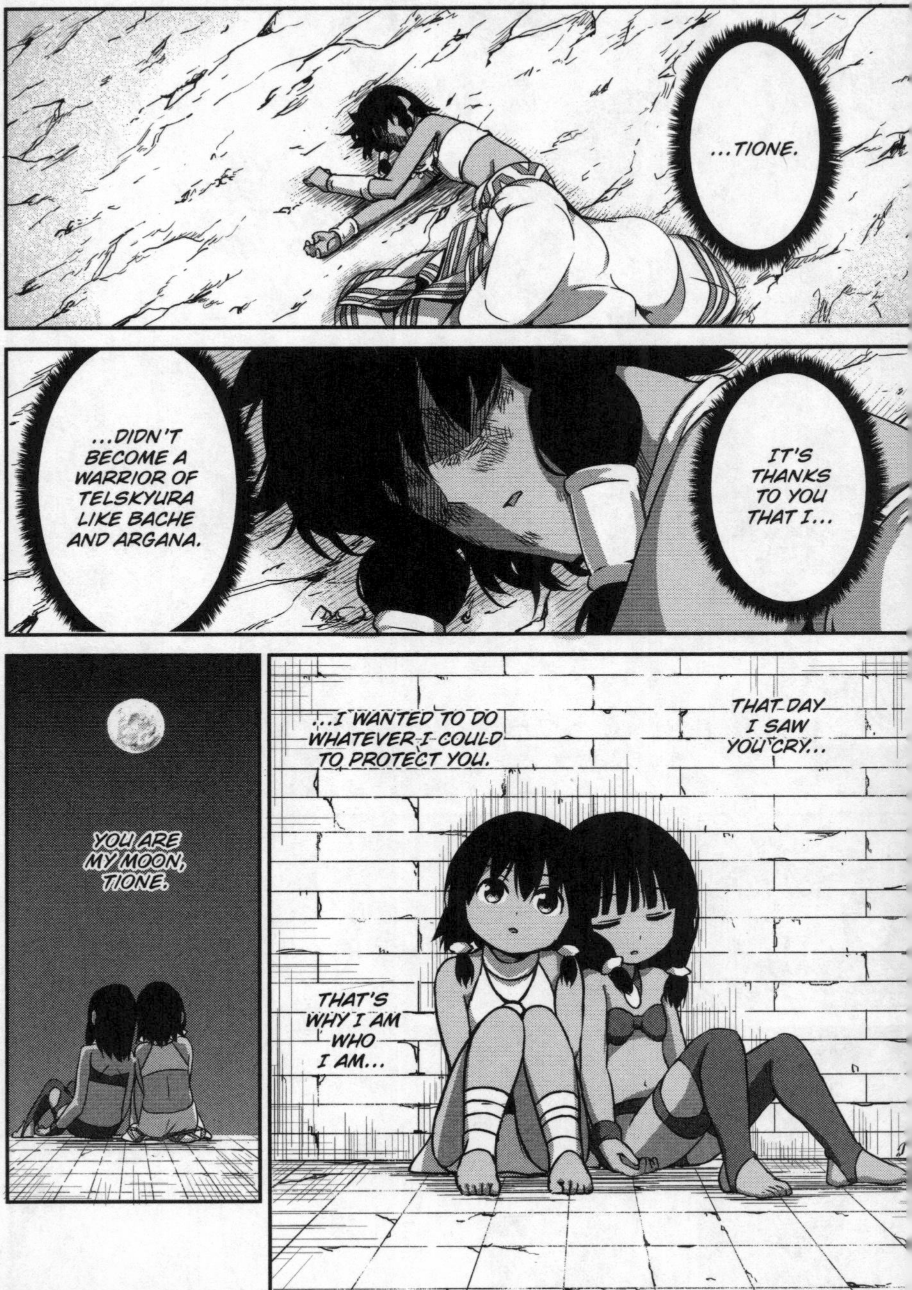
...TIONE.
IT'S THANKS TO YOU THAT I...
...DIDN'T BECOME A WARRIOR OF TELSKYURA LIKE BACHE AND ARGANA.
THAT DAY I SAW YOU CRY...
...I WANTED TO DO WHATEVER I COULD TO PROTECT YOU.
THAT'S WHY I AM WHO I AM...
YOU ARE MY MOON, TIONE.

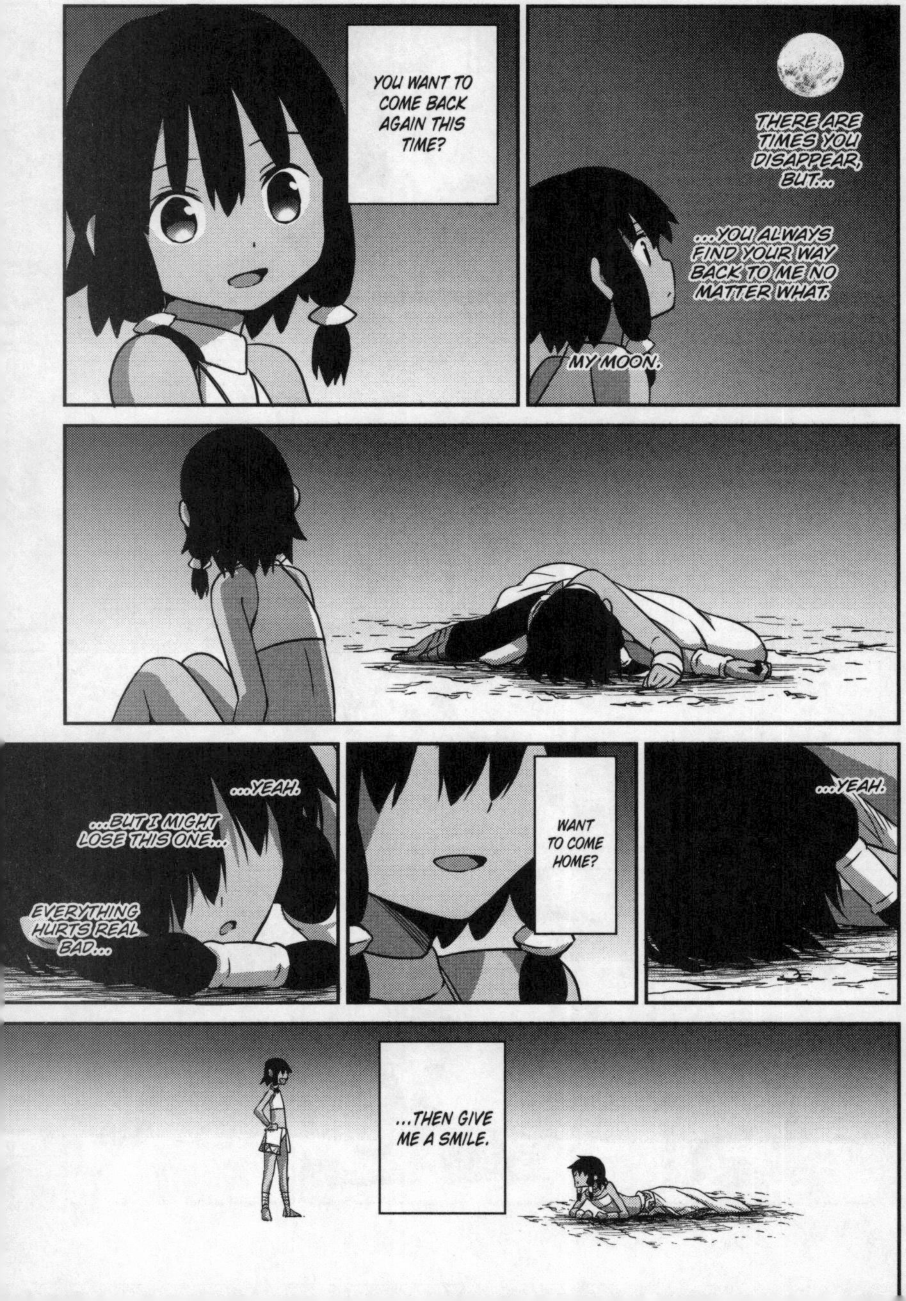
THERE ARE TIMES YOU DISAPPEAR, BUT...
...YOU ALWAYS FIND YOUR WAY BACK TO ME NO MATTER WHAT.
MY MOON.
YOU WANT TO COME BACK AGAIN THIS TIME?
...YEAH.
WANT TO COME HOME?
...YEAH.
...BUT I MIGHT LOSE THIS ONE...
EVERYTHING HURTS REAL BAD...
...THEN GIVE ME A SMILE.

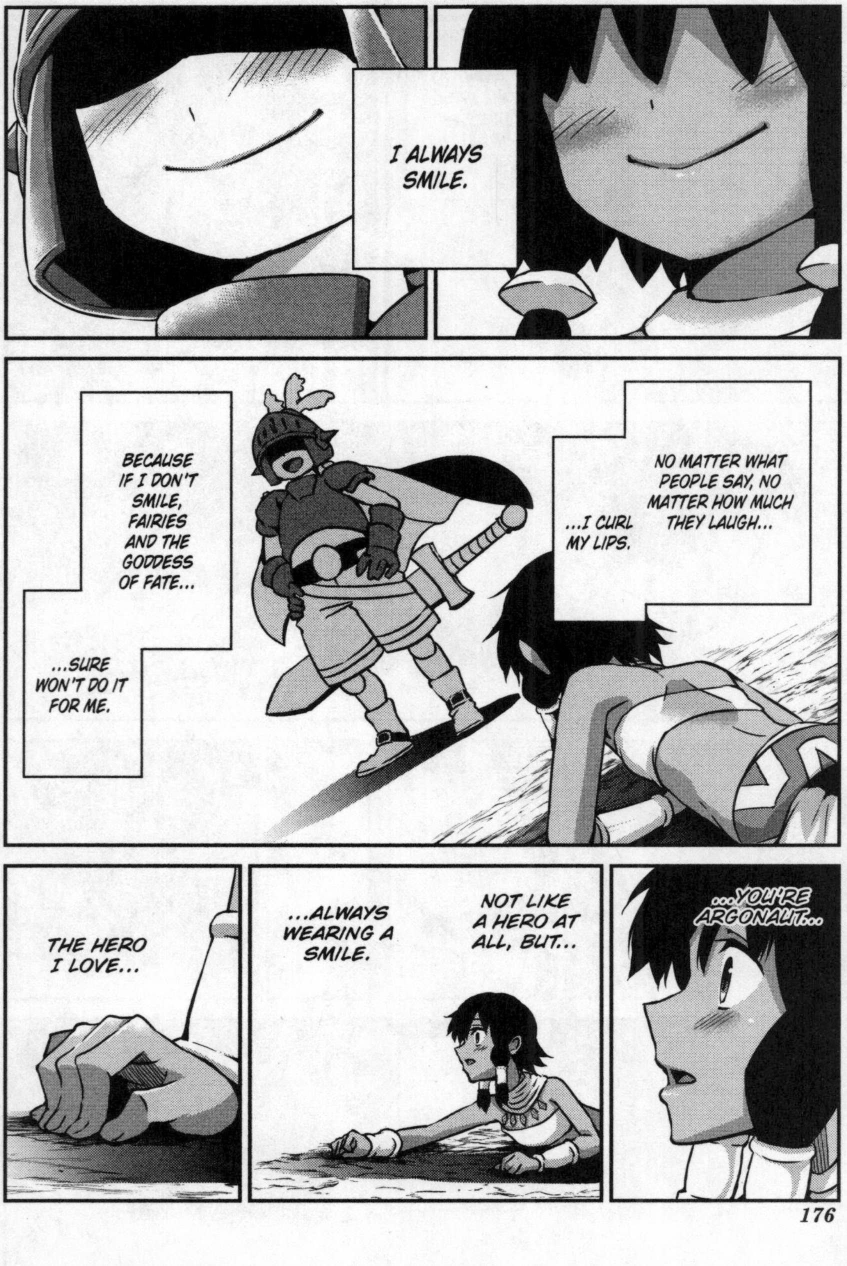
I ALWAYS SMILE.
NO MATTER WHAT PEOPLE SAY, NO MATTER HOW MUCH THEY LAUGH...
...I CURL MY LIPS.
BECAUSE IF I DON'T SMILE, FAIRIES AND THE GODDESS OF FATE...
...SURE WON'T DO IT FOR ME.
...YOU'RE ARGONAUT...
NOT LIKE A HERO AT ALL, BUT...
...ALWAYS WEARING A SMILE.
THE HERO I LOVE...

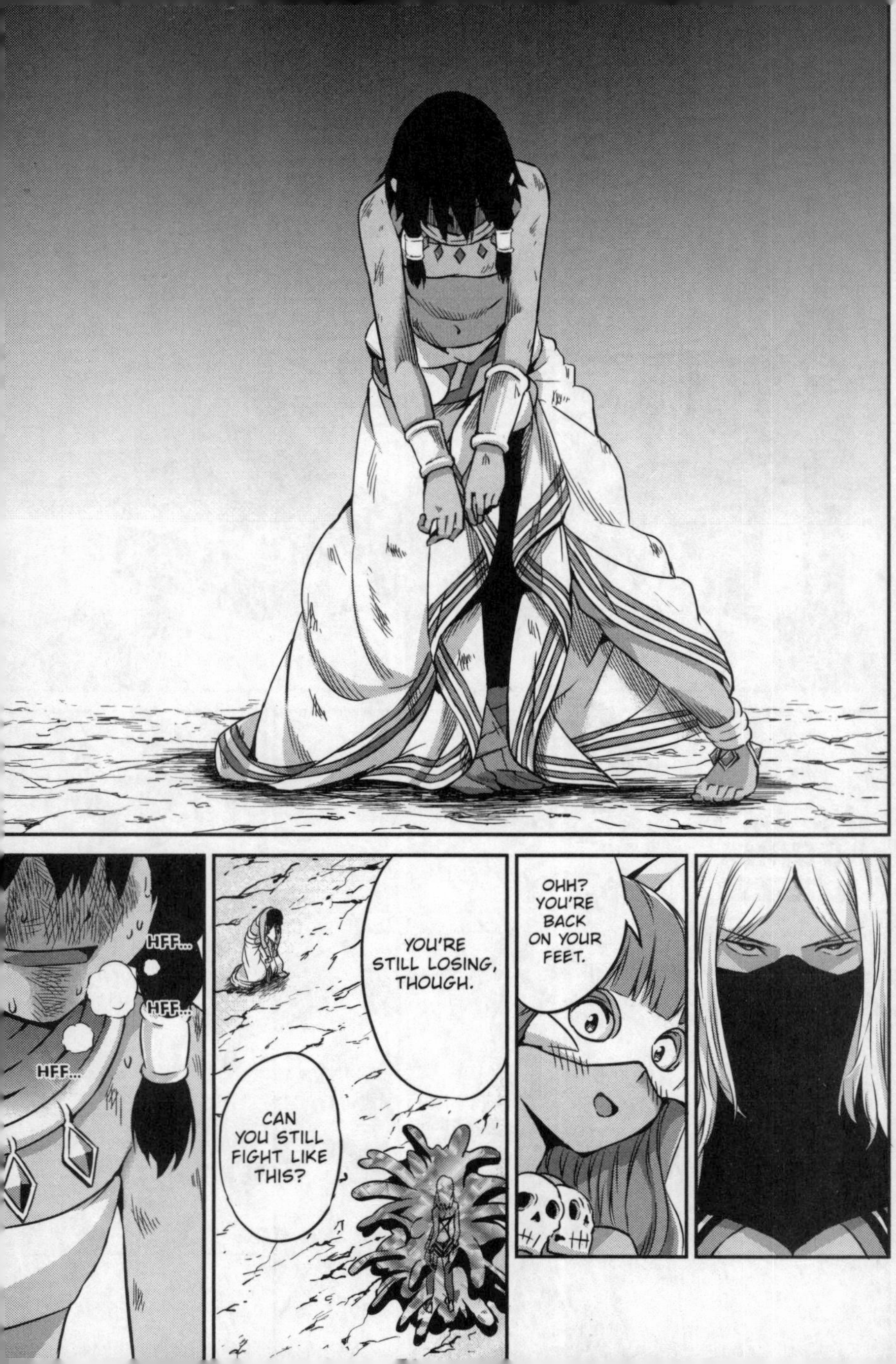
OHH? YOU'RE BACK ON YOUR FEET.
YOU'RE STILL LOSING, THOUGH.
CAN YOU STILL FIGHT LIKE THIS?
HFF...
HFF...
HFF...

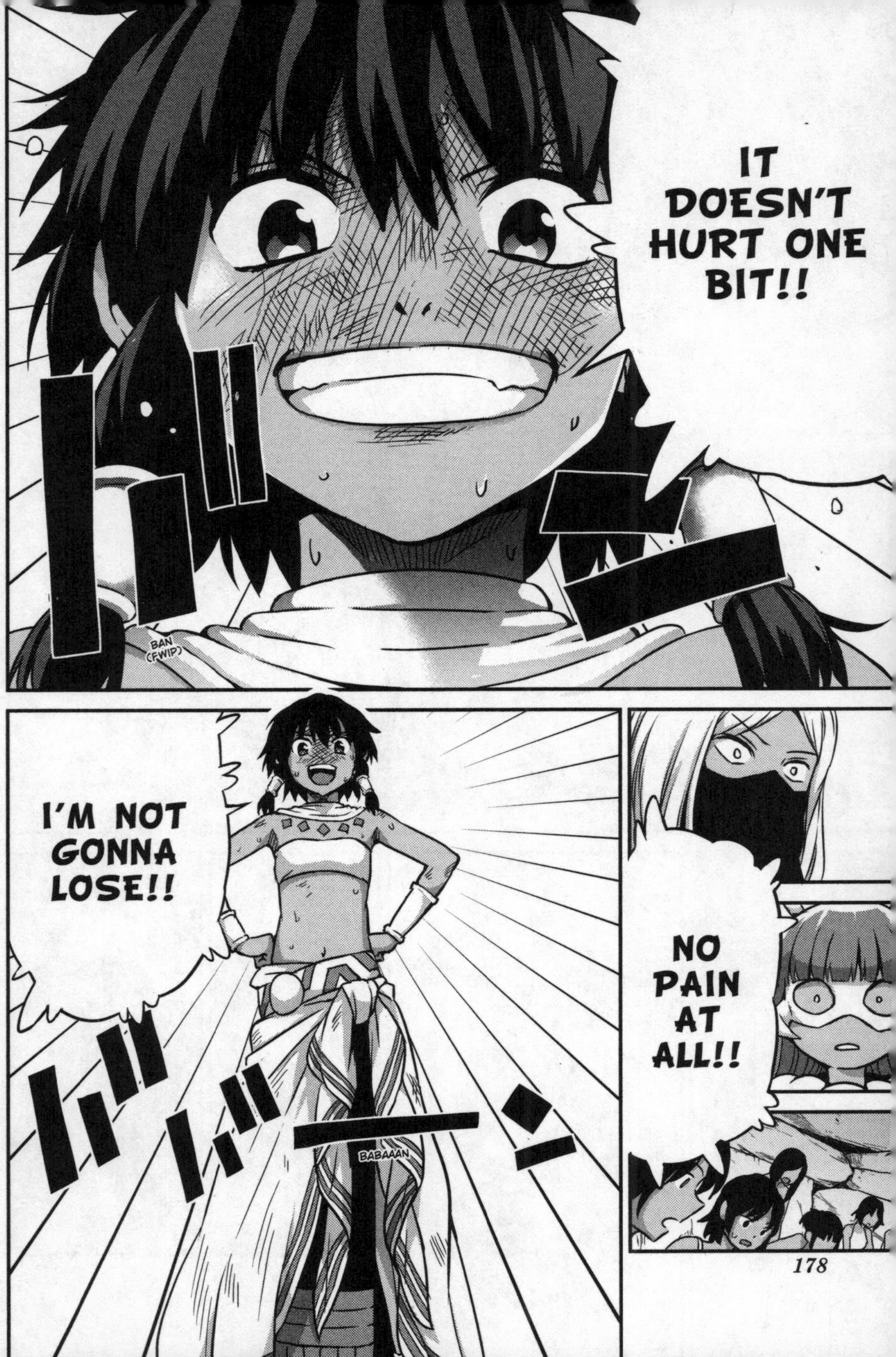
IT DOESN'T HURT ONE BIT!!
BAN (FWIP)
NO PAIN AT ALL!!
I'M NOT GONNA LOSE!!
BABAAAN

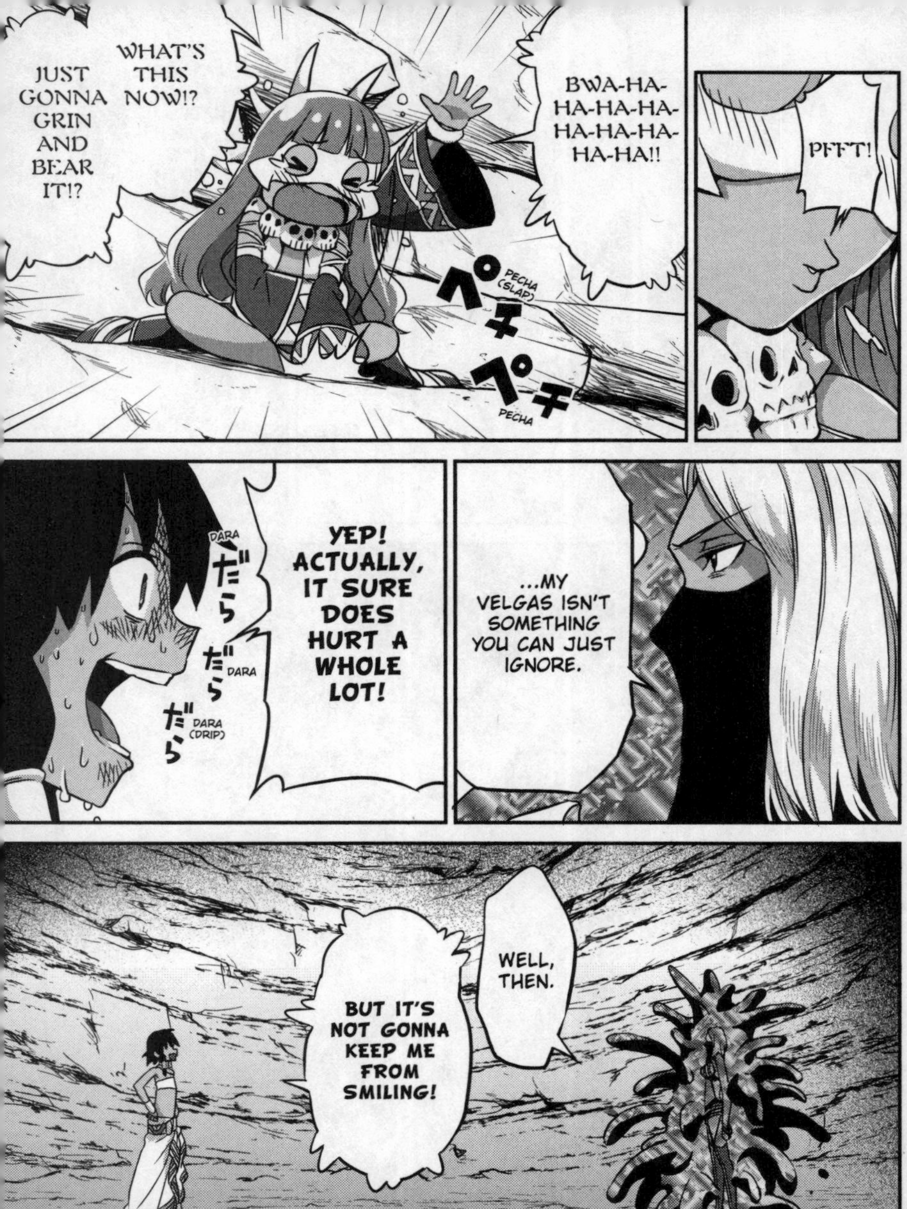
PFFT!
BWA-HA-HA-HA-HA-HA-HA-HA-HA-HA-HA!!
WHAT'S THIS NOW!?
JUST GONNA GRIN AND BEAR IT!?
PECHA (SLAP)
PECHA
...MY VELGAS ISN'T SOMETHING YOU CAN JUST IGNORE.
YEP! ACTUALLY, IT SURE DOES HURT A WHOLE LOT!
DARA
DARA
DARA (DRIP)
WELL, THEN.
BUT IT'S NOT GONNA KEEP ME FROM SMILING!

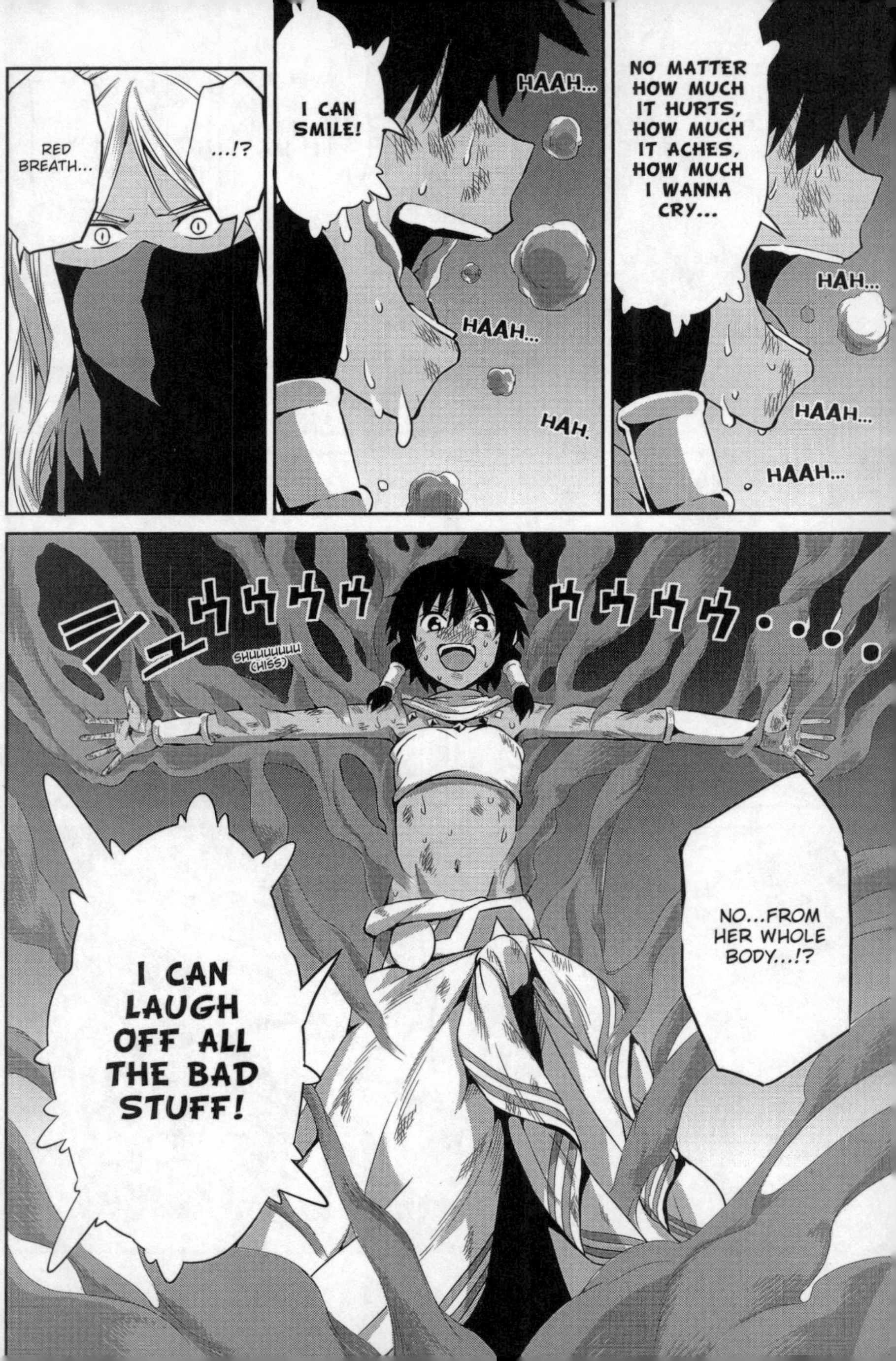
NO MATTER HOW MUCH IT HURTS, HOW MUCH IT ACHES, HOW MUCH I WANNA CRY...
HAH...
HAAH...
HAAH...
HAAH...
I CAN SMILE!
HAAH...
HAH.
...!?
RED BREATH...
シュウウウウ ウウウウ・・・・・
SHUUUUUUU (HISS)
NO...FROM HER WHOLE BODY...!?
I CAN LAUGH OFF ALL THE BAD STUFF!

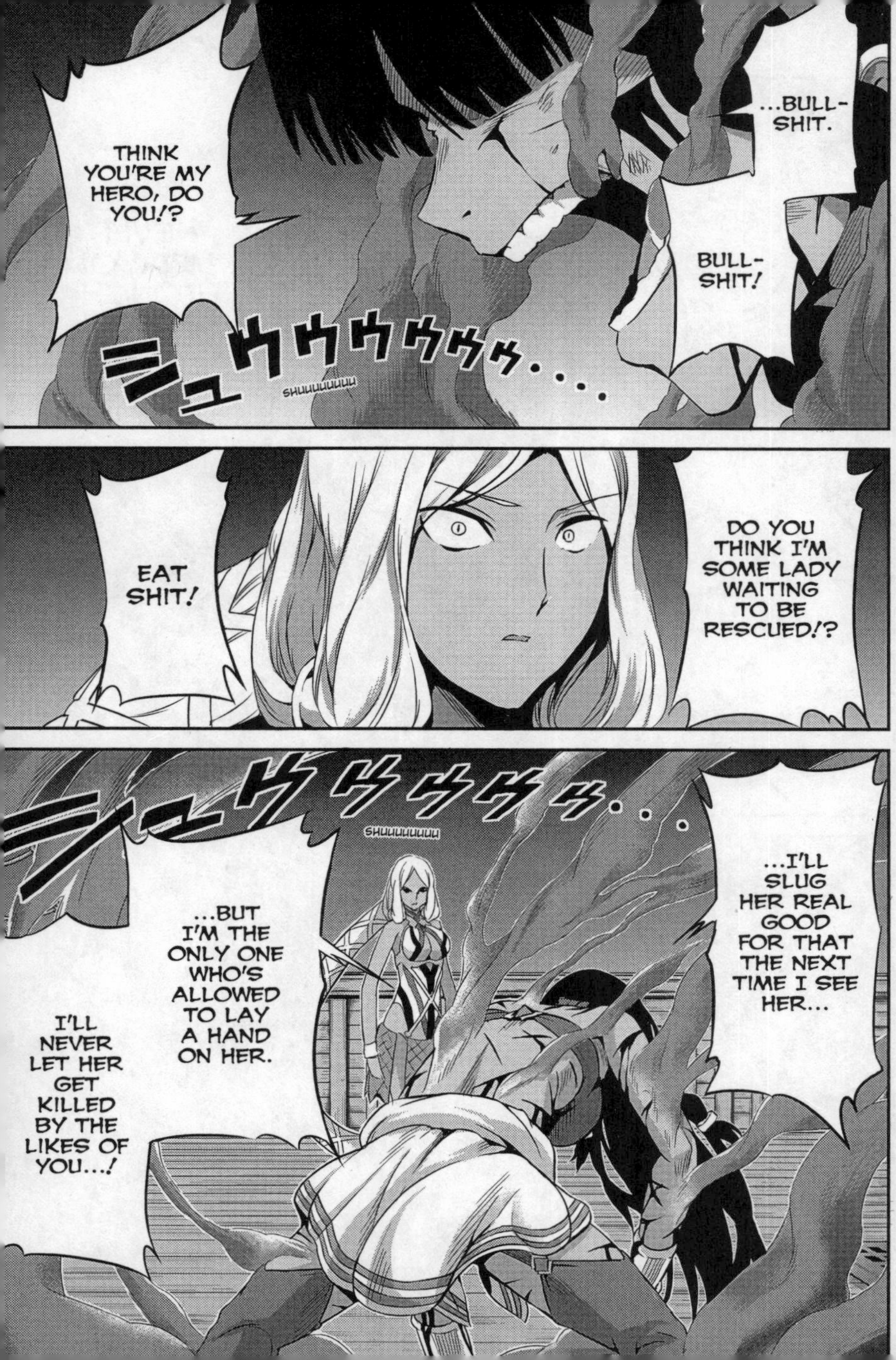
...BULL-SHIT.
BULL-SHIT!
THINK YOU'RE MY HERO, DO YOU!?
SHUUUUUUUU
DO YOU THINK I'M SOME LADY WAITING TO BE RESCUED!?
EAT SHIT!
SHUUUUUUUU
...I'LL SLUG HER REAL GOOD FOR THAT THE NEXT TIME I SEE HER...
...BUT I'M THE ONLY ONE WHO'S ALLOWED TO LAY A HAND ON HER.
I'LL NEVER LET HER GET KILLED BY THE LIKES OF YOU...!

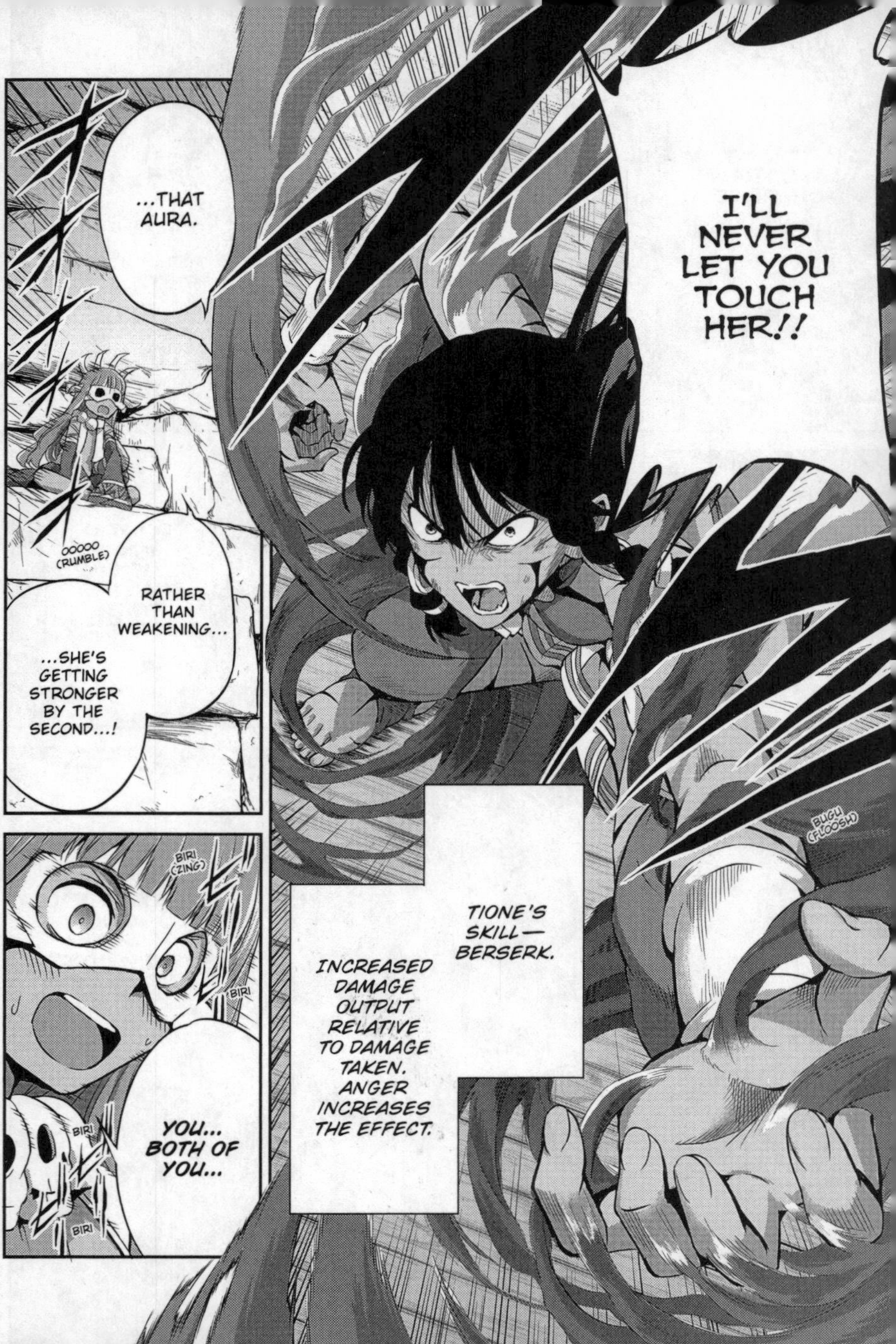
I'LL NEVER LET YOU TOUCH HER!!
BUGU (FLOOSH)
TIONE'S SKILL—BERSERK.
INCREASED DAMAGE OUTPUT RELATIVE TO DAMAGE TAKEN. ANGER INCREASES THE EFFECT.
...THAT AURA.
OOOOO (RUMBLE)
RATHER THAN WEAKENING...
...SHE'S GETTING STRONGER BY THE SECOND...!
BIRI (ZING)
BIRI
YOU... BOTH OF YOU...
BIRI
BIRI

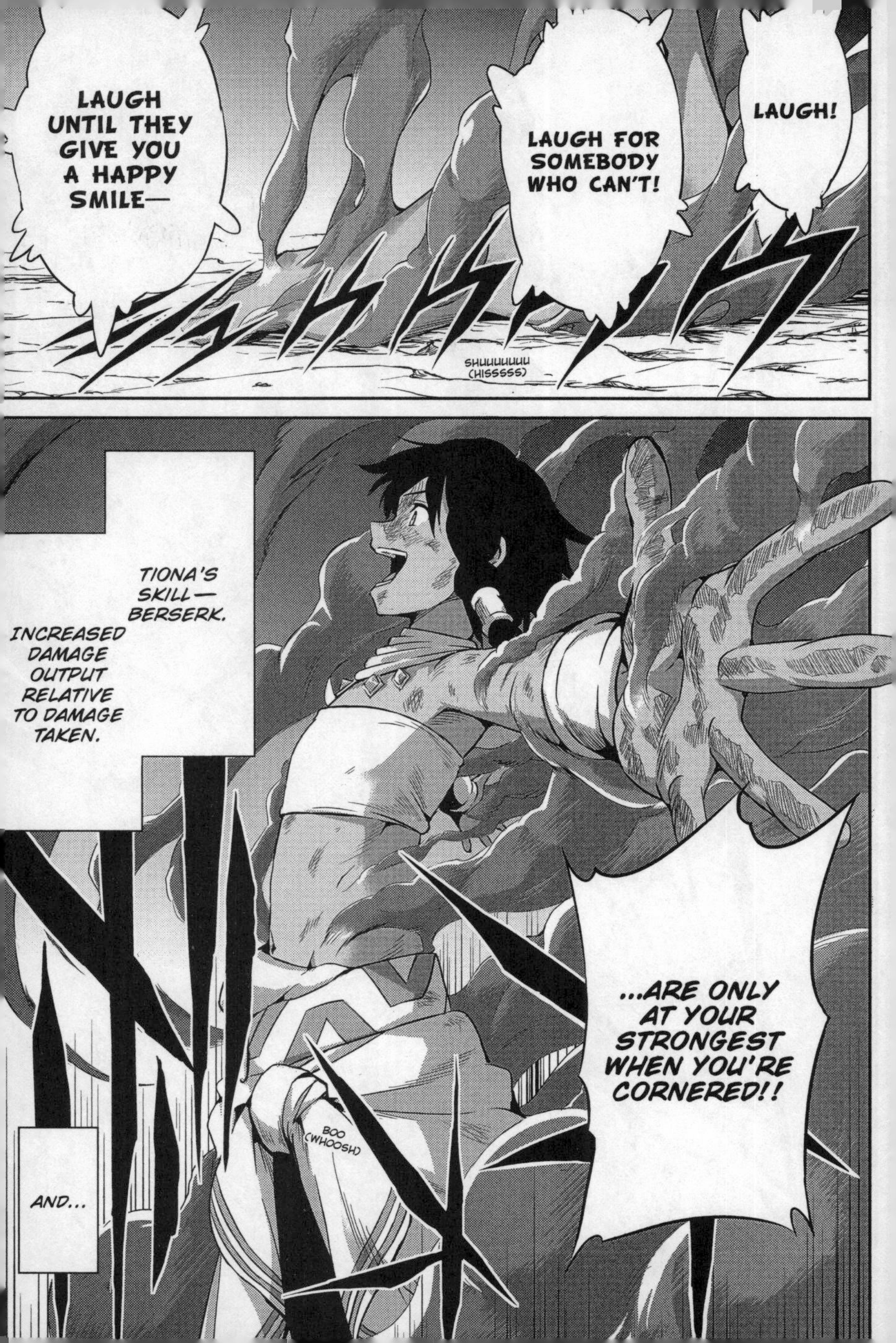
LAUGH!
LAUGH FOR SOMEBODY WHO CAN'T!
LAUGH UNTIL THEY GIVE YOU A HAPPY SMILE—
SHUUUUUUU (HISSSSS)
TIONA'S SKILL—BERSERK.
INCREASED DAMAGE OUTPUT RELATIVE TO DAMAGE TAKEN.
AND...
...ARE ONLY AT YOUR STRONGEST WHEN YOU'RE CORNERED!!
BOO (WHOOSH)

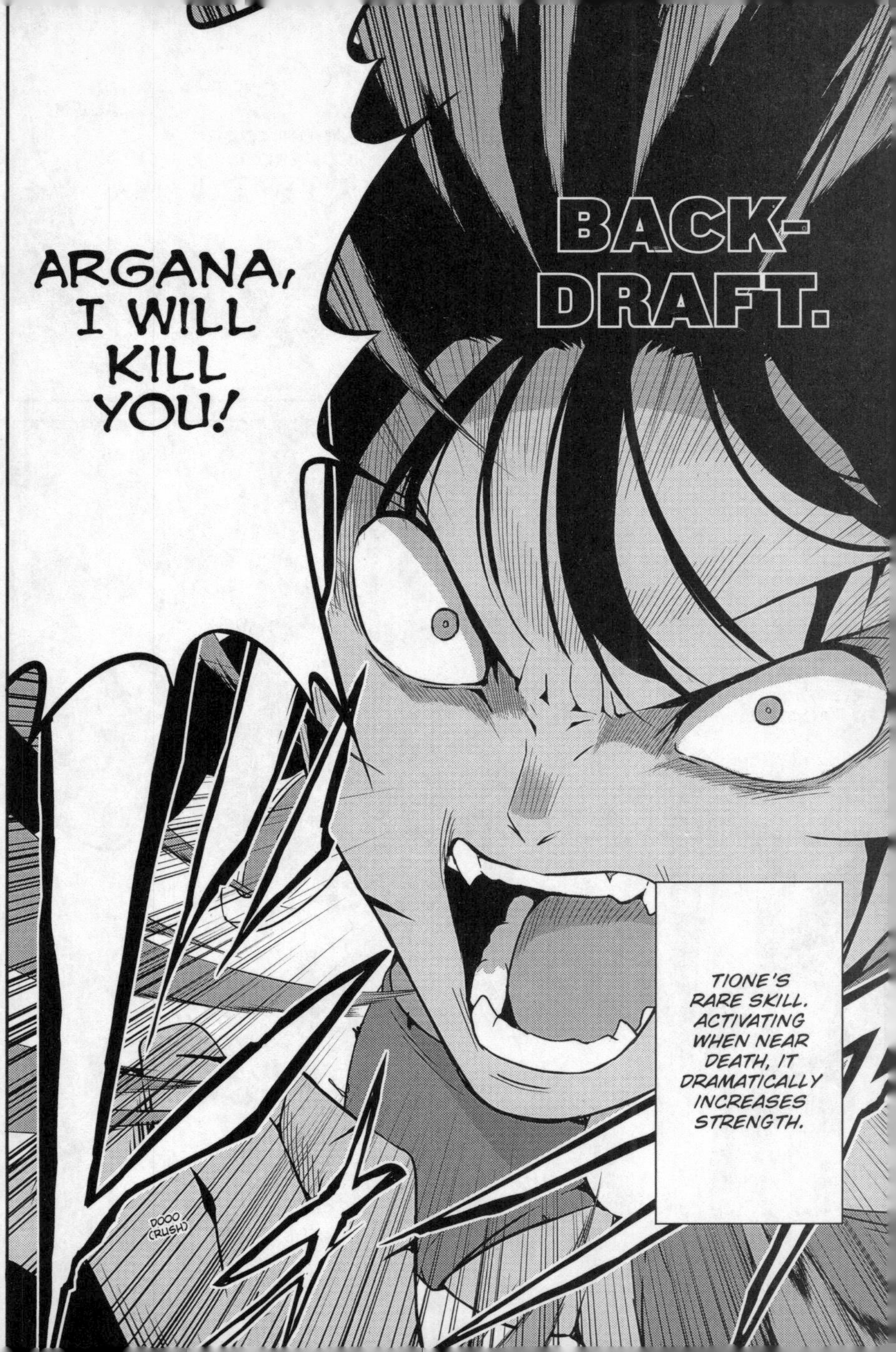
BACK-DRAFT.
ARGANA, I WILL KILL YOU!
TIONE'S RARE SKILL. ACTIVATING WHEN NEAR DEATH, IT DRAMATICALLY INCREASES STRENGTH.
DOOO (RUSH)

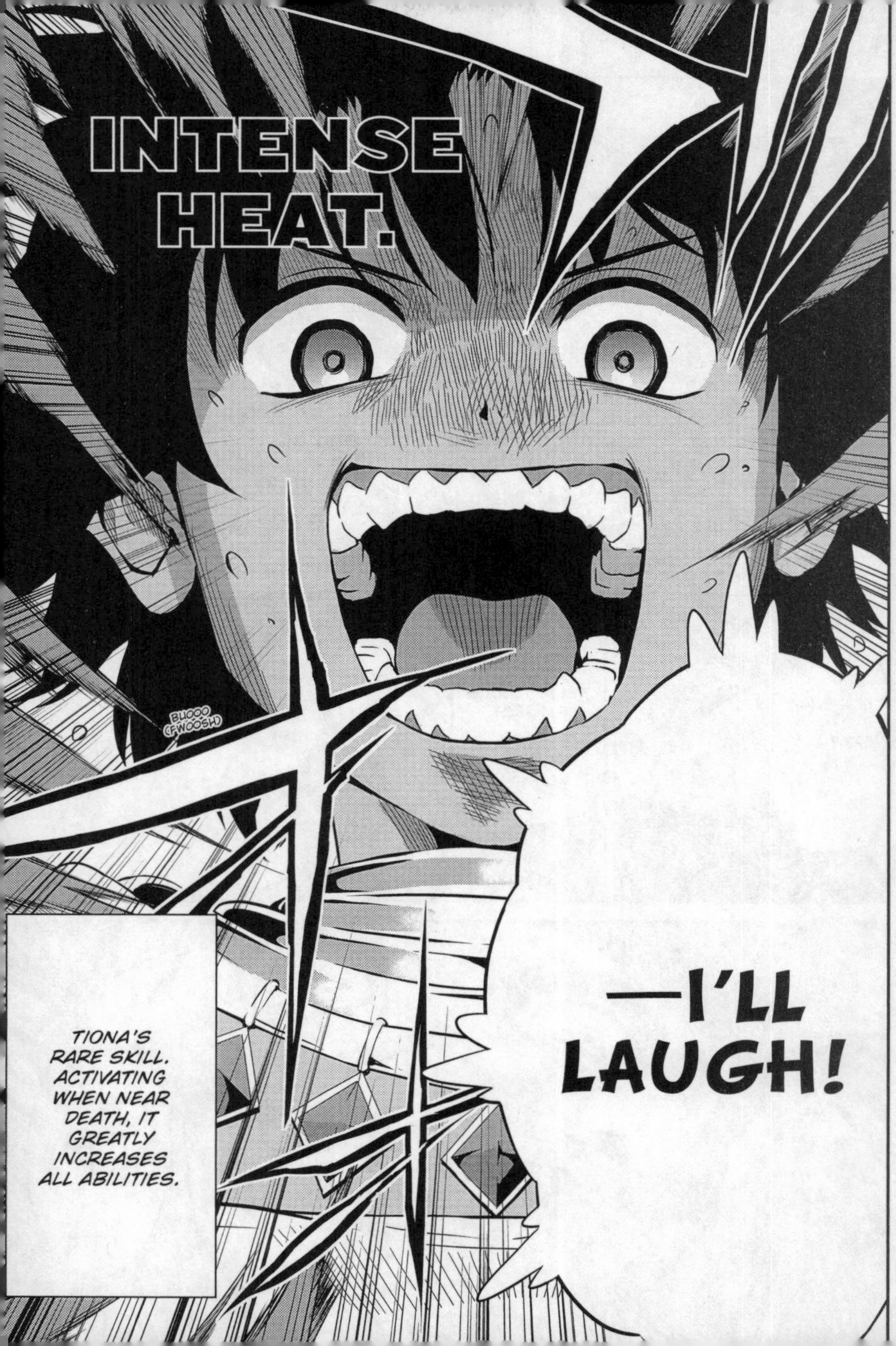
INTENSE HEAT.
BUOOO (FWOOSH)
—I'LL LAUGH!
TIONA'S RARE SKILL. ACTIVATING WHEN NEAR DEATH, IT GREATLY INCREASES ALL ABILITIES.

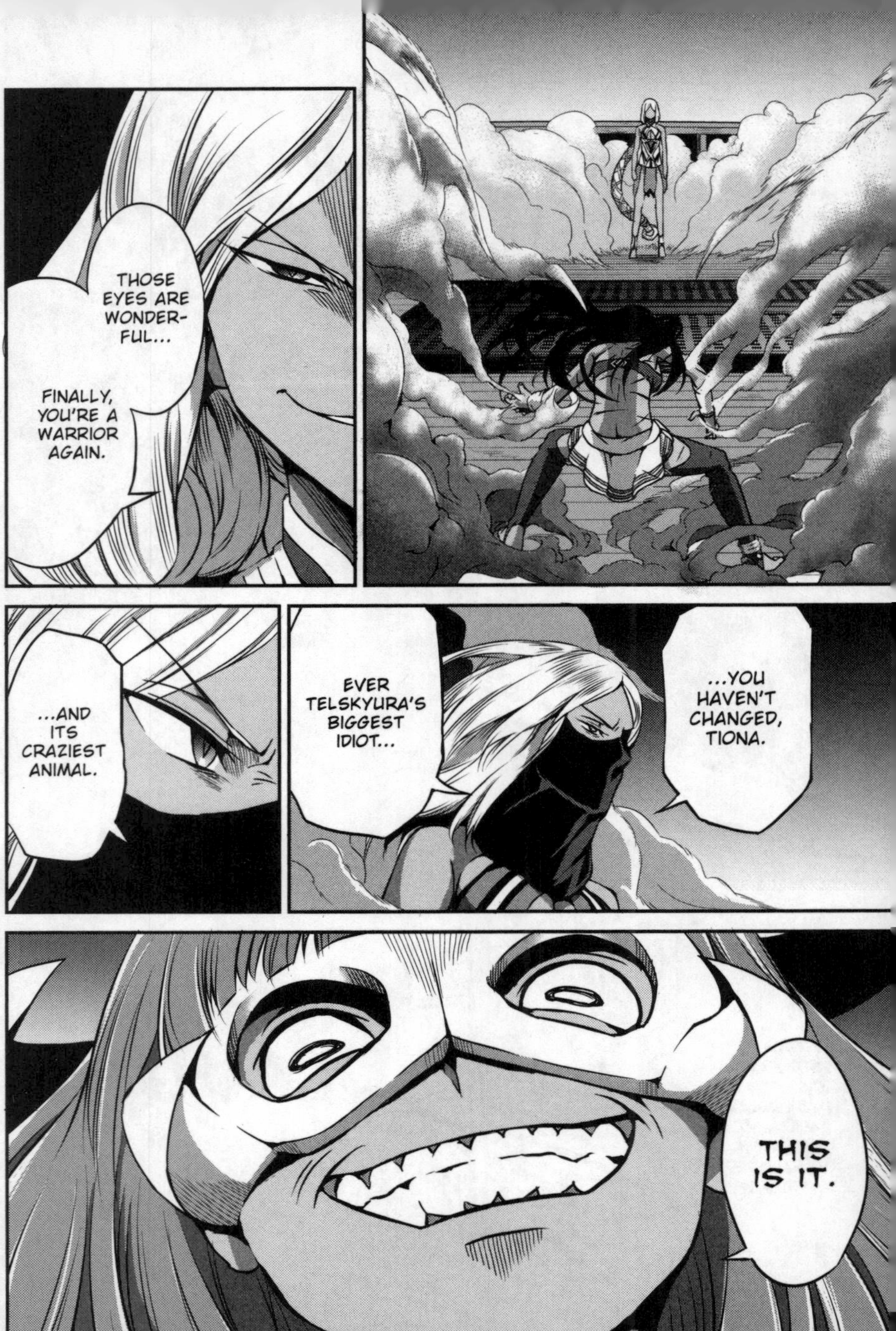
THOSE EYES ARE WONDER-FUL...
FINALLY, YOU'RE A WARRIOR AGAIN.
...YOU HAVEN'T CHANGED, TIONA.
EVER TELSKYURA'S BIGGEST IDIOT...
...AND ITS CRAZIEST ANIMAL.
THIS IS IT.

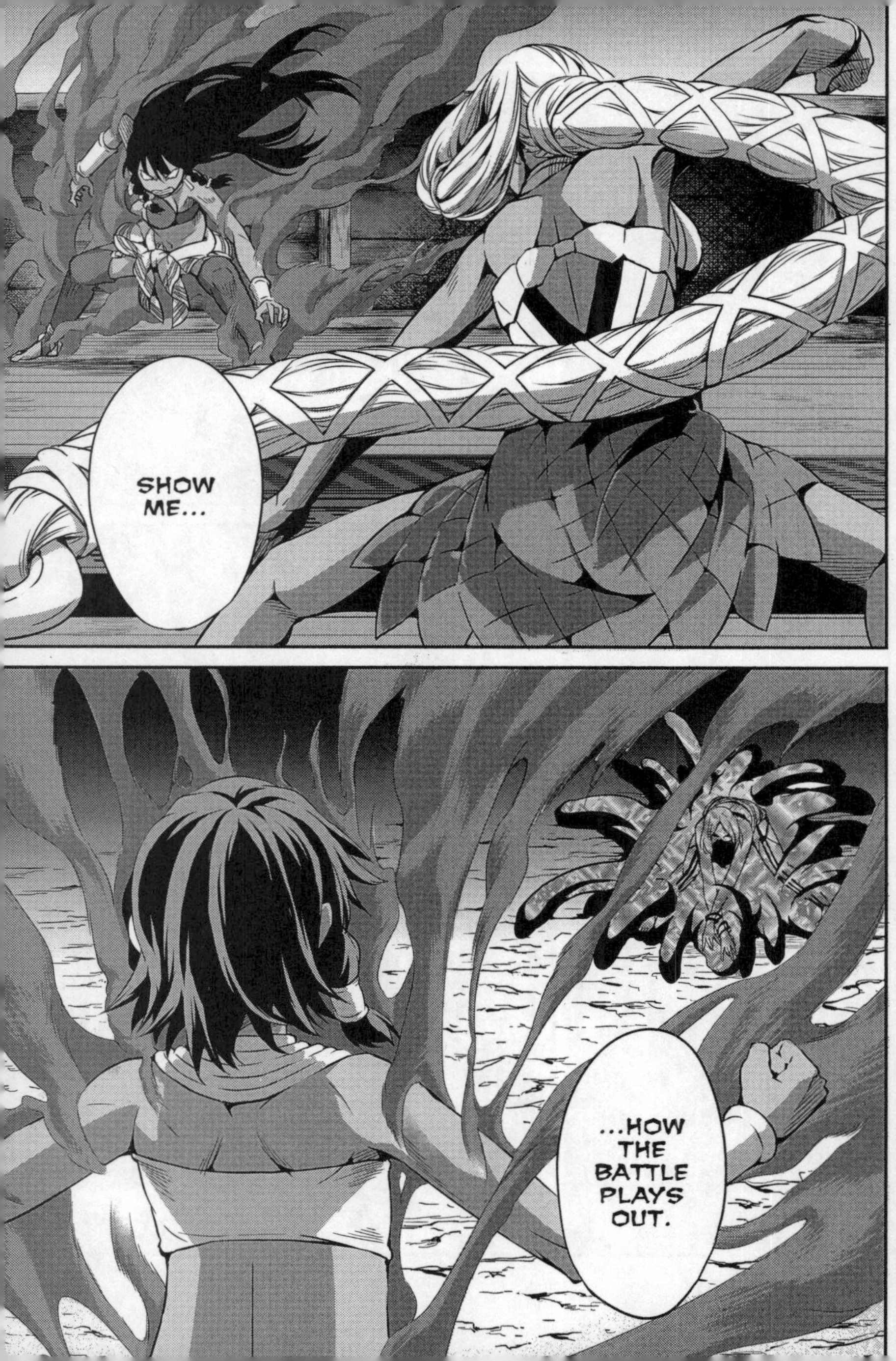
SHOW ME...
...HOW THE BATTLE PLAYS OUT.

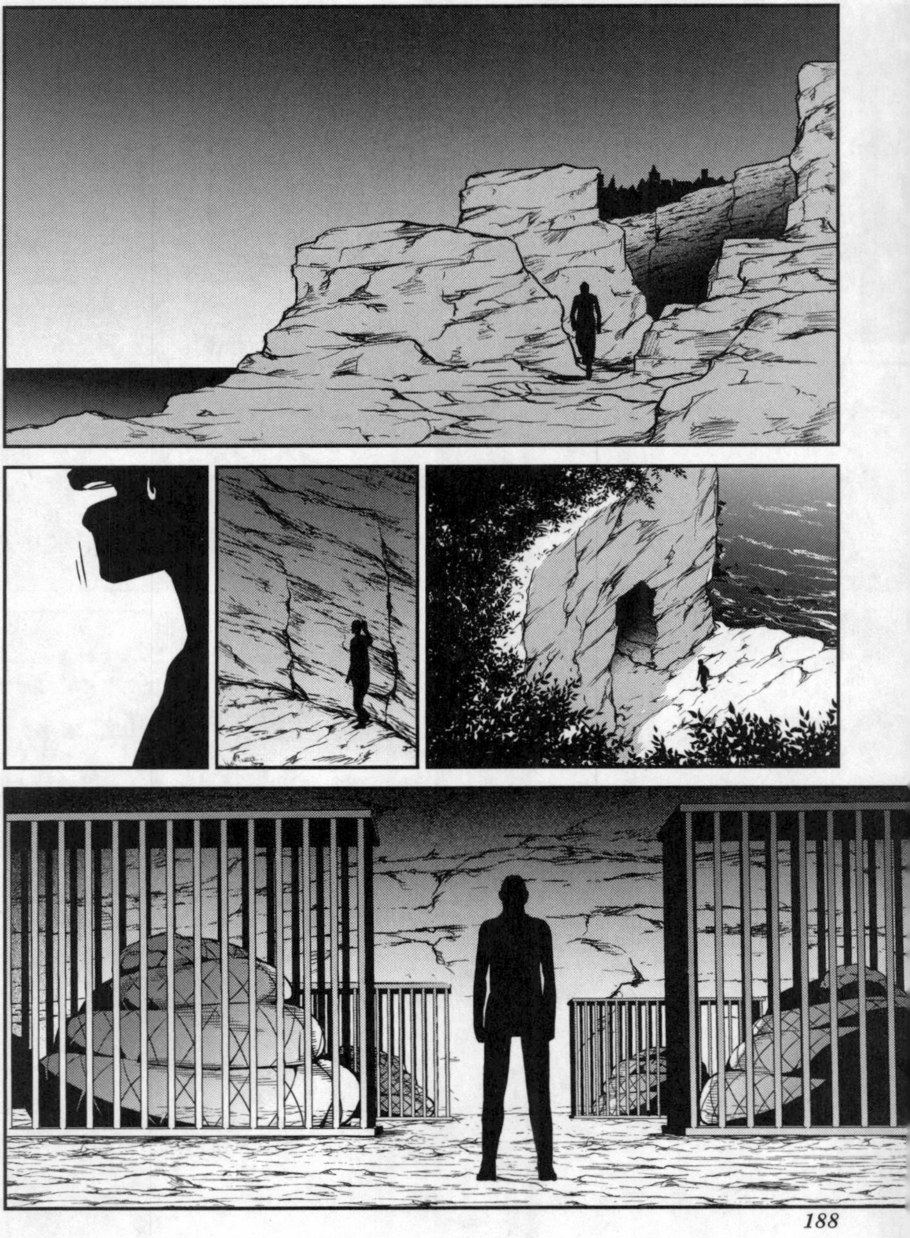

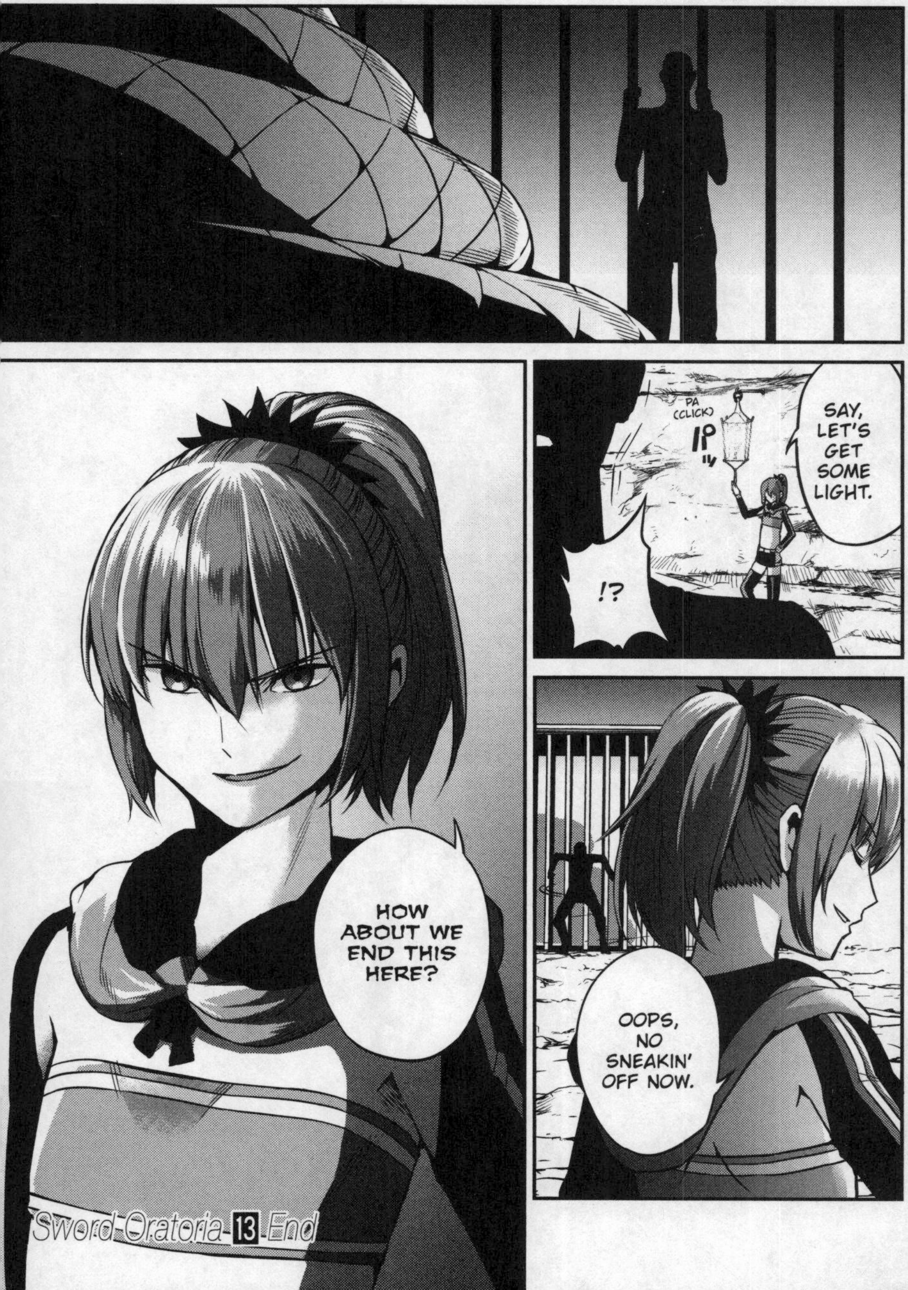
SAY, LET'S GET SOME LIGHT.
PA (CLICK)
!?
OOPS, NO SNEAKIN' OFF NOW.
HOW ABOUT WE END THIS HERE?
Sword Oratoria 13 End

Is it WRONG to try to PICK UP GIRLS IN A DUNGEON? ON THE SIDE

Sword Oratoria

AFTERWORD

THANKS FOR PICKING UP VOLUME 13! *SWORD ORATORIA*'S SECOND ARC ONCE AGAIN DIVES INTO TIONA AND TIONE'S STORY. IT'S FUN GETTING TO DRAW ALL THESE AMAZONS EACH TIME, BUT HAVING TO DO THE TAN SKIN TONE FOR ALL OF THEM HAS BEEN A REAL CHALLENGE (LOL). I WOULD'VE DIED IF IT WEREN'T FOR DOING THE FINISHING TOUCHES ON MY COMPUTER. THE TWINS' BATTLES HAVE REACHED THEIR PEAK, BUT THEY GET EVEN HOTTER IN VOLUME 14. PLEASE GIVE ME A BIT OF TIME TO COMPLETE THE NEXT ONE! I HOPE TO SEE YOU AGAIN IN VOLUME 14.

TAKASHI YAGI

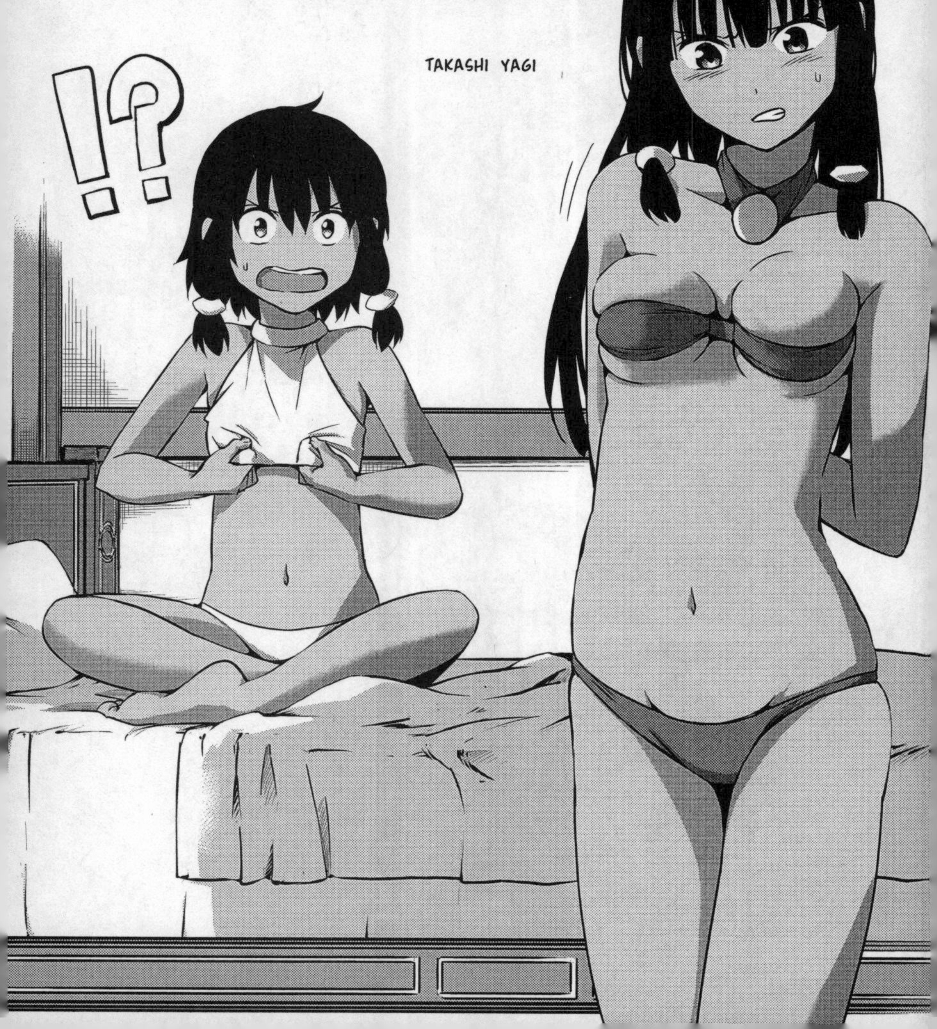
!?

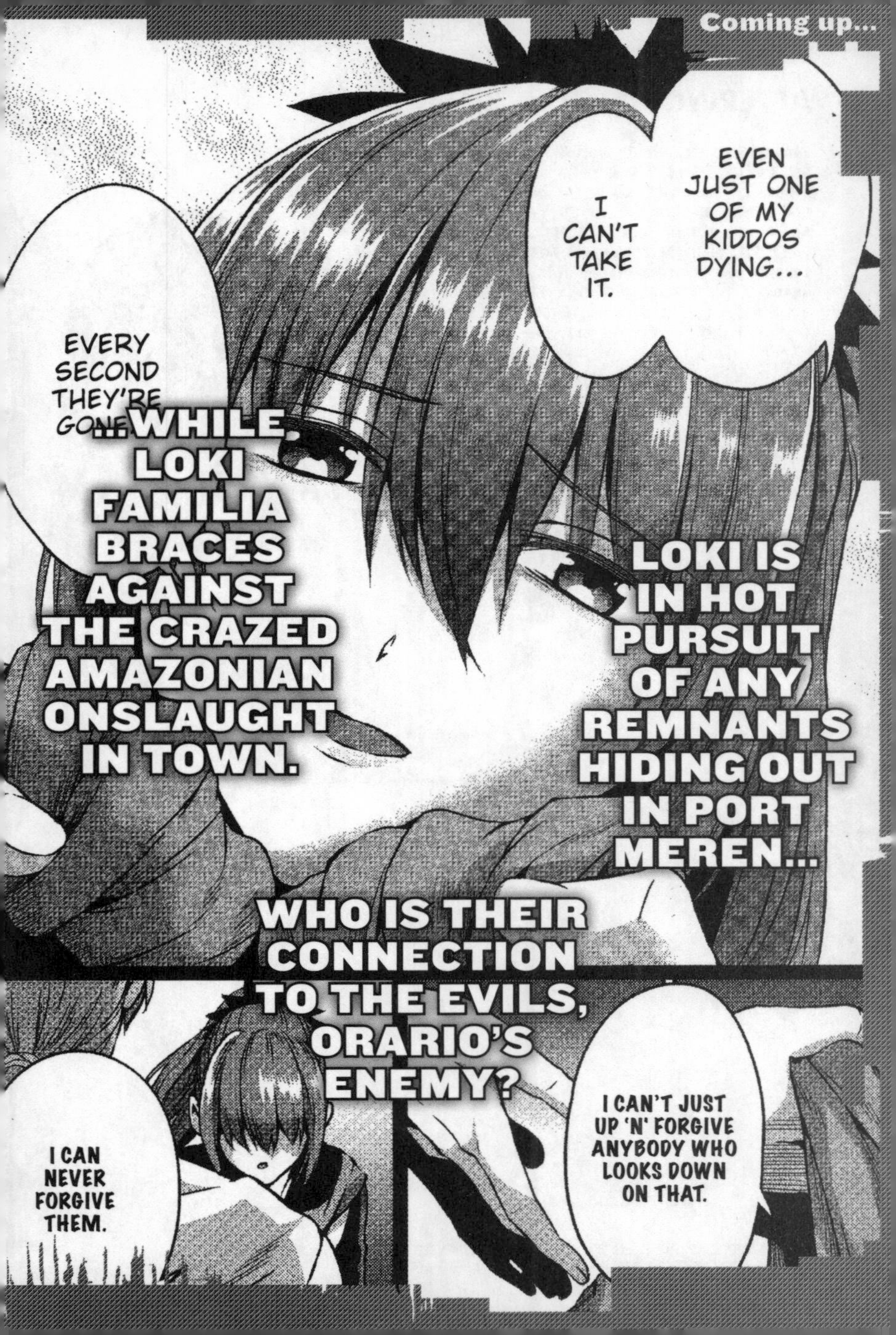
Coming up...
EVEN JUST ONE OF MY KIDDOS DYING... I CAN'T TAKE IT.
EVERY SECOND THEY'RE GONE...
LOKI IS IN HOT PURSUIT OF ANY REMNANTS HIDING OUT IN PORT MEREN...
...WHILE LOKI FAMILIA BRACES AGAINST THE CRAZED AMAZONIAN ONSLAUGHT IN TOWN.
WHO IS THEIR CONNECTION TO THE EVILS, ORARIO'S ENEMY?
I CAN'T JUST UP 'N' FORGIVE ANYBODY WHO LOOKS DOWN ON THAT.
I CAN NEVER FORGIVE THEM.

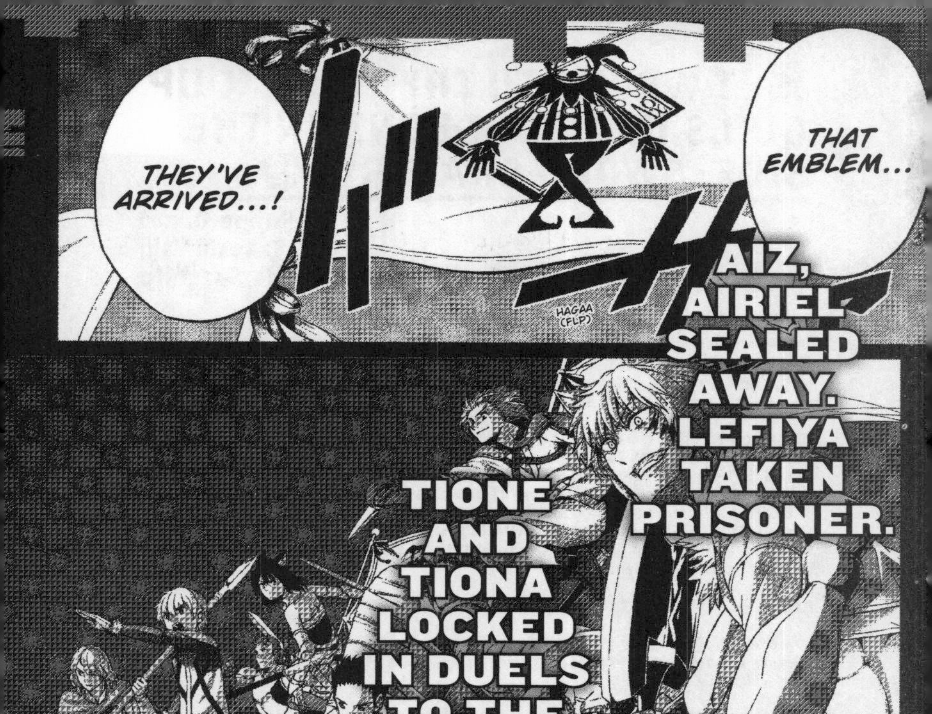
THAT EMBLEM...
THEY'VE ARRIVED...!
HAGAA (FLP)
AIZ, AIRIEL SEALED AWAY. LEFIYA TAKEN PRISONER.
TIONE AND TIONA LOCKED IN DUELS TO THE DEATH.
FROM THE BRINK OF DESPAIR COMES THE CAVALRY—!!

Is it WRONG to try to PICK UP GIRLS IN A DUNGEON? ON THE SIDE

Sword Oratoria 14

COMING WINTER 2020!

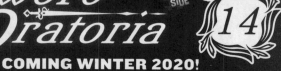

IS IT WRONG TO TRY TO PICK U GIRLS IN A DUNGEON? ON THE SIDE: SWORD ORATORIA ⑬

05/21

Fujino Omori
Takashi Yagi
Haimura Kiyotaka, Yasuda Suzuhito

Translation: Andrew Gaippe • Lettering: Barri Shrager

DUNGEON NI DEAI WO MOTOMERU NO WA MACHIGATTEIRUDAROUKA GAIDEN SWORD ORATORIA vol. 13
© Fujino Omori / SB Creative Corp.
Original Character Designs: © Haimura Kiyotaka, Yasuda Suzuhito / SB Creative Corp.
© 2019 Takashi Yagi / SQUARE ENIX CO., LTD.
First published in Japan in 2019 by SQUARE ENIX CO., LTD.
English translation rights arranged with SQUARE ENIX CO., LTD. and Yen Press, LLC through Tuttle-Mori Agency, Inc.

English translation © 2020 by SQUARE ENIX CO., LTD.

Yen Press
150 West 30th Street, 19th Floor
New York, NY 10001

Visit us at yenpress.com
facebook.com/yenpress
twitter.com/yenpress
yenpress.tumblr.com
instagram.com/yenpress

First Yen Press Edition: October 2020

Library of Congress Control Number: 2016946068

ISBNs: 978-1-9753-1310-4 (paperback)
      978-1-9753-1308-1 (ebook)

10 9 8 7 6 5 4 3 2 1

BVG

Printed in the United States of America